D0712381

Emerging Issues
in
Child Psychiatry
and
the Law

Library of Congress Cataloging in Publication Data
Main entry under title:

Emerging issues in child psychiatry and the law.

   Includes bibliographies and index.
    1. Children—Legal status, laws, etc.—United States.
2. Custody of children—United States. 3. Forensic
psychiatry—United States. 4. Child psychiatry—
United States. I. Schetky, Diane H., 1940-
II. Benedek, Elissa P. [DNLM: 1. Child Advocacy.
2. Divorce. 3. Ethics, Medical. 4. Forensic
Psychiatry—in infancy & childhood. 5. Juvenile
Delinquency. W 740 E53]
KF479.E44 1985   345.73'08   85-9920
ISBN 0-87630-393-9   347.3058

Copyright © 1985 by Diane H. Schetky and Elissa P. Benedek

Published by
BRUNNER/MAZEL, INC.
19 Union Square
New York, New York 10003

MANUFACTURED IN THE UNITED STATES OF AMERICA

Emerging Issues
in
Child Psychiatry
and
the Law

Edited by

Diane H. Schetky, M.D.
and
Elissa P. Benedek, M.D.

Brunner/Mazel, *Publishers* • New York

Foreword

This volume, like its predecessor, *Child Psychiatry and the Law,* pioneers a subject of great importance. The variety and depth of topics covered in *Emerging Issues in Child Psychiatry and the Law* put this book at the cutting edge. Indeed, these issues are not simply "emerging." Most of them have already "emerged" as topics of major concern for the field—as witnessed by recent professional and even media attention given them. As the social fabric changes, giving greater prominence to delinquency, divorce, children's rights, abuse, and neglect, greater emphasis has correspondingly been placed on the child as a witness, participant, and significant decision-maker in his or her own right.

Traditionally, the "dyad" has predominated in adult psychiatry. But in child psychiatry (and thus child psychiatry and the law) there is often a multiplicity of parties and interests. Relationships must be forged and conflicting interests adjudicated within triads, at times within tetrads, i.e., between children, parents, professional caretakers, and finally the state (including its multiple agents) acting as parens patriae or in fulfillment of the police power.

Controversies about child hospitalization and the requisite process "due" children (e.g., the *Parham* case) were among the issues that helped catalyze this field (see Chapter 16). Many months of debate went into formulating a position for psychiatry that could reconcile competing interests and protect children, while also not discourage needed care. One lesson from these debates was that despite the reliance now placed upon due process and the legal system to protect children's rights (and ensure that their best interests are served), mental health professionals still have a continuing role to play as "the guardian of last resort" for persons of dependent status and developing competencies. Many of the chapters in this book illustrate this point.

Complex issues, such as those discussed in *Emerging Issues in Child Psychiatry and the Law,* require general guidelines to act as beacons for society and professionals. However, as the following discussions and case histories in disparate areas illustrate, a "situationally based" approach to

v

ethics, assessment, and decision-making is clearly required in child psychiatry and the law. Melvin Lewis's comment in Chapter 4 applies more generally: "In the end, there is no perfect justice, and the 'best case' should be determined in each instance."

I know of no other systematic coverage for many issues addressed in this book. However, I also invite the reader to maintain a sense of openness and "tentativeness" about some of the conclusions reached. The area of child psychiatry and the law is in great flux; there is a lack of empirical data to inform us about what the best solutions really are to some of the problems discussed.

For the reader who digests this volume, it will also be apparent how profoundly social trends and mores are affecting relationships and even definitional matters in the field of child psychiatry and the law. This is true not only with respect to children and the law, but also for other special populations, such as the aged. Many of the issues touched upon in this volume thus teach lessons that are equally applicable for other dependent populations.

The authors are to be congratulated. *Emerging Issues in Child Psychiatry and the Law* joins its predecessor volume as a unique and useful guide for practitioners, students, and all others interested in child psychiatry and the law.

Loren H. Roth, M.D., M.P.H.
Professor of Psychiatry
Chief, Adult Clinical Services
Director, Law & Psychiatry Program
Western Psychiatric Institute
and Clinic
University of Pittsburgh
School of Medicine

Contents

Foreword by Loren H. Roth, M.D., M.P.H. v

Contributors xi

Introduction xvii

PART I. ETHICS

   1. Ethics in Child Psychiatry—An Overview 3
      Norbert B. Enzer

   2. Children's Capacities for Participation in Treatment Decision-
      Making 22
      Lois A. Weithorn

   3. Refusal of Treatment in Childhood Cancer 37
      Shirley B. Lansky

   4. Organ Transplants, Research, and Children 44
      Melvin Lewis

PART II. CHILD CUSTODY

   5. The Child Custody Dispute 59
      Barbara A. Weiner, Virginia A. Simons, and *James L.*
      Cavanaugh, Jr.

   6. Mediation: Its Implications for Children and Divorce 76
      Marilyn Ruman and *Marcia G. Lamm*

   7. Joint Custody: The Need for Individual Evaluation and
      Service 85
      Susan Steinman

   8. Father Custody 100
      Alan M. Levy

   9. Lesbian Mothers/Gay Fathers 115
      Donna J. Hutchens and *Martha J. Kirkpatrick*

10. Grandparents, Grandchildren, and the Law 127
    Richard H. Angell

11. Allegations of Sexual Abuse in Child Custody and Visitation
    Disputes 145
    Elissa P. Benedek and *Diane H. Schetky*

PART III. THE JUVENILE OFFENDER

12. Commentary: The Juvenile Justice System 159
    Melvin J. Guyer

13. Waiver of Juveniles to Adult Court 180
    Elissa P. Benedek

14. Treatment Alternatives in Juvenile Justice Programs: A Selected
    Review 191
    Rosemary C. Sarri

PART IV. SPECIAL ISSUES

15. Legal Issues and the Schools 217
    Kathleen M. Quinn

16. Psychiatric Commitment of Children and Adolescents: Issues,
    Current Practices, and Clinical Impact 229
    W. V. Burlingame and *Marc Amaya*

17. Psychiatric Approaches to Cults: Therapeutic and Legal
    Parameters 250
    David A. Halperin

18. Role Models for Violence 266
    Diane H. Schetky

19. Psychiatric Interventions with Children Traumatized by
    Violence 285
    Spencer Eth and *Robert S. Pynoos*

PART V. EMERGING ISSUES

20. The Baby as a Witness 313
    Lenore C. Terr

21. New Areas in Litigation for Children 324
    Gilbert W. Kliman

22. Emerging Issues at the Interface of Law and Medicine Concerning Children of the 1980s 332
    Judianne Densen-Gerber and *Jean Lothian*

Index 347

Contributors

MARC AMAYA, M.D.
Director, Children's Psychiatric Institute,
John Umstead Hospital;
Assistant Professor of Psychiatry, Duke University,
Chapel Hill, North Carolina.

RICHARD H. ANGELL, M.D.
Assistant Professor of Psychiatry;
Director, Training in Child Psychiatry,
Oregon Health Sciences Center,
Portland, Oregon.

ELISSA P. BENEDEK, M.D.
Director, Training and Research
Center for Forensic Psychiatry, Ypsilanti, Michigan;
Clinical Professor of Psychiatry,
University of Michigan,
Ann Arbor, Michigan.

W. V. BURLINGAME, Ph.D.
Director, Adolescent Unit of Children's Psychiatric Institute,
John Umstead Hospital;
Clinical Associate Professor of Psychology,
University of North Carolina.

JAMES L. CAVANAUGH, JR., M.D.
Director, Section on Psychiatry and the Law,
Rush-Presbyterian Hospital-St. Luke's Medical Center;
Associate Professor of Psychiatry, Rush Medical College,
Chicago, Illinois.

JUDIANNE DENSEN-GERBER, J.D., M.D.
Chairman, Odyssey Institute Corporation,
Bridgeport, Connecticut.

NORBERT B. ENZER, M.D.
Professor of Psychiatry,
Michigan State University,
East Lansing, Michigan.

SPENCER ETH, M.D.
Assistant Professor of Psychiatry; Coordinator
of Training with Children and Adolescents,
L.A. County U.S.C. Medical Center,
Los Angeles, California.

MELVIN J. GUYER, Ph.D.
Associate Professor and Director of
Family and Law Program, Department of
Psychiatry, University of Michigan Medical
School, Ann Arbor, Michigan.

DAVID A. HALPERIN, M.D.
Assistant Clinical Professor of Psychiatry,
Mt. Sinai School of Medicine, New York;
Consultant Psychiatrist, Cult Hot Line Clinic,
Jewish Board of Family and Children's Services and
Cult Information and Treatment Program,
Westchester Jewish Community Services.

DONNA J. HUTCHENS, J.D.
Lesbian Rights Project,
San Francisco, California.

MARTHA J. KIRKPATRICK, M.D.
Associate Clinical Professor,
Department of Psychiatry,
University of California, Los Angeles;
Assistant Faculty, University of California,
Los Angeles Psychoanalytic
Society/Institute.

GILBERT W. KLIMAN, M.D.
Associate Clinical Professor,
Director of Foster Care Study Unit,
Columbia University, New York.

MARCIA G. LAMM, M.A.
Clinical and Consulting Associate,
American Association for Mediated Divorce,
Encino, California.

SHIRLEY B. LANSKY, M.D.
Professor of Psychiatry,
University of Illinois at the Medical Center,
Chicago, Illinois.

ALAN. M. LEVY, M.D.
Clinical Associate Professor of Psychiatry, Department of Psychiatry,
College of Physicians and Surgeons, Columbia University, New York;
Director, Staten Island Children's Community Mental Health Center,
Staten Island, New York.

MELVIN LEWIS, M.B. B.S. (London) FRC Psych DCH
Professor of Pediatrics and Psychiatry;
Director of Medical Studies,
Yale University Child Study Center,
New Haven, Connecticut.

JEAN LOTHIAN
Odyssey Institute Corporation,
Bridgeport, Connecticut.

ROBERT S. PYNOOS, M.D., M.P.H.
Assistant Professor of Psychiatry,
University of California, Los Angeles, Neuropsychiatric Institute,
Los Angeles, California.

KATHLEEN M. QUINN, M.D.
Assistant Professor of Child Psychiatry,
Case Western Reserve University School of Medicine,
Cleveland, Ohio.

MARILYN RUMAN, Ph.D.
    Clinical Director,
    American Association
    for Mediated Divorce,
    Encino, California.

ROSEMARY C. SARRI, M.S.W.
    Professor of Social Work,
    University of Michigan,
    Ann Arbor, Michigan.

DIANE H. SCHETKY, M.D.
    Associate Clinical Professor,
    Yale University Child Study Center;
    Private Practice,
    Wilton, Connecticut.

VIRGINIA A. SIMONS, M.S.W.
    Clinical Coordinator, Center for Families in Conflict,
    Isaac Ray Center; Adjunct Faculty, Family Systems Program,
    Institute for Juvenile Research,
    Chicago, Illinois.

SUSAN STEINMAN, D.S.W.
    Project Director,
    Joint Custody Project,
    Jewish Family and Children's Services,
    San Francisco, California.

LENORE C. TERR, M.D.
    Associate Clinical Professor of Psychiatry,
    University of California, San Francisco;
    Lecturer in Law and Psychiatry,
    The Law Schools at University of California, Berkeley and Davis.

BARBARA A. WEINER, J.D.
    Executive Director, Isaac Ray Center,
    Rush Presbyterian, St. Luke Medical Center, Chicago;
    Assistant Professor of Law in Psychiatry, Rush Medical College;
    Adjunct Professor, Chicago Kent College of Law.

LOIS A. WEITHORN, Ph.D.
   Assistant Professor in Psychology, University of Virginia;
   Faculty, University of Virginia, Institute of Law,
   Department of Psychology,
   University of Virginia, Charlottesville.

Introduction

In 1980, *Child Psychiatry and the Law* was published (1). This volume was the result of the editors' experience of attempting to train colleagues in forensic child psychiatry and share their experience with practicing child clinicians. The editors lamented the fact that the existing body of knowledge in forensic child psychiatry had not yet been organized in an easily accessible, readable fashion for their students, practicing colleagues, and the many others who regularly dealt with the issue of the interface of child psychiatry and the law. *Child Psychiatry and the Law* was designed to alleviate the lack of learning materials and provide a core body of knowledge in the area of forensic child psychiatry.

The response to *Child Psychiatry and the Law* was enthusiastic and prompted the editors to develop *Emerging Issues in Child Psychiatry and the Law*. This text is intended to further expand the range of topics covered in *Child Psychiatry and the Law* and to provide an update of developments in child forensic psychiatry. Since adult, child, and forensic psychiatry are fields that have experienced rapid growth in the past decade, the authors are cognizant that it is not possible to cover all the issues that have emerged. Nor is it possible to anticipate those that will surface in the next decade.

Child Psychiatry and the Law covered four main areas. Part I focused on an introduction to forensic child psychiatry with chapters on the juvenile justice system, the court evaluation, and the expert witness. Part II highlighted issues in child custody, neglect, and adoption. In Part III, the major issues addressed were those of the juvenile offender with chapters on status offenders, delinquents, and juvenile murderers. Part IV addressed those special issues that seemed of paramount import in the late seventies and early eighties, including civil commitment, psychic trauma, and personal injury to children, as well as competency and criminal responsibility. The final chapter in this section was an attempt to summarize the legal issues impinging on the clinical practice of child psychiatry.

It is fair to say that virtually all new developments in the field of child psychiatry have legal implications and ramifications which ultimately affect clinical practice. The 1980s have witnessed a rapid expansion in the diagnostic techniques and treatment procedures available to clinicians working with children and families. DSM-III has afforded a whole new set of diagnostic criteria (2). Diagnosis in child psychiatry is becoming more sophisticated as it involves blood studies, CAT scans, specialized EEGs, and genetics studies. The availability of these techniques and others have now exposed the practitioner to liability for new sins of omission and commission. Treatment options increasingly invoke the use of medications, some of which have not been extensively used in children, and may lead the clinicians into uncharted waters with risk of side effects. As Slawson's malpractice survey of adult psychiatrists has demonstrated, the risk of being sued is highest when the psychiatrist is involved in inpatient work and prescribing medications (3). This risk increases as child psychiatrists adopt the newer psychopharmacologies and hospitalize more adolescents on short-term treatment units, leading to risks associated with premature discharge, suicide and homicide, and unlawful detention.

The 1980s have also been a period in which psychiatric practice has been subjected to more surveillance from the federal government, hospital administrators, third-party payers, and the public-at-large. This increased surveillance has led to greater legal regulation of the practice of child psychiatry, and to an increase in self-regulation and monitoring in the form of greater attention to ethical issues, peer review, and continuing medical education.

The last five years have also produced national, judicial, and legislative changes which have impacted on children and families. Judicially, we have seen more attention paid to the balance of power between children, families, and the state. For example, *Parham* has underscored parents' ability to make decisions for their children in regard to psychiatric hospitalization (4). On the other hand, the courts have struck down laws which limited the rights of adolescents to obtain treatment, specifically contraception, without parental consent. The Supreme Court's decision to raise the standard of evidence in termination of parental rights cases has made it more difficult for the state to intervene in family matters.

The 1980s have also witnessed the emergence of the field of infant psychiatry as a new subspecialty of child psychiatry. Forensic issues that pertain to infants and preschoolers are receiving increasing attention. Such issues include wrongful parity suits, rights to be well born suits, withholding aggressive medical treatment to handicapped children and infants as in the case of Baby Doe, the infant as a witness, the infant as party to civil suits relating to psychic trauma, and even legal representation for fetuses. Infant psychiatrists have contributed a wealth of new diagnostic techniques which have facilitated the evaluation of child physical and sexual abuse and increased our awareness of the prevalence of sexual abuse among this age group.

New legislation has focused on many areas of regulation such as parental kidnapping, grandparents' visitation laws, joint custody laws, the right to education for the handicapped, and the child's right to permanent placement. Outdated laws requiring corroboration in order to convict in cases of child sexual abuse have been replaced. Increasingly, courts have come to rely upon the expertise of the forensic child psychiatrist and the concept of the child's best interest in rendering decisions. Legislatures and courts have also become more involved in defining and curtailing the booming child pornography industry, and forensic child psychiatrists have assumed roles as lobbyists, contributing to greater public awareness of this issue. Unfortunately, all of these developments have not as yet been incorporated into residency training programs for child fellows or into continuing medical education for practicing clinicians.

A 1983 survey of 130 child training programs, conducted by the editors, revealed the following data: Among 74 respondents, only 40 programs had didactic time devoted to forensic child psychiatry. The average number of hours allotted to this important training was five hours per fellowship, with a range of two to 10 didactic hours for child fellowship training during the fellowship year. Only five programs responded that they offered child forensic fellowships. Many of the programs taught child forensic psychiatry as a part of the adult program, despite the fact that they were child fellowships. Thus, a child fellow in a psychiatry program might not receive any forensic child psychiatry training. Some directors volunteered that their fellows had training through experience in the juvenile courts or through evaluating patients who presented with problems relating to divorce, neglect, and adoption (5).

Interestingly, several training directors used the survey questionnaire to request training materials, including the development of a core curriculum in forensic child psychiatry. Other directors volunteered that their program offered forensic training through lectures and supervised experience in the areas of civil commitment, adoption, neglect, children of divorce, and the expert witness. No programs volunteered that any of the emerging issues of the 1980s covered earlier in this introduction were addressed.

The training directors are not alone in their neglect of many facets of forensic child psychiatry. Project Future, the American Academy of Child Psychiatry position statement of training needs of child psychiatrists, began with a special task force on forensic issues. The task force focused on manpower, service and training needs in the future, and made a variety of recommendations to the survey committee, including regional training centers, central development of training materials, a core curriculum, and core clinical experiences. As it was immediately apparent that service demands by juvenile courts far exceeded the ability of child psychiatry to respond to task force recommendations, it was strongly urged that involvement with the juvenile justice system be narrowed to take advantage of the medical skills of child psychiatry and focus on issues of diagnosis and treatment recommendations. The final draft of Project Future unfortunately watered down or omitted many of the more innovative recommendations of the task force and chose again to address the service needs of the juvenile justice system (6). The impact of this document on training and practice is still unclear.

In our opinion, child forensic psychiatry can no longer be ignored or neglected in the training and education of child practitioners. As in child neglect, ignoring issues does not lead to their disappearance but rather, with the passage of time, to predictable problems. We would again strongly recommend that *all* training programs devote ample time to child forensic psychiatry, with didactic and clinical components available to all trainees. We hope we have convinced the reader that the training experience and skills in child forensic psychiatry will improve the quality of practice available to patients and their families in the coming decades.

Emerging Issues in Child Psychiatry and the Law is divided into five sections. Section I, *Ethics*, covers many of the complex ethical issues encountered in the day-to-day practice of child psychiatry. This area has had inadequate coverage in the formal training of all psychiatrists. Special emphasis is given to some of the unique ethical problems that arise in our role as consultants to pediatricians dealing with acutely and chronically ill children.

Section II explores new issues in the area of children and divorce. It describes a variety of approaches to evaluating children and families in these difficult situations.

Section III again addresses the juvenile offender and reflects developments in this area.

Section IV concerns special issues not covered elsewhere, such as legal issues in the schools, civil commitment, cults, and problems relative to children's exposure to violence.

Section V deals with emerging issues and includes chapters on the baby as a witness, new areas of litigation with children, and an overview of emerging issues at the interface of law and psychiatry in the 1980s.

Child Psychiatry and the Law was dedicated to our patients in appreciation of what we have learned from them. This volume is dedicated to our trainees who used the material presented in *Child Psychiatry and the Law* and made further contributions to our knowledge of forensic child psychiatry. They show promise of becoming a part of that core of teachers and practitioners who devote their energies to forensic child psychiatry.

REFERENCES

1. Schetky, D., & Benedek, E. *Child psychiatry and the law, Volume I.* New York: Brunner/Mazel, 1980.
2. American Psychiatric Association. *Diagnostic and statistical manual of mental disorders* (Third Edition). Washington, D.C.: American Psychiatric Association, 1980.
3. Slawson, P. F. Psychiatric malpractice: The California experience. *American Journal of Psychiatry,* 1979, *136,* 650-654.
4. *Parham v. J.R.,* 99 S. Ct. 2493 (1979).
5. Benedek, E. P., & Schetky, D. H. Survey of Psychiatric Residency Training Directors. Unpublished.
6. Child Psychiatry: A Plan for the Coming Decades. *Washington, D.C.: American Academy of Child Psychiatry, 1983.*

Emerging Issues
in
Child Psychiatry
and
the Law

Part I

ETHICS

1

Ethics in Child Psychiatry—
An Overview

Norbert B. Enzer

The history of western medicine must be viewed as intricate and complex. Based on archaeological evidence, its roots are often traced to times prior to recorded history. That history is inextricably enmeshed in social, political, and religious history, and in the intellectual history of the western world, which is not directly "scientific." Lewis Thomas called medicine "the youngest science," for the actual impact of science on the care of patients is a relatively modern development (1). In the last couple of centuries, medicine has been influenced by all of the sciences and, more recently, by the phenomenal developments of technology. However, the practice of medicine and the behaviors of physicians have been directed by beliefs and by standards that often have had little to do with science.

Part of the history of medicine is the history of medical ethics. That history is an ancient one. The medical profession is proud of this heritage and has gone to great lengths to protect, perpetuate, and define and control the standards of behavior of its members. But the history of medical ethics is not solely within medicine. Certain theological and philosophical concepts of morality and human existence have contributed substantially, as have public policies, social values, and the law. There are some, particularly in more recent times, who have seen at least some of the ethical standards of medicine to be self-serving and not in the best interest of the individual patient or of the society as a whole. Such condemnations, which perhaps have some merit in specific situations or circumstances, do not adequately reflect the historical or even the more contemporary perspectives.

In 1950, Willard Sperry, then Dean of the Harvard Divinity School, wrote, "Of all professional groups, that of medicine has, on the whole, codified its ethics better than has any other of the kindred professions" (2). He continued,

I do not hesitate to say, then, that the ethics of accepted medical usage represents both in theory and in general practice the highest professional standard now recognized in our country. Lawyers, teachers and ministers have much to learn from the medical code itself and then from the scrupulous care given to the enforcement of that code. If the doctors fail us, morally, the whole level of our or professional morals will suffer accordingly. (3)

He further said,

The preeminence of medical ethics in the field of the several professions may well be due to its long history, a matter of twenty-five hundred years, and to its initial and still classic statement in the Hippocratic Oath. (4)

Although that code has an antiquated tone, even in its more modern translations, and some of its content is subject to controversy today, it did describe certain behaviors and attitudes that continue to be valued. It demanded a respect for and a responsibility to professional colleagues, it required physicians to teach those who wished to enter the profession, it made it a duty to help to the extent of knowledge, and it prohibited doing harm and established the notion of confidentiality. The code also suggested a high and, by implication, unique standard of personal conduct. Thus, even this ancient set of standards defined certain broad categories of responsibility of physicians to the profession and to patients that continue to have substantial relevance to current standards. It is noteworthy that so much of the material that was incorporated into the Hippocratic Oath stood for so long with so little change. However, during this twentieth century, and particularly during this half of the twentieth century, changes in social standards, society's values, the laws related to medicine, the economics of health care, and the almost unbelievable advances in science and technology have forced a reconsideration, not only of certain modern evolutionary corollaries of the ancient standards of ethics, but of those basic standards themselves.

The last 50 years have seen so many changes that these years seem almost discontinuous with our prior history. Our capacity to understand and diagnose illness, and particularly our capacity to effectively intervene to limit disability and to cure with both medical and surgical interventions using technology and materials, which in some cases were derived for quite different purposes, has been truly awesome. One might even call these years the beginning of therapeutic medicine. Although these advances should be cherished, they have created problems and dilemmas to which solutions are proving very difficult.

Medical ethics must be seen as having two meanings. In simple terms, it is a discipline or an area of study that deals with morality, moral obligations, and what is good or evil within the domains of medical care and research. It is also a set of moral principles and values, or a theory of moral values, that are intended to govern the conduct and behavior of physicians and are tantamount to rules, despite the lack of legal status. Transgressions have been viewed as the basis for some disciplinary action, although the procedures for the decisions are often very cumbersome and the ultimate punishments may appear trivial. Nevertheless, codes of medical ethics have provided patients and the public at large with a description of what they may expect from physicians and some assurance that the profession will exert control over its members.

What has become clear is that concise, explicit, and generally applicable statements are often disappointing. At the midpoint of the twentieth century, prior to most of the incredible advances in science and technology in such areas as molecular biology, genetics, immunology, neurochemistry, organ transplantation, pharmacology, imaging, and the host of developments in law, the organization of health care, and the mechanisms of funding of health care, Sperry wrote,

> The difficulty is that the book of words—i.e., the formal code of medical ethics—proposes general moral principles which should govern the doctor's decision, but sometimes seem to offer little help in difficult concrete situations such as that now before us. (5)

Throughout most of this history, the basic tenet has been that the physician will consider the individual patient before all else. Developments in high-technology medicine, and the often enormous costs involved, raise questions of resource allocation and the equity of access to the benefits of these developments. Furthermore, the cost of some care may have truly deleterious effects on others in the family or the community at large. Organ transplantation requires that physicians consider the donor as well as the patient, and creates a situation in which physicians sometimes essentially convert a healthy person, the donor, into a patient. Expanding knowledge in pharmacology creates an awareness that agents of great effectiveness may have long-term risks to the individual, and to subsequent generations. Given the scientific and technological developments, the current social and economic pressures, the greater understanding of multiple causality, and the recognition that many factors beyond the patient in the social and psychological environment of the family, the community, and the physical environment can influence outcomes and the level of disability, is it appropriate or even feasible that the traditional devotion to the individual be maintained regardless of all else? The dilemmas are substantial. If the decisions of a physician must take into account the relative benefit or harm to others, how many others and who will determine who should be considered? But, further, who will determine who will make the decision, even if it is clear who should be considered in regard to benefit or harm? Historically, in practice, these decisions, while certainly troublesome at times, were largely left in the hands of the individual patient and the attending physician. Although there were individual exceptions and some on institutionalized bases, e.g., the incompetent or unconscious patient, the patient and physician would negotiate the decisions between themselves with the patient predominating in regard to the matter of whom else to involve and the physician usually predominating in regard to clinical actions, although the right of the patient to refuse care was usually accepted. It is no longer as simple or as straightforward; many others—review committees, insurance carriers, the courts and others—are, in fact, involved in the decisions of who will receive care and how care will be provided.

Although the prohibition to "do no harm" is an oversimplification, it is the commonly held view of the bottom line of medical ethics. If "harm" is defined literally, physicians often do inflict harm. They do things to patients that are painful, limit functional capacity, and certainly a great many diagnostic and therapeutic procedures carry with them certain risks. They also do things that may be harmful to others or, at least, place others at risk. What is apparent is that to do nothing may also be harmful. It is not so much an issue of whether or not something is harmful, but, more often, which of several potential courses of action are the *least* harmful. Even in such extreme situations as those involving life and death, decisions are no longer as clear-cut as they appeared in the past. The concept of the quality of life has emerged as a consideration, which in some quarters, at least, is viewed as more important than life alone. It is clear that substantial controversy exists and is likely to continue. Even in situations not involving life and death decisions, there is no ethical issue of whether one course of action is good and the other evil, or more appropriately for medicine, whether one is helpful and the other harmful. But, all things are considered, such simple and clear-cut dichotomies are relatively uncommon.

The ancient principle of confidentiality and the legal concept of privileged communication that is its progeny have also been eroded. Health care insurance requires that agencies and groups of individuals that have no direct relationship to either the patient or the patient's family be provided with information that, in the past, was totally protected within the relationship between physician and patient. A recognition of risks to the public health or to individuals other than the patient in the community have led to laws and precedents that require physicians to divulge information that may have no bearing whatsoever on the specific care of the individual patient.

What is clear is that certain ancient standards of medical ethics are simply no longer applicable, are contrary to accepted social policy or practice, or are impractical.

Although not surprising, it is, nevertheless, important to recognize that particular attention to children by the medical profession is a recent development. To be sure there are notable exceptions: Itard's treatise on *The Wild Boy of Aveyron* (6), published in the late eighteenth century, and Heroard's journal of the early life of Louis XIII of France, published in 1868 (7), are but two examples. In the late nineteenth century, some physicians were beginning to develop a particular interest in children and there were signs of the emergence of the specialty of pediatrics in this country. Textbooks were being written and a few medical schools appointed faculty in the area of child health. But it is really in the twentieth century that a consistent progressive growth has occurred in medical concern and knowledge regarding children, the illnesses of children, and child development. Medical history has, in many ways, paralleled a similar growth in attention to children in other fields of intellectual endeavor, psychology and education particularly, and a growing concern with the lives and fates of children in our society at large. Broad concerns regarding child welfare have included such specific issues and problems as those presented by the juvenile offender, the exploitation of children in the work force, and the lack of educational opportunities.

Traditionally, children, those individuals below the legal age of majority, have been seen as the property of their parents or legal guardians who had the responsibility to protect and provide for their care. In regard to health care, children have been treated as almost an extension of their parents. Although the concept of parens patriae, derived from the English courts, has provided the State with the right to intervene on behalf of children should parents fail in their responsibilities to care for and protect them or if discipline became cruel, in practice, until recently, courts have been reluctant to exercise the parens patriae authority except in the most extreme situations. In the health area, again until recently, the interventions of the State have been limited and have mostly involved such specific situations as immunization, or rather clear-cut clinical issues such as blood transfusions. By way of example, it was not until 1974, with the passage of the National Child Abuse Prevention and Treatment Act, that there was a truly national policy regarding this specific threat to the health and safety of children. Prior to 1974, despite the parens patriae authority, reporting and interventions were sporadic and infrequent.

Our society's views of children have changed dramatically since the late nineteenth century. Although it had long been true that society did not confer on children the rights of adults, it might be suggested that with the

The Code can be viewed as based on three assumptions. First, children are dependent but the course of development and indeed the expectations of society move them progressively toward greater independence and autonomy. Biological, psychological, social, and economic factors combine to create a situation in which children and most adolescents in our society must depend upon adults for the better part of the first two decades of life. While one could deal at length with the specifics of dependency, it is essentially self-evident that in our society children cannot provide for their materials needs, and that they require interactions with adults for healthy personality development, for acquisition of useful and satisfying skills, and for the development of socially acceptable patterns of behavior and attitudes. However, dependency is not an "all or none" phenomenon. The total dependency of the human infant gives way gradually but progressively. As development proceeds, adaptive skills increase, knowledge of the world expands, interests and talents are elaborated, communication becomes more refined and sophisticated, social relationships broaden, cause and effect relationships become clear, the capacity to delay gratification is increased, and so on.

Children also develop the capacity to make judgments and choices and to solve problems. Even young children, provided they can be made to understand the nature of choices and their consequences, often have the capacity to make decisions on their own behalf even in situations of more than trivial importance. Age alone is not the principle determinant of a child's capacity for decision-making. However, perhaps capacity should not be the sole determinant of whether or not a child should make a particular decision. One might say that although a particular child has the capacity to understand a situation and the alternatives, and the capacity to make a decision, he or she may not make it wisely or in a way that will truly be appropriate. Surely, many adult decisions are not wise or appropriate and, yet, society would not deprive them of the right to make a mistake. Furthermore, children are not in a position to implement many decisions that affect their lives. More often they lack the authority and the material resources to do so. Thus, regardless of decisions, children and most adolescents must rely on others. Some decisions should not be left wholly in the hands of children, not because of a lack of wisdom or appropriate self-interest or their lack of authority or resources, but because the process of decision-making itself may place an undue burden upon a child that might have noxious or painful consequences on other aspects of a child's life, development, or relationships.

Second, children are uniquely vulnerable. Dependency itself creates certain vulnerabilities. More often the young child whose physical or psychological needs are not being met by caretaking adults cannot, on his own, seek fulfillment from other sources. Physical size and strength differences create a vulnerability not only to physical abuse but to intimidation and coercion as well. But the very nature of the psychosocial relationships between children and adults and the child's sense of an adult's omnipotence and omniscience further enhances the potential for intimidation and coercion or for disturbances in psychosexual and psychosocial developments. The issue of a child's vulnerability is not limited to the relationship with adults; it includes relationships with other children as well. Further, vulnerability is not limited to the intentional actions of others; it includes family decisions to move to another community, illnesses or death of a family member or even a pet, and a child's own failure at school or on the playground. Children have special vulnerabilities to the physical environment, e.g., lead in the atmosphere, malnutrition, and certain drugs. Because of dependency and vulnerability, adults, especially parents, have a special moral and practical obligation to children, which, like the development of a child's capacities, changes over time.

Third, even with dependency and their unique vulnerabilities, children and adolescents are individual human beings with their own truly unique characteristics, strengths, weaknesses, interests, and talents and, as such, are entitled to be taken seriously and respected. Their rights must be considered and observed, unless so doing would involve "untenable risks or betrayal of caretaking responsibility," a phrase used at several points in the Academy's Code of Ethics.

The Code of Ethics includes 17 principles. These principles are accompanied by a set of "Clarification Notes." Throughout, the Code recognizes the special importance of family relationships, but it establishes as the "primary concerns of child psychiatrists" the welfare of the individual child or adolescent patient. It also establishes competence as an ethical responsibility, as did the ancient Hippocratic Oath, at least by implication.

While a complete description and discussion of all 17 principles of the Code cannot be accomplished in this chapter, some features will be summarized and others will be discussed at more length. In addition to clearly establishing the "welfare and optimum development of the individual child or adolescent patient or of the population of children or adolescent patients" being served by the child psychiatrist as the "primary" concern, the Code requires that the child psychiatrist make judgments that are "determined by the needs of the child or adolescent patient or population" and that are "assessed in the context of the family and community life" (10). It recognizes the vulnerability of children to certain interactions with others and makes it an ethical responsibility of child psychiatrists to "reduce any deleterious effects of the behavior of others" (11).

The Code places substantial emphasis on the value of the individual, charges child psychiatrists with the responsibility of enhancing "the dignity and the self-respect of all of those served," and demands respect for the "social, economic, ethnic, racial and sexual context within which they [child or adolescent patients] live" (12). Although the phrase "double agent" is not used in the code, there is a recognition that child psychiatrists are usually "retained" by parents, guardians, or agencies with varying degrees of responsibility for the care of the child or adolescent. However, at several points the Code requires that judgments, decisions, and actions not be determined or influenced by the source of compensation (13). It specifically prohibits the participation of a child psychiatrist in "attempts to control or change the behavior of children or adolescents" if, in the opinion of the child psychiatrist, "those efforts ignore individuality or are counter to the needs of the child or adolescent, or impede optimum development, or involve efforts solely directed toward conformity" (14).

Recognizing that child psychiatrists have the potential for substantial influence, based upon the unique relationships with children, adolescents, and their families, and their professional status, the Code requires the use of that influence "to foster optimum development and well-being of children and families" and prohibits using that influence principally for personal gain or aggrandizement. Coercion intended to gain agreement to participation in evaluation or treatment efforts that may be inappropriate for the needs of the clinical situation or of the child or family but may benefit the child psychiatrist are prohibited, and "any action that involves exploitation of a child, parents or others involved for the physician's personal advantage is clearly unethical" (15).

The Code makes an ethical commitment to advocacy on the behalf of children and families. In a formal sense, this commitment may be the first of its kind in medicine, although in practice, medicine in general, and specifically child psychiatry, has accepted the role of advocate for a long time. The Code makes this a responsibility of individual child psychiatrists. (16). But there are other issues not addressed in the Code which deserve comment. Michels makes the point that a profession has the responsibility to be an advocate for itself if it serves an important social need and that it needs to assure society that it will continue to attract, develop, and monitor future professionals who can continue to serve the community and advance knowledge. As Michels indicates, these are ethical responsibilities of professional groups and professional organizations and it is the individual responsibility of each professional to participate in these organizational efforts. (17).

The Code devotes considerable attention to two broad and related issues—consent and confidentiality—both of which are particularly complex in the provision of psychiatric care for children and adolescents. Others who provide medical and surgical care for children have grappled with these issues, as have those not directly involved in such work.

In 1981, the American Academy of Pediatrics sponsored a Conference on Consent and Confidentiality in Adolescent Health Care. Participating in the conference was a broadly interdisciplinary group of individuals including physicians representing several specialties (including child psychiatry), attorneys, social workers, behavioral and social scientists, theologians, philosophers, congressional staff persons, and adolescents. The rich and, at times, conflicting discussions were summarized in a publication in 1982. That report outlined 12 "broad principles on which conference participants largely agreed," which included the following:

- With respect to adolescence, there exists an enduring need to balance delicately the relative rights and needs of minors to confidential health services with the relative rights and responsibilities of parents toward the offspring.
- Adolescents, unless fairly adjudged incompetent, should participate in decisions pertaining to their health.
- Even when adolescents seek health care on their own consent, they should be encouraged to involve their parents, unless there is a compelling reason not to do so. (In that case, an alternative adult advisor is appropriate.)
- Chronological age is not a suitable yardstick to determine an adolescent's maturity and capacity to give informed consent. Developmental criteria are far more telling, as applied on an individual basis.
- Adolescents generally should be entitled to confidentiality in their own health care, and that presumption should be overridden only by good reason.
- Parental notification should be encouraged but not made mandatory in the provision of adolescent health care, especially inasmuch as the absence of guaranteed confidentiality could deter many young persons from seeking and receiving necessary service. (18)

Other principles involved issues relating to the access to health care and access to and consent regarding health care records. The principles themselves suggest some of the complexities but the fact that unanimous agreement of the participants was lacking further illustrates that the resolution of these issues is difficult and that debate will continue.

The Code of the American Academy of Child Psychiatry differentiates, as did the above mentioned conference, between consent for care and consent for the release of information. Although these are separable, the issue of consent is generic. Prior to the last few decades, the issue of consent in regard to unemancipated minors received little attention. In fact, the issue of "informed consent" is quite modern and in the past, and for most of history, "consent" was by implication. Seeking the attention of a physician implied consent but, for the most part, patients reserved the right to refuse care. Parents had the responsibility to consent for their dependent children and adolescents and although the requirement, both ethical and legal, to inform them emerged as a responsibility of the physician, it is much more recently that the issue of the minor's role in consent decision making has emerged.

Gaylin described, in the *Journal of American Academy of Child Psychiatry*, the issue of proxy consent and pleaded for psychiatrists to become familiar with the numerous issues involved. He stated,

> There is no issue that presents as anguished a conflict as that of proxy consent. If one examines those values which have a high priority in our present culture, certainly one would list life itself; the family; health (and here it is used in its most constricted sense); and somewhere down the line but certainly high on our priority list, certain aspects of autonomy, dignity, and privacy. The problems of proxy consent in terms of the child ask for a balance in these respective rights against each other. There is no conclusion in this area which cannot lead to distress. There is no conclusion worthy of adopting that will not lead to distress. Any position in a complex area such as this which does not produce anxiety is probably too simple to be argued, too unworthy to be held. Similarly, conclusions recommended must always be tentative; of the time; and must be receptive to immediate modification and constant reexamination. (19)

Nevertheless, Gaylin supports a "paternalistic" approach to the decisions regarding the health and mental health care of children.

> In this paper, however, I am not dealing with the mentally ill, the prisoner, the mentally retarded, the senile or the unconscious; I am dealing with the child. The most rigid antipaternalists may want to restrict the definition of child to its extreme (under 7, 5, 2 years). Inevitably one would end up with some population who are to be considered "children," and as such may be assumed to be childish. Here such paternalism is not only necessary, but desirable. To be a parent, one must obviously behave in a parental fashion. To be parental to a child does not imply the condescension or presumption that it does with an adult. The parent is an authentic instrument of paternalism with a minor child. (20)

Miller has discussed "four senses of autonomy" in an attempt to resolve the conflict between paternalism and autonomy in decision making regarding consent in health care. Although he was addressing issues in life and death situations involving adults, his perspectives may be of substantial value in child psychiatry. Drawing on the works of others, Miller described the four senses of autonomy as follows:

- *Autonomy as Free Action.* Autonomy as free action means an action that is voluntary and intentional. An action is voluntary if it is not the result of coercion, duress or undue influence. An action is intentional if it is the conscious object of the actor.
- *Autonomy as Authenticity.* Autonomy as authenticity means that an action is consistent with a person's attitudes, values, dispositions and life plans. Roughly, the person is acting in character.
- *Autonomy as Effective Deliberation.* Autonomy as effective deliberation means action taken where a person believed that he or she was in a situation calling for a decision, was aware of the alternatives and the consequences of alternatives, evaluated both, and chose an action based upon that evaluation. Effective deliberation is of course a matter of degree; one can be more or less aware and take more or less care in making decisions. (21)
- *Autonomy as Moral Reflection.* Autonomy as moral reflection means acceptance of the moral values one acts on. The values can be those one was dealt in the socialization process, or they can differ in small or large measure. In any case, one has reflected on these values and now accepts them as one's own. This sense of autonomy is deepest and most demanding when it is conceived as reflection on one's complete set of values, attitudes and life plans. It requires rigorous self-analysis, awareness of alternative sets of values, commitment to a method for assessing them and an ability to put them in place. (22)

Miller describes each of these as essentially independent aspects of autonomy and of more or less importance depending upon the specifics of the situation. Each of these, if applied to children and adolescents, may be useful in specific situations but surely will not result in rules or standards that can be helpful all the time. As indicated earlier, children and even adolescents may be very vulnerable to coercion, intended or not. Since children and adolescents are continuing to develop and their attitudes, values, dispositions, and life plans are changing, autonomy as authenticity may be seen as having little value. Yet, those who work with and observe children carefully often can describe a number of constant characteristics of even a young child. Depending upon the developmental level and cognitive capacity, a child may be quite capable of effective deliberation, although they, like some adults, may need substantial help in understanding the situations and the alternatives. Autonomy as moral reflection may have substantial limitations when applied to children and adolescents as the capacities and awareness required develop relatively late.

In regard to the issue of consent regarding evaluation, treatment, or prevention involving a minor or unemancipated child or adolescent, the Code of the American Academy of Child Psychiatry states, "The formal responsibility for decisions regarding such participation usually resides with the parents or legal guardians" (23). It acknowledges that the agreement of the patient may be important in regard to clinical activity, but it is not required ethically. It is the responsibility of the child psychiatrist to assist the child patient in developing as much understanding as possible. In those situations, often defined by statute or special situation, where a child or adolescent seeks and consents to the care of a child psychiatrist on their own behalf, it is the responsibility of the child psychiatrist to help the patient "recognize the influence of their relationship to family members and the consequences of their decision" (24). From a clinical perspective, involvement of the family may be valuable and usually should be encouraged, although not necessarily required. The similarity with one of the principles from the Conference on Consent and Confidentiality should be noted.

In considering the issues of confidentiality in the psychiatric care of children and adolescents, one must recognize the clinical importance of the environment in which the child lives. It is not simply a tradition that psychiatric care of children requires some level of involvement of parents, at least, and, often, of others in the family, as well as the school, and, depending upon the situation, individuals in a variety of other agencies or institutions, e.g., courts, child protective services, social welfare departments, or community mental health units. For the purposes of evaluation, information may be needed from several sources, and treatment programs often require the cooperation, if not the participation of others, necessitating that they be informed about the ongoing activities of the treatment provided by the child psychiatrist. The questions of who needs to be involved, who is to make the decisions regarding involvement and the release of information, and what information is to be released must be addressed.

The responsibility for consent in the care of the unemancipated child or adolescent with regard to release of information rests with the parents or guardians, except in certain specific situations. Although the Code suggests that the information released should be sufficient to create "as thorough an understanding as can be usefully grasped and therapeutically utilized in the care of the child," it also requires that the "specific confidences of the patient and the parents, or guardians or others involved should be protected unless this course would involve untenable risks or betrayal of caretaking responsibility" (25). The Code further requires the child psychiatrist, "regardless of the locus of decision, attempt to inform the child or adolescent of the need and intent to release information and . . . seek his/her concurrence even though such agreement is not required" (26). The fundamental responsibility regarding the nature and content of the information, except in particular situations, rests with the child psychiatrist. In those situations where specific confidences are so important as to severely threaten the child or others, the child psychiatrist should seek permission to breach confidentiality but, if that is not possible, must inform the persons involved that, even without permission, information would be released.

There are some situations in which confidentiality is exceedingly limited. Such is the case when child psychiatrists agree to evaluate a situation involving a child or adolescent for a court. Under such circumstances, the child psychiatrist is obliged to answer all questions posed in the court that could be addressed by the clinical evaluation. As such, it is the child psychiatrist's responsibility to inform all parties of the lack of confidentiality beforehand.

There are some situations not directly addressed by the Code. Child psychiatrists may be requested to release information to courts or other agencies not previously involved regarding children who have been under care for some time. Such situations may pose rather difficult dilemmas. Perhaps one of the most frequent of these situations involves custody disputes or the termination of parental rights. The basic question is if the agreements that earlier evaluation and treatment were based upon did not include provisions for the release of information in regard to such matters, then can "new" authorizations to release information apply to information previously available to the child psychiatrist? Certainly psychiatrists and other physicians regularly do release information developed previously regarding an adult patient when that patient requests that it be done. That is certainly legal and probably does not raise an ethical issue unless there was information of which the patient was not aware. However, in those situations where a child has been involved in psychotherapy with a child psychiatrist, is it morally right that even with the consent of parents, the child psychiatrist release information given in confidence by the child prior to the parent's authorization and notification to the child? There is no question that to do so may alter or jeopardize the therapeutic relationship with the child and have a negative effect on the child.

The Code does address an issue that is related. Principle XII states,

Where required to do so by the laws of a state, as in cases of child abuse or neglect, or in other situations where the safety and welfare of the patient or children or others involved are in jeopardy, the child psychiatrist may divulge confidences. However, in such cases the parties involved must be thoroughly informed in advance of these requirements. (27)

The child psychiatrist may ethically refuse to comply with a legal requirement if there is sufficient reason in regard to the welfare and optimum development of the involved child or children to do so. However, to do so might clearly place the child psychiatrist in legal, but not necessarily ethical, jeopardy. In situations such as those mentioned above, it would seem a logical extension of Principle XII that a child psychiatrist called upon to release information, even if ordered to do so by a court, might ethically refuse to do so, while recognizing the risk of being held in contempt of court. Hopefully, such dilemmas can be resolved through negotiations, but law and ethics may, at times, conflict.

Although the Code recognizes the parental rights *and* responsibility to make decisions regarding consent for treatment and for the release of information, it does require child psychiatrists to attempt to inform the minor or unemancipated child or adolescent and to seek their agreement. There are two areas in which the Code specifies that regardless of the decisions of parents, the refusal of a child, who is able to understand, to agree to participation should be overriding. These involve the participation in research "where risk is significant" (28), and in professional educational activities (29).

As has been the case in the past, the American Academy of Child Psychiatry hopes the Code will serve as a standard for the profession and as an assurance to the public that standards will be maintained. It probably serves those goals rather well. The public's expectation that if an individual child psychiatrist were to transgress or breach the Code, meaningful action would result is probably not well addressed by the Code itself or by present mechanisms of enforcement. In fact, no code in medicine has "worked" particularly well in this regard. Necessary due process requirements, confidentiality, and the lack of clarity of what can be brought before ethics committees or other groups charged with the responsibility of "enforcement" have made procedures very cumbersome. Furthermore, since codes of ethics are not laws, transgressions can be dealt with in only limited ways and what might appear relatively meaningless punishments, such as the withdrawal of membership privileges in a national professional organization.

Codes of ethics are better viewed as having educational value both within the profession and beyond it. Although, like medicine as a whole, child psychiatry has viewed itself as a highly ethical profession, it has devoted relatively little formal effort to educating its members and those seeking to enter the field in the principles of ethics or the means by which ethical issues might be discussed, debated, and resolved. Although that is changing throughout medicine, child psychiatry and, indeed, all of medicine, needs to deliberately and explicitly bring more of these matters to residency programs, fellowships, and continuing education programs. It is clear that despite the good intentions of the drafters of the codes of ethics and the professional organizations that endorse and attempt to enforce them, there are times when the codes fail both the profession and the public. In some cases, statutes have replaced ethical standards in order to provide more specific assurances to the public and more meaningful reactions to transgressions. It is also clear that issues change and standards become outdated as science and technology create new dilemmas. Winslade has reviewed historical ethical changes in psychiatry and the various forces that have seemed to prompt change. Concluding his discussion, he writes,

> It is difficult to predict the shape and direction of future change, but it seems inevitable that the general trend toward legal regulation and political control of health systems will be felt quite strongly in psychiatry. For this reason, it is especially urgent that persons interested in psychiatry devote increasing attention to ethical issues. The substantive and often perplexing problems involved in examining and revising fundamental assumptions and values must be confronted directly and thoughtfully by psychiatrists, other health professionals and their critics. These explorations must not be conducted in isolation. Rather, they require an atmosphere of common concern about issues and mutual respect for different assumptions, methods and values. (30)

Education in the ethics of child psychiatry should surely go beyond an exposure to the Code of Ethics of the American Academy of Child Psychiatry. As indicated earlier, there remain many unsettled issues and new ones will arise. Case discussions, considerations of the involvement of children in instruction, research in child psychiatry training programs, and discussions involving the development of public policy all are fertile areas for education. The involvement of practitioners from other fields beyond child psychiatry in such work offers the possibility of broadening awareness and modeling an approach to the actual decision-making in clinical situations that raise ethical issues. Further, such educational efforts offer the opportunity of refining and updating the standards themselves.

This overview has not addressed all of the ethical problems that may and do arise in the psychiatric care of children and adolescents, nor does it attempt to anticipate specific issues that may arise in the future. It has also not fully addressed all of the issues in which there may be conflicts between law, ethics, and good clinical practice. Among the many such issues are requirements such as the judicial review procedures that have been established in some jurisdictions regarding the hospitalization of children and unemancipated minors. Many child psychiatrists believe that such requirements establish adversarial relationships that often compound clinical difficulties.

One might well suggest that just as child psychiatry has an obligation to pursue new knowledge and techniques regarding the diagnosis and treatment of the psychiatric illness of children and adolescents, and to work toward better, more equitable access to improved care, it has a similar obligation to continue to develop and improve the ethical standards of the profession.

REFERENCES

1. Thomas, L. *The youngest science. Notes of a medicine-watcher.* New York: Viking Press, 1983.
2. Sperry, W. L. *The ethical basis of medical practice.* New York: Paul B. Hoeber, 1950.
3. *Ibid.,* p. 83.
4. *Ibid.,* p. 84.
5. *Ibid.,* p. 93.
6. Itard, J. M. G. *The wild boy of Aveyron* (trans. G. Humphrey and M. Humphrey). New York: Appleton-Century-Crofts, 1962.
7. Aries, P. *Centuries of childhood: A social history of family life.* (trans. R. Baldick). New York: Knopf, 1965.
8. Blom, G. E. The international year of the child: Guest editorial. *Journal of the American Academy of Child Psychiatry,* 1979, *18,* p. 416.
9. *The code of ethics.* Washington, D.C.: The American Academy of Child Psychiatry, 1980, Preamble.
10. *Ibid.,* Principle I.
11. *Ibid.,* Principle II.
12. *Ibid.,* Principle V.
13. *Ibid.,* Principle VIII.
14. *Ibid.,* Principle XIV.
15. *Ibid.,* Principle III and Clarification Note regarding Principle III.
16. *Ibid.,* Principle IV.
17. Michels, R. The responsibility of psychiatry to society. In C. K. Hofling (Ed.), *Law and ethics in the practice of psychiatry.* New York: Brunner/Mazel, 1981.
18. Moore, R. S., & Hofmann, A. D. (Eds.). *American Academy of Pediatrics conference on consent and confidentiality in adolescent health care.* Evanston, IL: American Academy of Pediatrics, 1982, p. 3.
19. Gaylin, W. Who speaks for the helpless—The question of proxy consent. *The Journal of the American Academy of Child Psychiatry,* 1979, *18,* 419-436, p. 434.
20. *Ibid.,* p. 432.
21. Miller, B. L. Autonomy and the refusal of lifesaving treatment. *The Hasting Center Report,* 1981, August, p. 24.
22. *Ibid.,* p. 25.
23. *The code of ethics.* Washington, D.C.: The American Academy of Child Psychiatry, 1980, Principle VI, p. 25.

24. *Ibid.*, Principle VIII.
25. *Ibid.*, Principle VII.
26. *Ibid.*, Principle X.
27. *Ibid.*, Principle XII.
28. *Ibid.*, Principle XV.
29. *Ibid.*, Principle XVI.
30. Winslade, W. J. Ethics and ethos in psychiatry: Historical patterns and conceptual changes. In C.K. Hofling (Ed.), *Law and ethics in the practice of psychiatry*. New York: Brunner/Mazel, 1981, p. 62.

2

Children's Capacities for Participation in Treatment Decision-Making

Lois A. Weithorn

In our society, parents are authorized to make most important life decisions for their minor children. Typically, parents can and do make decisions in the "best interests" of their children. However, in recent decades, legal policy has evolved such that a range of "exceptions" to the traditional doctrine of parental consent now exists (1, 2). Certain exceptions permit children an increasing role in legal decision-making regarding their own health and well-being. As we have refined our ethical analyses and recognized the complexity inherent in doctrines such as paternalism and autonomy as applied to children, there has been an increasing attempt to define the circumstances under which minors should be involved in decisions affecting their own welfare (3, 4, 5).

Together with these trends is our growing recognition, based upon research and practice, of the clinical implications of involving children in personal health decision-making. Applications of research findings suggest that inclusion of children in certain phases of the treatment process (e.g., through access to information, or an active role in the decision-making process) may facilitate that treatment process and increase positive psychological adjustment (6, 7).

These developments lead us to a set of critical questions regarding children's capacities for participation in treatment decision-making. How capable are children of various ages and developmental stages of participating in personal treatment decisions? How do particular psychological and psychiatric disorders affect such capacities? Given the relevant legal, ethical, and clinical issues, what strategies are appropriate and useful in involving children in such decisions? This chapter is an attempt to address these questions through a review of the current state of relevant knowledge. However, I will first examine in greater detail those legal, ethical, and clinical issues that have focused greater attention upon questions of minors' capacities in treatment decision-making.

LEGAL ISSUES

Primary responsibility for the care, upbringing, and welfare of children in our society rests with children's parents who are provided with discretion in carrying out this responsibility. This discretion is protected by the legal doctrines respecting family privacy and parental autonomy, limiting the state's power to interfere with parental decision-making and activities concerning their children (8, 9). Such discretion, however, is not absolute. It is based upon presumptions 1) that parents can and will act in their children's best interests; 2) that there are no conflicts of interests impinging upon the parents' decision-making or characterizing the relationship between parent and child; and 3) that there are no countervailing interests of the state or the child which outweigh parental interests in family privacy (10, 11, 12).

When one or more of these presumptions is violated, state intervention into family affairs may occur. The most frequently cited instance of such intervention is in the case of child abuse, where parents are viewed as having failed to act in their child's best interests by harming or permitting harm to befall the child. The related concept of conflict of interests is perhaps best exemplified in the case of organ donation, where a parent may be faced with the dilemma of whether to place the health of one child at risk for the well-being of another (13, 14). Also relevant to this concept is the notion that when minors are capable of exercising autonomy, their preferences may not coincide with those of their parents (15). Countervailing state interests may include the government's interest in promoting the health of its citizens, which might lead to a waiver of the parental consent requirement, for instance, in the treatment of minors with venereal disease (the assumption being that such a waiver would increase the likelihood that minors will seek treatment, which would prevent the spread of a contagious disease). The courts have also held that in some instances, minors have interests in liberty, autonomy, and privacy, separate from those of their parents.

Whereas state intervention into the family is often characterized by a court serving as or appointing a substitute decision-maker for the parents, more recently such intervention may be characterized by an expansion of the minor's legal decision-making role. For example, the U.S. Supreme Court has held that it is unconstitutional for a state to permit parents veto power over their minor daughter's access to an abortion if their daughter is "mature enough and well-enough informed to make her abortion decision" (16). While a judge may overrule the parental veto for immature minors, in the case of mature minors, the minor's preference prevails. The Supreme Court has also supported minors' access to contraceptive devices and services (17). Many states have statutes permitting minors of particular ages independent access to other forms of treatment, such as outpatient mental health care, or treatment for substance abuse (18). And, to date, there remains a "patchwork" of state laws governing mental hospitalization of minors (19). Some states consider a "voluntary" admission of a minor voluntary only if the minor consents to the hospitalization. If the minor does not consent, or is not competent to consent, admission can be sought only through a judicial hearing. Other states permit parental "voluntary" admissions of minors, and still others have any of several variations of these procedures and policies.

Closely related to the concept of consent for treatment is the notion of consent for research participation. These concepts merge when we focus attention on research expected to be of direct benefit to the subject (i.e., "therapeutic" research) (20). Recent federal regulations defining protection for children as human subjects of biomedical and behavioral research require that research review committees ensure that "adequate provisions are made for soliciting the assent of the children, when in the judgment of the [review committee] the children are capable of providing assent" (21). *Assent* requires a significantly lower level of cognitive sophistication than does consent (22). It is clear, however, that although the research review committees are given discretion in waiving the requirement of children's assent under certain conditions, the emphasis clearly is upon involving the child in the research participation decision, if the child is capable of meaningful decision-making.

In summary, legal policies of recent years have led to an expansion of minors' roles in personal treatment decision-making in several areas. These expansions are not "across the board," that is, they do not apply to all treatment situations. Rather, they apply to those circumstances where legal policymakers have determined that some exceptions to our presumptions about the functioning of families exist, or that countervailing policy goals outweigh the protection of parental autonomy. Typically, these expansions of minors' decision-making autonomy hinge on either a presumption (e.g., based on age) of competency of the minor or a case-by-case judicial or clinical finding of competency. Given the disparity among states with respect to the ages cited in statutes, and given the emphasis on case-by-case determinations of competency in some instances, it is clear that the application of empirical research on children's decision-making capacities may assist the law in reaching informed judgments about such competencies.

ETHICAL ISSUES

Basic ethical imperatives often conflict, presenting us with ethical dilemmas, i.e., situations where either of two conflicting courses of action are ethically justifiable. Further, depending upon our personal values and the values of our reference group (e.g., our professional discipline), we may weigh one or more ethical principles more heavily when analyzing the appropriate course of ethical behavior. Regarding questions of consent to treatment, the values that most often conflict are those of autonomy and beneficence (23). Autonomy is that principle that respects each individual's basic right to determine his or her own destiny, i.e., to "self-govern." Beneficence is the principle that presents us with an affirmative duty to do good for others. When we, as health care providers, perceive that the exercise of an individual's autonomy interferes with our ability to care for them, the principles may collide. Paternalism is that process where we may decide to limit an individual's autonomy, on the bases that we know better than the individual what is in his or her best interest and that it is our duty to act on that knowledge.

Unquestionably, there are no easy shortcuts to deciding when it is *more* ethical to respect autonomy or to act paternalistically. Rather, each instance requires careful analysis of individual factors. However, one variable that appears vital to the equation is that of the individual's capacity for self-determination, i.e., his or her competency to decide. In our society, where we presume the competency of adults, the doctrine of informed consent requires that we respect the treatment decisions of adults, regardless of whether we agree with their preferences. It is only when their competency is questioned that we consider overriding personal preferences. And while the competency of psychiatric patients frequently used to be considered, de facto, to be impoverished, no such sweeping presumptions are now appropriate. In *Winters* v. *Miller*, for example, a federal court stated that:

> A finding of "mental illness" even by a judge or jury and commitment to a hospital does not raise even the presumption that a patient is incompetent or unable adequately to manage his own affairs. . . . (24)

Today, we presume that psychiatric patients are competent, unless there is case-by-case evidence that sheds doubt on such assumptions. Based on prevailing legal and ethical policy in the United States, there is not sufficient justification for overriding the treatment preference of a psychiatric patient on the basis of serving the patient's best interest, unless the patient is incompetent to decide. Other rationales, however, such as protecting society from a dangerous individual, do permit coerced treatment under certain circumstances (25).

In the case of minors, however, there remains a range of perspectives regarding their capacity for autonomy. Traditionally, the law presumed incompetence on the part of minors (26). However, as the above legal analyses and the empirical data reviewed below suggest, such a blanket presumption is no longer appropriate. Rodham notes that the presumption that all children are incapable of autonomy

> ... obscures the dramatic differences among children of different ages and the striking similarities between older children and adults. The capacities and the needs of a child of six months differ substantially from those of a child of six or 16 years. (27)

From an ethical standpoint, we need to balance respect for parental authority (i.e., "natural" paternalism) with both our own paternalism as health care professionals, and with a respect for the minor's capacity for autonomy. As that capacity increases, most typically with age and concomitant maturity, we must give increasing weight to the minor's preferences. Ethical imperatives may hold professionals to an even higher standard of conduct than the law. Thus, while a clinician may be legally authorized to provide treatment on the request of a third party (e.g., a parent), she may decide, based on an ethical analysis, to refrain from treating because the proposed focus of the treatment, a mature minor, prefers not to be treated. Capacity for autonomy and paternalism can be viewed as continual, with delicate balances maintained so that individual preferences are overridden to the minimum extent necessary to protect an individual, given the specific limitations in that individual's decision-making capacities. It remains clear that evidence regarding the capacities of minors will be helpful to professionals who must assess the appropriateness of paternalistic actions in the treatment of minors.

CLINICAL ISSUES

This chapter has focused on the legal and ethical issues relevant to the increasing involvement of children in decisions regarding their own health and mental health care. However, applications of basic research, as well as analyses of research in the treatment context, strongly suggest that there are important *clinical* advantages to increasing the participation of children in such decisions.

Facilitating positive psychological adjustment is a goal that motivates most of the efforts of mental health professionals. And, while ameliorating physical disorders may be the primary goal of other health professionals, facilitating positive psychological adjustment should be a corollary goal, in part because we now recognize how closely physical and psychological health are intertwined (28). Thus, the growing body of research indicating that a sense of control over what happens to one facilitates such positive psychological functioning is quite relevant to the efforts of professionals (29-32).

A sense of control may be achieved in many ways. When a patient is competent to make a decision regarding treatment, and otherwise situated to provide effective consent, he or she may be given autonomy either in deciding on the direction of a treatment regimen, or in deciding whether or not to enter treatment (33). When the direction of treatment is determined by another (e.g., a child whose parents should most appropriately decide, or a psychiatric patient who has been adjudicated incompetent), any of several strategies may be used to increase the patient's sense of involvement. The patient may be consulted about the options, with preferences and concerns solicited, regardless of where the final decision-making authority rests. If the eventual choice is contrary to the patient's preferences, a discussion of the rationale for the choice, and how the concerns were taken into account, may facilitate a sense of participation. Along similar lines, a child may be permitted to participate in certain corollary choices, such as whether to attend therapy sessions on Tuesday or Thursday, if such a choice is available. If a medication appears to be making her too sleepy during the day, and a slightly lower dosage is proposed by the physician, then this may be discussed with the child and her preference sought prior to making the dosage adjustment.

Perhaps most important, however, is the use of *information* as a mediator in attaining a sense of control (34). Access to information about treatment, its purpose, nature, and course, appears to have a range of positive effects on children and the treatment process. For example, research with pediatric oncology patients, among others, strongly indicates that in the absence of direct control over treatment decisions, access to information serves to enhance the sense of personal control (35-40). Information appears to reduce uncertainty and increase predictability in the environment. Not surprisingly, research findings suggest that involving patients in treatment decisions through access to information increases treatment compliance and reduces premature termination (41-47). Overall, there appears to be growing support for the belief that involving children in treatment decisions in some manner is beneficial both for their psychological well-being and for the ultimate success of the treatment endeavor (48). The nature and extent of such involvement may be determined by factors such as the legal, ethical, and clinical issues that are relevant, and the age, maturity, and desired role of the child in question (49, 50).

CHILDREN'S COMPETENCY TO CONSENT

Although the biological and psychological immaturity of children, as compared with adults, is indisputable, the categorical presumption that all individuals younger than age 18 are incapable of making reasonable decisions regarding their own welfare does not hold up against the relevant empirical data. Rodham points out that the delineation of adulthood at ages 18 or 21 were initially arbitrary and reflective of concerns that are now irrelevant (51). For example, prior to increases in the weight of armor worn by young men, the ages of 14 and 15 were the legal equivalents of our age of majority in medieval England, since capacity to bear arms was the responsibility of adults (52).

The traditional presumption of incompetence of all minors has gradually eroded in most legal circles. Although U.S. Supreme Court Chief Justice Warren E. Burger retains this perspective (53), it is apparently not shared by all of his colleagues on the Supreme Court, as evidenced by the references to minors' competency in recent abortion decisions (54). In his dissent in the 1972 case of *Wisconsin* v. *Yoder* (55), the late Justice William O. Douglas went so far as to cite the research of cognitive developmental psychologists as support for his notion that the children on whom the case focused, aged 14 and 15, had the requisite intellectual and cognitive maturity to make the important life decision of whether to withdraw from public school to assert free exercise of religion.

In fact, the research cited by Justice Douglas does appear directly relevant to questions of competency to consent to treatment. Competency is one of three conditions necessary for a treatment decision to be considered legally valid. The other conditions are "voluntariness," i.e., that the patient can decide free from coercion and unfair persuasions and inducements; and the disclosure of information, i.e., that the consent was knowledgeable (56). The predominant legal standard for competency emphasizes that the patient must have an "appreciation" of the nature, extent, and probable consequences of the treatment to which he has consented (57). Although the law gives little elucidation to the definition of the term "appreciation," it appears to refer to a "higher" level of understanding, beyond comprehension of mere factual information, requiring the individual to think abstractly and draw inferences about the implications of the proposed treatments for herself (58, 59). In practice, however, a standard emphasizing comprehension of factual information probably typifies how the notion of competency is construed.

Roth, Meisel, and Lidz (60), Meisel (61), and Lidz et al. (62) have reviewed several additional standards of competency. They point out that the application of one standard versus another in setting the criterion for competency at a higher or lower level depends on the context and the policy issues involved. The "rational reasons" or "reasonable decision-making process" standards examine the process used by an individual in reaching a treatment decision. Application of behavioral decision-making theory would suggest that one strategy for assessing this process is evaluating the degree to which one utilizes the information disclosed regarding the risks, benefits, and related consequences of the alternative treatments. The "evidence of choice" test requires only that patients express a preference regarding the proposed treatments; no demonstration of understanding or adequate reasoning is necessary. Finally, the "reasonable outcome" standard examines the degree to which the choice made by the patient is reasonable. Clearly, this is the most subjective standard, since what is considered to be a reasonable choice to one person may not appear to be reasonable to another.

Weithorn (63) and Grisso and Vierling (64) reviewed the psychological abilities and skills that appear to be required to make competent treatment decisions, given the application of various standards, as noted above. Relying upon Piagetian research (65), these authors suggest that most adolescents will have the requisite cognitive skills to demonstrate competency even according to the highest standard: appreciation. This standard requires that patients comprehend information about future possibilities resulting from each of several choices, necessitating the ability to conceptualize abstract ideas (66). The highest stage of cognitive development, according to Piaget's framework, formal operational thinking, permits reasoning about multiple abstract possibilities, hypothesizing about the consequences of each, and choice among the various courses of action (67). Such operational structures develop during pre- and early adolescence, and reach an equilibrium at around age 14. This would suggest that most adolescents are as capable as adults of such cognitive operations, since thinking does not progress to a higher stage of cognitive development subsequently. Rather, further development is characterized more by differentiation of skills and development of specific areas of interest (68).

Although little empirical research exists that directly tests the above proposals in the treatment context, that which has been conducted is strongly supportive. Weithorn and Campbell (69) compared children aged nine and 14 to adults aged 18 and 21. All subjects were presented with four hypothetical "dilemmas" describing two medical and two psychological disorders. In each dilemma, subjects were given detailed information about the nature, purpose, risks, and benefits of several alternative treatments, and were asked to choose among them for the hypothetical story character who was faced with the decision. A series of standardized questions followed, and responses were scored according to an extensive set of quantitative coding criteria developed to permit assessment of competency according to each of the standards noted above.

The findings strongly supported the hypothetical predictions. In general, the performance of the 14 year olds was strikingly similar to that of the adults according to all standards of competency; factual understanding; inferential understanding (i.e., appreciation); reasoning process; reasonable outcome; and evidence of choice. The nine-year-old subjects, however, performed significantly less well on the understanding and reasoning scales. Yet, despite such performance, they did not differ from the adolescents and adults, in most instances, with regard to the choices they selected! In all instances, the nine year olds evidenced a preference.

More focused analysis of the findings reveals several interesting trends. For example, whereas the adolescents and adults appeared to understand most of the treatment information disclosed to them (approximately 89% by the adults), the nine year olds appeared to comprehend approximately 69% of the information presented to them (70). Thus, while the youngest subjects clearly were not capable of as complete comprehension as the adults and adolescents, they did demonstrate an impressive level of understanding. Along the same lines, while they failed to take into account the diversity of risks and benefits disclosed, compared with the adults and adolescents the nine year olds tended to consider the few most salient, and arguably, most reasonable and important variables in making their decision (e.g., take the medication because otherwise you can continue having seizures and hurt yourself) (71). They attended less to factors such as side effects and discomforts, emphasizing instead the importance of alleviating whatever symptomatology was present. Typically these children presented quite sensible rationales for their judgments.

These findings suggest that where appropriate from legal, ethical, and clinical standpoints, most normal adolescents are capable of making competent treatment decisions. Younger children, perhaps as young as age nine, are also quite capable of meaningful involvement in the decision-making and treatment processes, despite their somewhat less mature cognitive capacities. Related research (72) suggests that children as young as six may be capable of such participation.

THE IMPACT OF PSYCHOLOGICAL AND PSYCHIATRIC DISORDERS UPON THE COMPETENCY OF CHILDREN

The research described above involved normal children as subjects. At present, I am undertaking a similar project with psychiatric inpatients, examining the capacities of children, adolescents, and adults to consent to psychiatric hospitalization. To date, no studies have empirically investigated the questions of both developmental differences and differences due to presence of a psychological or psychiatric disorder. However, findings from related research, described below, permit us to make some initial predictions regarding the capacities of children suffering from mental health problems.

Researchers at Hahnemann Medical College have examined the problem-solving skills of normal and mentally disordered persons of various ages. These investigators were not studying competency to consent to treatment, but certain of their findings are relevant. In particular, they examined the "consequential thinking" (i.e., decision-making process) applied by subjects to interpersonal problems. They found that normal children and adolescents did not differ significantly from same-aged psychiatric patients, with respect to this measure (73). However, adolescents labeled "impulsive" were found to be less likely to consider the consequences of interpersonal behavior than normal adolescents (74). When adult psychiatric patients were compared with normal adults, significant differences were found to exist (75). It is not clear why the adult patients would be less skilled than their normal control group, while the child and adolescent psychiatric patients would not. No further specificity regarding the diagnostic characteristics of the groups was provided. These findings, while providing some indication of how psychiatric patients might reason generally about interpersonal problems, do not directly address the question of competency to consent to treatment.

Other researchers have investigated the competency of patients to participate in treatment decision-making. Unfortunately, much of the research on psychiatric patients does not compare such patients to control groups of nonpatients or medical patients. Such comparisons are essential, since studies have demonstrated that medical patients demonstrate incomplete recall and understanding of disclosed information (76, 77, 78). Studies that find that psychiatric patients also demonstrate such incomplete recall and comprehension may naively label such patients "incompetent," without realizing that the general population may function at a similar level. Those studies that compared psychiatric patients empirically to medical patients found that the groups do not differ significantly on most measures (79, 80, 81). Although some of the studies without control groups report deficiencies in psychiatric patients' comprehension, others do not (82, 83, 84). Yet, within a psychiatric patient sample, type of disorder has been found to differentiate patients on competency measures. Roth and colleagues found that patients diagnosed as psychotic performed significantly more poorly on a measure of competency to consent to electroconvulsive therapy than did patients with nonpsychotic diagnoses (85, 86). Unquestionably future research must focus on the relative capacities of psychiatric patients of identified diagnostic groups as compared with medical patients or nonpatient control groups. At this point, however, we may conclude that the data suggest that some psychiatric patients (particularly those with cognitive disorders) may be less competent than normals or medical patients. The data do not, however, support the notion that psychiatric patients in general are less competent than appropriate control groups.

There are several implications of this research for the competency of children and adolescents with mental health problems. First, and most importantly, our state of knowledge to date is still too rudimentary to draw conclusions. Second, what data exist do not indicate that the types of psychological or psychiatric impairments experienced by children and adolescents necessarily interfere with competent decision-making. A large percentage of children in psychiatric inpatient facilities are diagnosed as having conduct disorders and other problems not expected to impair cognitive capacities necessary for comprehension and decision-making (87). Few children in such facilities experience psychotic disorders, for example. Impulsive children may be less able to consider a range of consequences in decision-making (88), but may be able to demonstrate adequate understanding, as would be required by the more prevalent legal notions of competency. In short, the need for more focused data, which examine the capacities of the population of interest in comparison to appropriate control groups, is essential before we can further speculate as to the implications of the existing data base for the competency of children with mental health disorders.

STRATEGIES FOR INVOLVING CHILDREN IN TREATMENT DECISIONS

Whether or not a patient is capable of independent treatment decision-making, and whether or not the relevant legal standards permit such autonomous decisions, there remain a range of clinically useful strategies for involving the minor in the treatment decision or treatment process. As noted above, even if a minor is not given independent decision-making authority, it is, in most instances, in that minor's best interests to have some role in the decision or process.

Such participation can be achieved through encouraging joint decision-making within families (89). The professional can facilitate parent-child communication by assisting families in working together to reach important treatment goals. Merely having access to information about the ultimate decision can be psychologically beneficial to children. The information may be provided by the parent(s) or the professional, with each strategy having certain advantages.

Certain types of professional relationships, such as those between a psychotherapist and patient, and in some cases between physician and patient, lend themselves to an ongoing collaboration between practitioner and child. Once a decision has been made to establish a professional relationship, that relationship can be conceptualized as a working partnership. Koocher (90) and Melton (91) suggest that children's input into the planning of therapeutic strategies and goal setting be incorporated into the treatment process wherever possible. As previously noted, such collaboration and access to information may reduce premature termination and increase treatment compliance.

There remains a great need for data to elucidate questions regarding the capacities of minors, particularly emotionally disturbed minors, to make informed treatment decisions, but several conclusions are possible. First, it is clear that most school-aged children, including those with serious psychological difficulties, are capable of meaningful *participation* in the treatment process and in decision-making, although their specific role will depend on the circumstances, their age and maturity, and the clinical issues involved. There are a variety of strategies that may be employed in involving children in such processes. Most importantly, whether or not the law requires the involvement of minors in such decisions, it appears to be in their best interest, and in the interest of facilitating therapeutic goals, to include the children in the process in an appropriate manner.

REFERENCES

1. Wadlington, W. J. Consent to medical care for minors. In G. B. Melton, G. P. Koocher, & M. J. Saks (Eds.), *Children's competence to consent*. New York: Plenum, 1983.
2. Wilkins, L. P. Children's rights: Removing the parental consent barrier. *Arizona State Law Review*, 1975, 31-92.
3. Mnookin, R. H. *Child, family and state*. Boston: Little, Brown, 1978.
4. Wadlington, W. J., Whitebread, C. H., & Davis, S. M. *Children in the legal system*. Mineola, NY: The Foundation Press, 1983.
5. Weithorn, L. A. Involving children in decisions affecting their own welfare. In G. B. Melton, G. P. Koocher, & M. J. Saks (Eds.), *Children's competence to consent*. New York: Plenum, 1983.
6. Melton, G. B. Decision making by children: Psychological risks and benefits. In G. B. Melton, G. P. Koocher, & M. J. Saks (Eds.), *Children's competence to consent*. New York: Plenum, 1983.
7. Weithorn, L. A. Developmental factors and competence to make informed treatment decisions. *Child and Youth Services*, 1982, 5, 85-100.
8. Mnookin, 1978.
9. Wadlington, 1983.
10. Mnookin, 1978.
11. Wadlington, 1983.
12. Weithorn, 1982.
13. Wadlington, 1983.
14. Weithorn, 1982.

15. In re Green, 292 A. 2d 387 (Pa., 1972).
16. Bellotti v. Baird (II), 443 U.S. 622 (1979).
17. Carey v. Population Services International, 431 U.S. 678 (1977).
18. Wilkins, 1975.
19. Weithorn, L. A. Voluntary Admission to Mental Health Facilities: Children's Capacities for Self-Determination. Paper presented at the American Psychological Association Convention, Anaheim, CA, 1983.
20. Weithorn, L. A. Children's capacities to decide about participation in research. IRB: A Review of Human Subjects Research, 1983, 5(2): 1-5.
21. Additional Protections for Children Involved as Subjects in Research, 48:46 Federal Register 9614 (March 8, 1983).
22. Weithorn, L. A. Children's capacities in legal contexts. In N. D. Reppucci, L. A. Weithorn, E. P. Mulvey, & J. Monahan (Eds.), Children, mental health and law. Beverly Hills: Sage Publications, 1984.
23. Beauchamp, T. L., & Childress, J. F. Principles of biomedical ethics. New York: Oxford University Press, 1983.
24. Winters v. Miller, 446 F. 2d 65 (2d Cir. 1971), p. 66.
25. Wexler, D. B. Mental health law. New York: Plenum, 1981.
26. Wadlington, 1983.
27. Rodham, H. Children under the law. Harvard Educational Review, 1973, 43, 487-514.
28. Stone, G. C., Cohen, G., & Adler, N. E. Health psychology—A handbook. Washington: Jossey-Bass, 1979.
29. Abramson, L., Seligman, M., & Teasdale, J. Learned helplessness in humans: Critique and reformulation. Journal of Abnormal Psychology, 1978, 87, 49-74.
30. Arnkoff, D. B., & Mahoney, M. J. The role of perceived control in psychopathology. In L. C. Perlmuter, & R. A. Monty (Eds.), Choice and perceived control. Hillsdale, NJ: Lawrence Erlbaum, 1979.
31. Averill, J. R. Personal control over aversive stimuli and its relationship to stress. Psychological Bulletin, 1973, 80, 286-303.
32. Seligman, M. E. P. Helplessness: On depression, development and death. San Francisco: W. H. Freeman, 1975.
33. Weithorn, 1983 (see Reference 5).
34. Ibid.
35. Cassileth, B. R., Zupkis, R. V., Sutton-Smith, K., & March, V. Information and participation preferences among cancer patients. Annals of Internal Medicine, 1980, 92, 832-836.
36. Kellerman, J., & Katz, E. The adolescent with cancer: Theoretical, clinical and research issues. Journal of Pediatric Psychology, 1977, 2, 127-131.
37. Kendall, P. C., Williams, L., Pechacek, T. F., Graham, L. E. et al. Cognitive-behavioral and patient education interventions in cardiac catheterization procedures: The Palo Alto Medical Psychology Project. Journal of Consulting and Clinical Psychology, 1979, 47, 49-58.
38. Koocher, G. P. Promoting coping with illness in childhood. In J. C. Rosen, & B. J. Solomon (Eds.), Prevention in health psychology. Hanover, NH: University Press of New England, in press.
39. Nannis, E. D., Susman, E. J., Strope, B. E., Woodruff, P. J. et al. Correlates of control in pediatric cancer patients and their families. Journal of Pediatric Psychology, 1982, 7, 75-84.
40. Vernick, J., & Karon, M. Who's afraid of death on a leukemia ward? American Journal of Diseases of Children, 1965, 109, 393-397.
41. Melton, 1983.
42. Day, L., & Reznikoff, M. Social class, the treatment process, and parents' and children's expectations about child psychotherapy. Journal of Clinical Child Psychology, 1980, 9, 195-198.
43. Francis, V., Korsch, B. M., & Morris, M. J. Gaps in doctor-patient communication II: Patients' response to medical advice. New England Journal of Medicine, 1969, 280, 535-540.
44. Holmes, D. S., & Urie, R. G. Effects of preparing children for psychotherapy. Journal of Consulting and Clinical Psychology, 1975, 43, 311-318.

45. Lewis, C. E., Lewis, M. A., Lorimer, A., & Palmer, B. B. Child-initiated care: The use of school nursing services by children in an "adult-free" system. *Pediatrics*, 1977, *60*, 499-507.
46. Mazucca, S. A. Does patient education in chronic disease have therapeutic value? *Journal of Chronic Disease*, 1982, *35*, 521-529.
47. Roter, D. L. Patient participation in the patient-provider interaction: The effects of patient question asking on the quality of interaction, satisfaction, and compliance. *Health Education Monographs*, 1977, *5*, 281-315.
48. Weithorn, 1983 (see Reference 5).
49. *Ibid.*
50. Melton, 1983.
51. Rodham, 1981.
52. Weithorn, 1982.
53. *Parham* v. *J.R.*, 442 U.S. 584 (1979).
54. Weithorn, L. A. Abortion Decisions by Minors: How Mature is "Mature Enough?" Paper presented at the American Psychological Association Convention, Anaheim, CA, 1983.
55. *Wisconsin* v. *Yoder*, 408 U.S. 205 (1972).
56. Meisel, A., Roth, L. H., & Lidz, C. W. Toward a model of the legal doctrine of informed consent. *American Journal of Psychiatry*, 1977, *134*, 285-289.
57. Weithorn, 1983 (see Reference 5).
58. Weithorn, 1982.
59. Appelbaum, P. S., & Roth, L. H. Clinical issues in the assessment of competency. *American Journal of Psychiatry*, 1981, *138*, 1462-1467.
60. Roth, L. H., Meisel, A., & Lidz, C. W. Tests of competency to consent to treatment. *American Journal of Psychiatry*, 1977, *134*, 279-284.
61. Meisel, A. The "exceptions" to the informed consent doctrine: Striking a balance between competing values in medical decisionmaking. *Wisconsin Law Review*, 1979, 413-488.
62. Lidz, C. W., Meisel, A., Zerubavel, E., Carter, M. et al. *Informed consent: A study of decisionmaking in psychiatry.* New York: Guilford, 1984.
63. Weithorn, 1982.
64. Grisso, T., & Vierling, L. Minors' consent to treatment: A developmental perspective. *Professional Psychology*, 1978, *9*, 412-437.
65. Inhelder, B., & Piaget, J. *The growth of logical thinking.* New York: Basic Books, 1958.
66. Weithorn, 1982.
67. Inhelder & Piaget, 1958.
68. Piaget, J. Intellectual evolution from adolescence to adulthood. *Human Development*, 1972, *15*, 1-12.
69. Weithorn, L. A., & Campbell, S. B. The competency of children and adolescents to make informed treatment decisions. *Child Development*, 1982, *53*, 1589-1598.
70. Weithorn, 1983 (see Reference 12).
71. Weithorn & Campbell, 1982.
72. Lewis, C. E., Lewis, M. A., & Ifekwunigue, M. Informed consent by children and participation in an influenza vaccine trial. *American Journal of Public Health*, 1978, *68*, 1079-1082.
73. Spivack, G., Platt, J. J., & Shure, M. B. *The problem-solving approach to adjustment.* San Francisco: Jossey-Bass, 1976.
74. Spivack, G., & Levine, M. *Self-regulation in acting-out and normal adolescents* (Report M-4531). Washington, D.C.: National Institutes of Health, 1963.
75. Platt, J. J., & Spivack, G. Studies in problem-solving thinking of psychiatric patients: Patient-control differences and factorial structure of problem-solving thinking. Proceedings of the Eighty-First Annual Convention of the American Psychological Association, 1973.
76. Bergler, J., Pennington, C., Metcalfe, M., & Freis, E. Informed consent: How much does the patient understand? *Clinical Pharmacology and Therapeutics*, 1980, *27*, 435-439.
77. Kennedy, B. J., & Lillehaugen, A. Patient recall of informed consent. *Medical Pediatric Oncology*, 1979, *7*, 173-178.
78. Robinson, G., & Merav, A. Informed consent: Recall by patients tested post-operatively. *Annals of Thoracic Surgery*, 1976, *22*, 209-212.

79. Grossman, L., & Summers, F. A study of the capacity of schizophrenic patients to give informed consent. *Hospital and Community Psychiatry,* 1980, *31,* 205-207.
80. Soskis, D. A. Schizophrenic and medical inpatients as informed drug consumers. *Archives of General Psychiatry,* 1978, *20,* 126-131.
81. Stanley, B.H., Stanley, M., Lautin, A., Kane, J., & Schwartz, N. Preliminary findings of psychiatric patients as research participants: A population at risk? *American Journal of Psychiatry,* 1981, *138,* 669-671.
82. Appelbaum, P. S., & Gutheil, T. G. Drug refusal: A study of psychiatric inpatients. *American Journal of Psychiatry,* 1980, *137,* 340-346.
83. Appelbaum, P. S., Mirkin, S. A., & Bateman, A. L. Empirical assessment of competency to consent to psychiatric hospitalization. *American Journal of Psychiatry,* 1981, *138,* 1462-1467.
84. Roth, L. H. Competency to consent to or refuse treatment. In L. Grinspoon (Ed.), *Psychiatry 1982: The American Psychiatric Association annual review.* Washington, D.C.: American Psychiatric Association, 1982.
85. Roth, L. H. An empirical study of informed consent in psychiatry. Final Report: NIMH Grant No. R12-MH 27553. Rockville, MD., 1980.
86. Lidz, C. W., Meisel, A., Zerubavel, E., Carter, M., Sestak, R. M., & Roth, L. H. *Informed consent: A study of decisionmaking in psychiatry.* New York: Guilford, 1984.
87. Weithorn, 1983 (see Reference 11).
88. Spivack & Levine, 1963.
89. Weithorn, 1983 (see Reference 5).
90. Koocher, G. P. Competence to consent: Psychotherapy. In G. B. Melton, G. P. Koocher, & M. J. Saks (Eds.), *Children's competence to consent.* New York: Plenum, 1983.
91. Melton, G. B. Children's participation in treatment planning: Psychological and legal issues. *Professional Psychology,* 1981, *12,* 246-252.

3

Refusal of Treatment in Childhood Cancer

Shirley B. Lansky

Advances in cancer treatment have been dramatic over the past 20 years. Nowhere is this more evident than in the treatment of childhood cancer. Statistics now available indicate an overall survival rate of 50% for childhood cancer patients and, in certain illnesses, that rate increases to an 80%-90% survival. This improvement has come about through aggressive anticancer treatment modalities, primarily chemotherapy and radiotherapy.

Cancer treatments are rigorous and often accompanied by undesirable side effects. Frequently, unsuspecting parents bring their child to the attention of a physician with what appears to them to be a minor problem, such as a painless swelling, and are confronted with the frightening news that the child has cancer and will need a prolonged period of treatment (one to three years). Additionally, in some cases, surgery may be indicated, which, in its most mutilative form (such as that of osteosarcoma), can include the loss of a limb. Thus, it may not be surprising that some parents refuse treatment. In addition to fear, refusal is often based on a feeling of hopelessness, despite the favorable statistics, about the ultimate outcome of the illness. This can be occasionally traced back to the parents' prior exposure to an adult cancer patient, who may have had a long, protracted, painful course, and ultimately succumbed despite treatment.

During a five-year period, 14 cases of childhood cancer were seen at the University of Kansas in which treatment was not carried out because of the parents' and/or the child's refusal. Some families refused on the basis of religious beliefs. Others sought unconventional treatment such a laetrile. Refusal by the patient was seen most often in adolescents who disliked the side effects and the inconvenience of treatment. The case examples described below highlight the four different sets of circumstances that were seen in these families and the general philosophy used in managing the cases. The four categories of refusal are: 1) the parent refuses therapy for a child with a good prognosis; 2) the parent refuses therapy for a child with a poor prognosis; 3) the child refuses therapy; and 4) therapy is refused by parent and the child is also abused.

PARENT REFUSES THERAPY FOR A CHILD WITH A GOOD PROGNOSIS

Case 1

A five-year-old girl was referred to the hospital for treatment of acute lymphoblastic leukemia. The symptoms and findings she had at diagnosis put her in that group of patients who have at least a 50% chance of disease-free survival expected. The mother was noted to be remarkably casual during this initial period and displayed none of the anxiety usually seen in parents. She came to the hospital irregularly and frequently appeared intoxicated. On one occasion, the nursing staff discovered the mother and her boyfriend engaged in sexual play in the child's bed (which was in an occupied, three-bed ward). By the end of the first week, the mother stated that she did not want the child treated any longer as it was a bother for her to come into the hospital. She commented, "She can heal herself." A fortuitous visit by the grandparents confirmed the suspicions that the mother was a heavy drug user. Further family history disclosed that the child had been used by the mother to manipulate the grandparents, i.e., she would not let the little girl visit unless the grandparents gave the mother money. A court order was obtained, and the judge placed the child in the custody of the grandparents for the three-year duration of the child's treatment. The child was alive and disease-free at the last inquiry.

PARENT REFUSES THERAPY FOR A CHILD WITH A POOR PROGNOSIS

Case 2

This youngster was diagnosed with acute myelogenous leukemia at age six. When first seen, the father, a mechanic for a major airline, announced that he believed in faith healing. During the diagnostic period, he was belligerent and hostile to the staff, whom he described as "worldly." He also said he did not want any "secular" literature left in the room, which consisted of disease-related materials and basic hospital information always given to the family. He announced that the biggest problem the family had was the mother's lack of faith that the child would be healed.

Numerous attempts were made to reach the father. One of our parent advocates, who belonged to the same religious group, spent time with him. The father told her that she obviously did not have enough faith or her child would not have died. The family minister was called in to talk to the father. He, too, was dismissed as having inadequate faith. By dealing with the father in as supportive and unthreatening a manner as possible, we were able to keep the child in the hospital for three weeks, the duration of the first course of treatment. At the end of the three-week period, the father told his wife that the boy should be taken to a faith healer. The mother was afraid of the father, but also understood the need for treatment. She urged the staff to keep the child in the hospital for the entire duration of treatment (three years) as she was afraid her husband would use airline passes to take the child out of the country once he was dismissed from the hospital. By this time, the child was near the end of the first treatment (induction therapy) period, and was in remission and doing well. One Sunday afternoon, the parents requested that he be permitted to go out of the hospital for a short visit. The house officer on duty, not recognizing the implications, granted the request. The family took the boy out and did not return him to the hospital.

The family was called repeatedly, but refused to return the child for further treatment. The father said he would consider bringing the child in at a later time for a bone marrow examination to "prove" that faith had cured him. Four months later, we were notified that the boy had been sent to school, appeared to be extremely ill, and was not getting any treatment. The teacher reported the case to Protective Services, and treatment was ordered. At this time, the child had orbital cellulitis, mastoiditis, and leukemia in relapse. The child was court ordered to be confined to the hospital and had a deteriorating course over a three-month period. The parents visited occasionally. The father maintained that the child was cured. The mother refused to talk to anyone.

The terminal event was a central nervous system hemorrhage. The parents were called and came in smiling, saying that they had been asking for an event to demonstrate their faith. They maintained a smiling vigil by the bedside and, following the child's death, refused to permit the body to be taken to the morgue for several hours because they were anticipating a miracle (interpreted as waiting for him to rise from the dead).

Following the child's death, the staff carried out the usual procedure of calling the family to indicate their concern and provide assistance if the family wished it. These overtures were met with hostility. However, periodically over the next two years, one of the parents would call a physician or nurse clinician who had been involved in their child's care and request information about some aspect of pediatric oncology, but not necessarily related to the disease or treatment of their son. During these calls, they refused to discuss anything other than the specific question posed. This was viewed by the staff as a method of maintaining contact, and it was surmised that even this highly structured conversation provided comfort for them.

THE CHILD REFUSES THERAPY

Case 3

A young man, 18 years of age, was diagnosed with osteosarcoma and had an amputation of the right leg. He began a course of chemotherapy and, after approximately six months of treatment, said he was not returning.

He was the oldest child of a farm family. During adolescence he had done very well in managing his sick father's farm, as well as planning an independent farm. The loss of his leg, the vomiting, and weight loss accompanying his chemotherapy interfered with his responsibilities on the farm. He had been the mainstay of the family and now saw himself as the biggest burden. His outlook was depicted by a statement made to one of the physicians treating him, "On the farm, when you have a lame horse, you shoot it." Subsequently, he refused to continue chemotherapy. Talks with him and his family were fruitless, and he left the hospital. All attempts to contact him were unsuccessful.

THERAPY IS REFUSED BY PARENT AND THE CHILD IS ALSO ABUSED

Case 4

A five-year-old girl was operated on for a hemangiopericytoma of the chest. Five years later, the disease recurred. The mother had abandoned the family when this patient was two years old. The father was disabled, weighed 500 pounds, and had problems with heart disease and diabetes. It was difficult to persuade the father to bring this child in for treatment, and therapy was frequently refused. During one of her hospital stays, she informed the staff that the father had sexually abused both her and her older sister. Her sister escaped the home by getting married at age 16. This girl was the only child left at home. At age 10, she had full responsibility for household maintenance and was the father's sexual object. She was taken into protective custody. In spite of court-ordered treatment, she developed brain metastases and died.

These cases highlight the four circumstances under which refusal of treatment occurred: 1) parent's refusal with a child with a good prognosis; and 2) Parent's refusal with a child with a poor prognosis; 3) the child refuses therapy; and 4) the therapy is refused by the parent and the child is also abused. Each circumstance led to different recommendation for clinical management. Clinical recommendations also influenced the juvenile court responses to staff requests. The treatment plan was thus interactive. The precedents that appeared to be operative in managing these difficult questions included the following principles: Parents cannot refuse proven life-saving treatment for a child (1). However, parents can refuse high-risk treatments that are potentially effective but whose efficacy has not been conclusively demonstrated (2). When the statistical cure rate for the illness was greater than 50%, and the odds for survival were favorable, the request for a court order was pursued. When the prognosis was less than 30% with treatment, the court was not requested to order treatment.

The second circumstance—poor prognosis—is the most difficult category for several reasons. First, prognosis deals with statistics, and thus is no assurance that a particular child may not fall into the small group who do respond to treatment. Second, over the past 25 years progress in the treatment of malignancies has occurred at a rapid rate and new effective treatments are being developed continuously. Thus, successful treatment is followed by statistical documentation. In other words, a disease with a 20% - 30% prognosis today may see a new treatment six months later that increases the survival rate to greater than 50%. One could, therefore, argue that in these cases, a court order for treatment should also be sought. In the second case, it was the secondary complications of leukemia in relapse—principally, infection—that prompted the teacher to report the case. The pitiful plight of the child influenced the order for treatment, which included chemotherapy as well as attention to the multiple infections.

In the third case the patient's age, 18 years, prevented an appeal to the juvenile court even though the prognosis was favorable. The fourth case included the additional element of sexual abuse. By requesting the court's assistance, the child was removed from the home and put into protective custody, which allowed continuation of therapy.

While a great deal of progress has been made in reporting child abuse to the juvenile authorities, there is still reluctance on the part of many professionals to report parents who refuse conventional therapy to the courts. The severity of the illness and discomfort of treatment, in addition to the question of how well this particular child fits into the statistical probability of cure, generate a reluctance among some caregivers to begin the unpleasant legal process.

When the treatment team has weighed the question of the validity of refusal of treatment and has decided that the parents' or child's wishes (3, 4) should not be followed, they are faced with the difficulties inherent in any attempt to act in the interests of the child against his or the parents' wishes. Work in the area of child abuse and neglect is gradually modifying the once widespread view that parental rights are sacred. However, when the questions of a catastrophic, life-threatening illness, which requires prolonged and aggressive treatment, arise, some juvenile courts may be more sympathetic to the parents' suffering than to the benefit of treatment for the child. When it is the child's wish to discontinue treatment, then the issue of his or her ability to exercise informed consent arises.

Given the many questions and few certainties, how is the clinician to proceed in taking care of these children? Tentative guidelines have emerged from the work with the children and families described above. When parents wish to discontinue treatment with a child with a good prognosis, recourse to the juvenile court is indicated. Prompt reporting of these children as cases of medical neglect ideally results in the child's reentering treatment. However, even under the best circumstances, valuable time is lost due to the nature of the legal proceedings, which potentially alters the child's prognosis for survival.

In a child with a poor prognosis and with unproven but possibly effective treatment modalities, we do not notify, and do not recommend notifying, the juvenile court of the parents' action in discontinuing treatment against medical advice. When aggressive treatment may result in little or no benefit to the child, the child's best interests may be better served by maintaining rapport with the parents and in providing the child and family with as much support and symptomatic relief as possible. This course of action has resulted in maintaining support services to and contact with patients and families who might otherwise be lost to follow-up.

We will undoubtedly be faced with an increasing number of patients and/or families where recommended treatment is refused for one reason or another. The most desirable course is to be able to educate both the child and the parents in the value of the recommended cancer treatment. However, if this approach is unsuccessful, and if the child has a good prognosis with treatment, then one should not be hesitant about reporting these families to the juvenile court. It might appear impossible for the same pediatric oncology team that reports to the court to later provide emotional support to the same family. However, continued efforts to work with the family, in our experience, can usually be resolved. The same approach has been used effectively in cases of child abuse for several years.

The concept of providing continuing emotional support is a critical one for families who have chosen to discontinue treatment for a child with a poor prognosis. Maintaining frequent contact with the medical center, as well as mobilizing community services such as visiting nurses, is also an important aspect of treatment.

It is no longer acceptable to take at face value a decision by the parents to either discontinue treatment and "let the child die in peace," or seek unconventional or unproven treatments. Working to secure any treatment that is in the child's ultimate best interest is as crucial in cancer treatment as in any other childhood disorder where there is a significant probability of control or cure (5).

REFERENCES

1. Case. C. G. Custody of a minor (Refusal of Rx in childhood cancer). *New England Journal of Medicine*, 1979, *379*(2), 1053.
2. Macklin, R. Consent, coercion, and conflicts of rights. *Perspectives in Biology and Medicine*, 1977, *20*, 360.
3. Rozovsky, G. E. Can a minor consent to treatment. *Dimensions in Health Sciences*, 1977, *54*, 10.
4. Rombro, R. A. Minor's capacity to consent to medical treatment. *Maryland State Medical Journal*, 1978, *27*, 43.
5. Lansky, S. B., Vats, T., & Cairns, N. U. Refusal of treatment. *American Journal of Pediatric Hematology/Oncology*, 1979, *1*, 277-282.

4

Organ Transplants, Research, and Children

Melvin Lewis

Organ donation for transplantation in children is becoming increasingly common. To serve this need a nationwide transplant hotline, 800/24-DONOR, sponsored by the North American Transplant Coordination Organization (NATCO), is available to physicians who need to procure a kidney or an extrarenal organ. While death is necessary for the donation of organs such as the liver, this is not the case in kidney transplant. Consequently, an important question arises about consent for kidney donation by a child.

Since kidney donation by a minor entails virtually no possibility of direct, tangible benefit to the donor (although the expectation is that the donation will so benefit another), kidney donation by a minor may be considered in one respect as research (i.e., a contribution for the good of someone *other* than the person involved) (1). If that is the case, the critical question in research is how the child's understanding of the procedure and risks involved applies to organ transplants.

The preadolescent's cognitive level is usually insufficient for the child to comprehend fully the risks, discomfort, and nature of the procedure, or reasons given for its necessity. Informed consent in preadolescents is therefore impossible. Consequently, the notion of a lower standard called "assent" has been invoked (2). Yet even assent requires: 1) a minimum basic understanding of what is going to be done to one; 2) some comprehension of the purpose of the action, i.e., to help another person recover from an illness; and 3) an ability on the part of the child to say *yes* or *no* to the "invitation" (if that is the right word) to undergo the operation.

To meet even these lower requirements, it is still necessary that the child be able to consider multiple, and sometimes complex, paradoxical factors simultaneously (e.g., risks *and* benefits), weigh the relative merits of various options, and consider factors not immediately present (e.g., consequences that may occur at a remote time). Thus, it again becomes important to define and assess the degree to which this is possible in a child at different stages of development.

At what point on the developmental curve does the child become mature enough in his own right to make the decision for himself? At what point can the child participate (assent/dissent) in the decision? And when does the child have no real capacity to participate? In general, 14 years seems a safe point at which a sufficient level of cognitive development can be expected to exist that would allow informed consent (3). Below age seven, in general, the level of cognitive development is such that the child can usually have but little understanding. Between seven and 14 the level of maturity is variable. Put another way, between seven and 14 the child has an *increasing* maturity; consequently, the child's assent or dissent becomes *increasingly* important during the period seven to 14 years of age.

At the same time, the child's assent is not a simple, autonomous matter. The child is still dependent on the parent or custodial adult in many respects and understandably will tend to follow the dictates and wishes of that adult. Therefore, the adult has a special responsibility (as always, but especially during this age period) to listen carefully to the child's feelings, fears, and frustrations, to respond to them, and to take them into account in making a decision (4). Provided there is no evidence of incompetence, neglect, or abuse, the parent or custodial adult should remain the decision-maker for these children.

Since there is such a dependent relationship between child and parent, the question arises of whether it is advisable in these circumstances to include another, relatively more independent, decision-maker (5). Such a decision-maker would presumably not only have no conflict of interest, but also be a strong, unambivalent advocate of the child's best interests and the child, in turn, would have no special, deep ties to that person. The advocate would assess whether the conditions of minimal chance of harm to the child donor, coupled with maximum chance of great benefit to the other, obtained; ascertain that the child was appropriately informed; and determine the child's assent or dissent. A test for the degree to which these tasks had been successfully accomplished might be whether the child at a later date, when maturity is achieved, would have reason to sue the advocate for having made a bad judgment or for having advised treatment in the event that a bad outcome occurred (i.e., actual harm to the donor). One could ask further questions, e.g., should the judgments of the advocate be monitored, and if so by whom?

The impetus for these questions is the fact that in many instances there are no right or wrong answers to what is better or best for a child or for the child's family. There is a wide range of preferred values that influence decisions, and no single person is well-enough endowed to make the wisest decision in every case.

At the very heart of the problem is the core issue of the validity, if any, of informed consent or assent by the child (6). In the first place, information is rarely given to the child with complete impartiality, and almost never heard impartially by the child (7). The informant may appear awe-inspiring, magesterial, persuasive, intimidating, rewarding, or gratifying to the child. The child may have previously unconsciously responded with acquiescence to numerous predecision requests for compliance, thus paving the way selectively for the final compliance; or the child, having already decided precipitously and impulsively, may simply elect to "hear" only that information that "confirms" the immediate decision.

If the child's judgment is fallacious, to what extent is the substitute judgment of a parent or a guardian ad litem truly representative of and fair to the child donor's best interests? Who can test the validity of the parents' or the guardian's competence? In what way can the competence be tested? Certainly, when a substitute person (guardian ad litem) is authorized to speak on behalf of the child, that guardian must be open to the adversarial process.

What if the child adamantly, or even not so adamantly, refuses to consent or assent? What weight is to be given to that refusal?

While arbitrary cutoff ages may simplify the task of the judge, justice for an individual child may not be done through such a rule. Yet case-by-case judgments often require such an enormous amount of detailed knowledge and expertise that here, too, justice may not be done through simple unavailability. At the same time, this difference is important—the difference between a relatively arbitrary approach that will satisfy the largest number (somewhat akin to a public health approach to a population) and the individual approach of a physician toward his or her (donor) patient.

In the end, there is no perfect justice, and the "best case" should be determined in each instance. While the age of 14 for consent and seven for assent are reasonable guidelines, they should not be written in stone. Other mitigating factors, including intelligence, maturity, and the social context in which the potential donor child lives and will live, may be important (8).

Finally, society *does* have an interest in the values it wishes to promulgate and those it eschews. Perhaps it is reasonable in these circumstances to empower a panel that represents society to sanction parents who must, in the last analysis, make decisions for children who are not capable of informed consent. The panel might consist of the same constituents that currently form Institutional Review Boards for biomedical research. The charge of that panel would be to ensure that the parents are competent, informed, and have a more or less conflict-free, benign relationship with the child; and that the child has been reasonably informed and heard. The judgments of the panelists, who would be "average citizens," comparable to a jury, would be based on average social expectations and usual legal limitations. The panelists would be free to call in experts. The approval of the panel would be sufficient and any further intervention by the state would ordinarily be unwarranted. Such a procedure would obviate the necessity for either the parents or the hospital staff to sue each other, and would eliminate the need for a court to oversee each decision. Only in the event that the parents were found significantly incompetent would it be necessary to invoke a guardian ad litem and judicial review.

INSTITUTIONAL REVIEW BOARDS

The above suggestion is based, in part, on the model of the Institutional Review Board (IRB) (9). The purposes of the Institutional Review Board are:

> The ethical conduct of research involving human subjects requires a balancing of society's interests in protecting the rights of subjects and in developing knowledge that can benefit the subjects or society as a whole.... Investigators should not have sole responsibility for determining whether research involving human subjects fulfills ethical standards. Others who are independent of the research must share this responsibility, because investigators are always in positions of potential conflict by virtue of their concern with the pursuit of knowledge as well as the welfare of the human subjects of their research.
>
> ...(T)he rights of subjects should be protected by local review committees operating pursuant to Federal regulations and located in institutions where research involving human subjects is conducted. Compared to the possible alternatives of a regional or national review process, local committees have the advantage of greater familiarity with the actual conditions surrounding the conduct of research. Such committees can work closely with investigators to assure that the rights and welfare of human subjects are protected and, at the same time, that the application of policies is fair to the investigators. They can contribute to the education of the research community and the public regarding the ethical conduct of research. The committees can become resource centers for information concerning ethical standards and Federal requirements and can communicate with Federal officials and other local committees about matters of common concern. (10)

PRACTICAL CONSIDERATIONS IN PREPARING A CONSENT FORM

The consent form is merely documentation of a dialogue that should have already occurred between the investigator and the prospective subject. A piece of paper, however detailed, is no substitute for discussion with prospective subjects.

The consent form should be a statement addressed to the subject which gives reasonable information about the study, its procedures, benefits, risks, and alternatives, to enable him or her to make an intelligent decision about participation. The consent form should be worded in the second person and written in language that the prospective subject can be expected to understand. It should be concise, literate, and be proofread carefully for errors in spelling and grammar.

The consent form must not sound coercive. It may not include any language through which a subject is made to waive or to appear to waive any legal rights or to release the institution or its agents from liability for negligence.

All subjects invited to participate in a research protocol must be given the opportunity for informed consent. For these purposes, control subjects including *normal volunteers* are always viewed in the same way as other subjects. Even if the research plan is to treat *control subjects* with standard accepted diagnostic and therapeutic maneuvers, consent invariably will be required owing to special systems of monitoring effects.

If a procedure is performed solely for purposes of identifying a population of research subjects, consent is required. The investigators may wish to present prospective subjects with a consent form describing only this procedure and stating as its purpose a determination whether the subject will be eligible for participation in further studies. A separate consent form may then be presented to those who are found to be suitable. In such situations, while soliciting consent to the diagnostic maneuver, the investigator will be expected to show potential subjects the consent form they will be asked to sign if they prove to be suitable subjects for further study.

If there are two or more consent forms, label each clearly as to which subject population is addressed (i.e., patient/subject, normal controls, family members).

The most common reason for delay of approval of a protocol is an improperly prepared consent form—either incomplete information or coercive, confusing, or unintelligible language. The following points should be covered on all consent forms except in cases where the point is irrelevant to the proposal:

Invitation

The subject must be clearly invited to participate in the study, e.g., "You are invited to participate in a study of...." To request participation does *not* convey that the subject has a choice.

Purpose

The purpose of the study should be expressed in lay terms. It should be clear to the subject that this is research.

Selection of Subject

The subject should be informed as to why he or she has been selected. This may be because of a specific disease or condition that the subject or one of his or her relatives has, or because he or she is free of a specific disease—a normal control.

Procedures

The subject must be informed exactly what his or her participation will involve, with particular attention to the way it will be experienced by the subject. This should include the length and frequency of hospitalizations if this will be necessary; number, length, and frequency of visits to the investigator; types of medication; types and numbers of tests; amount of blood to be withdrawn (in terms a lay person can understand, such as ounces or small tubes); questionnaires; videotaping; diets; withholding of standard treatment; and follow-up studies. It should be made clear which of these procedures are being done in the interests of research and which in the interests of providing diagnosis, prevention, or therapy. Of the various maneuvers done in the interests of practice, which are "standard" and which are "investigational"? Of the various diagnostic maneuvers—e.g., laboratory tests—which are extra in that they would not have been done during customary therapy or would not have been done as often?

Risks and Inconveniences

There should be a description of any reasonably foreseeable risks, discomfort, or inconveniences to the subject; this description should match that provided elsewhere in the protocol. These may include side effects of drugs, hazards of procedures, or withholding of a therapy of proven value. The subject should be told what will be done to minimize risks and counteract side effects, and which, if any, side effects might be irreversible. In addition to the known risks of being in the study, there may be unforeseeable complications and the subject should be made aware of this fact.

If *randomization* is used to develop subsets of the subject population, this process should be defined and its implications must be stated on the consent form. If a *placebo* is part of the research design, the full implications must also be detailed on the consent form.

In any *double-blind* study the subject must be informed that neither the investigator nor the subject will know which medication the subject is receiving during the study. In case of *cross-over studies* the implications must be explained. The consent form must also contain the information that the key to the codes will be kept where there is a 24-hour service, e.g., the Pharmacy Department. In an emergency, the medications being taken as part of the study may be identified by telephoning the Pharmacy Department. The principal investigator must provide the subject with an identification bracelet or wallet card that includes the information that he or she is participating in a double-blind study, the identification number of the study, the name and phone number of the investigator, the subject's code number in the study, and the message that in an emergency the code may be broken or information about the drug may be obtained by contacting the Pharmacy Department (phone number should be provided) at any time of day or night.

In studies involving *investigational drugs*, it may be desirable to include information on the consent form that in any emergency, information about the drugs may be obtained by contacting the Pharmacy Department. When appropriate, the subject should also be informed that he or she will be provided with a card identifying the subject as being in a study involving an investigational drug. The card should include the name of the investigational drug, the identification number of the study, the name and phone number of the investigator and a phone number that may be called at any hour of day or night for further information about the drug.

Benefits

Research, by definition, is not designed to provide direct health-related benefits to the subjects. Most commonly, the purpose of research is to develop knowledge that may produce benefits in the future for persons who resemble the subject. This should be made clear on the consent form. Some protocols involve the performance or administration of various diagnostic, preventive, or therapeutic maneuvers or modalities—e.g., protocols designed to assess the safety and efficacy of investigational practices. In such cases, informed consent also requires a reasonable statement of the direct health-related benefits one hopes to produce for the subjects.

It should be made clear whether the subject will be offered continuing access to an investigational therapy after completion of the study; if so, will it be provided free or will the subject be expected to pay for it?

Economic considerations

The net financial consequences of participation in the project should be made clear. Using terms as specific as the protocol will permit, how much more (or less) money will the subject (or the third-party payer) be expected to pay as a consequence of the subject's participation in the protocol?

Alternative Treatments

If there are alternative therapies, the consent form should at least state that they exist and offer a discussion of their relative advantages and disadvantages. In some cases it may be appropriate to provide a statement of the nature of the alternatives—e.g., surgery, radiation therapy; however, it is usually not necessary to provide a full account of their risks and benefits in the consent form. In some cases it may be appropriate to state that one reasonable alternative open to the prospective subject is to choose against accepting any therapy designed to produce either cure or remission.

Confidentiality

Steps taken to assure confidentiality should be explained in the consent form. Limits on confidentiality such as FDA inspection of medical records in studies involving investigational drugs and devices should also be explained.

Disclosure

The subject should be informed about the names of disclosure of information obtained during a study. When a study is of a diagnostic or therapeutic modality, information is routinely entered in the subject's medical record, discussed with the subject, and transmitted to anyone else whom the subject designates. If the intent of a study is not directly related to diagnosis or therapy of a particular subject, he or she has the right to decide whether or not such information shall be entered into the medical record or transmitted directly to the private physician.

The nature of some studies requires that the full purpose not be revealed to the subject until the study is completed. Such deliberate withholding of information is permitted if the subject is informed that this is the case and agrees. This must be clearly stated in the consent form, along with the plan for when and how the complete information will be shared with the subject. Research based on deception or incomplete disclosure must always be fully justified and cleared by the Institutional Review Board.

Some particularly sensitive research may require a federal confidentiality certificate which affords protection of the investigator's records against subpoena.

Compensation and Medical Therapy

Federal regulations require, for any research involving more than minimal risk, an explanation of whether any compensation and/or medical treatments are available if injury occurs and, if so, what they consist of or where further information may be obtained.

A) For protocols in which the risks of physical injury are presented by procedures or modalities performed or administered solely for research purposes (no investigational practice), state in the consent form in language appropriate for the proposed subject population:

> Medical therapy will be offered at no cost to you for any physical injuries sustained as a consequence of your participation in this research. Federal regulations require that you be informed that—in the event of injuries—no additional financial compensation is available.

B) For protocols in which the risks of physical injury are presented by investigational practices, the investigator should decide which injuries or complications will be treated at no cost to the subjects. Those for which free medical therapy will be provided should be identified clearly in the consent form. They should be distinguished clearly from those for which therapy will be provided at the expense of the subject or his or her insurance carrier. The style of distinguishing these matters should be appropriate to the particular consent form. The following information should be transmitted—stated in appropriate lay language:

First, there should be an identification of the risks of physical injury to which the subject will be exposed that differ qualitatively or quantitatively from those connected with standard forms of therapy. It should further be pointed out—when appropriate—that there is a possibility that in the course of the studies new adverse effects of the investigational (drug, device, procedure, etc.) that result in physical injury may be discovered. Then it should be stated that medical therapy will be offered at the institution at no cost to the subject for the physical injuries that are identified in this paragraph. It should further clarify that the subject (or his or her insurance carrier) will be expected to pay the costs of medical care for physical injuries and other complications not mentioned in this paragraph. It should explain why—because physical injuries and other complications not mentioned in this paragraph are either associated with the subject's disease or commensurate with the complications expected of the usual therapies for the disease. Finally, it should be stated: "Federal regulations require that you be informed that—except as specified in this paragraph—no financial compensation for injury is available."

Questions

Since subjects often need time to decide about participation, it is often appropriate to include the following statement: "Before you sign this form, please ask any questions on any aspect of this study that is unclear to you. You may take as much time as necessary to think this over." If the proposed procedures are complex or hazardous, patients should be encouraged to discuss them with their own physician or anyone else they wish before making a decision. Additionally, the investigator responsible for the research should give a phone number on the consent form where he or she can be reached by the subject in case of questions or problems that arise.

For some protocols it may be necessary to identify a person other than the principal investigator whom the subject should contact for answers to questions about the research and research subjects' rights or in the event of a research-related injury.

Disclaimer

Subjects should be informed that they are free 1) to decide whether or not to participate, and also free 2) to withdraw from the study at any time unless the nature of the investigation, once commenced, precludes this. They should be assured that if they prefer not to participate or decide to withdraw, 3) they will still receive standard treatment if such a statement is appropriate. There should also be assurance 4) that a decision not to participate will not adversely prejudice future interactions with the institution; this is particularly important when a dependent relationship exists between the investigator and the subject, such as physician-patient, employer-employee, or faculty-student. If withdrawal or nonparticipation in the study would result in transfer of the patient to another service or institution, this must be made clear.

In some studies, abrupt withdrawal from a study may be dangerous to a subject. In such cases, this danger must be explained and it must be made clear that the subject should not withdraw without first discussing such action with the investigator.

Signatures

Spaces should be provided for the signature of the person who consents to participate in the study or the relative who consents on behalf of the individual who will be the subject of the study. There should also be a space for the signature of the person who obtains the consent. If this will be done by someone other than the investigating physician, it should be so indicated on the consent form. If the subject is a child old enough to understand, the child is additionally invited to sign the consent form after the procedures have been explained.

Continuing Contact

Following the signatures on the consent form there should be a statement about whom to contact in the event that questions arise during the conduct of the research or the subject believes he or she has sustained a research-related injury. The name and telephone number of the principal investigator should be given. In some cases, it may be more suitable to identify some other person for the subject to contact.

A signed copy of the consent form should be placed in the subject's hospital medical record, if applicable. If the subject has a medical record in the institution but the principal investigator does not wish to include the consent form therein, the reasons for this must be specified in the protocol. Examples of exceptions might include research irrelevant to the medical record or violations of confidentiality. In all cases, a copy showing the signatures must be given to the subject, and another retained in the investigator's files.

When appropriate, the following additional elements may be included in the consent form. Such elements include, but are not limited to:

1) A statement that the particular treatment or procedure may involve risks to the subject (or to the embryo or fetus, if the subject is or may become pregnant) that are currently unforeseeable.
2) Anticipated circumstances under which the subject's participation may be terminated by the investigator.
3) A statement that significant new findings developed during the course of the research that may relate to the subject's willingness to continue participation will be provided to the subject.
4) The approximate number of subjects involved in the study.

CONSENT PROCEDURES FOR CHILDREN

Procedures should be described for obtaining the assent of the child (when capable) as well as the permission of the parent or guardian. The term *assent* refers to a child's agreement as distinct from the term *consent*, which is legally valid. These transactions are essentially those used to obtain informed consent. Children who are capable of meaningful assent should be provided with a fair explanation of what their participation will involve. Those children who have reading skills sufficient to understand the consent form may be invited to sign the form. In instances where the intervention offers no prospect for direct benefit to an individual child, procedures should not be done over the deliberate objection of the child. The right of a minor to refuse to participate in any investigational practice or standard therapy varies according to many factors, including his or her age, illness, and alternative therapies.

There may be some circumstances under which adolescents may consent without parental involvement to participation in minimal risk studies (e.g., questionnaires, withdrawal of a very small amount of blood). Justification for dispensing with parental consent must, however, be provided in the protocol and this remains within the discretion of the Institutional Review Board to approve.

Protection of Subjects

In general, when research involves a significant departure from routine, one or both parents should be invited to be present for purposes of comforting the child and, if necessary, intervening on behalf of the child.

Consent form. The invitation to participate should be addressed to both the parents and child. This may be worded as follows: You (your child) are invited to participate in a study.... It is not necessary to continue this format throughout the entire consent form.

A space should be provided for the signature of the minor (when appropriate), as well as for the parent or guardian.

In some cases it may be of value to develop an assent form addressed to the child in a language he or she may be expected to understand.

EPILOGUE

Final regulations were published by DHHS in March 1983. An excellent interpretation of these latest regulations is provided by Levine (11).

REFERENCES

1. Weithorn, L. A. Children's capacities to decide about participation in research. *IRB*, 5, 1-5, 1983.

2. NCPHSBBR: National Commission for the Protection of Human Subjects of Biomedical and Behavioral Research. Report and Recommendations on Research Involving Children. (DHEW Publication No. (OS) 77-0004). Washington, D.C.: U.S. Government Printing Office, 1977.
3. Inhelder, B., & Piaget, J. *The growth of logical thinking*, trans. A. Parson & S. Milgram. New York: Basic Books, 1958.
4. Pence, G. E. Children's dissent to research—A minor matter? *IRB*, 2:1-4, 1980.
5. Gaylin, W., & Macklin, R. Who speaks for the child? In W. Gaylin (Ed.), *Who speaks for the child?* New York: Plenum, 1982.
6. Melton, G. B., Koocher, G. P., & Saks, M. J. (Eds.). *Children's competence to consent.* New York: Plenum Press, 1983.
7. Fellner, C. H., & Marshall, J. R. Kidney donors. In J. Macaulay & L. Berkowitz (Eds.), *Altruism and helping behavior.* New York: Academic Press, 1970.
8. Saks, M. J. Social psychological perspectives on the problem of consent. In G. B. Melton, G. P. Koocher, & M. J. Saks (Eds.), *Children's competence to consent.* New York: Plenum Press, 1983.
9. Levine, R. J. *Ethics and regulation of clinical research.* Baltimore, MD: Urban and Schwarzenberg, 1981.
10. The National Commission for Protection of Human Subjects of Biomedical and Behavioral Research. Institutional Review Boards: Report and recommendations. DHEW Publication No. (OS) 78-0008. Washington, D.C.: Department of Health, Education and Welfare, 1978, pp. 1-2.
11. Levine, R. J. An interpretation of the new regulations. *IRB*, 5:2-5, 1983.

Part II

CHILD CUSTODY

5

The Child Custody Dispute

Barbara A. Weiner, Virginia A. Simons, and James L. Cavanaugh, Jr.

In a child custody dispute no one wins. This is one point that psychiatrists and attorneys can agree upon. The dispute is a means for parents to ventilate their anger and distrust of each other using their most powerful weapon—their children. With the divorce rate approaching 50%, and with more fathers desiring custody, it is likely that there will be a continual increase in the number of contested custody cases from the present rate of approximately 15% (1). The transition from a single family unit to two family units, for the one million American children each year whose parents divorce, is often difficult (2, 3, 4, 5). This is especially true for those children who were or continue to be the subject of custody disputes. The pressures created as a result may psychologically impair the child, and require him or her to need mental health services. In addition, the growing numbers of these cases also increase the likelihood that the psychiatrist will be called upon as an evaluator in contested cases.

For the psychiatrist who takes on the role of evaluator, the choices are usually very limited. The issue is often not what is in the child's best interests, but what choice will be the least detrimental to the child. The clear-cut cases of one "good" parent and one "bad" parent are usually not referred. The contested cases frequently involve a choice between two parents who are almost equal in their parenting skills or lack thereof. At the time of the evaluation, the family will be under tremendous emotional strain, which has probably been continuing for many months. These evaluations are also very draining for the psychiatrist, who must wade through charges and countercharges to reach a result that may seem less than satisfactory. Yet psychiatrists and other competent mental health professionals must undertake to involve themselves in these painful cases. Without the objective input of professionals, who can focus on the needs of the child, the child, who is the weapon, will be lost in the battle.

This chapter attempts to provide the reader with an understanding of what is required to perform a competent custody evaluation, as well as brief discussion of the legal issues.

POINTS OF INVOLVEMENT

There are three time periods in the legal process when the custody or visitation issues may be litigated: 1) predivorce, 2) divorce, and 3) postdivorce.

Predivorce

The issues of custody or visitation may arise on an emergency basis when the family first separates. One party may seek the court's assistance in being awarded temporary custody or visitation. This period is often critical because the pattern that is established may be finalized at the time of the divorce.

Divorce

A contested trial will occur if the parties cannot resolve the issues of custody or visitation. These trials are often lengthy (taking three or more days) and sometimes require the children to take the stand or speak to the judge in chambers about their preferences. In addition to being very expensive, the trial often represents a high point in the parents' anger and bitterness toward each other. When a contested custody case goes to trial, the attorney will always seek the testimony of experts to establish why his client should have the primary custody. It should be borne in mind that the issue of custody also has great financial implications. Usually the marital home and child support go with the children.

Postdivorce

After the decree has been entered, circumstances may arise that encourage one party to seek a change in custody or visitation arrangements. These can include remarriage, developmental changes of the child, the child expressing a preference to be with the other parent, or other factors. In most instances the parties will agree. However, where there is a disagreement, the courts become involved. Once the party seeking change establishes a realistic basis for the court to address this issue, a new trial is usually involved.

Although the number of contested custody cases remains small, the amount of predivorce and postdivorce litigation is enormous. In many states there will be as many of these types of cases each year as there are people seeking divorce (6, 7).

THE LEGAL STANDARDS

In almost every American jurisdiction today the standard for determining who shall have custody of the child is based on the child's best interests (8, 9). This standard rejects the earlier "tender years doctrine," in which the mother was automatically presumed to be the person able to provide for the needs of a young child. Under the "best interests of the child" standard, the parents are viewed equally at the outset by the courts. To determine what is in the child's best interests, the statutes specify that the court consider:

1) the wishes of the parents regarding custody;
2) the wishes of the child regarding his custodian;
3) the interaction and interrelationships of the child with his parent or parents, his siblings, and any other person who may significantly affect his interest;
4) the child's adjustment to his home, school, and community;
5) the mental and physical health of all involved individuals; and
6) whether there is physical violence or threats of physical violence by the child's potential custodian, directed at either the child or another member of the household.

In addition, the court will consider other factors such as caretaking arrangements, each parent's capacity for meeting the needs of his child, and which parent can provide the most stable living situation for the child. In the majority of states, a child over a certain age (usually 16) can decide which parent he wishes to live with and the court will agree, regardless of the above factors.

The law also provides that the noncustodial parent is entitled to visitation, unless such visitation would endanger the child's physical or emotional health. Visitation is also supposedly determined by the child's best interests but there is also universal recognition that noncustodial parents are entitled to access to their children.

In order to seek a modification of a custody judgment, most states provide that no changes can occur within a specified time (usually two years), unless the child's environment may seriously endanger his physical or emotional health. This type of limitation encourages families to accept the initial custody decision and not continue to litigate these issues.

THE EVALUATION

The evaluation is a multiphased process that should be done in a systematic manner. To become involved in a contested custody case, a psychiatrist is required to possess a thorough knowledge of child development, good clinical skills, and also the ability to present findings and recommendations in an articulate fashion. For some this is easy, but for most this is often a difficult task and one not usually taught in residency training. Yet it is one which *should* be undertaken. Only when competent professionals become involved can the needs of the child be forcefully and effectively presented to the court.

Before Accepting the Case

At the outset, the psychiatrist should understand what the attorney is requesting and whom he is representing. For example, does the attorney want a complete evaluation with a written report, or is he seeking an informal opinion that will benefit his client? Is the attorney hoping the psychiatrist will be able to mediate this matter and help the family reach a resolution or is he seeking therapy for his client? Is the attorney anticipating that this case will go to trial, and does he want a complete evaluation? Once the parameters of the evaluation are understood by all parties, the psychiatrist should then decide if he wishes to take the referral and on what basis. For example, the psychiatrist may want to insist on having access to all parties and all records relating to the family. In addition, the psychiatrist may want to emphasize that the report will focus on the child's needs. This is, of course, the ideal and most ethically sound manner in which to proceed (10, 11).

Once these matters are resolved, the psychiatrist should discuss his fees for both the evaluation and any time spent in giving a deposition or at trial. Attorneys are not surprised when an expert requests the full fee or part of it in advance in these types of cases. Alternatively, one may request payment at the time of service or prior to release of report or testifying. This has the advantage of assuring that one is compensated for one's time. It also underscores the fact that one is being paid for time and skills rather than for an opinion.

Beginning the Evaluation

This is a time of great tension for the family. Hopefully, the evaluation or its recommendations will provide some therapeutic relief as the parents are forced to focus on their children rather than on their disputes with each other. For some, the questioning of the evaluation process gives the parents "new lenses" through which to see their children and their own situation. This may result in the parents becoming more conscientious and/or realistic about addressing their situation. In other instances, the evaluation can provide the attorneys with information about the needs of the child and help suggest workable solutions.

Although there is no uniformly right way to conduct an evaluation in a custody or visitation dispute, its orchestration is crucial to the outcome. What follows are general guidelines.

Initial Screening

In addition to taking a marital history, the personal and family history of each parent, and the history of the physical and emotional development of each child, there are certain other areas that should be explored at the outset since they may influence the direction of the evaluation. The following questions should be included:

1) Are there any charges of physical or sexual abuse?
2) Is there a history of alcoholism, drug abuse, or previous psychiatric hospitalizations?
3) Is anyone presently in therapy or were they in therapy? Why? With what results?
4) Are the children showing adjustment problems?
5) If the custody disputes center only on one or two children in the family, why is there no dispute about the other children?

Should any of these issues arise, they should be thoroughly explored, including obtaining supporting documentation.

In addition, there are a few other factors that seem to indicate a greater likelihood of conflict and stress. The most notable is if the parents have filed for divorce but remain under the same roof. This will greatly increase the tension within the household and place tremendous stress on the children. If the parties have a history of numerous court appearances, there is a greater likelihood of conflict and ongoing pressure. Finally, if one of the parties has had multiple attorneys, this will often indicate more problems than in the usual case. All of this information can help the psychiatrist to organize the evaluation.

The Interviews

Neutral entry into a family disrupted by conflict, competition, defensiveness, and hypersensitivity is a delicate matter and influences the family's acceptance of the evaluation process and the competency of the evaluator. At the outset, the parties should be clearly told what the psychiatrist's role is, and that the evaluator will be making recommendations that he believes best address the needs of the child or children. The evaluation's purpose, process, limitations, and procedures should be explained. Any child old enough to understand what the evaluation is about should also be given an explanation of the process. All parties should understand the limits of confidentiality and sign a witnessed waiver of confidentiality.

Each family member should be interviewed alone and in subgroups. Thus, children should be seen with their mother and also with their father. Attention must be paid to the time spent with each family member, and attempts made to keep it equal. Thought should be given in scheduling the order of the interviews. The care taken in attending to the sensitivities of the family members and in increasing their comfort level as much as possible offers its own calming effect. When the referrals are made by the court, resistance and guardedness become more prevalent, in part because tne children may have been exposed to more overt conflict.

A stance of neutrality must be demonstrated in the psychiatrist's non-verbal interactions with the family. Questions can be seen as threatening or critical, and general politeness can be interpreted as friendliness and support for one side or the other; therefore, the psychiatrist must be careful to be fair and open to information, tolerate animosity, and listen sympathetically, but remain consistently focused on the task of getting the information and impressions that are needed. A tolerance for the parents' distress is needed in order to reduce their anxiety enough to get a clear picture of the full range of their positive and negative qualities as parents. Open discussion regarding concerns for the children, future planning, and airing of accusations by each parent should occur during the individual interviews with the parent. Discussing both parents' accusations can become stressful and, at times, may be too stressful to be pursued in one session. But if parents are not given the opportunity to counter accusations, the information gained can be compromised. At times, confronting parents with these accusations can become a pivotal point in the interviewing process.

Parents going through the divorce process often distort facts in order to justify their situation and to distance themselves from their spouse. Many times these distortions lead to faulty assumptions. For example, a male parent can think that his spouse was a bad parent because she was a poor wife. Also parents may anticipate that they will be vindicated in some magical way by the evaluation.

The Team Approach

Probably the most ideal way to conduct a child custody evaluation is through a team approach, though we recognize this may often not be possible. The team will usually consist of a psychiatrist and a psychiatric social worker or psychologist. Working alone during these evaluations is time-consuming and exhausting. The team permits a division of duties and allows for full case discussions, which often bring new insights as to possible recommendations. More objectivity can be gained through multiple observations, and the potential for agreement by two professionals has added advantages should the case go to trial. However, caution must be taken in team formation and in the division of labor in the evaluation. It is important that all the professionals are not only well-qualified and experienced, but that they are also comfortable working with each other and as part of a team. There is no room for competitive personalities in this type of approach.

Care must also be taken to avoid duplication of work. The team can decide initially how to divide the work, and then, as the evaluation progresses, consult each other. Having the input of another person at the time of formulating recommendations makes the process easier, and also permits the possibility of exploring areas that might not occur to a single evaluator. Impressions of the family can also be confirmed if they are seen by more than one team member, giving the evaluator more confidence in the recommendations formulated. This approach can be designed in such a way to speed the evaluation process and make it less costly.

Focus on the Child

Recent research on children of divorce indicates that in any divorce, children generally experience diminished parenting (12, 13, 14). Parents frequently become narrowly focused, are tense and preoccupied with their ongoing conflicts, and often do not consider their child's needs. Focusing on the child can psychologically shift the orientation from spousal conflict to concern for the child.

When focusing on the child, the evaluator must analyze those factors the state laws define as the ones to be considered in determining a child's best interest (see the section on The Legal Standards). This can be accomplished by having the parent describe the child's history, perceptions of the child, and what the parent has to offer the child. In addition to love, warmth, and affection, can the parent encourage the child's development and recognize problems that may need remediation? Has the parent thought of realistic childcare arrangements? Does he or she recognize what the child will need at different developmental stages? Can this parent provide the guidance and discipline that may be required? If the child has problems, then can the parent address these in an effective manner?

To discuss in careful detail each child's history, development, current and future needs, hobbies and interests heightens the position of the child in the family by forcing the parent to recognize the child's needs. The evaluation process may result in the more perceptive and sensitive parent becoming more conscientious and caring toward the child during this stressful period. Other parents, however, will remain rigidly conflicted about the divorcing process, with no ability to recognize the child's interests or needs as separate from their own.

In addition to the information gained from the interviews with the parents, the interviews with the child are usually very revealing. Many experts believe the child *should not* be asked directly with which parent he prefers to live.* Generally the child will be defensive and protective of both parents. Questioning the child about his activities with each parent will provide insights into the relationships. The interactions during the interview of the child with each parent will also provide a great deal of information. This interview will provide many nonverbal cues to the relationship between each parent and the child. This is particularly true of the very young child who cannot yet verbalize feelings.

As part of the evaluation we find it helpful to give parents a list of suggestions on how to act during this time (see Table 1).

Table 1
Pointers for Separated and Divorced Parents

1. Tell your children, in a protective but honest way, what is happening and the plans for them. Then expect to answer any questions as calmly and patiently as you can. Some questions will come immediately, others will come later. Reassure the children that it is *not* their fault, but a problem between the parents.
2. Provide stability and try to keep things as much the same as possible for the children. If possible, stay in the same home, neighborhood, and school. Continue to pay special attention to comforting rituals: bedtime stories, special family events, such as holidays or birthdays, remembering favorite activities, favorite toys, or other special things that will comfort children.
3. Recognize that a child needs to respect both parents—don't criticize or berate the other parent in front of the children. Try not to argue in front of the children. This will increase their fears and insecurity and ultimately affects the child's self-esteem.
4. Recognize that the child needs each parent. Don't compete for your child's affection or try to force your child to take sides. If you do, you will cause increased anxiety for the child and in the long run you will lose your child's respect and affection.   (cont'd.)

---

*Others believe the child's preference should be made explicit and, in some states, the law demands that the child's preferences be articulated. The evaluator must help the child understand that while his wishes will be taken into consideration, the ultimate decision is not his.

5. Try very hard to put aside personal injuries, anger, and grievances and work out reasonable flexible arrangements for custody, visitation, and support. Try to live up to your end of the bargain, even in those difficult times when you feel unsupported or when your ex-spouse is uncooperative.

6. Visitation is critical to a child. Arrangements should be made considering the child's age, developmental stage, and needs. Changes will be needed as the child grows older. Regular, dependable visitation is important if the child is to have confidence in the noncustodial parent. Thus, visitation commitments should be kept except when there is a real emergency to justify cancellation. If changes are made, the parent making the changes should explain to the child the reasons for such changes. If a child refuses to go on visits, or seems upset after visits, explore the reasons. Try to work out a solution or seek counseling assistance.

7. Divorce requires a substantial period of adjustment. Visitation schedules must be made considering work schedules, school and child care facilities, as well as the activities of the child.

8. The noncustodial parent should maintain regular contact with the child via the telephone when not visiting. This parent should be aware of how the child is doing in school and in after-school activities and have a real sense of the child's daily life. The custodial parent should be cooperative with the noncustodial parent's access to the child.

9. Turn to your friends or family, not your children, for consolation. This is the time to use any support network you have—family, friends, or community organizations. Try to reduce your stress as this will ease the stress on the children, too.

10. Permit the children to discuss their feelings. Be more sensitive to their behavior. Either being "too good" or "acting up" may be a sign that professional help is needed. Don't hesitate to get professional help for either yourself or your child. This is a difficult period and professional support can help ease the transition. It is wiser to act preventively than to wait for acute distress.

The Home Visit

The home visit provides a more expeditious way of conducting a custody evaluation that will provide more accurate information. Home visits increase the psychiatrist's understanding of the conditions in which the child lives and offer a more reality-oriented framework than can be offered in the office visit alone. The child's level of comfort in each household can be seen, and familial interactions are bound to be more spontaneous. In addition, there may be important information revealed in a home visit that neither parent mentions in the office. For example, in one case the visit revealed that a seven-year-old boy was sharing a single bed with his grandfather who was a dialysis patient. This was in a family that could have easily afforded some alternative sleeping arrangement. Another visit revealed a situation where all the furniture had been removed from a very expensive home to avoid the other parent having access to it. The children were sleeping on floor mats. Obviously this parental behavior had an immediate effect on the children's sense of security.

Although psychiatrists have traditionally avoided such visits, they provide an efficient way to conduct an evaluation and allow a great deal more information to be gathered than can be gleaned from an office visit.

Other Sources of Information

In addition to interviews with the involved family members, it might be advisable in some cases to include interviews with other family members or people who are familiar enough with the situation to provide additional data. In almost all cases, older siblings who are not part of the custody dispute need to be seen. Their reactions can strongly influence family members and their insights are usually quite useful. Sometimes grandparents may have important information to provide. If it is proposed that a grandparent become a primary caretaker while the custodial parent works, then the grandparent should be interviewed. Housekeepers also can provide valuable information and often confirm concerns about a child that may not be recognized by the parents. Boyfriends, girlfriends, and significant others should also be interviewed.

In addition to these significant others, reports from or conversations with teachers, pediatricians, and any involved therapists are critical. Sometimes the family clergyman can also provide objective information from an historical perspective of what has occurred over time. Obviously, when conducting any of these interviews, the possible biases of the party must be weighed. Yet these sources often can confirm or expand the data base during formulation of clinical impressions.

Synthesizing the Information

Since most evaluations will involve parents who are fairly equal in terms of their parenting skills, synthesizing the information to reach a reasonable recommendation is frequently the most difficult part of the evaluation. This is often complicated by the fact that the alternatives for the involved children often seem so limited. In such cases, where a team approach has been used, the process is usually easier. The team can usually reach a consensus through comprehensive discussions and the evaluators can feel more confident that the broadest base of information has been utilized in reaching the final conclusions.

The recommendations come at one point in time; however, change in the family is inevitable. The shifts that will occur during the divorce and postdivorce process are unpredictable. Thus, the evaluator must recognize these limitations and be honest about them at the time of making the recommendations. The evaluator must rely heavily on his or her own clinical skills and experience in this type of work, since good research data on the impact of divorce on children are only beginning to be published (15, 16, 17). Emphasis must be placed on those factors carrying the most weight: the parenting qualities of the mother and father, the child's total adjustment, signs of attachment between the parent and child, and the child's preferences. The recommendations should include any suggestions about visitation or the treatment needs of any involved family members, in addition to the custody recommendation. If the evaluator thinks there may be problems later, the parents should be alerted as to what signs to watch for in their child. Once a recommendation has been reached, the evaluator should outline what factors supported his decision. This will permit the writing of a logical report and the rational presentation of coherent opinions for examination in court if necessary.

EVALUATOR-ATTORNEY INTERACTIONS

Writing the Report

Once the evaluation is completed, a report should be written that concisely states recommendations and provides the reasoning. We suggest dividing the report into four parts: 1) summary; 2) interviews conducted and materials considered; 3) observations and comments; and 4) conclusions.

The summary restates the issues to be addressed and provides a one- or two-sentence synopsis of the recommendations. Usually we include recommendations relating to custody, visitation, and treatment needs of any involved family member(s). However, the risk of putting the summary first is that some people may not bother to read the entire report. The section on interviews conducted and materials considered includes a listing of each person interviewed and the dates, along with all the information and reports reviewed. Telephone conversations with significant others or teachers, for example, are also included. This demonstrates the entire data base and the thoroughness of the evaluation process. The observations and comments section describes the evaluator's findings in some detail. Finally, the conclusion summarizes how the evaluator reached the specific recommendations and why.

When writing a report, it is important to keep in mind the specific medical-legal purpose. Thus, it would generally be inappropriate to give a full developmental history unless this specifically influenced the conclusions.

Psychiatric terminology should be explained when it is used. Specific diagnoses of the involved parties should not be made unless treatment for specific disorders is recommended. Thus, if a conclusion is reached that one parent is somewhat "neurotic" or a "borderline personality," then there is no point in attaching that label in the report. It will have no meaning to the attorneys unless specifically related to the custody visitation recommendation or a need for treatment. Bear in mind that the report will be read and critiqued by the parties. Thus, their strengths *and* weaknesses should be described. The report should be a thorough explanation of the consultant's reasoning and fully support his recommendations.

Conferences

It is ideal to hold a conference with the attorney to discuss the findings. If the consultant is acting as an independent expert, he will want to hold a conference with all the involved attorneys. These conferences permit an opportunity to explore recommendations and may allow amplification of views that are not appropriate to put in writing (see the section on A Working Model). If the consultant is going to testify, he should insist on having a conference with the attorney to prepare him for trial with sample questions the attorney will ask and which he expects will be asked on cross-examination.

Testimony

Should the psychiatrist be required to testify, he must remember that he is there as an expert, *not* as an advocate. It is the attorney's job to win the case; the evaluator's job is only to provide the court with opinions based on professional experience and knowledge. The psychiatrist should try to present his views in language that a high school student would understand, and, above all, to be *organized*. Also, the psychiatrist should not be afraid to admit that psychiatry is not an exact science, or that he could be wrong. Consultants should explain that they are giving their professional opinion based upon their training and experience. Finally, the psychiatrist must understand that the attorney is there to advocate his client's position. This may require that he try to discredit the clinician. This should not be taken personally, and the consultant should respond calmly to any harassment. This is part of the attorney's job and not an adverse reflection on one's professional credentials.

ASSISTING THE FAMILY IN REACHING AN AGREEMENT

There will be a few instances when a family seeks advice from an evaluation and agrees at the outset to abide by the consultant's recommendations. This is rare. There are other instances where a psychiatrist may be contacted to act as a mediator. In that case he will be addressing all the issues that surround the separation and divorce to attempt to help the parties reach a consensus between themselves regarding how to divide their property or arrange for the caretaking of their children (18, 19, 20). Mediation involves skills that often require training. It is sufficient to note briefly that in those cases where the parents are amenable to proceeding in an orderly and rational manner, mediation may have a great deal to offer. The parties reach an agreement, which both are more likely to view as fair, and since they were involved in the process together, they are more likely to uphold their respective agreements.

Most families involved in contested custody cases are not amenable to mediation. If the parents could communicate effectively with each other in the first place, then they would have been able to resolve the custody issues without pursuing a custody evaluation. One of the psychiatrist's tasks during the evaluation is to seek some movement toward problem solving and future solutions for the parents. The evaluation may be the first time the parents have spent a concentrated amount of time discussing the meaning of separation and divorce in terms of the effects on their child. It could be the first time either parent acknowledges that the future will be different and plans will need to be made to adjust to life without the present spouse or the current home. Focusing the parents on the needs of their child can force them to reevaluate their present situation and their future plans. This can encourage parents to gain insight into the needs of their child and to develop realistic approaches to meeting those needs.

In some cases it may be beneficial, at the end of the evaluation, after the report is written, to have a conference with the parents (without the attorneys) to explain the evaluator's findings and recommendations. This is not to reiterate what has been said earlier, or to refute the allegations of the other spouse, but to help sensitize the parents to their child's needs and find ways to help them realistically address those needs. Unfortunately, in many cases, the parents will be so involved in their anger toward each other that there is little likelihood of progress and such a conference will accomplish nothing. Yet, during each evaluation, the evaluator should attempt to explore possible solutions that will meet the child's needs and, hopefully, simultaneously satisfy the parents. Even if this results in only a few nonjudicial settlements, the effort will have been worthwhile.

RECOGNIZING THE PSYCHIATRIST'S LIMITATIONS

When undertaking a child custody evaluation, the psychiatrist needs to recognize certain limitations. Three obvious limitations come to mind: 1) inability to predict long-term outcome; 2) problems with confusing an evaluation with treatment; and 3) lack of knowledge about the legal consequences of the recommendations developed.

1) When conducting an evaluation, the psychiatrist is looking at the family at only one point in time. Thus, the recommendations are based on the data available at that point and the child's current needs and stage of development. Yet changes may warrant a change in custody and, thus, a reevaluation may be necessary at some future point. When doing an evaluation, the psychiatrist should stress that the recommendations are based on the present available facts and be direct in acknowledging limitations at predicting long-term outcome.

2) A psychiatrist should not attempt to provide an evaluation of a family when he is currently treating a family member. It is appropriate to be an expert in testifying as to the good parenting skills of the patient or the needs of a child being seen in therapy, but the only way the evaluation can be viewed as impartial is if it is done by an evaluator, who has not had any previous professional involvement with any family members. Thus, past treatment of a family member should disqualify the psychiatrist from the role of child custody evaluator. It is also advisable that once the evaluation is completed, the therapist not provide treatment to a family member unless the custody matter is settled.

3) Finally, the therapist should recognize that recommendations may have legal consequences. Thus, evaluation efforts should be directed toward addressing the needs of the child. The evaluator should advise the parents to consult their attorney(s) about the recommendations. This is particularly important if the evaluator has served as a mediator and there is little or no involvement with attorneys. Whether, for example, something is deemed "child support" or "alimony" can have great tax consequences. The psychiatrist (evaluator) should, therefore, focus on the needs of the child, and the attorneys should try to implement those recommendations while simultaneously advising the spouse-client on how to protect that client's interests.

A WORKING MODEL—THE ISAAC RAY CENTER

In September 1980, a new program, called the Center for Families in Conflict, opened in Chicago as part of the Isaac Ray Center, Rush Medical College, to provide comprehensive child custody evaluations in contested custody or visitation cases. This fee-for-service program utilizes a team of a child psychiatrist and a psychiatric social worker to evaluate the family and make recommendations relating to custody, visitation, and treatment needs of any family members. Cases are only undertaken by the Center with the agreement of the attorneys, of both parents, or by court order. The Center's approach is unique in three respects: 1) it utilizes a team approach; 2) home visits are routine when the children are younger than 10 years of age; and 3) a conference is held with all the involved attorneys and includes the attorney for the Center.

The evaluation incorporates all the elements described earlier in this chapter. It begins with an initial screening by the social worker. A psychiatrist is then selected from a panel of university-affiliated, board-certified child psychiatrists to participate in the evaluation. The team then decides how it will divide tasks and proceed with the interviews. At the initial screening, releases of information are signed and the social worker begins to collect reports from the school, the pediatrician, any therapists who have been involved with the family, and for any previous psychiatric hospitalization. As new information becomes available, which requires a different approach, the initial decision on how to proceed with the evaluation can be changed. These changes might include more interviews by the psychiatrist to confirm or rule out major psychiatric problems or may involve obtaining psychological testing or medical subspecialty consultations.

A visit to each parent's home will occur when the child is under 10 years of age. Sometimes this is done by the social worker alone, and sometimes the psychiatrist panelists participate in the visit. Those psychiatrists who do participate in the home visit report this to be an expeditious use of their time. The psychiatrist can interview most of the involved family members during one block of time and obtain a more realistic view of what the family is like within the home environment. After this home visit, the team confers to decide how to proceed further. They determine who else needs to be interviewed, who should be seen again, and what additional documentation is needed.

In most cases, *each* team member will have time alone with *each* family member. This has the advantage of allowing each professional to formulate an opinion. Many times the impressions will be similar, and this helps confirm for the team members the consistency of their views. This process also enhances the objectivity of the evaluation. Once all the data have been collected and the interviews completed, the team meets to formulate its recommendations. Sometimes consultation with the Center's attorney is necessary during this process to help define the limits of what can be legally implemented, and what types of recommendations are likely to be accepted by the attorneys or the court.

The evaluation report is then written by the team members in the format described earlier. Each report is reviewed by the Center's attorney. This is to be sure that the conclusions are supported by the information contained in the report and that the construction of the report is such as to be understandable to nonmental health professionals. A conference is then scheduled with all the involved attorneys. The entire evaluative process averages from 12 to 20 hours of time, including the time spent in the conference and dictation.

The report is released at the conference. It is not released before the conference to assure the attorneys' attendance. The conference permits the evaluation team members to explain their findings and recommendations. This meeting also permits an elaboration on the information contained in the report and allows the team to emphasize the needs of the child. By attending the conference the attorneys are given the opportunity to explore in a nonadversarial setting possible solutions to the contested custody or visitation dispute.

In our opinion, the conference, combined with the quality and thoroughness of the evaluation and report, is the reason 90% of the cases thus far have settled out of court. This is a much higher percentage than was initially anticipated, given that our population is one that is invested in the custody dispute. Also, our clients usually have a long history of arguing over custody and visitation issues. Most of the cases that did not settle involved a situation where one of the attorneys did not attend the conference, or the attorney for the Center was not present when the conference occurred. These variables are currently being further analyzed in relationship to the outcome of the evaluation process.

We also believe it is important that the Center's evaluation process provides a "way out" for the attorney. He can explain to his client, who usually will trust the attorney's judgment, that the Center's staff is well qualified and that the court is likely to follow their recommendations. This gives the attorney more leverage in working out a solution. Progress toward settlement is more likely if the attorneys are experienced in the divorce area. Divorce attorneys, because of their knowledge in this area, will force their clients to have more realistic expectations about the outcome.

We have also found that the Center's attorney plays an important role in the conference. She serves as a bridge between the mental health professionals and the divorce lawyers. She can direct the lawyers toward workable solutions because of her previous experience in this area, and encourage possible questions, which help the team further explain their reasoning. Even without this "neutral" attorney, a conference is highly recommended and presents the best chance of reaching a settlement. In addition, in cases where there is an attorney for the child, it is likely that if the guardian ad litem accepts the recommendations, both parties (or the court if necessary) will accept the findings.

The Center's approach is to provide a thorough evaluation by mental health professionals with experience in understanding families and their dynamics. The Center has been successful with this approach, because of the ability of the professionals to communicate with the legal community regarding the availability of the service, and the fact that an attorney is part of the program. These facts tend to diminish the ambivalence of the legal community, which often mistrusts psychiatrists. Recently the Center began providing short-term counseling to families with problems relating to separation and divorce, in addition to the Center's evaluation project.

REFERENCES

1. Wallerstein, J. S., & Kelly, J. B. *Surviving the breakup.* New York: Basic Books, 1979.
2. *Ibid.*
3. Hetherington, E. M., Cox, M., & Cox, R. *The aftermath of divorce.* In J. H. Stevens, Jr., & M. Mathews (Eds.), *Mother-child, father-child relations.* Washington, D.C.: NAEYC, 1978.
4. Levitin, T. Children of divorce. *Journal of Social Issues,* 1979, *35,* 1-182.
5. Luepnitz, D. A. *Child custody: A study of families after divorce.* Lexington, MA: Lexington Books, 1982.
6. Freed, D. J., & Foster, H. H. Family law in fifty states: An overview. *Family Law Quarterly,* 1983, *16,* 289-383.
7. Zuckman, H. L., & Fox, W. F. The ferment in divorce litigation. *Journal of Family Law,* 1973, *12,* 515-605.
8. Freed & Foster, 1983.
9. Zuckman & Fox, 1973.
10. Group for the Advancement of Psychiatry. *Divorce, child custody and the family* (Report #106). New York: Mental Health Materials Center, 1980.
11. Goldzband, M. G. *Consulting in child custody.* Lexington, MA: Lexington Books, 1981.
12. Wallerstein, 1979.
13. Hetherington et al., 1978.
14. Levitin, 1979.
15. Wallerstein, 1979.
16. Hetherington et al., 1978.
17. Luepnitz, 1982.
18. Haynes, J. M. *Divorce mediation.* New York: Springer, 1981.
19. Winks, P. L. Divorce mediation: A nonadversary procedure for the no-fault divorce. *Journal of Family Law,* 1981, *19,* 615-653.
20. Silberman, L. J. Professional responsibility problems of divorce mediation. *Family Law Quarterly,* 1982, *16,* 107-145.

6

Mediation: Its Implications for Children and Divorce

Marilyn Ruman and Marcia G. Lamm

Divorce mediation is a process that utilizes the skills of a mental health professional and an attorney who work together to assist couples to reach mutual resolutions of the legal and emotional issues of divorce or separation. The American Association for Mediated Divorce (AAMD), founded and directed by Dr. Marilyn Ruman and located in Encino, California, advocates a co-mediation team approach, in which an impartial attorney and an impartial mental health professional meet with both husband and wife to assist them in resolving conflicts, reaching decisions, and negotiating agreements regarding the dissolution of their marriage. The desired result of a mediation is a settlement agreement that has been totally shaped by the couple which recognizes their legal rights and responsibilities as individuals, as well as their mutual interests as a couple. This agreement is submitted to the court for jurisdiction and is binding as to property settlement, support, and child custody.

The 1970s brought with them great advances in legislature in the areas of divorce and custody. Laws were passed in many states advocating no-fault divorce, community property, and joint custody. The psychiatric community became aware of the need for cooperative and amicable resolutions to these issues, and it became increasingly evident that the traditional adversarial approach to divorce was no longer effective. In 1973, in Los Angeles, and similarly in Santa Clara County, California, Hennepin County, Minnesota, and Dane County, Wisconsin, the courts began experimenting with the referral of highly contested custody and visitation matters to Conciliation Court, in an attempt to encourage parents to work out their own agreements. The conciliation courts were successful in resolving these disputes and, in 1976, in Los Angeles and San Francisco, the courts began referring all contested custody and visitation matters to the Conciliation Court prior to trial (1).

AAMD was founded in response to the increased demand for mediation services in custody matters, and later expanded to the need for complete divorce mediation services. AAMD advocates and uses a co-mediation team model of mediation. The mental health professional handles the emotional aspects of the divorcing process as it affects the negotiation of a settlement. The lawyer advises the couple of legal rights and parameters of family law, but does not act as an advocate for either party. During the mediation process, the mental health professional reduces the emotional anxiety and emotional conflicts that impede the parties' abilities to explore legal and financial alternatives with the attorney.

THE MEDIATION PROCESS

Couples are carefully screened at an initial consultation to determine whether they are suitable candidates for mediation, and to provide them with sufficient information to allow them to determine if mediation is the alternative of choice for them. If the mediators feel that there is a great deal of attachment or ambivalence about separation between the spouses, a recommendation for outside therapy or that the couple seek separate counsel may be made. Those who are unwilling or unable to cooperate fully in making their own decisions because they have unresolved conflicts with each other or because they are too weak, insecure, or mentally ill to fully take part in the mediation are not good candidates for the process. Mediators should be particularly cautious about clients whose "balance of power" in their relationship is so skewed that one of the spouses may be intimidated into passivity by the other. In addition, the spouses must agree to full disclosure and to make available all information regarding their finances, assets, liabilities, plans regarding the children, and other commitments that may be relative to the mediation process. The final and most compelling criterion for selection of mediation clients is that they are willing and desirous of mediating a settlement agreement.

An estimate of mediation fees is calculated by the attorney and mental health professional and is based on the amount of time (sessions) needed to mediate all of the issues in the divorce. Over a five-year period, the majority of our clients reported that the estimates quoted by the AAMD were significantly lower than those quoted by their family attorneys. If the couple decides to proceed and they meet the selection criteria, they are asked to sign a Pre-Mediation Agreement, which delineates the understandings AAMD has with the couple regarding the rules of mediation, their understandings of the roles of the attorney and mental health professional, and the fees for mediation. The initial consultation is also used to review all the issues that are unique to each couple's divorce.

In each of the subsequent meetings, the issues of the dissolution are examined and the mediators help the couple reach resolutions step by step. Couples are encouraged to review a draft of the agreement with their own separate attorneys. When all parties are agreed to the settlement, the final document is submitted to the court for filing and the court's jurisdiction binds the individuals to compliance. The mediation process encourages maximum participation on the part of individuals to make decisions about their own divorce. The probability of compliance is psychologically but-tressed by the couple's belief that they made their own decisions and do not have to live with the arbitrary decisions of a judge.

DIVORCE, MEDIATION, AND THE LEGAL SYSTEM

The dramatic increase in divorce rates in the 1960s and early 1970s, the bureaucratic overloading of the court system, and the research indicating the consequences of divorce for children have necessitated that a different view of divorce be taken by the legal system. Couples are encouraged to reach their own decisions and settlements regarding their dissolution, par-ticularly with regard to children, custody, and parenting issues. This change of attitude in the legal system has set the stage for mediation as a viable and constructive alternative to the traditional adversarial divorce.

The 1972 Uniform Marriage and Divorce Act was drafted by the National Conference of Commissioners in Uniform State Laws advocating "irretriev-able broken marriage" as the sole cause for divorce (2). Although the Act was not adopted by the American Bar Association, it represents the changing view of divorce in America in the 1970s. As a result, "no-fault" statutes were created in many states that provided that a marriage that is irretriev-ably broken may be dissolved without the necessity of proving fault of either of the parties. The statutes are based on the premise that involved individuals have a basic right to determine the disposition of their marriage. Although the courts were traditionally skeptical about making divorce "too easy," recent research has indicated that no-fault laws have not contributed to an increase in divorce rates (3). In 1981, Faynes reported that 47 states had adopted a form of "no-fault" divorce that did not require either party to prove fault on the part of the other spouse (4).

Community property statutes have also been adopted in several states in an attempt to decrease the conflicts in marital dissolutions around property issues. The California court system reserves the right to divide community property by dividing assets as it "deems property to effect a substantially equal distribution of property" (5). However, another California statute provides that if no demand for money, property, costs, or attorneys fees is made in petition, no financial declaration is required (6).

The legal system has encouraged the use of conciliation courts to defuse litigation and conflicts around child custody and visitation. For example, a California ruling mandates that all divorce matters involving conflicts around custody issues must be set for mediation prior to hearing, for the purpose of reducing acrimony and to ensure a close and continuing relationship between the children and both of their parents (7). The court provides mediation services and guidelines for mediators to provide this service.

Many opponents of the adversarial system of divorce have argued that although legal rights may be decided by the court system, emotional rights are ignored in the combative litigation process. Still others have questioned whether legal rights are actually protected. For example, in highly conflicted cases, where attorneys are unable to settle differences between the parties, judges often intervene and make arbitrary decisions that may or may not be in the "best interests" of everyone involved. Spencer contends that judicial resolution of custody issues not only results in the imposition of an external set of values, but also serves as a means of punishing a parent whose values the judge did not share (8).

Mediation now offers an alternative to the traditional adversarial approach to divorce. Although mediation is a legal process, it provides a comprehensive and humane opportunity for the divorcing couple to intrinsically and wholly shape the outcome of their divorce and future as individuals and parents.

CHILDREN AND THE LAW

The divorcing process is especially hard on children. Often children are used as pawns by parents and attorneys to manipulate support and property division rulings, to get even with the other parent, or to serve as messengers on a battlefield between two warring parents. Visitation and custody battles are the source of much pain for parents and future emotional problems for children. In the early 1980s, several states created laws that recognize that the best interests of children are served by continued interaction with both parents. When a child is denied access to either parent, he is the one who suffers most.

Children of divorce generally are troubled with psychological feelings of omnipotence alternating with feelings of helplessness. They may manifest a sense of suffering, blame, and responsibility, and a fear that they will be abandoned (9). Loss of access to a parent is often a consequence of an embittered battle between parents, misplaced anger at arbitrary judicial decisions, and a sense that through the divorce a parent has lost the rights and privileges of parenthood. In addition, the authors have observed that fathers who go through mediation are much more likely to adhere to support agreements than those who go through an adversarial divorce. We believe this is true because both parents have an equal part in creating an agreement and come out of the divorcing process with a feeling that they had a part in creating their commitments.

Clinical practice with divorcing families provides mental health professionals with abundant data to support the opinion that the emotional and psychological needs of both parents and children are neither addressed nor resolved in the traditional adversarial divorce. In fact, the court system often serves to intensify a battle between spouses, often escalating conflictual areas of parenting as well.

Traditionally, the courts have favored the mother for custody and have permitted limited visitation schedules for the father. Many states, including California, now advocate joint custody and acknowledge that children have strong emotional bonds with both parents and suffer greatly from the loss of either parent.

CUSTODY MEDIATIONS

Part 1

AAMD makes use of a three-part mediation process culminating in the formulation of a Co-parenting Agreement. The first section of the Agreement delineates the philosophy behind a cooperative parenting arrangement between the two parents. It includes a paragraph that describes the nature of the parental relationship as one that is formed to serve, through mutual cooperation, as a source of love and support for the children. The Agreement specifies that both parties recognize that it is in the best interests of the children to continue to provide them with the maximum opportunity to spend time and develop a close, bonded relationship with each parent.

Part 2

The second part of the Co-parenting Agreement is designed to maximize the caretaking responsibilities of both parents so that their contributions are significant to the raising of the child. The Agreement stipulates that all decisions regarding the guidelines for standards of development, education, and health, as well as any major medical or legal decisions, be discussed and mutually agreed upon by both parents. It is further stipulated that each parent contribute time and energies on a daily basis toward the children's day-to-day care when they live with that parent. Minor decisions and care-taking responsibilities are delegated to the custodial parent who is designated by contract to be responsible for the children at that time.

Agreements vary as to the specificity of structure imposed regarding times and days of responsibilities. Those couples who are able to remain flexible and communicative about custodial schedules are not encouraged to form an agreement that will be too rigid or binding for their circumstances. For those couples who have more difficulty in communicating or express a desire to have a formal structure of custody that both can rely on, mediation may help them formulate an Agreement with specific days and times for the exchange of the children. Often holidays and vacations are also stipulated in the Agreement.

When there are conflicts between the parties, the parties are encouraged to refrain from exhibiting any demeaning behavior or destructive attitudes toward each other in the presence of the children. Often we find it useful to include in the Agreement that both parents are responsible for controlling their behavior by not provoking, belittling, or criticizing each other, and by not giving advice unless it is requested. At times, we have found it advisable to limit the nature of communication between the parents to communication about the children, and, minimally, to restrict behavior to that which exhibits common courtesy and respect for one another.

Part 3

The third part of the Co-Parenting Agreement contains the support arrangement. We have found that it is very helpful to mediate the conflicts the couple has regarding parental obligations and responsibilities well before financial support issues are discussed. Traditionally, emotional and financial issues often cloud and complicate issues of custody and caretaking. Mediation allows these issues to be separated and delineated so that the children are not used to barter for property or money. Since property and money are loaded issues in many divorces, mediating the emotional and practical issues surrounding caretaking and parenting relationships and obligations serves to give plenty of opportunity for the couple to practice and succeed at conflict resolution and to perceive that they may each be able to draw what they need from one another without putting the children up as ante.

The Agreement provides that in the event that either of the parents feels that his or her interaction has deteriorated, that communication is impossible, or that the couple is in a deadlock and incapable of resolving a difference between them, they: 1) delay a decision until such time that they both feel they can agree upon a decision; or 2) submit the problem to mediation to be resolved with the aid of a mediator.

THE EMOTIONS OF CHILDREN IN DIVORCE

Children exhibit a variety of symptomatic behavior during a divorce. According to Ware (10), the age of a child is a significant determinant of what reactions the child will have. Ware has observed that infants, toddlers, and preschoolers may exhibit excessive crying, difficulties in toilet training, or intense fear of the dark. They may also experience difficulty with sleeping habits. Early elementary school children may experience intense fears of abandonment, rage toward one or both of the parents, and difficulties in adjusting to school routines. Preteens often become extremely introverted in an attempt to mask feelings of loneliness, fear, and mistrust. Because peers are so important to preteens, they may also experience shame and embarrassment with their friends.

Divorce is often the first time that many children face the idea that their parents might not always be there for them. They experience feelings of loss, uprootedness, anger, and protectiveness of both parents. Children also experience separation anxiety from one or both parents and a profound fear that they will be abandoned. For this reason, we have found it to be very important to include the children in the mediation process. Often they are seen once or twice by a therapist on our staff. In addition, we ask that the parents discuss their plans, share the various parts of the Co-parenting Agreement and indicate their own input, and be sure to let the children know how they are included in these plans, although they will not be jeopardized by making the decisions for themselves.

Mediation is an opportunity for parents to become well educated about the needs of children as they go through the divorce process. It is important to acknowledge children's despair in this period of high transition. Children are usually the ones who are unintentionally forgotten and misunderstood in a divorce. Often both parents are in a highly emotional period of their lives and tend to overlook their children's emotional needs. Mediation encourages parents who have agreed upon a joint custody arrangement to monitor and discuss the children's emotional reactions to these changes —especially during the first year of separation until they stabilize and internalize a sense that they truly still have two parents and two homes.

Children often feel responsible for the divorce. They think that they caused their parents to fight. We have been given reasons for divorce that include: "We didn't go to bed when we were told and they started to fight over it." It is important for parents to reassure children that the parents' incompatibilities had nothing to do with the children and that they are very much loved and cared about by both parents.

There is a strong tendency among divorcing parents to criticize each other, to sabotage each other's parenting styles, and to demean or even attack each other in front of the children. In addition, children are often used as informants. It is very important to avoid placing the children in the middle of any conflict between the parents. It is best not to discuss methods of parenting or disciplinary styles around the children.

PARENTS AND THE MEDIATION PROCESS

Parents have indicated that one of their worst fears during divorce proceedings is that they will lose their children. Both fathers and mothers experience tremendous anxiety and fear of loss when another lover is present, when the other parent is threatening to keep the children with him or her, when there is conflict over visitation, or when their children seem to "prefer" one parent to the other.

Mediation operationally addresses the assumption that divorce is not the end of the family life cycle, but a phasic period that needs to be managed as a crisis that threatens the continuing existence of the family. Mediation is based on the proposition that although the divorce ends a marriage, it doesn't end the family. AAMD (11) believes that the mediation process should help couples restructure a bi-modal family unit. The negotiation and conflict resolution process are designed to increase the couple's ability to maintain a collaborative relationship as parents to their children. Although impartial as to the outcome of the settlement agreement, most mediators agree that even though parties are entitled to become ex-spouses, no children should have to have an "ex-parent."

Fathers often experience feelings of insecurity and inadequacy in taking on parental and caretaking responsibilities for the first time. They may feel that they are ill equipped to perform the day-to-day functions required of a single parent. Often fathers try to play the "good parent," in an attempt to win the affections of their children, by neglecting the disciplinary and directive parts of parenthood and assuming only those roles that will gratify and entertain their children. Unfortunately, the "Disneyland Dad" is more than a myth. Mothers are often stuck with the day-to-day chores and caretaking responsibilities without help from fathers. In effect, both parents lose the opportunity to share the responsibilities and real parenting with each other, and the children lose the opportunity to experience the full range of involvement with their parents.

Fathers often profit by information regarding the nature of parenting. We find ourselves telling fathers over and over again to spend a fixed amount or time alone every day with the children, to freely express emotions, fears, doubts, uncertainties, to be clear about what expectations and requirements there are of each child, to explain questions they might have about divorce, to get involved with the children's daily lives and social activities, and to minimize changes in everyone's lives as much as possible.

Mediation also helps parents deal with the loaded problems of the "other person." Often one parent will request that the children not be around the "lover." We have found that this is often rooted in jealousy and insecurity, rather than in a sincere desire to protect the children. We usually recommend that in order for the children to have a close and meaningful relationship with either parent, it is important that they are a part of both their parents' lives. To significantly impede this involvement really serves to leave the children out in the cold. A reasonable division of time alone and time together with the new person is generally the outcome of mediation, once the underlying emotions of jealousy, fear of loss, and insecurity recognized and resolved.

CONCLUSION

Numerous studies have pointed out that the more conflicts there are between parents, the more children suffer from divorce, and that the more access children have to both parents, the less potential there is for emotional damage. Divorce is potentially destructive to children, but perhaps future research will indicate that the major variable is not divorce, but the destructive fallout from a combative divorce. Divorce mediation may provide a means for children and parents to avoid the rubble of the "broken family."

REFERENCES

1. McIsaac, H. Mandatory conciliation custody/visitation matters: California's bold stroke. *Conciliation Courts Review*, 1981, *19*(2), p. 73.
2. Irving, H. H. *Divorce mediation: A rational alternative to the adversarial system.* New York: Universe Books, 1981.
3. Wright, G. C., Jr., & Stetson, D. M. The impact of no fault divorce law reform on divorce in American states. *Journal of Marriage and the Family, 1978, 40*(3) 575.
4. Haynes, J. M. *Divorce mediation: A practical guide for therapists and counselors.* New York: Springer, 1981.
5. California Code of Civil Procedure, Section 4800.
6. California Code of Civil Procedure, Section 4364.
7. California Code of Civil Procedure, Section 4607.
8. Spencer, J. M., & Zammet, J. P. Mediation, arbitration: A proposal for private resolution of disputes between divorced or separated parents. *Duke Law Journal, 1976, 76*(5) 807.
9. Despert, L. *Children of divorce.* New York: Dolphin, 1962, p. 171.
10. Ware, C. *Sharing parenthood after divorce.* New York: Viking Press, 1982, pp. 80-87.
11. Ruman, M., & Lamm, M. G. Divorce mediation: A team approach to marital dissolution. *Trial,* 1983, *19*(3), p. 86.

7

Joint Custody: The Need for Individual Evaluation and Service

Susan Steinman

The concept of joint custody, in which both divorced parents share responsibility, authority for decision-making, and time with their children, has gained increasing acceptance over the past five years. This approach to the complex psychological and legal problems that attend child custody decisions is a response to dramatic changes in society and in the family.

During the 1970s and early 1980s, as more and more women with children entered the work force, parents began to share the traditionally separate nurturing and breadwinning roles more equally. At the same time, however, the rising divorce rate created unprecedented numbers of divorced parents and their children. No-fault divorce laws, a major factor in this increase, contributed to the growing movement to make child custody decisions less adversarial. These social changes set the stage for joint custody as an alternative to the traditional practice of awarding custody of the children to the mother, with the accompanying rigid visitation rights and child support orders to fathers.

The dissemination of findings from the divorce research of the past decade provided data to support a public policy that encouraged both continuing contact between children and both parents after divorce and parental cooperation. The longitudinal work of Wallerstein and Kelly (1) underlined postdivorce family relationships as being more salient to the child's adjustment than the fact of the divorce itself, and emphasized two major factors in the child's recovery from the divorce trauma: 1) a continuing relationship with both parents, and 2) the reduction of anger and conflict between the parents. While this research did not directly examine joint custody, the findings provided support for an overall approach that would protect children from disruption of their relationship with the noncustodial parent and from the ongoing hostility between parents, which is greatly exacerbated by the adversarial nature of legal custody decision-making.

The concept of joint custody has aroused considerable controversy among legal and mental health professionals. The absence of long-term data and experience with joint custody has allowed decision-making to be influenced by personal and professional biases, and, in some cases, very passionate feelings. Most professionals and judges can agree, however, that the adversarial approach is destructive to children and to postdivorce family relationships. In this context, joint custody, along with the growing practice of divorce mediation, offers hopeful alternatives that deserve further exploration.

DEFINITIONS

Joint custody has no standard operating definition, which often creates confusion for the parents, lawyers, counselors, and judges who must evaluate its viability. It is distinguished from the traditional approach by the following assumptions and values: 1) Both parents are viewed as important in the psychological and day-to-day life of the child; 2) parents share the authority for making decisions about the children; 3) parents cooperate in sharing authority and responsibility for raising their children; and 4) children spend a significant amount of time living with each parent.

How these ideas are put into practice is up to the parents and the professionals whose roles are to assist them. Mental health and legal professionals, and some statutes, distinguish between "joint legal custody," which refers to equal input into major decisions about the child, and "joint physical custody," which refers to where the child lives. What joint custody really means—practically, psychologically, and legally—needs further exploration.

LEGAL AND SOCIAL POLICY CONTEXT

Prior to California's joint custody statute of 1980, joint custody was essentially an extrajudicial phenomenon. During the 1970s, small but increasing numbers of divorcing parents made informal joint custody arrangements for the care of their children after divorce, independent of the legal system. These de facto joint custody arrangements generally did not have the sanction of the court, as most judges felt there was no legal authority to grant joint custody and did not, in any case, see it as a viable arrangement.

Joint custody legislation brought legal approval for families who chose and implemented these arrangements on their own, regardless of social policy and legal practice. While two states passed laws making joint custody an option, California was the first state to encourage joint custody. This policy resulted in a proliferation of joint custody legislation nationwide, such that 32 states now have some form of joint custody statute. Some states simply make joint custody an option, other states prefer joint custody and do not require parental agreement for a joint custody order, and several states have made joint custody a presumption even in the absence of parental agreement (2).

This legislative movement has had several effects. First, the laws established expectations for and shaped the attitudes of divorcing parents to decide about custody of their children outside the court system, thus influencing a growing number of parents and professionals to explore the joint custody option. Second, it is functioning as a corrective to the judicial and professional bias against joint custody to create more receptivity on the part of mental health and legal professionals. Third, laws preferring joint custody put legal pressure on disputing parents who come to court for resolution to work out a joint custody arrangement. (It is estimated that only 10% to 15% of divorcing parents come to court to resolve child custody issues. It is this population that is more directly affected by the law as interpreted and applied through the decision of the judge.)

The major social policy issue is whether joint custody should be approached as either a socially approved option or a custody solution imposed on parents by the legal system. It is clear that this policy issue reaches far beyond the available data we have on joint custody.

JOINT CUSTODY LITERATURE

In the past six years, a growing body of popular literature has brought the arguments in favor of joint custody before the public and professional communities for consideration. In *The Disposable Parent* (3), Roman and Haddad strongly advocated making joint custody a legal presumption. Several books have subsequently been written for parents, which describe the advantages of sharing custody and making practical suggestions for developing and managing a joint custody arrangement (4–7). While this literature has been an important educational resource for parents considering joint custody, it is based primarily on professional and personal opinions.

Few empirical studies to date have examined joint custody, and even fewer have directly assessed the children involved. In a study of divorced fathers, Greif (8) found that those fathers with joint custody were less depressed and more satisfied in their postdivorce relationships with their children than were visiting fathers. Ahrons (9) studied 41 parents who had joint legal custody, and found that while co-parental relationships varied in the degree of conflict and cooperation and the kinds of arrangements, it was possible for parents to cooperate in childrearing matters while discontinuing the intimate spousal relationship. Ilfeld, Ilfeld, and Alexander (10) tracked 414 divorce cases through court records in Los Angeles County, and found that relitigation was half as frequent among joint legal custody awards as among sole custody awards. They concluded that because relitigation is an indication of parental conflict, joint custody must be the better alternative. No direct contact was made with the parents or children, so it was impossible to determine what types of arrangements the families had or how they were working.

Studies of joint custody that include direct assessment of the children's experiences of joint custody are extremely limited. Abarbanel (11) studied four San Francisco Bay Area families using a case study approach. She found the parents to be generally satisfied and most of the children to be adjusting well. She identified four factors that seem to make joint parenting work: 1) commitment to the arrangement; 2) parents' mutual support; 3) flexible sharing of responsibility; and 4) agreement on the implicit rules of the system.

Luepnitz (12) studied 50 parents—16 custodial mothers, 16 custodial fathers, and 18 joint custody parents—along with their children. She found that child adjustment did not differ by custody type, and that joint custody offered a number of advantages to parents and children. She concluded that the findings did not support a presumption of maternal custody, and pointed to the need for further research on how joint custody works for children of different ages and with varying degrees of parental motivation.

Our study of San Francisco Bay Area families who arranged joint custody extrajudicially prior to the law in California, and who maintained it over a number of years, found that the parents were generally satisfied, while the children's experiences were more mixed (13). Joint custody offered significant benefits to parents and children, but it also required considerable effort and commitment on the part of both parents and children. In this group of highly motivated and satisfied parents, about one-third of the children were having significant adjustment problems and appeared to be burdened by the arrangement, even after a number of years. We concluded that joint custody arrangements should be determined with the child's individual needs and capacities foremost in mind, and that further research was necessary to better understand which children and parents would benefit from joint custody and for which it would constitute a serious stress.

The available literature suggests that joint custody is a viable option, and that parents can separate their intimate spousal relationship from their parenting relationship in order to develop a respectful, cooperative relationship for childrearing. It also suggests that it is possible for children to live in two homes and remain positively attached to two parents who no longer want to be married to one another. It is clear, however, that more systematic research with larger and broader samples is needed in order to gain information about how joint custody works for children of different ages, personalities, and family circumstances. Our understanding of how joint custody actually works has been limited thus far to studies in which parents were highly motivated to undertake joint custody and committed to making it work. With joint custody legislation now being applied to parents who are unmotivated and even bitterly hostile to one another, it is especially urgent that we understand how joint custody works for parents and children in less-than-ideal circumstances.

ISSUES TO CONSIDER IN EVALUATING JOINT CUSTODY

My research with joint custody families over the past six years at Jewish Family and Children's Services in San Francisco has helped to clarify the benefits and demands of joint custody for divorcing parents and their children.* The following discussion is based on our study of 24 families who arranged joint custody prior to the law and were highly motivated to make it work (14).

Advantages and Disadvantages for Parents

I found that the overriding motivation and advantage for the parents committed to joint custody was to share the pleasures and burdens of childrearing. The working mothers in the study greatly valued the time off to pursue their careers and reorganize their adult social life. In general, the women who valued their work as a source of identity and self-esteem seemed able to relinquish the role of full-time parent more easily. For fathers, joint custody was a way to preserve a close relationship with their children and to maintain an important adult role.

Joint custody seems to help the motivated parent diminish the sense of loss, personal failure, and disruption of adult role and identity that often accompanies divorce. These parents greatly value their former spouse as parent to their child, despite the disappointment and anger they may feel toward the spouse as husband or wife.

---

*Joint Custody Study Project, Jewish Family and Children's Services, San Francisco, funded by the San Francisco Foundation and the Joint Custody Project sponsored by the Jewish and Family and Children's Services, San Francisco, and the Center for the Family in Transition, Corte Madera, California. The latter project is funded by the San Francisco Foundation Jewish Community Endowment Fund of the Jewish Community Federation, Zellerbach Family Fund, The Morris Stulsaft Foundation, and the Benjamin and Mae Swig Foundation.

For parents who maintained the joint custody arrangement over a number of years, these psychological and practical advantages outweighed the disadvantages. The stresses reported by these parents, and those observed in the newly developed arrangements of our current population, while varying according to personalities and life circumstances, most often included the ongoing contact with the former spouse. While these parents were generally able and motivated to contain their anger at one another to protect the child and the co-parental relationship, conflicts and latent feelings periodically erupted. Some parents reported that while shared parenting allowed a more gradual and less immediately painful emotional separation, it may also have fed the fantasies of reconciliation that lingered under the surface. Another strain was the sense of discontinuity engendered by part-time parenting, (e.g., following through on rules and routines), both in their personal lives and in their relationships with their children.

Tasks of Co-Parenting

While joint custody can offer important psychological and practical advantages for parents whose personalities, life- and work-styles, and basic values support it, it is a complex, intricately balanced system of relationships, which requires commitment and work to maintain. Both new and long-term joint custody parents report that living with joint custody is more complicated than the concept might suggest.

The major work of co-parenting is to put aside the marital and divorce-engendered anger and cooperate around the child, rather than use the child (albeit unconsciously) to punish the other parent. The specific tasks of co-parenting after divorce include decision-making, communication, handling differences and conflict, and building new boundaries.

Making decisions together about the major aspects of the children's lives is the cornerstone of joint custody. While day-to-day decisions were left to the independent judgment of each parent, these parents consulted one another and made joint decisions on issues of health care, school, religion, or major problems. They accepted the premise that parents have equal authority over and influence on the development of their children. They clearly understood the distinction between major decisions, which required discussion and negotiation, and daily decisions, which were "off limits."

Communication is another important task of co-parenting. Parents who made a positive adaptation to joint custody over the long run learned to limit the frequency and content of discussion to what is essential for child-rearing, and to avoid emotionally charged issues. While co-parental discussion can increase continuity and coordination between homes, it can also stir up anger and tension. Among newly divorced parents, in their struggle to disengage and develop ways of coping with feelings of anger, depression, anxiety, and guilt, communication can be very distressing and old arguments can be re-ignited very quickly. Very little communication occurs at this stage. Because contact is so painful, these parents tend to communicate only when necessary and only about concrete issues, such as schedules.

Joint custody parents need to develop ways of coping with their differences in childrearing ideas and behavior. The parents with smoothly running arrangements were clear about their differences and able to tolerate them. They were able to distinguish important from unimportant differences with respect to the child's well-being, and to restrain themselves from criticizing the other parent. Their skills in problem solving allowed them to resolve conflicts by finding a mutually acceptable solution, rather than by trying to prove the other parent inadequate.

The underlying psychological task for joint custody parents is to build a new set of boundaries that will allow them the emotional and territorial distance necessary to disengage from the intimate marital bond, while leaving open a channel for communication and cooperation around the children. This requires a respect for the privacy and autonomy of the other parent, and the ability to not interfere in the ex-spouse's relationship with the child.

CHARACTERISTICS AND CAPACITIES OF PARENTS LIKELY TO WORK OUT JOINT CUSTODY

The following parental characteristics and capacities, together with a commitment to the concept of joint custody as a fair and moral solution and commitment to their children, have been important in sustaining the dynamic joint custody arrangements. While these characteristics may not be demonstrated during the acute divorce crisis, we have found it useful to keep them in mind when evaluating the parents' potential for successful implementation of joint custody.

1) A sense of basic respect and trust for one another as parents. Despite the failure as a marriage partner, each spouse considers the other parent to be a decent person and a good enough parent;
2) Appreciation of the value of the other parent to the child;
3) Empathy for the sense of loss experienced by the child and other parent;
4) Basic congruency of childrearing values;
5) Capacity to tolerate existing differences;
6) Capacity to let go and not interfere in the other parent-child relationship;

7) Personal flexibility to accommodate to the needs of the arrangement, the child, and the other parent, as well as to other changes;
8) Capacity to suppress anger and divert it away from the children;
9) Capacity to take responsibility for their role in the divorce and for their current life and not project blame onto the other parent;
10) A sense of parity with the other parent;
11) Ability to maintain a "conflict-free sphere" around the children (and protect them from co-parental conflict); and
12) Appreciation of "time off" from parenting.

THE CHILDREN'S EXPERIENCE OF JOINT CUSTODY

During the past decade, research on the effects of divorce on children has consistently emphasized the importance of postdivorce family relationships in how children adapt to divorce. Regular and frequent contact with both parents, and a civilized relationship between divorced parents, have been positively associated with the child's ability to resume developmental progress. While joint custody seems to address these two requirements, direct assessment of how children adjust within a dual-home living arrangement is very limited. The question of whether the benefits to the child of being closely involved with both parents outweighs the strains of moving between parental homes remains to be explored. Our study indicated that the strengths and vulnerabilities of the individual child need to be considered when making decisions about which families will be good candidates for joint custody.

By the time we interviewed them, these children had lived in a dual-home joint custody arrangement for a number of years. While a more detailed report on the psychological experience of the 32 children (ages four and a half to 15) in this study has been published elsewhere, our findings on the benefits and strains of joint custody for these children and their overall adjustment can be summarized as follows (15).

Benefits

The major benefit of joint custody to these children was their clear sense of being loved and wanted by both parents. They were secure in the knowledge that they were important in their family; the fact that both parents put forth a great deal of effort to jointly care for them enhanced their sense of self-esteem. Because they had physical access to both parents and the psychological permission to love and be with both parents, they were protected from crippling loyalty conflicts and problems of identification.

Parental Differences

Most of these children whose parents shared basic childrearing values adapted well to the minor personality differences and childrearing styles between their two parental homes. When parents were clear about their differences—and, more importantly, not angry about those differences—the children adapted with minimal conflict and confusion. However, in the few families in which parental hostility and conflict continued to involve the children, the children were significantly troubled by it.

Switching Homes

Whether or not shifting between parental homes is a source of anxiety and insecurity for joint custody children has been of primary concern. Most of the children in this study were able to remember their schedules and make the transition between homes with a minimum of distress. They exhibited an overall sense of mastery of the arrangement, and many had developed adaptive ways of coping with the emotional and cognitive demands of the transitions. However, about one-quarter of the children found the alternation of homes to be anxiety-provoking and disorganizing. They worried about themselves, their parents, and their possessions, and demonstrated a general sense of insecurity. The group included four- to five-year-old girls who were anxious and angry about switching houses, and a group of seven- to nine-year-old boys who felt confused and insecure about their ability to keep track of things and who were having learning problems at school.

Continuity of School Life and Friendships

Most of the parents in this study lived in close geographical proximity so that the children were able to attend the same school or day-care program and to maintain contact with their peers. This continuity was very important, particularly to the school-age and adolescent children. With the disruption caused by the divorce and the frequent changes necessitated by living in two homes, school was a source of stability and continuity that they consciously valued.

The adolescents in the study (and to a lesser extent the preadolescents) felt that the previously prescribed dual-home arrangement interfered with their increased involvement in peer life and school-based social activities. This, in combination with their developmental need to loosen emotional bonds with parents, made the arrangement antithetical to their needs and, as they became teenagers, there was a shift toward a primary-home arrangement.

Changes Over Time

Follow-up interviews were conducted 12 to 18 months after the initial series of interviews. We were interested in what precipitates change and how parents and children adapt, but we did not expect to find major changes because the arrangements had been maintained over a number of years, and because the parents had generally felt satisfied with and committed to the arrangement.

Surprisingly, one third of the families had shifted to an arrangement where the children lived in one primary home. The children continued to visit their other parent, and the parents continued to make major decisions jointly. The factors triggering this shift from a dual-home to a primary-home arrangement seemed to be a geographical move, remarriage and the birth of a new baby (remarriage alone did not have this effect), and entry of the child into adolescence.

ISSUES IN EVALUATING DISPUTED JOINT CUSTODY

Recent legislation has put urgent pressure on legal and mental health professionals to assess for whom and under what circumstances joint custody is likely to work. Unfortunately, we have no data on how joint custody works among parents who undertake it as a result of legal decisions, or what helps differentiate joint custody that works well from that which works poorly or is abandoned.

Our current research and service project for families considering joint custody is designed to contribute such data. In this second project, we are studying the process of decision-making and implementation of joint custody in 50 divorcing families who are within the first year of filing for marital dissolution. We are following the course of the arrangement and the psychological and legal outcome for the children and their parents in two subgroups: "nondisputing parents," parents who have mutually agreed to joint custody without court involvement; and "legally disputing parents," parents who are in legal dispute about joint custody, where one parent wants joint custody and the other is opposed, or where both parents seek sole custody and a third party recommends they explore joint custody.

We are examining the factors that differentiate those parents who overcome their initial resistance to joint custody and develop the capacities and resources to manage the arrangement from those who cannot. A major issue for these parents is the overriding anger at the spouse for the hurt experienced during the marriage and divorcing process. Frequently, this intense anger, the projection of blame for the divorce, and the wish to punish provide a fertile breeding ground for distortions about the spouse as parent.

The spouse is devalued as a parent and there is an absence of basic trust and respect between the parents. There is an attempt to repair a damaged sense of self-esteem via criticism and blame of the other parent. Spouses may not be equally angry or mistrustful; the spouse who is left may be more angry, while the partner who wanted the divorce may be more guilty.

It is difficult to assess, during the initial post-separation crisis, when parental functioning may be at its lowest point, whether the fear, anger, and distortion will diminish over time, or whether parents are likely to remain enmeshed in a hostile, punitive relationship with the child acting as the vehicle for punishment.

Helping parents separate marital- and divorce-engendered anger from their evaluation of their child's needs, and supporting their ability to put those needs first, are major issues in working with initially disputing parents. Will time and supportive, educational intervention diminish the hostility and conflict between these parents? Or are they enmeshed in a hostile and unremitting battle? Are the parents' childrearing and other basic values congruent? Do parents value the child's relationship with the other parent, or is the other parent seen as damaging to the child? Can parents progress in resolving the emotional issues of the divorce, rebuild their parenting capacities, and move forward toward a more satisfying life? Can parents organize and coordinate childrearing activities and responsibilities so the child's growth can be enhanced by their joint effort, or will the child be burdened by parental conflict and miscommunication? Are the parents flexible enough to observe and problem solve around the changing needs of the child?

A more systematic data analysis of failed joint custody arrangements is still in progress. However, some of the special problems associated with joint custody that cannot be implemented or sustained, or which are subject to continuing relitigation, can be said to include: 1) intense and unremitting hostility and conflict that cannot be diverted from the children; 2) history of physical violence in the relationship; 3) extreme lack of respect for the other parent; 4) major emotional disturbance of one or both parents; 5) alcoholism; 6) differences in childrearing experienced as violation of important values; and 7) the inability of one parent to accept the reality of the divorce (which often changes with time).

A mediated legal agreement or court order cannot create the parental resources and capacities necessary to cooperate in joint custody. However, supportive intervention through mediation and counseling may help parents work on developing these skills.

TASKS AND DEMANDS FOR THE CHILD

We need to differentiate the characteristics of the children who can make a positive adjustment to joint custody from those who cannot. Joint custody requires children to be flexible and make adaptations that would be difficult for many adults. Joint custody children must be able to handle transitions from home to home and parent to parent. They must cognitively master the arrangement and achieve a sense of security and belonging in each home. Children will differ in how they manage these tasks.

Age-Related Differences

The child's age may affect adjustment to joint custody, especially as it relates to the effects of shifting between parental homes. While joint custody might diminish the sense of loss and abandonment and the worry about the absent parent that young children are particularly vulnerable to after separation, would this benefit outweigh the strain of making transitions from parent to parent? Would the distress and anxiety observed among young children at leaving their primary caregiver be a temporary reaction that would fade over time, or would it have lasting effects? Would the stress of transition be reduced as parental tension is reduced?

School-age children face the developmental tasks of learning and establishing friendships with peers, as well as consolidating their sexual identification with the same-sex parent. While the greater cognitive development, which includes a clearer sense of time and geography, of this age group makes the arrangement easier, there are also increased social and academic demands. The joint custody child may need to be naturally well-oriented, organized, and able to concentrate in order to meet both the demands of school and life in two homes. There are indications that support and coordination between joint custody parents are particularly important for children who are less competent in these areas.

We also need to observe whether joint custody affects how school-age children establish and maintain friendships. Depending on the child, the schedules, and the proximity of homes, maintaining continuity with friends outside of school may require a socially active child and one whose parents facilitate this contact with friends. Some joint custody parents report that while they see their child only part-time, that time is intensified and exclusive. It is unclear whether this would create less opportunity for peer interaction outside of school, or would require extra effort on the part of the child and parent.

For adolescents, increased involvement with school life and social activities, along with a desire for increased independence and control of their lives, may make a prescribed dual-home arrangement antithetical to their needs. As teenagers become increasingly independent and able to travel between homes, they may find that living in one primary home and more flexible time with the other parent is a desirable alternative.

Individual Differences

Children differ in their characteristic responses to change. Information on individual differences and on how particular strengths and vulnerabilities might affect a child's experience of joint custody would be useful in developing appropriate arrangements.

The kinds of arrangements (e.g., time schedule, geographical proximity, transportation) may certainly be significant in how children manage the dual-home arrangement. Further information on whether one type of arrangement is better than another, and for which children, would be useful. In our first study, it was impossible to tell how a child was doing by looking at the particular time schedule. In 50% of the families, the children split the week between their two homes (usually three days in one home and four days in the other). Another 25% had a week-to-week schedule. The remaining families had arrangements that ranged from alternating homes each day, every two weeks, every three months, alternate weekends, to alternate years with the other parent. The one schedule that was clearly problematic was the year-to-year arrangement in which the children, ages nine and 10, changed schools, neighborhoods, and lifestyles to live one year with the mother in a rural area and one year with the father in a cosmopolitan town several hundred miles away.

Geographical proximity between parental homes was perhaps the most consistent dimension that both parents and children believed to be crucial. From the children's point of view, the proximity of their parents' homes was very valuable, as was the proximity to their school. Many of the children, who knew the geography well, had confidence in their ability to negotiate the distance between homes and had a sense that their parents were accessible. To the children who did not have a clear cognitive map, and who did not feel a sense of mastery over the arrangement, the distance between homes was a source of insecurity.

While we need to learn more about how the specific types of arrangements support or burden children, at this point geographical proximity, particularly in relation to maintaining the continuity of school, friendships, and neighborhoods, should be given high priority in planning for joint custody.

IMPLICATIONS FOR POLICY AND RESEARCH

Joint custody is a process, not a panacea. The purpose of this process is the reorganization of a family structure to support the child's growth while helping parents move on to more satisfying lives. Deciding upon and implementing joint custody require a consideration of the needs and capacities of the individual child and his or her parents at a particular time in that child's life, rather than the imposition of a standard legal formula.

At the present time, our data on joint custody are very limited. Until our current study, research had focused on extrajudicial arrangements made by highly motivated parents. We learned from these studies that joint custody can be a satisfying arrangement that helps ease the sense of loss and diminished self-esteem for children and parents. Yet, even in families where parents are committed to making joint custody work, it is not an easy arrangement or one that all children will master.

A careful examination of joint custody arrangements made by court order, after mediation or counseling efforts have failed to help parents reach agreement, is still in progress at the Jewish Family and Children's Services. (In California, mediation is mandatory when parents are in dispute over child custody or visitation.) Preliminary impressions of the continuing emotional distress and relitigation activity, and the emotional and behavioral problems of the children, indicate the need for a more cautious approach with respect to developing state policy that imposes joint custody on such families. Where joint custody is imposed on parents who remain enmeshed in conflict even after intervention, the children may remain caught in the crossfire of their parents' battles, and decisions about their lives may be delayed because of their parents' inability to agree.

The available data seem to indicate a policy that encourages co-parental cooperation and protects the child's ongoing relationship with both parents. The traditional legal prescription of maternal custody with restrictive visiting patterns for fathers and children should not be replaced with an equally rigid prescription of joint custody. Divorcing families may be better served by a commitment to the development of child-focused mediation and counseling services.

Our data suggest that most divorcing parents may require some degree of help to implement joint custody. Services to help divorcing parents resolve child-related conflicts and decide upon an arrangement, as well as to help provide education and support to parents and children embarking on joint custody, would seem to be an important adjunct to joint custody legislation. Such services should 1) help parents actively participate in evaluating and deciding about child custody arrangements; 2) provide an opportunity to identify and work on impediments to a workable joint custody arrangement; 3) help parents develop skills in problem solving, communication, and decision-making around the children; 4) facilitate the parents' separation of child-related issues from anger toward spouse and emotional distress around the divorce; and 5) provide a forum for parents to return to, when changes occur in their own and their children's lives, as these changes may renew the anxiety and anger of the earlier post-separation crisis.

As research data on the course and outcome of joint custody over time are reported, and we continue to gather clinical and court experience, we can build a body of knowledge to better guide decision-making in joint custody and to refine services for divorcing families exploring this new postdivorce arrangement.

REFERENCES

1. Wallerstein, J. S., & Kelly, J. B. *Surviving the break-up: How parents and children cope with divorce.* New York: Basic Books, 1980.
2. For a description of all the states' joint custody legislation, see Folberg, J. *Joint custody and shared parenting,* Appendix A., Washington, D.C.: Bureau of National Affairs, Association of Family Conciliation Courts, 1984.
3. Roman, M., & Haddad, W. *The disposable parent.* New York: Holt, Rinehart & Winston, 1978.
4. Woolley, P. *The custody handbook.* New York: Summit Books, 1979.
5. Galper, M. *Co-parenting: Sharing your child equally, A source book for the separated or divorced family.* Philadelphia: Running Press, 1978.
6. Ware, C. *Sharing parenthood after divorce.* New York: Viking Press, 1982.
7. Ricci, I. *Mom's house, dad's house: Making shared custody work.* New York: Macmillan, 1980.
8. Greif, J. Fathers, children and joint custody. *American Journal of Orthopsychiatry,* 1979, *49*(2), 311-319.
9. Ahrons, C. Joint custody arrangements in the post-divorce family. *Journal of Divorce,* 1980, *3*(3), 189-203.
10. Ilfeld, F., Jr., Ilfeld, H., & Alexander, J. Does joint custody work? A first local look at outcome data of relitigation. *American Journal of Psychiatry,* 1982, *62,* 139.
11. Abarbanel, A. Shared parenting after separation and divorce: A study of joint custody. *American Journal of Orthopsychiatry,* 1979, *49*(2), 320.
12. Luepnitz, D. A. *Child custody: A study of families after divorce.* Lexington, MA: Lexington Books, 1982.
13. Steinman, S. The experience of children in a joint custody arrangement: A report of a study. *American Journal of Orthopsychiatry,* 1981, *51*(3), 403-414.
14. *Ibid.*
15. *Ibid.*

8

Father Custody

Alan M. Levy

This chapter will present the various issues involved in the consideration and selection of fathers as custodial parents. Nothing stated in this chapter should be understood to be an argument for or against such a custodial decision, but rather an illumination of one possible choice among others in a most complex and difficult process. If this chapter has a bias at all, it is for the equality of fathers in consideration for custody. When fathers and mothers are truly considered on an equal footing, the decision-making process will emphasize factors other than sex, and may point the entire process in the direction of joint or shared custody, rather than a single-parent preference.

HISTORICAL PERSPECTIVE

The historical background for current child custody considerations has been ably presented elsewhere and will not be repeated here (1, 2, 3). Today, the controlling legal standard guiding most custody decisions is "the best interest of the child." In some states, there are statutes specifically stating that neither parent has a greater right to the child. In recent years, there has been a shift away from considerations of which parent should be preferred to considerations of what would be best for the child.

The best interest concept, however, is not without its own problems. It has yet to be well defined. While no controlling guidelines exist as to what constitutes the best interest of the child, sample laws that define this are available (4). The behavioral science equivalent to the legal statements defining "best interest" would be found in considerations of what constitutes a psychological parent and how one might conduct a custody study that leads to a custodial recommendation. Discussions of these issues are currently available (5, 6, 7).

IS THERE SEXISM IN CHILD CUSTODY DECISIONS?

In spite of the passage of new legislation and the promulgation of more modern guidelines in the area of child custody, many judges still think in outmoded terms such as "tender years" or presumption of maternal preference. Attitudes and habits change slowly.

, It has been pointed out that more and more fathers, unwilling to accept their alleged parental incompetence or the greater capability of their wives, are seeking custody (8). No-fault divorce laws and laws providing for a nonsexist view of parental competence have led to a dramatic departure from traditional domestic litigation. As a result, lawyers are more willing to pursue cases of male custody, and increasing numbers of fathers are seeking to become primary custodians. This has led to an increasing rate of success for fathers in contested child custody cases. In spite of the new laws, strong vestiges of maternal preference remain, and many fathers, who would be excellent parents, are discouraged from seeking custody. Many mothers are also still implicitly encouraged to seek custody when this, in fact, may not be their primary desire or interest (9). A guidebook on family law, published by the Family Law Committee of the Minnesota State Bar Association in 1971, stated that

> . . . except in rare cases the father should not have the custody of the minor children of the parties. He is usually unqualified psychologically and emotionally; nor does he have time and care to supervise the children. A lawyer not only does an injustice to himself but he is unfair to his client, to the state and to society if he gives any encouragement to the father that he should have custody of the children. A lawyer who encourages his client to file for custody, unless it is one of the classic exceptions, has difficulty collecting his fees, has a most unreasonable client, has taken the time of the courts and the welfare agencies involved, and has put a burden on his legal brethren. (10)

Although the statutes of many jurisdictions provide that either party is entitled to custody, lawyers and speakers humorously clarify this to mean that "the mother will always receive custody of the children regardless of her sex." The father must be able to convince the judge or jury, by a preponderance of the evidence, that he is so knowledgeable in the needs of his children that their best interests will obviously be served by their custody being awarded to him (11).

Slovenko (12) reminds us that over the past century, child custody decisions have clearly given priority to the mother. It is observable that among human and animal species it is generally the mother who cares for and protects the young. Slovenko states that the father, as a rule, recognizes that the mother can better render care and that the children usually wish to be with the mother. Consequently, the father does not request custody or possession of the family home in the divorce action. The father may also recognize that a custody dispute is a futile endeavor. Surveys of sample cases indicate that maternal custody is awarded in 85% to 95% of the cases (13).

Ploscowe, Foster, and Freed (14) have also indicated that the mother gets custody in the majority of the instances. They estimate that the mother receives custody in approximately 80% of the cases, the father in 10% of the cases, and both parents (joint custody) or relatives are made guardians for the other 10% of the children.

Salk (15) feels that when mothers are awarded custody based on unscientific notions that females are better equipped to rear children than males, children and fathers are deprived of their constitutional rights and there is a negative psychological implication for everyone in the family. He was encouraged by the American Psychological Association, Council of Representatives, in their January 1977 meeting, when they voted "that it is scientifically and psychologically baseless as well as a violation of human rights to discriminate against males because of their sex in child custody assignment" (16).

A research questionnaire sent to lawyers, psychiatrists, psychologists, and social workers revealed a clear-cut tendency to maintain different criteria when dealing with a mother rather than a father (17, 18).

HISTORICAL PERSPECTIVE OF FATHERHOOD

An examination of fatherhood and fathering from an historical viewpoint will be helpful in understanding some of today's attitudes toward fathers. Ross (19) points out that psychoanalytic theorists have allowed little place for fatherhood in the developmental scheme of things. It almost seems as if to be a parent one must be a woman. He adds that like everyone else, psychoanalysts tend to defy nature's facts and to exclude men from the creation and care of children. The emphasis has been on dyadic relationships (mother-child). Now we realize that it must not be just a father-child dyad, but a triadic or family relationship. Ross goes on to point out that at times it seems that the professional community has succumbed to the kind of primitive myths described by Bettelheim (20) whereby procreation and parenthood are relegated to the realm of women alone. The father, Ross says,

had for many years remained the forgotten parent in the psychoanalytic literature, treated in passing perhaps as some austere and remote overlord uninvolved in the direct care of his children and in their emotional growth. Within the past decade, however, the psychoanalytic literature has begun to reveal a slowly growing appreciation of a father's active, positive part in his children's development as well as the influence of his own paternal needs and strivings with regard to his sons and daughters. The lines of developing relationship between the father and children running from the preoedipal through the oedipal, post-oedipal and latency periods and on into adolescence and adulthood need to be drawn systematically with reference to gender identity, generative development, self and object differentiation, etc. For instance, the second year is vital in cementing self and gender identity and the father plays a central part in these processes. (21)

Lamb (22) reminds us that cultural presumptions and cultural change probably account for both the earlier devaluation of the paternal role and the recent interest in it. He goes on to say:

Cultural realities alone are not, however, responsible for the emphasis that psychological theorists placed on maternal influences. An influential and disparate group of scholars drawn from anthropology, behavioral biology, comparative psychology, ethnology and a new field, social biology, argued that the traditional division of parental roles and responsibilities should not be viewed as accidents of cultural organization. Instead they argued that these roles were "natural," that is they were determined, at least in part, by biological predispositions and imperatives. The facts that women alone lactate and that males tend to be little involved in child care throughout mammalian species were viewed as a sufficient reason for concluding that women were biologically destined to assume primary responsibility for both caretaking and socialization. (23)

In addition, Lamb states that most arguments concerning the biological basis of sex differences in parental behavior drew on evidence concerning the role of hormones in the establishment of maternal behavior in rats. Few even acknowledge that the relevance of this evidence was questionable. He further says:

There is every reason to believe that among humans societal prescriptions are at least as important in the regulation of parental as of sexual behavior. There is no reason to believe that a specific constellation of hormones is either necessary or sufficient for the elicitation of human parental behavior. As has been argued elsewhere, most biological predispositions are biases or tendencies rather than imperatives. The biological tendencies are such that they would be trivial if not supplemented by social forces. They could be reversed readily if they were contradicted rather than reinforced by cultural influences. The resulting behavior patterns or sex differences are the joint product of biological influences and social learning. (24)

In the late 1960s, however, values began to change, according to Lamb, for the following reasons:

1) The focus on mother-infant and mother-child relationships became so extreme and imbalanced that researchers were forced to ask whether fathers could legitimately be deemed irrelevant entities in socialization.

2) A second reason for the ascendent interest in both fathers and families was that the traditional family structure itself appeared to be in mortal danger of displacement.

3) It was increasingly apparent that modern fathers do not wish to be peripheral figures in the lives and socialization of their children. Indeed, the vast majority of young men want to be intricately involved in relationships with their children. The women's movement has raised the consciousness of both men and women and has led women to demand that their husbands play a more active role within the family so that they too can pursue their own aspirations outside of the home.

4) Although full-time mothers obviously spend more time with their children than working fathers do, there is a tendency to exaggerate the extent of interaction between mothers and children. The evidence suggests that even when mother and child are in the same room, interaction can be relatively infrequent. Much of the time involved in caretaking is taken up by activities (laundry, food preparation, etc.) that do not involve interpersonal interaction.

5) Students of both cognitive and social development have come to realize that the amount of time adults spend with children is not linearly related—perhaps not related at all—to the amount of influence they have. Empirical and theoretical considerations indicate that the amount of time spent with the parent is a poor predictor of the quality of the infant's relationship with either mother or father. The quality of the interaction and of the adult's behavior are far more important than the quantity.

6) Finally, there has been a revolution in the way in which children—especially infants—are conceptualized. Where theorists once portrayed infants and children as the passive recipients of social influences, they now recognize that children play an active

role in eliciting and shaping social interactions and in constructing subjective conceptualizations of the social world. This realization has led social scientists, particularly in the study of infant and social development, to wonder whether they have underestimated the capacity of infants to establish formatively significant relationships with persons other than their mothers. (25)

THE ROLE OF FATHERS IN CHILD DEVELOPMENT

The assumption concerning mothers' preeminence in infancy has been so strong that investigation of father-infant relationships has been attempted only in the past few years (26). However, fathers can no longer be deemed the forgotten contributors to child development, and the father is not, as Margaret Mead said, "a biological necessity but a social accident" (27).

Some claim that there is a hierarchy among attachment figures such that most infants prefer mother over father, but these preferences probably develop as mother is the caretaker. This preference pattern may well disappear or be reversed when the father shares caretaking. In fact, empirical evidence fails to confirm the existence of monotrophy, and measures of attachment confirm that most infants are strongly attached to both parents from the second half of the first year of life (28, 29). It was also found that in the second year of life, a boy is often more attached to his father than to his mother (30) and, in stress-free situations, infants appear to show no preference for either parent.

Fathers and mothers represent different types of experience from early in the child's life (31). From infancy, children's fathers engage in physically stimulating and playful interaction, whereas mothers engage in conventional play and are primarily responsible for caretaking. Infants and young children from the first year on prefer playing with their fathers. It is thought that the range of affects and modulation of affect are taught by the father (32). Fathers are traditionally more directly involved in the rearing of sons than daughters, which has been a consistent finding of research. Fathers believe that mothers should be responsible for the socialization of daughters. They are especially unwilling to deal with female sexuality and menstruation (33).

Although studies of differences between maternal and parental roles help to identify their effect on children's development, one must not lose sight of the similarities or exaggerate the differences (34). Father caregiving is good in the presence of mother caregiving and then more potent when in combination. The functional diversity is optimal. Recent research has pointed to the similarities in the capacity of males and females to be responsive to their infants.

All theorists propose that fathers have a major impact on sex role development through modeling and identification. Fathers appear to demand conformity to the cultural norms more than mothers (35). Some say that fathers have a greater interest in sex differences than mothers and exert a stronger influence in general sex typing. Fathers appear to have a preference for boy babies and discourage feminine behavior in boys (36). The father's masculinity and status in the family are correlated with masculinity of sons and femininity of daughters; however, this depends on sufficient interaction with the children. The most influential father is the one who takes his role seriously and interacts extensively (37).

The evidence in the area of parental influence on achievement and intellectual development is inconclusive. However, it can be stated that boys with nurturing fathers excel in intellectual tasks through their identification with the father. Underachieving boys often have inadequate relationships with their fathers. A father's attitude often affects his daughter indirectly through the mother. Highly nurturant fathers have been found to have highly positive impacts on their daughters' cognitive development, while maternal influence on cognitive development is poorly understood (38).

Another way to learn about the effect of fathers on development is to study their absence from the family. When fathers are absent, it leads to daughters having difficulty in their interactions with males—early absence being most disadvantageous—though the effects do not show up until adolescence. The effect of father absence on boys appears to be more in the area of school performance (39). It is also noted (40) that children identify with their mother's attitude toward their father in his absence. Studies of father absence, then, confirm that the father influences sex roles, morality, achievement, and psychosocial adjustment. Research clearly supports the advantage of high levels of father-child interaction even when parents are divorced (41).

To sum up, dyadic models, although simpler to conceptualize, seriously distort the psychological and sociological realities of the environment in which children develop. Intact families comprise numerous reciprocal relationships, role demands, and expectations. The father role is largely defined by the father's position in the family system, therefore a father affects child development both directly and indirectly, including the influence on his wife's behavior (42). Herzog puts it this way:

> The father fulfills many roles. As a husband he monitors, absorbs, elicits, limits instinctual drives and derivatives from the mother. He replenishes her affective well and allows her to attach a bond and establish a symbiosis with and then affect phase specific disengagement from the child. He serves as an external referent and alternative

in the separation-individuation process. As a parent he nurtures, disciplines, serves as a model for identification and serves as a love object. His libidinal and aggressive availability which is clearly available in different men and a function of their previous experience and caretaking determines how well or poorly he can function in all these regards, as well as whether or not he will be a good enough father. It appears from newer work that the father is also crucial in the formation of the child's sense of self and consolidation of core gender identity. (43)

It is interesting to note that from 1975 to 1980, the study of the father and his role has generated over 450 chapters, articles, and papers (44)!

A FATHER AS A SINGLE PARENT

Fathers can become single parents through widowhood, divorce and separation, or adoption, with divorce and separation rapidly replacing death as a major cause of single parenthood. As stated previously, estimates of custody awards to mothers range from 85% to 90%; however, changing social attitudes have resulted in increasing numbers of children being reared by fathers. The number of children under 18 years of age living with a single-father caretaker has been estimated to be between one and three million (45, 46).

Berry (47) reports that demographic data about single fathers reveal them to be at a higher socioeconomic level and to have a higher than average income with a higher educational level. These fathers also rate high in economic and social stability. Berry goes on to say that most studies suggest that single-parent fathers are highly nurturing, assertive, and confident, with a high degree of organization in their lives. With their assumption of single parenthood, fathers report significant changes in their living routines and living priorities, as well as their attitudes toward their careers. In some cases a complete change of lifestyle is reported. The first year of single parenthood is reported to be the most difficult. Smith and Smith (48) found that fathers made the transition to single parenthood more easily when they: 1) actually had experience in childrearing; 2) received some education about children and child development; 3) participated earlier in household responsibilities; 4) were actively involved in discipline of their children prior to the separation; and 5) had nurturing, supportive interaction with their children.

Berry states that:

It would seem logical to assume that children of single male parents undergo experiences and consequences much like those of children who reside solely with their mother following separation or divorce. The bulk of data would suggest that children of single fathers experience some transitory problems involving insecurity and that some behavioral problems ensue immediately after the family breakup. The reason for the lower instance of reported child problems from fathers is apt to be a result of two variables: namely a high need to present an image of competence and/or the fact that the fathers, particularly those in the United States, have gone through a highly selective process as the result of biases of the court. (49)

Some studies (50, 51) indicate that fathers, as single parents, report a lower incidence of problems with children's behavior and fewer incidents of problems of running the household. Additionally, they found that fathers use extended families, professionals, and community support very well.

A male single parent frequently encounters prejudice in his neighborhood, day-care centers, schools, and from professionals, and is frequently asked why he and not the mother has the children. Teachers, aware of a child living with a father, keep an eye open for signs of emotional disturbance, poor nutrition, and ill health (52). Because of the lack of social sanction and institutionalization of the single parent role, the custodial father is still viewed as an anomaly of society. As a single parent he is not expected to participate in childcare and nurturing, he may not learn the behavior necessary to meet the child's needs, and father custody thus becomes a self-fulfilling prophecy (53, 54).

In order to be prepared for single parenthood, fathers need information about childcare, classes and groups on parent education and child development, changes in the legal system, financial assistance, and public education.

Nonetheless, single male parents manage well in making adequate adjustments to single parenthood (55, 56). It is said that the males who do care for children are already a select, highly motivated, interested group. They are confident and have knowledge of childcare. However, most fathers can be successful single parents (57). It is necessary that fathers be prepared for childcare and have the resources to support it. The same recommendation, incidentally, would apply to mothers. In fact in one study (58), it was found that there was no statistical difference between groups of single-parent fathers and groups of mothers in regard to their coping and lifestyles. The fathers felt capable and successful in their abilities to be the primary parent (59, 60), and they expressed confidence and satisfaction in their role. Fathers with custody have been studied from the viewpoint of whether they receive custody by adjudication (seekers of custody) or by allocation (assenters). It was found that more fathers passively accept single-parent status than sought it. But those fathers who sought custody were more successful in parenting roles, adjusted to it more readily, and enjoyed it more. The explanation lay in the history of each father-child relationship prior to divorce (61).

FATHERS AS PRIMARY NURTURING PARENTS

Fathers as supplemental parents have been a focus in the literature for some time (62). It is only quite recently, however, that studies have been reported on fathers as primary parents (63, 64). Pruett (65, 66) studied 17 intact families in which the father was the primary nurturing parent. The children's ages ranged from two months to 24 months. He focused on the infants' development, the psychodynamics of the fathers, their nurturing patterns, and their relationships to the infants' mothers. Pruett found that "children raised by men can be vigorous, competent and thriving infants who may be especially comfortable with and interested in stimulation from the external environment" and that "these men are capable of forming intense reciprocal nurturing attachments so critical in the early life of the thriving human organism." He did not feel that the father's style of nurturing was merely that of a mother substitute or "wife-mirror" (67, 68).

ASSESSMENT OF FATHERS FOR CUSTODY

The assessment of a father for custody should include: 1) the father's motivation for custody; 2) an evaluation of the father as a psychological parent and his ability to fulfill the child's needs; and 3) the consideration of such special issues as the age and sex of the children.

1) Motivation for seeking custody is varied. In a study of 80 single fathers (69), the reasons given for seeking custody were as follows: considered self as better parent, 35%; love of children, 16%; wife did not want children, 15%; simply wanted children, 8%; wife unable emotionally to care for children, 4%; wife unable to physically care for children, 4%; no response, 18%. Other reasons seen for seeking custody are: genuine interest in the children; a feeling of having been wronged or a sense of loss and rejection; the need to be vindictive and use custody proceedings to harass and intimidate; and economic gain. The psychological impact of divorce and threatened loss of custody often create a regressive crisis in one or both parents, making the search to explain motivation very difficult indeed. Perceived injury to self and/or children can lead to various types of regressive behavior including lying, acting out, and even near psychotic behavior (70). It may be difficult and risky to feel confident about one's understanding of motivation, especially as it is unlikely that there will be much time to make the assessment.

2) The assessment of whether or not a father is a psychological parent or can meet the best interests of the child is no different from a similar assessment of the mother. The ways of conducting the evaluation and what to look for have been dealt with at length and need not be repeated here (71–75).

3) Special questions with respect to age and sex of the child arise in regard to single-parent custody. These deal with the advisability of a father's caring for an infant or child of the opposite sex. The question of the father's caring for an infant should be the same as it would be for a mother: Is the capability and the desire to care for the infant present? Does the father appear knowledgeable about what is required to care for the child and how should this be done? Is he aware of the infant's needs and does he have the where-with-all to satisfy those needs? Sex of the parent by itself is not a guarantee of anything, nor should it alone rule either parent in or out.

Should a boy be with his father and a girl be with her mother? Or, does it make much difference? A definite answer to this question is difficult to give. A study of 60 families (76) suggests that children living with the opposite sex parent are less well adjusted than the children with the same sex parent. However, in both father and mother custody families, authoritative parenting by the custodial parent was positively linked with the child's competent social behavior. Psychoanalytic theory emphasizes the importance of the child's identification with the same sex parent, but it also emphasizes the importance of the opposite sex parent to provide a realistic foil for oedipal aims and their resolution. Possible problems of a father-daughter relationship in a single-parent family are developmental distortions in oedipal resolution and superego development. However, some father-daughter twosomes may provide developmental advantages, if the child's talents are recognized early and encouraged (77).

Parents may know how to interact more comfortably and effectively with children of the same sex, although we know from surveys that both mothers and fathers have a lot of questions regarding child development in general and especially regarding questions of sexuality (78). Another possible problem arises when a child of the opposite sex comes to represent a substitute for the absent spouse. If this occurs, the expectations and interactions of the custodial parent and the opposite sex child might lead to a relationship that is coercive and demanding (79).

Other sex-related differences in children have been noted. In general, boys tend to be more immature, aggressive, and act out more readily. Friction between father and son was found to be less than between mother and son. However, Santrock and Marshak (80) point out that regardless of the custodial arrangement, the quality of the ongoing relationship with the custodial parent is the critical factor for both boys and girls. They go on to state that many other factors must be considered: reliance on external support systems (day-care, relatives, and friends); existence and quality of child and custodial parent's ongoing relationship with the ex-spouse; and the personality makeup of the child and both parents. To this list one could add any special needs or vulnerabilities that that child may have (school problems, health problems, mental retardation, etc.), and/or special circumstances or problems for either parent.

There does not appear to be an easy or clear formula for general use in deciding whether it is better to place children with the same sex parent or not. Each case must be thought out separately, taking into account the many existing variables.

EFFECT OF FATHER CUSTODY ON MOTHERS

Mothers, socially conditioned to expect custody of their children, but who lose it, are often devastated. They suffer not only a loss of the child but also a loss of parenthood status. Since they have "failed" in their role as mother they often question their femininity and womanhood, feeling rejected, despised, and socially unacceptable. The injury suffered by the loss of the child may be perceived as having occurred to the self and/or to the child. Depending on the individual parent involved, this may trigger various regressive and affective responses such as denial, depression, anger, hostility, vindictiveness, and a ferocity of actions and allegations that approaches psychosis. For those mothers whose self-esteem and self-concept are still intact, the loss will be managed with greater equilibrium. When the specter of possible custody loss arises by a father's legal action—even when it is for joint or shared custody—many mothers feel so threatened and injured that regressive responses appear, causing them to draw closer to the children, interfere with the child's relationship with the father, make wild accusations about the father, or otherwise falsify and distort the family situation.

SUMMARY

In recent years the social roles of both men and women have changed substantially, as have the patterns of childcare and ideas of what constitutes the optimal development of a child. It will, however, be some time before the newer ideas become the norm. Many women (and men) are still caught in the changeover and, consequently, may be expected to react as they did in the past.

Given the massive evidence that supports and elucidates the father's important role in child and family development and maintenance, there seems to be little left but sentimental tradition to buttress the concept of maternal or single-parent preference in custodial disputes. Indeed, the era of shared parenting should now take center stage in our thinking and planning for families of divorce.

REFERENCES

1. Derdeyn, A. Child custody contests in historical perspective. *American Journal of Psychiatry*, 1976, *133*(12), 1369-1376.
2. Orthner, D., & Lewis, K. Evidence of single-father competence in childrearing. *Family Law Quarterly*, 1979, *13*(1), 27-47.
3. Zasnaldin, J. The emergence of a modern American family law: Child custody, adaptation and the courts, 1796-1851. *Northwestern University Law Review*, 1979, *73*, 1038-1089.
4. Bernstein, B. E. Lawyer and counselor as an interdisciplinary team: Preparing the father for custody. *Journal of Marriage and Family Counselling*, 1977, *3*(3), 29-40.
5. Musetto, A. *Dilemmas in child custody.* Chicago: Wilson-Hall, 1982.
6. Westman, J., & Lord, G. Model for a child psychiatry custody study. *Journal of Psychiatry and Law*, Fall, 1980, 253-269.
7. Levy, A. Assessment in child custody. In E. Mahon, & J. Sours (Eds.), *The assessment of the child and adolescent.* New York: Jason Aronson, in press.
8. Orthner & Lewis, 1979.
9. *Ibid.*
10. Zasnaldin, 1979.
11. Bernstein, 1977.
12. Slovenko, R. *Psychiatry and law.* Boston: Little, Brown, 1973.
13. *Ibid.*
14. Ploscowe, M., Foster, H. H., Jr., & Freed, D. *Family law: Cases and materials* (2nd ed.). Boston: Little, Brown, 1973.
15. Salk, L. On the custody rights of fathers in divorce. *Journal of Clinical Child Psychology,* Summer, 1977, 49.
16. *Ibid.*
17. Woody, R. H. Sexism in child custody decisions. *Personnel and Guidance Journal,* 1977, *56*(3), 168-170.
18. Woody, R. H. Fathers with child custody. *The Counseling Psychologist,* 1978, *7*(4):60-63.
19. Ross, J. M. The roots of fatherhood: Excursions into a lost literature. In S. Cath, A. Gurwith, & J. Ross (Eds.), *Father and child.* Boston: Little, Brown, 1982.
20. Bettelheim, B. *Symbolic wounds.* Glencoe, IL: Free Press, 1954.
21. Ross, J. M. In search of fathering. In S. Cath, A. Gurwith, & J. Ross (Eds.), *Father and child.* Boston: Little, Brown, 1982.
22. Lamb, M. E. Fathers and child development: An integrative overview. In M. E. Lamb (Ed.), *The role of the father in child development.* New York: John Wiley & Sons, 1981.
23. *Ibid.*
24. *Ibid.*, pp. 3-4.
25. Lamb, 1981.
26. *Ibid.*
27. Fitzgerald, H., & McCread, C. Fathers and infants. *Infant Mental Health Journal,* 1981, *2*(4), p. 214.
28. Lamb, 1981.
29. Fitzgerald & McCread, 1981.
30. Gunsberg, L. Selected critical review of psychological investigations of the early father-infant relationship. In S. Cath, A. Gurwith, & J. Ross (Eds.), *Father and child.* Boston: Little, Brown, 1982.

31. Herzog, J. On father hunger: The father's role in the modulation of aggressive drive and fantasy. In S. Cath, A. Gurwith, & J. Ross (Eds.), *Father and child*. Boston: Little, Brown, 1982.
32. Lamb, 1981.
33. *Ibid.*
34. *Ibid.*
35. *Ibid.*
36. Gunsberg, 1982.
37. Lamb, 1981.
38. *Ibid.*
39. *Ibid.*
40. Atkins, R. Discovering daddy: The mother's role. In S. Cath, A. Gurwith, & J. Ross (Eds.), *Father and child*. Boston: Little, Brown, 1982.
41. Wallerstein, J. S., & Kelly, J. B. *Surviving the breakup*. New York: Basic Books, 1980.
42. Herzog, 1982.
43. *Ibid.*, p. 173.
44. Fitzgerald & McCread, 1981.
45. Berry, K. The male single parent. In J. Stuart, & L. Abt (Eds.), *Children of separation and divorce*. New York: Van Nostrand Reinhold, 1981.
46. Hanson, S. Single custodial fathers and the parent-child relationship. *Nursing Research*, 1981, *30*(4), 202-204.
47. Berry, 1981.
48. Smith, R., & Smith, C. Child rearing and single-parent fathers. *Family Relations*, 1981, *30*, 411-417.
49. Berry, 1981, p. 38.
50. Ambert, A. Differences in children's behavior toward custodial mothers and custodial fathers. *Journal of Marriage and the Family*, February 1982, 73-86.
51. Santrock, J., & Marshak, R. Father custody and social development in boys and girls. *Journal of Social Issues*, 1979, *35*(4), 112-125.
52. Berry, 1981.
53. Smith & Smith, 1981.
54. Mendes, H. Single fathers. *The Family Coordinator*, 1976, *25*, 439-444.
55. Smith & Smith, 1981.
56. Gasser, R., & Taylor, C. Role adjustment of single-parent fathers with dependent children. *The Family Coordinator*, 1976, *25*, 397-401.
57. Smith & Smith, 1981.
58. Defrain, J., & Eirick, R. Coping as divorced single-parents: A comparative study of fathers and mothers. *Family Relations*, 1981, *30*, 265-274.
59. Mendes, 1976.
60. Orthner, B., Brown, T., & Ferguson, D. Single-parent fatherhood: An emerging family lifestyle. *The Family Coordinator*, 1976, *25*, 429-437.
61. Orthner & Lewis, 1979.
62. Pruett, K. D. Infants of primary nurturing fathers. *Psychoanalytic study of the child*, (Vol. 38). New Haven: Yale University Press, 1983. (a)
63. *Ibid.*
64. Pruett, K. D. Two year followup of infants of primary nurturing fathers in intact families. Presented to the Second World Congress of Infant Psychiatry, Cannes, France, 1983. (b)
65. Pruett, 1983 (See Reference 62).
66. Pruett, 1983 (See Reference 64).
67. Pruett, 1983 (See Reference 62).
68. Pruett, 1983 (See Reference 64).
69. Chang, P., & Deinard, A. Single-father caretakers: Demographic characteristics and adjustment processes. *American Journal of Orthopsychiatry*, 1982, *52*(2), 236-243.
70. Schuman, D. The psychiatric aspects of custody loss. In J. Stuart, & L. Abt (Eds.), *Children of separation and divorce*. New York: Van Nostrand Reinhold, 1981.

71. Musetto, 1982.
72. Westman & Lord, 1980.
73. Levy, in press.
74. Levy, A. The divorcing family: Its evaluation and treatment. In D. Shaffer, L. Greenhill, & A. Ehrhardt (Eds.), *Clinical Guide to Child Psychiatry.* New York: Free Press, 1984.
75. American Psychiatric Association. Child custody consultation: A report of the task force on clinical assessment in child custody. Washington, D.C.: American Psychiatric Association, 1982.
76. Santrock & Marshak, 1979.
77. Berlin, I. Vicissitudes of father and daughter relations in single-parent families. *Psychiatric Opinion*, October, 1979, 9-11.
78. Orthner & Lewis, 1979.
79. Santrock & Marshak, 1979.
80. *Ibid.*

9

Lesbian Mothers/Gay Fathers

Donna J. Hutchens and
Martha J. Kirkpatrick

Thousands of lesbians and gay men are the parents of children born to them through heterosexual relationships and marriages.* When a child's heterosexual parent discovers that the other parent has entered into a same sex relationship, he or she may often attempt to limit the parenting role of the lesbian mother or gay father. Challenges to an individual's parental rights may also be initiated by other relatives or governmental entities on the basis of a parent's homosexuality. A custody or visitation proceeding that is based on a parent's sexual orientation creates intense emotional trauma, as well as significant legal problems. The system that decides whether or not a parent is to be allowed custody or visitation with his or her children is a system that often reflects the homophobia of the society. Often, judges who determine how the interests of the children can best be served will share the stereotypes common in society about lesbians and gay men. There is, therefore, a serious risk that the parent will not be evaluated fairly and objectively in terms of his or her parenting role and what will serve the best interests of the children.

The legal standards applied to a child custody case, as they are articulated in judicial opinion and statutory language, vary considerably depending on the nature of the proceeding. Proceedings in which the custody of minor children is at issue fall into three types: *custody proceedings* between the biological parents; *guardianship proceedings* where a person other than a biological parent seeks custody of the children; and *neglect proceedings* or termination of parental rights where the state or the county seeks to

---

*It has been estimated that there are approximately 1.5 million lesbian mothers in the United States (1).

remove the children from the home and place them under the control of the court. Almost every state has statutes that set out the legal standards to be applied to the determination of custody of a minor child in each of these types of proceedings. Common to all of the statutes is the fact that the statutory language is vague and places a great deal of discretion in the judge.

The sexual orientation of a parent can be an issue, if not the predominant issue, in all of these proceedings. Although some states may have, by custom or statute, a list of the factors that are considered relevant in the determination of custody, no state currently excludes evidence regarding the sexual orientation of a parent (2). There are states, however, in which appellate courts have made it clear that a parent's homosexuality, in and of itself, is not grounds for depriving the parent of the custody of the children (3). In states that have such case law, a trial court may consider the parent's sexual orientation as one factor in the total case. The trial judge is only prohibited from deciding that homosexuality, by itself, precludes an award of custody or visitation to a lesbian mother or gay father.

Several recent cases appear to take a contradictory view. For example, in North Dakota (4) and Kentucky (5), appellate courts have recently overruled awards of custody to lesbian mothers. In each of these cases, the appellate court based its opinion on some factor connected to the mother's sexual orientation. The most disturbing aspect of each of these cases is that there was no factual evidence of any harm to the children. In fact, after hearing the evidence, the trial judge placed custody with the mother. Each appellate court based its reversal on what the justices perceived to be potential future harm to the children.

When the issue of which parent should have custody of the minor children is brought before a court, most states apply the "best interest of the child" standard. This means that a judge is vested with broad discretion to determine a placement that is consistent with what he or she believes to be in the best interest of the children. Where the challenge to custody or visitation is made by someone other than the other parent, there is usually an additional requirement that there be a finding of detriment to the child or a lack of parental fitness.

The application of these legal standards to custody and visitation cases where one parent is homosexual has produced remarkably different results (6). Clearly, some of the discrepancy in the outcome of these custody cases can be explained by the differences in the factual context in which a case arises. In all likelihood, however, stereotypes about homosexuals and their parenting abilities have also played a significant role.

A careful review of lesbian mother and gay father cases discloses three major categories of presumptions about homosexuality that have significantly influenced custody and visitation cases. First, homosexuals are assumed to be psychologically and sexually maladjusted. This stereotype is demonstrated by court orders that limit the homosexual parent to visitation and place conditions on the exercise of those visitation rights. The most common conditions are that the homosexual parent's partner not be present during visitation (7), and that the children not be allowed to visit overnight (8). These restrictions are based on the assumption that the parent will either engage in sexual behavior in the presence of the children or expose the children to some form of sexual advance.

The second and third categories of judicial concern involve the presumed negative effects of homosexual parenting and social stigma. The presumed negative effects include the belief that the children will become homosexual, will have confused gender identity, or will develop the attitude that a homosexual lifestyle is acceptable (9). Finally, many judges hesitate to award custody to an admittedly good parent because of the potential that the children will be stigmatized by the custodial parent's sexual orientation (10).

The very real and damaging effects of these stereotypes are that they often result in custody awards or visitation orders that do not serve the best interests of the children involved. Where the trial court's determination is based on the judge's preconceived notions about homosexuality, an honest evaluation of parental abilities and relationships with the children is precluded. There may, in fact, not be any concrete connection between the parent's sexual orientation and a negative impact on the children. The resulting custody arrangements may even harm the children. For example, some children are removed from the home of their primary psychological parent solely on the basis of that parent's sexual orientation.

The use of expert testimony becomes extremely important in lesbian mother and gay father cases. Such testimony has three functions: 1) to confront general stereotypes about homosexuality; 2) to evaluate the particular parties; and 3) to evaluate the parent-child relationship (11). The first type of expert testimony is needed to confront widespread assumptions about lesbians and gay men. The expert must be familiar with the scientific research that contradicts common stereotypes about sexual behavior, e.g., that lesbians and gay men are maladjusted and promiscuous, may sexually harm their children, or may engage in sexual activity in front of their children (12). Second, expert testimony is needed to confront stereotyped views about the effects of homosexual parenting on the children, which include beliefs that children will grow up to be homosexual, will lack heterosexual role models, will have confused sex identification, or will be hampered in their moral development (13). Finally, expert testimony may be helpful in dealing with assumptions that children in the custody of a lesbian or gay parent will be harmed by being socially stigmatized, having fewer contacts with peers or neighborhood adults, or being exposed to ridicule (14).

The second and third types of expert testimony are needed to evaluate the particular parties in the case and their relationships with the children. This use of experts—to make recommendations regarding custody or visitation based on interviews and psychological testing with the parties involved—is familiar to many lawyers and psychiatrists who work with custody cases. The evaluation of the client should focus on her or his general emotional stability, parenting ability, relationship with the children, home atmosphere, ability to cope with the problems of living as a lesbian or gay man in this society, and understanding of the problems and questions that might arise for the children regarding his or her sexual orientation (15).

The effect of a parent's homosexuality on his or her children is a question that most psychiatrists are poorly prepared to answer. The social and legal climates have been so condemnatory that until the last decade, parents with homosexual proclivities always denied that aspect of their lives. Consequently, there was no opportunity to explore this question clinically or through research studies. Psychiatrists trained prior to the 1970s, who wished to consider this question, would have been unable to find relevant literature. The only available case studies were of homosexuals, primarily men, who had been in psychiatric treatment. Only a rare report (16) included the information that some of these people were parents.

PSYCHOLOGICAL FUNCTIONING OF HOMOSEXUALS

Studies of nonpatient populations (17-27) began to emerge as homosexual men and women became less fearful of revealing themselves in the more tolerant social climate of the Liberation and Civil Rights Movements in the 1960s. These large-scale studies culminated in the 1978 publication of Bell and Weinberg's (28) monumental survey of approximately 600 homosexual men and 300 homosexual women.

All these studies weigh heavily against the assumptions our society has made about homosexuals. First, there is no evidence for a homosexual personality or character structure. The diversity within the homosexual community is as great as within the heterosexual community. Second, the researchers did not find evidence of greater neuroticism or unhappiness in homosexuals when matched with heterosexuals living similar lives. Bell and Weinberg (29) found that the most valuable data emerged when they compared groups with common relationship styles, i.e., close-coupled, open-coupled, etc. They found the most unhappiness and difficulty with coping in the isolated individuals, regardless of sexual orientation, while the close-coupled of both groups had similar levels of successful coping and perceived satisfaction in life. Comparative studies on psychological test batteries also failed to show homosexuals to be less well adjusted than comparable heterosexuals. While there is a group of homosexual males who are preoccupied with anonymous sex, this is not true of all male homosexuals (30).

All the evidence we have available to date recommends that homosexual orientation by itself does not prophesy psychological status, coping mechanisms, lifestyle, or degree of stability. The preponderance of data to this effect prompted the American Psychiatric Association to remove homosexuality from the *Diagnostic and Statistical Manual of Mental Disorders* in 1973 (30a). The investigators listed above agree that homosexual individuals are as likely or as unlikely as heterosexuals to achieve the levels of emotional maturity and stability necessary for satisfying and responsible lives.

PARENTAL BEHAVIOR

Studies of homosexual parents and their children began to appear over the last decade. However, only a few primarily anecdotal surveys of homosexual fathers are currently available (31, 32). The majority of studies concern lesbian mothers and their children. Some data arose from evaluations during custody disputes (33). Other data were prompted to fill the gap of relevant data to advise the courts (34–39). Some clinical experience with mothers and children has also appeared (40, 41).

The findings from these studies show lesbian mothers to be very unlike the stereotypes of masculine or male-hating women, and, instead, very like their heterosexual counterparts. The lesbian mothers studied had married at the same average age and for the same reasons (i.e., love of husband and desire for marriage) as the heterosexuals. They had had children out of a desire for them and at the same average age as the heterosexuals. Even the length of the marriages that produced the study children was the same in both heterosexual and homosexual groups in several studies (42, 43).

The lesbian mothers were more likely to be associated with either a lesbian organization or a feminist organization than the heterosexual mothers, but their daily support system did not depend on the lesbian community. Their identity and friendship patterns evolved from their role as mothers and this identity was the most salient feature of their lives (44). They were rarely interested or involved in activities in the lesbian community that cater to women without children. For the lesbian mothers, as much as for heterosexual mothers, the overriding concerns were childcare, housing, financial security, and medical care (45, 46). Several lesbian mothers maintained close friendships with their ex-husbands, who helped with childcare. Many mothers, both homosexual and heterosexual, complained about the unreliability of ex-husbands' child support payments and involvement with the children. The lesbian mothers in one study (47) were more concerned than the heterosexual mothers that their children have adequate male figures in their lives. Many regularly arranged events for their children that included male relations or friends. In some communities, lesbian mother support groups have emerged to provide both social support and activities.

While some courts have curtailed the lesbian mother from living with her lesbian partner, mothers who had live-in partners seemed less harried and were able to provide more family interaction for their children. Jealousies and competition arose especially if children were unprepared for the new partner (48, 49). No evidence was found that lesbian partners attempted to enact the role of a male partner, but rather, when integrated into the family, they were seen as aunts or big sisters. Household chores and activities performed with the children did not imitate heterosexual role stereotypes, but were divided according to time and talent. Thus, the lesbian mother family tended to organize along egalitarian rather than authoritarian lines.

Several studies (50, 51, 52) evaluated the mothers on the Bems Sex Role Inventory (53) and found the lesbian mothers scoring similarly to heterosexual mothers on the femininity scale. This further suggests that lesbian mothers, no less than heterosexual mothers, are successfully socialized in feminine and maternal interests and capacities.

PARENTING STYLES

No lesbian mothers preferred their children to become homosexual. "I hope he's heterosexual; its an easier life in this society" was a frequent response. Other mothers indicated an acceptance of whatever object choice their children might make, with the hope the child would have the independence and strength to assert his or her individuality. Hoeffer (54) studied mothers' reports of encouraging sexual traits and behavior, and found the heterosexual and lesbian mothers to be similar in their encouragement. Some lesbian mothers were willing to accept some cross-gender sex role traits and behaviors, while heterosexual mothers showed a greater tendency to emphasize socially defined gender differences. Both mothers encouraged nonsex-type toys for both boys and girls. Both groups of mothers also reported more involvement with daughters' play than sons'. Mucklow and Phelan (55) examined lesbian and heterosexual mothers on self-confidence, dominance, and nurturance scales. No significant differences in mean scores were found.

In summary, no studies to date have confirmed either a difference in lifestyle or parenting style between lesbian mothers and heterosexual mothers.

THE CHILDREN'S DEVELOPMENT

The court's concern with the best interest of the child demands that it be assured that no harm will come to the child from the presence of a homosexual parent and that healthy development will be facilitated. The court's fear that children might be sexually molested, disordered in gender identity or object choice, or suffer from stigmatization has arisen from assumptions without a data base. Child molestation involves primarily heterosexual males and female children. Gender identity, the inner sense of being male or female, develops in the first three to four years of life, and ordinarily is stable for life. While it is unclear how gender identity is formed, correct parental assignment of the child's gender is known to be crucial. The psychologically formative forces are in the parenting figures' interaction with the child, rather than with each other.

Homosexuals, like heterosexuals, are raised predominantly by heterosexual couples. There is no evidence that the absence of a father in and of itself leads to either gender disorder or homosexuality. There is less certainty about the timing for object choice consolidation, although early childhood is clearly the crucial period. While the specific forces leading to homosexual or heterosexual preference are unclear, they would appear to be multiple, diverse, and dependent on inner fantasies as well as external influences. An opportunity to have significant relationships with members of both sexes and to feel valued for one's gender-appropriate characteristics promotes healthy development, but these experiences need not be with a live-in parent. Grandparents, uncles, aunts, family friends, and caretakers provide figures for both identification and for necessary childhood romantic fantasies. No specific family constellation is required for either heterosexual or homosexual development.

Studies of the consequences of homosexuality in parents have not been able to identify any specific characteristics or pathology of their children. Green (56) examined 21 children being raised in seven lesbian households as part of child custody litigation. His data showed that 15 children drew a person of their own sex first on the Draw-A-Person Test, one did not draw, and five drew a person of the opposite sex. The preferred peer group of 19 of these children was a peer group of the same sex. The favorite toy of 20 children was consistent with conventional sex-typed toy preferences and the vocational choices for all 21 were within the typical range of sex types in our culture. The four oldest children reported erotic fantasies of a heterosexual nature. These measures are the most reliable indicators available of sexual identity and object choice. Green concluded that these findings do not differ appreciably from those of children raised in more conventional settings.

Hoeffer's (57) study also included measures of the children's sex-role traits and behaviors. Sex-role traits were measured by asking the children to rate themselves on five male-valued traits (outgoing, adventuresome, never cries, strong, likes to be the leader) and five female-valued traits (aware of others' feelings, gentle, behaves, neat, quiet) on a four-point scale for ideal and real self and same gender peers. Sex-role behavior was measured by Block's Toy Preference Test (58). The boys of both groups of mothers did not vary on sex-role traits or sex-role behavior, and both groups of boys chose an androgynous sex-role trait profile as their ideal. However, the boys of lesbian mothers rated themselves higher on two female valued traits, awareness of others' feelings and gentleness, than had the boys of heterosexual mothers. Both groups of boys gave their peers higher scores on male-valued traits than themselves. Girls in the two groups did not differ on sex-role behavior. The girls of lesbian mothers rated themselves higher on two male-valued traits, adventuresome and likes to be leader, than did the girls of heterosexual mothers. Both groups of girls chose androgynous ideals. Hoeffer felt that all mothers were more effective models for daughters than for sons. She also concluded that the trend in boys of rating their peers ahead of themselves in masculine values resulted from father absence, since both groups of boys showed this finding. This trend was not, however, compared with responses of boys in families with fathers present.

Mandel et al. (59) examined children on similar variables. They found that girls of lesbian mothers were slightly more likely to show interest in masculine occupations. Boys in both of their groups were very similar and conventionally masculine. The majority of children in both groups reported an interest in getting married and having a family. The Draw-A-Person Test and toy and activity preferences showed no differences.

Kirkpatrick et al. (60) used similar measures of the children's sexual identity. The results of the Draw-A-Person Test, reports of toy and activity preferences, peer relationships, and future plans were similar in the two groups. Kirkpatrick et al. included a blind evaluation by a female psychologist and a male child psychiatrist of each child's general psychological functioning, as well as gender identity. Each child was rated on the Rutter Scale (61) following examination. Approximately 10% of each group was rated as severely disturbed. Of the two boys so rated, one from each group, both drew cross-sex figures on the Draw-A-Person Test and both had histories of brief periods of feminine behavior, dressing, and interests. Both boys had physiologic defects that had disrupted their early infancy. The severely disturbed girls did not draw cross-sex figures and had no common features in their histories. There were no significant differences in the ratings of the two groups of children in regard to psychological status, nor could any correlations be drawn between problems presented and the mothers' lesbianism.

We do not have controlled studies of an adolescent population where measures of object choice would have more validity, nor do we have longitudinal studies. These would help us better understand how parental homosexuality is perceived and used at various stages of psychological development. While we assume any parental characteristics has some effect on the child, we cannot assume that we know what the effect of this characteristic will be. Most probably, responsible parenting, including the capacity to perceive and respond to the growing child's changing needs, is the overriding variable.

Clinical work with children going through the experience of discovering their mother's lesbianism (62, 63) shows that many were initially shocked and confused. Older boys, especially, tended to display initial anger, often displaced onto the mother's partner. The children were able to make good use of a group to discuss their confusion and fears. Fears related primarily to their own sexual futures. While some were more open to possible homosexual exploration, there was no evidence of change in sexual orientation.

STIGMATIZATION

This area is inadequately explored. None of the controlled studies reported on children's feelings of discrimination (64-67). Adolescent studies will, hopefully, yield more information. We do not have clinical reports that suggest that discrimination has been instrumental in producing emotional problems in adolescence.

SUMMARY

Courts evaluating custody or visitation, where parental homosexuality is an issue, need expert testimony on the effect of this parental characteristic on the children. It is important that the courts be advised that current studies of homosexual parents and their children show no significant differences from heterosexual divorced parents and their children. By the measures available, no evidence is found of developmental difficulties, gender disorders, or increased likelihood of homosexuality in these children. The possibility of stigmatization has not been researched, but no clinical material has come to light implicating stigmatization as a source of pathology. While parental homosexuality, like all parental characteristics, must have some effect on the child, what this effect may be or whether it is harmful or beneficial probably depends on other overriding variables, such as the quality of parent-child relationship and the capacity of the parent to perceive and respond effectively to the child's changing needs.

REFERENCES

1. Hunter, N., & Polikoff, N. Custody rights of lesbian mothers: Legal theory and litigation strategy. *Buffalo Law Review*, 1976, *25*, 691.
2. *E.g., Immerman v. Immerman*, 176 Cal. App. 2d 122, 1 Cal. Rptr. 298 (1959) [evidence of homosexual conduct is relevant]; *Smith v. Smith*, 3 Fam. L.Rep. (BNA) 2693 (N.Y. Fam. Ct. 1977) [lesbianism is one factor that must be considered]; *Medeiros v. Medeiros*, 8 Fam. L.Rep (BNA) 2372 (Vt. Super. Ct. 1982) [homosexual relationship is a factor that should be considered].
3. *E.g., Nadler v. Superior Court*, 255 Cal. App. 2d 523 (1967); *D.H. v. J.H.*, 418 N.E. 2d 286 (Ind. Ct. App. 1981); *Bezio v. Patenaude*, 410 N.E. 2d 1207 (Mass. Sup. Jud. Ct. 1980); *Miller v. Miller*, 405 Mich. 809 (1979); *People v. Brown*, 49 Mich. App. 358, 212 N.W. 2d 55 (1973); *Doe v. Doe*, 222 Va. 736 (1981).
4. *Jacobson v. Jacobson*, 50 U.S.L.W. 2425 (N.D. 1981), also reported in 8 Fam. L. Rep (BNA) 2154 (1982).
5. *S. v. S.*, 608 S.W. 2d 64 (K. Ct. App. 1980).
6. Compare *M.P. v. S.P.*, 169 N.J. Super. 425, 404 A. 2d 1256 (1979); *A. v. A.*, 514 P. 2d 358 (Or. App. 1973); and *Schuster v. Schuster* and *Isaacson v. Isaacson*, 90 Wash. 2d 626, 585 P. 2d 130 (1978) with *D.H. v. J.H.*, 418 N.E. 2d 286 (Ind. Ct. App. 1981); *Newsome v. Newsome*, 42 N.C. App. 416, 256 S.E. 2d 849 (1979) and *Ashling v. Ashling*, 42 Or. App. 47, 599 P. 2d 475 (1979).
7. *E.g., Irish v. Irish*, 102 Mich. App. 75, 300 N.W. 2d 739; *L. v. D.*, 630 S.W. 2d 240 (Mo. Ct. App. 1982); *Newsome v. Newsome*, 42 N.C. App. 416, 256 S.E. 2d 849 (1979); *DiStefano v. DiStefano*, 60 A.D. 2d 976, 401 N.Y.S. 2d 636 (1978); *Scarlett v. Scarlett*, 252 Pa. Super. Ct. 641, 390 A. 2d 1331 (1978).
8. *E.g., Kalla v. Kalla*, 614 P. 2d 641 (Utah 1980); *J.L.P. v. D.J.P.*, 643 S.W. 2d 865 (Mo. Ct. App. 1982).
9. See more detailed analysis in Hitchens, D., & Price, B. Trial strategy in lesbian mother custody cases: The use of expert testimony. *Golden Gate University Law Review*, 1978-1979, *9*, 451-479.
10. *Ibid.*
11. *Ibid.*, pp. 451-63.
12. *Ibid.*, p. 454.
13. *Ibid.*, pp. 455-59.
14. *Ibid.*, pp. 460-61.
15. *Ibid.*, pp. 461-62.
16. Curran, D., & Parr, D. Homosexuality: An analysis of 100 male cases seen in private practice. *British Medical Journal*, 1975, *5022*, 797-801.
17. Hopkins, J. A. The lesbian personality. *British Journal of Psychiatry*, 1969, *115*, 1433–1436.
18. Hopkins, J. A. Lesbian signs of the Rorschach. *British Journal on Projective Psychology and Personality Study*, 1970, *15*, 7-14.
19. Rosen, D. H. *Lesbianism: A study of female homosexuality*. Springfield, IL: Charles C. Thomas, 1974.
20. Riess, B. F., & Safer, J. M. Homosexuality in females and males. In E. Gomberg, & V. Franks (Eds.), *Gendered and disordered behavior*. New York: Brunner/Mazel, 1979.
21. Seigelman, M. Adjustment of male homosexuals and heterosexuals. *Archives of Sexual Behavior*, 1972, *2*(1), 9-25.
22. Siegelman, M. Adjustment of homosexual and heterosexual women. *British Journal of Psychiatry*, 1972, *120*, 558-563.

23. Saghir, M., & Robins, E. *Male and female homosexuality: A comprehensive investigation.* Baltimore, MD: William & Wilkins, 1973.
24. Thompson, N., McCandless, B. R., & Strickland, B. R. Personal adjustment of male & female homosexuals and heterosexuals. *Journal of Abnormal Psychology,* 1971, *78,* 237-240.
25. Adelman, M. Comparison of professionally employed lesbians and heterosexual women in the MMPI. *Archives of Sexual Behavior,* 1977, *7*(3), 191-201.
26. Armon, V. Some personality variables in overt female homosexuality. *Journal of Projective Techniques,* 1960, *24,* 292-309.
27. Freedman, M. *Homosexuality and psychological functioning.* Belmont, CA: Brooks/Cole, 1971.
28. Bell, A., & Weinberg, M. *Homosexualities: A study of diversity among men and women.* New York: Simon & Schuster, 1978.
29. *Ibid.*
30. Mattison, A., & McWhirter, D. *The male couple.* Englewood Cliffs, NJ: Prentice-Hall, 1984.
30a. American Psychiatric Association. *Diagnostic and statistical manual of mental disorders* (2nd ed.). Washington, D.C.: American Psychiatric Association, 1973.
31. Miller, B. Gay fathers and their children. *The Family Coordinator,* 1979, *28,* 544-552.
32. Bozett, F. Gay fathers: Evaluation of the gay father identity. *American Journal of Orthopsychiatry,* 1981, *51*(3), 552-559.
33. Green, R. Thirty five children raised by homosexual or transsexual parents. *American Journal of Psychiatry,* 1978, *135,* 692-697.
34. Hoeffer, B. Children's acquisition of sex-role behavior in lesbian mother families. *American Journal of Orthopsychiatry,* 1981, *51*(3), 536-544.
35. Mandel, J., Hotvedt, M., & Green, R. The lesbian parent: Comparison of heterosexual and homosexual mothers and children. Paper presented to the American Psychological Association, New York, NY, August, 1979.
36. Kirkpatrick, M., Smith, K., & Roy, R. Lesbian mothers and their children: A comparative study. *American Journal of Orthopsychiatry,* 1981, *51*(3), 545-551.
37. Lewin, E. Lesbianism and motherhood: Implications for child custody. *Human Organization,* 1981, *40*(1), 6-14.
38. Miller, J. A., Jacobsen, R. A., & Bigner, J. J. The child's home environment for lesbian vs. heterosexual mothers: A neglected area of research. *Journal of Homosexuality,* 1981, *7*(1), 49-56.
39. Mucklow, B., & Phelan, G. Lesbian and traditional mothers' responses to adult response to child behavior and self concept. *Psychology Reports,* 1979, *44*(3), 880-882.
40. Pagelow, M. Heterosexual and lesbian single mothers: A comparison of problems, coping and solutions. *Journal of Homosexuality,* 1980, *5*(3), 189-204.
41. Hall, M. Lesbian families: Cultural and clinical issues. *Social Work,* 1978, *23*(5), 380-385.
42. Mandel et al., 1977.
43. Kirkpatrick et al., 1981.
44. Lewin, 1981.
45. Miller et al., 1981.
46. Pagelow, 1980.
47. Kirkpatrick et al., 1981.
48. Hall, 1978.
49. Lewis, K. G. Children of lesbians: Their point of view. *Social Work,* 1980, *25*(3), 198-203.
50. Hoeffer, 1981.
51. Mandel et al., 1979.
52. Kirkpatrick et al., 1981.
53. Bem, S. L. The measurement of psychological androgeny. *Journal of Consulting and Clinical Psychology,* 1975, *42,* 155-162.
54. Hoeffer, 1981.
55. Mucklow & Phelan, 1979.
56. Green, 1978.
57. Hoeffer, 1981.
58. Block, J. Toy Preference Test. Unpublished manuscript.

59. Mandel et al., 1979.
60. Kirkpatrick et al., 1981.
61. Rutter, M., & Graham, P. The reliability and validity of the psychiatric assessment of the child: I. Interview with the child. *British Journal of Psychiatry*, 1968, *114*, 563-579.
62. Hall, 1978.
63. Lewis, 1980.
64. Hoeffer, 1981.
65. Mandel et al., 1979.
66. Kirkpatrick et al., 1981.
67. Mucklow & Phelan, 1979.

10

Grandparents, Grandchildren, and the Law

Richard H. Angell

Until approximately the past 20 years, grandparents had no legal rights to visitation with their grandchildren. Now almost all states have enacted statutes giving visitation rights to grandparents, and three remaining states have such legislation pending (1). This remarkable change has been accompanied by modifications in the criteria used in custody and visitation decisions. Further, the increasing divorce rate has led to a major shift in the configuration of American families. Demographically, a growing number of younger grandparents and older generations are available to their grandchildren; yet, they have frequently found access to their descendents complicated, as when the child's family is disrupted by death, divorce, remarriage, or adoption.

These sociological shifts have occurred at the same time the legal system has shown increased willingness to recognize the value to the child of continuing close relationships, such as with a grandparent. Familiarity with grandparent visitation laws will benefit mental health professionals, who will be increasingly called upon to evaluate the contribution of the grandparent-grandchild relationship to the child's welfare. Expert witnesses may be hindered in evaluating this relationship by the modest amount of empirical research in this area and by training that emphasizes dyadic relationships within the nuclear family and ignores the extended family.

This chapter will include a review of the evolution of law regarding grandparents' rights from common law to statutory laws. Areas of continuing debate, such as the effect of adoption on grandparent visitation rights, animosity toward the grandparent, and custody awards to grandparents, deserve emphasis as they demonstrate shifts in the competing principles of parental rights and the best interest of the child. The demographic and sociological characteristics of grandparents as "a third party," as well as the psychological aspects of the grandparent-grandchild relationship, will be reviewed, followed by some practical aspects of the psychiatric evaluation of this relationship.

GRANDPARENT VISITATION RIGHTS—FROM COMMON LAW TO STATUTORY LAW

Common Law

The immediate family being disrupted by the loss of a parent, death, divorce, or adoption constitutes a crisis in a child's life. In these circumstances, the child, as well as other family members, often draws support from extended family relationships. At such time, the child's close relationships to other significant persons, such as grandparents, may be jeopardized and thus add to the child's loss. For example, the custodial parent might move or object to relatives having access to the child. The legal question of whether the grandparent has the right to secure visitation with the grandchild over the custodial parent's objection may then arise.

Under common law the grandparent generally had no access to the grandchild. Historically, the decisions reached in matters of visitation and custody in British courts of law were based on the principle of absolute parental authority (2), and parental objection was sufficient to deny grandparents visitation. A landmark case in establishing this principle was *The Succession of Reiss* in 1894 in which a grandparent petitioned for visitation rights (3). The courts found that the grandparents had no legal rights to visitation with their grandchild over the custodial parents' objection. The reasons given for this ruling derived from an affirmation of the supremacy of parental authority, and served as an important precedent from 1894 until the recent past. Salient details of this case were as follows: The father of two children, ages six and eight, was living with his mother and other family members. His wife had been dead approximately six years. The mother of his deceased wife sought visits with her grandchildren in her home. The father agreed to allow her to visit them in his home, but refused to send them to her house. A lower court ordered both the father and the mother-in-law to alternate the visits weekly between the two homes. Later, the Louisiana Supreme Court reversed this judgment. While the court recognized that "without a doubt it is desirable that the ties of affection that nature creates between the ascendents and their grandchildren be strengthened and increasing," it went on to elaborate the following basic reasons for denying visitation:

1) The parent's obligation, ordinarily, to allow the grandparent to visit the child is moral, not legal.

2) The judicial enforcement of grandparent visitation rights would divide proper parental authority, thereby hindering it.

3) The ties of nature are the only efficacious means of restoring normal family relations and not the course of measures that follows judicial intervention.

4) The best interests of the child are not furthered by forcing the child into the midst of a conflict of authority and ill-feelings between the parent and grandparent.

5) The parent alone, in cases of conflict, should be the judge, without having to account to anyone for the motives in denying the grandparent visitation. (4)

Subsequent decisions in other jurisdictions followed these same arguments (5). In *Odel* v. *Lutz*, for example, we read that

> The court docs not have the power to compel the parents to allow the grandmother the right of visitation merely because the relationship is that of grandparent. Their right, if it can be called that ... is no different from that of any third person or stranger. (6)

Grandparents were effectively denied legal standing in court, no matter how compelling the facts of a specific case were in favor of a grandparents' visitation. Only when there were cases of "downright wrong and inhumanity," as noted in the *Succession of Reiss*, did the courts have a right to intervene in family life. Most case law did not recognize cutting off grandchild access to grandparents as "so grave an issue."

To summarize, the common law denial of grandparents' access to grandchildren was based on parental rights. This included almost total parental authority over children, without interference from the state as long as the adults were fit parents. Children's interests are usually acknowledged in common law cases in terms of their right to be spared the conflict between parents and grandparents. Grandparents' rights to seek visitation were limited to cases in which the grandparent had prior custody of a grandchild, or had petitioned for custody when the parents were found to be unfit, or when the parents were in the process of a divorce proceeding. In these situations, grandparents were in a position to be granted visitation privileges. Subsequent adoption of the grandchild resulted in the termination of prior visitation privileges. Although most case law did not recognize cutting off grandchild access to a grandparent as a threat to his/her welfare, there was common recognition that hostile relationships between parents and grandparents created an emotional atmosphere that did not serve the best interest of the child. It is interesting that the assumption has been made that visitation under such circumstances would be detrimental to the child when no such assumption has been made about visitation to hostile parents following a divorce.

Common law principles were modified sufficiently over time to accommodate the best interests of the child standards instead of adhering strictly to the principles of parental authority. In the case of *Williams* v. *Miller*, a 10-year-old girl lived with her mother and aunt after her parents separated shortly after her birth (7). She had continued to live with her aunt after her mother remarried and moved away. A maternal grandmother had frequent visits with the girl. When the child's mother died, the father was granted custody and the aunt was given visitation rights. The maternal grandmother continued frequent visits with the girl until the aunt's poor health interfered and the father refused to allow visits by the grandmother. The trial court's denial of visitation to the grandmother was later reversed by the Pennsylvania Supreme Court. This court not only recognized that to deny visitation to the grandchild would cut her off from contact with the maternal side of the family, but also acknowledged the special quality of the grandparent-grandchild relationship. The Pennsylvania Court quoted the New Jersey opinion, which stated that the "visits with the grandmother are often a precious part of a child's experience and there are benefits which devolve upon a grandchild from the relationship with his grandparents which he cannot derive from any other relationship" (8). Animosity alone was not held to be a sufficient reason in the *Williams* v. *Miller* case to bar the grandparent from visitation because the custodial parent could easily use this as an objection. The effect on the well being of the child of continuing animosity between the custodial parent and the grandparent was held to be a sufficient reason to stop visitation, but only if detrimental effects on the grandchild could be shown.

The case of *Benner* v. *Benner* (9) dealt with a child who lived with her grandmother and her mother, the custodial parent. After the mother disappeared, the father was awarded custody of the child and he allowed visitation privileges with the maternal grandmother. Following his remarriage, the father sought to end visitation privileges with her. The appellate court upheld the visitation order, noting that the child had lived with the grandmother for about three years and would suffer considerable emotional disturbance if she were cut off from contact with the grandmother. It was also noted that the father had previously agreed to visitation in the prior custody decision.

Exceptions in Common Law

There are some situations in which common law tends to be more favorable to the rights of grandparents to maintain access to their grandchildren. One such situation is when a grandparent has been awarded custody of a grandchild during a divorce proceeding. If the grandparent subsequently loses custody, the courts have been willing to grant visitation to the grandparents. For example, in *Warren* v. *Warren*, the paternal grandparents were granted custody of a grandchild in a divorce decree (10). The natural father was subsequently given custody and the grandparents were denied visitation. The court of appeals changed the lower court's order to allow the grandparents reasonable visitation. Because the grandparents had been given legal custody, they had standing in court to seek visitation with their grandchild, which the court held was in the child's interest.

Grandparents have been in a more favorable position to secure visitation with grandchildren when the parents are found to be unfit because of the difficulty of applying the fitness of the parent standard. Ironically, in this situation the grandparents might be in a better position to seek custody than visitation, especially if they previously provided continuous care for the child for a reasonable period of time (11, 12).

To summarize, common law denial of grandparents' access to grandchildren was derived from several principles. First, parents' rights included the right to nearly total authority over the child, without interference from the state, as long as they were fit parents. Children's interests were acknowledged in terms of their right to be spared the conflict between parents and grandparents, and their right to have authority vested in their parents. Grandparents who had custody of a child, or who petitioned for custody when parents were found to be unfit or were in divorce proceedings, were in a position to be granted visitation privileges. However, subsequent adoption of a child usually resulted in termination of such visitation privileges if the custodial parent objected. Under parens patriae, the state could interfere in family life if there were "cases of downright inhumanity demanding judicial intervention," but matters of grandparent visitation were not "so grave an issue." Although these principles effectively blocked grandparents' access to grandchildren, trends toward the limiting of absolute parents' rights, the increasing emphasis on the "best interests of the child" in custody and visitation matters, and the contribution of meaningful relationships, such as with grandparents, to those best interests all set the stage for a legal alternative, namely, a proliferation of grandparent visitation statutes.

Visitation Statutes—Threshold for Judicial Intervention

Most statutes identify specific changes in the child's family that allow the grandparents to petition for visitation. Initially, statutes justified judicial intervention when the disruption was major; namely, when one or both parents died. Subsequently, the right of intervention was extended in some states by statute to include divorce, separation, abandonment, family dissolution, parental nonsupport of a child, parents living in separate habitations, adoption, and a child being placed in foster care. While a change in the child's family status is still a requirement for the courts to intervene, such intervention is no longer a "grievous wrong," as specified in the *Succession of Reiss* (13). The justification increasingly has become that the state may intervene when there is a change in the status of a child's family in order to protect the child's right to a continuing relationship with the grandparent, even against the wishes of the parent. An extension of this trend would be for grandparents to have the right to petition in a situation in which there were "kindly family relations," and both natural parents objected to visitation with their own natural child. Just such a statutory provision is being advocated by Grandparents, Inc., in California (14).

Criteria—Best Interests of the Child

Decisions in cases of grandparent visitation, as in other matters of visitation and custody, have increasingly made reference to the best interests of the child standard (15, 16, 17). Unprecedented emphasis on child development has also increasingly influenced the courts. This has been manifested in part in the value placed on a child's continuous, uninterrupted relationships, which has emerged as a major component of the best interests of the child standard. In addition to awareness of the harm done to children when their strong emotional attachments are broken, blood relationships with relatives are thought to have "intrinsic value":

> An adopted person may not in many respects be cut off from his natural family. If affection and regard remains [sic] between members of a natural family, the law, should not in the name of consistency, undertake to thwart the expression of a natural family of those feelings when the encouragement thereof does not hinder the adoptive relationship. (18)

The natural ties between relatives are most often put in terms of the best interests of the child to know his or her "roots." Natural ties between kin provide a child not only with important relationships, but also with a sense of family identity and knowledge of his heritage. It can be seen, however, that the best interest of the child standard may bring into conflict the following principles: the importance to a child of "psychological parents"; the value of important kin relationships and family identity; and the right of a child to have his life protected by parental authority. The conflict between these principles is clear in the Tribal Child Welfare Act of 1978

(19). This law, which is based on the importance of kin and culture, gives authority to tribes to determine the best interest of Indian children, especially those who have been living in non-Indian foster homes. Courts are faced in custody disputes with weighing the effects of this law against the best interests of the child to continue a relationship with a "psychological parent" who is non-Indian.

It is important to emphasize that it is the child's right to continued involvement with his grandparents that is the dominant principle in most current grandparent visitation statutes. The value to the grandparent to have access to grandchildren, although mentioned in court opinions, has not been given weight as an independent standard or principle. The dramatic development of visitation statutes is striking evidence of grandparents' political power in advocating their own interests in terms that the court does recognize, namely, the best interests of the child standard.

Grandparents as a Third Party

Just as there has been a trend to broaden the circumstances in which a third party, such as grandparents, can petition the courts for visitation, so has the notion broadened of who the third party can be. The first visitation statutes addressed the rights of natural grandparents and gradually have been extended, in some states, to natural great-grandparents, other relatives, and even nonrelatives who have had a meaningful relationship with the child. Under French and Swiss law, third party means anyone other than the father, mother, and grandparents, but these parties have no legal right to access to the child. To gain this right, they must prove before court authorities exceptional circumstances, such as a documented period of child care. French law, however, provides that grandparents are a separate class of persons who do have the right of visitation with grandchildren, even when the parents object (20).

In American courts distinctions between grandparents and other persons appear to be increasingly diminished. Attempts continue to be made to specify qualifications of the third party. For example, Zaharoff (21) suggests that

> blood or adoptive relatives, any person with whom the child has resided for a period of six months or longer, and any person who has a substantial interest in the child's welfare, should have a right to petition the courts for access to the child.

His view is that limiting petitioners to grandparents is overly restrictive and artificial. This presents the courts and mental health professionals with the challenge of defining which relationships are most important. The courts continue to debate what constitutes a meaningful relationship in terms that encompass increasing emphasis on psychological dimensions as opposed to blood ties. It has become common to speak of the psychological parent as distinct from the biological parent. To date, however, the courts have not yet spoken of the "psychological grandparent." The trend to broaden the group of third parties who may petition for visitation implicitly minimizes any special attributes of the grandparent-grandchild relationship. An extension of visitation rights may intensify conflict over the principle of preserving the autonomy and integrity of the family.

Adoption

When a child is adopted, the right of access to biological grandparents remains a controversial issue, since most states have not yet created specific statutes to deal with it (22). For example, a child may be adopted by other relatives or nonrelatives if both parents are deceased. The most common situation is for a custodial parent to remarry and for the stepparent to adopt children. Under existing statutes, grandparents could petition for visitation. However, in many states when the stepparent adopts the child, the adoption statutes, which terminate all prior parental rights, are in conflict with the grandparent visitation statutes. After adoption, the natural parents' legal relationship ends and, by extension, so does that of the natural grandparent. Thus, adoption has been regarded as a bar to grandparent visitation when adoption statutes are interpreted as terminating all rights of blood relatives, including those of grandparents. Grandparents cease to have any legal relationship with the child. In *Deweese* v. *Crawford* (23), the paternal grandparents sought visitation with their grandchildren after their son and his wife were divorced and she had been granted custody. The grandparents' contact with the grandchildren continued until their son died. The wife's new husband then adopted the children, and access to the grandchildren was blocked. The court found that they were not legal grandparents since the adoption had severed all blood ties.

States have responded to the competing interests of the child, the grandparent visitation statutes, and adoption statutes in various ways. Adoption is not always regarded as an absolute bar to visitation where it is "in the child's best interests." In *Scranton* v. *Hutter* (24), the court showed concern for grandparents who lost their own child and, because of the remarriage of the remaining parent, were cut off from their grandchild. This court reasoned that the New York and California adoption statutes define the effects of adoption only in terms of succession of property:

Unquestionably the substitution of adoptive for natural parents serves a great number of social objectives. On the other hand the law should not and cannot ignore the fact that an adoptive person may not in many aspects be cut off from his natural family. If affection and regard remain between members of a natural family, the law should not, in the name of consistency, undertake to thwart the expression of those feelings when the encouragement thereof does not hinder the adoptive relationship. (25)

The court further reasoned that

where the child has been adopted by grandparents instead of by a stepparent, there is an even less reason to sever contact with the natural family and that the expression of grandparent visitation rights after adoption is consistent with a growing awareness of the need for an adoptive child to know his roots. (26)

Those states that deny visitation to the adopted child weigh more heavily the belief that adoption is strengthened when all ties with the natural family are severed. Such natural family ties are viewed as a threat to the adoptive parents' authority, which might have the social effect of discouraging adoption. Some courts have stated concern that the child may be confused by having three or four sets of grandparents (27). A practical concern sometimes expressed is that the natural parents of a child who has been adopted may seek contact with the child, and grandparents might make it easy for the natural parent to have contact with the child during visits with the grandparents. Those courts that view visitation awards to grandparents as a threat to the adoptive parental authority appear to draw from common law tradition, which views a division of parental authority as a threat to the best interests of the child. When there is conflict between the grandparent and the adoptive parents, this approach asserts that the parent is in the best position to judge whether such conflicts harm the child's welfare sufficiently to end visitation.

Other courts have used a technical interpretation of grandparents' relationship to the adoptive parents to deny visitation after an adoption proceeding, on the grounds that the natural grandparents are no longer the legal grandparents of the adopted child. Therefore, the natural grandparents have no rights to visitation (28).

In the situation where the child is adopted by two strangers, natural parents have all parental rights terminated and, again, no legal relationship is recognized between the grandparents and the grandchild. It has been suggested that the best course in this situation is for the court or court staff to attempt to get consent from the adopting parents to continue visitation (29).

Animosity Between the Parties

In contrast to common law traditions, animosity between the parents and grandparents under statutory visitation laws is not a sufficient reason to deny grandparent visitation. In determining the best interests of the child, courts have been willing to balance the effects of animosity against the benefits of continuing a preexisting relationship between the grandparent and the grandchild. As in the case with divorce proceedings, the hostile custodial parent is not thought to be an objective judge of what is in the child's best interests. When animosity exists between the grandparents and parents, the court may order visitation and retain jurisdiction in order to oversee the effects of the visitation and to make modification in the visitation order as needed.

Child's Preference

The child's preference in grandparent visitation cases is given the same weight as in custody cases. The opinion of an older child will be considered favorably, especially if a positive preference is stated. When a child states negative feelings about visiting with his grandparents, the courts have been willing to look at the possibility that the child is caught in loyalty conflicts with his parents and is unable to state a preference without fear of offending or angering them. The child's preference in these cases may be given less weight. In some cases, children may have been brainwashed by parents into rejecting their grandparents and this also must be taken into consideration.

GRANDPARENTS, GRANDCHILDREN, AND THE FAMILY

Demographics

The improved status of grandparents in the courts has been accompanied by several notable demographic changes. At the turn of the century, when grandparents' demands for visitation rights were first heard in the court, only 4% of the population was over the age of 65 (30). By 1975, life expectancy had increased to 72 and 10.5% of the population was over 65 (31). Not only is there a larger population of grandparents, but there have been changes in the timing of life stages that have had a major effect on the age at which grandparenthood is reached. Because the stage of child rearing has been completed earlier, the average age for a woman to become a grandmother is now in the mid-forties (32). Another change is that parents now look forward to 13 to 16 "empty-nest" years, rather than the two to three years that was typical in the early 1900s (33). Four- and five-generation families, rather than three-generation families, will become the norm (34). Increased longevity makes it likely that grandparents will have five living grandchildren within their lifetime (35).

Grandparent is no longer synonymous with an old, feeble person. The Little Red Riding-Hood of today would more likely meet grandmother going to work or jogging than find her bedridden. Not only are grandparents younger, they are healthier for a longer time, better educated, and more financially secure than their counterparts in the past (36). Because of the differential longevity of women over men and women's lower rate of re-marriage, more older women will be living alone, and probably close to at least one child.

It is estimated that three-fourths of persons over 65 have living grand-children. A further three-quarters of these see their grandchildren at least once every week or two (37), and about half of them see their grandchildren every day or so. Only a small minority of grandparents are living with grandchildren. This is consistent with evidence that the proportion of par-ents over 65 who live with their children has declined. However, the num-ber of adult children who live within 10 minutes of their children has increased (38).

Two other demographic factors must be noted in relation to grandparents and the law: namely, the well-known increase of divorce rates, and the increase in single-parent families. As a consequence of higher divorce rates, more and more children are no longer living with their natural parents and ready access to their grandparents becomes more complicated. From the demographic evidence described thus far, there are more grandparents potentially available to press their interests in continuing a relationship with grandchildren at a time when legal access to them has become more difficult.

Older persons, in general, have achieved a higher level of self-awareness and this has resulted in a burgeoning of national and local advocacy groups. Law schools have responded to the legal issues that have surfaced with the elderly by routinely including studies of case decisions and laws affecting the elderly. We can conclude that from a political, as well as demographic, standpoint grandparents do not appear to be an ordinary "third party." Legislatures' responsiveness to their claims suggest that they have been unusually effective politically, and legislatures and the courts may have been more responsive to grandparents' status than the social sciences.

Grandparenting

Given the effective legal advocacy of grandparents, and a strengthened position in the eyes of the law, what clarity can be found in the social science literature regarding the grandparenting role and the psychological importance of this relationship to the child? Although information about geriatric populations has grown considerably, surprisingly little information is available regarding grandparenting and its significance to children and the family. Studies of grandparenthood are limited in number and often lack uniform attention to important class and cultural variables (39). For this reason generalizations are difficult to make.

Early studies of families dealt with household members, mainly power and authority relationships (40), a focus that corresponds well with the courts' past emphasis on parental authority. Both emotional and instrumental relationships between extended family members were ignored, especially after Parsons' description of the nuclear family in the forties as the dominant family configuration (41). The commonly accepted thesis was that the nuclear family was cut off from extended family ties as a consequence of urbanization and industrialization, and extended family were relegated to what Goode calls the "classical myth of Western nostalgia" (42). As divorce rates began to climb, public policy and professional research responded to the concern that the isolated conjugal family unit was succumbing to impossible demands, much as Parsons had predicted in the forties.

Both the nostalgic view of extended family and common beliefs about the dominance of the nuclear family have come under increasing attack (43). Shanas (44) attacks the myth that older persons in contemporary American society are alienated from and peripheral to their families, particularly from their children. Many studies indicate that a modified extended family is the most common family configuration. It is important to note that there are wide variations, however, between American ethnic groups and the proximity of kin and frequency of contact (45). For example, in one study, 74% of Italian-American respondents visited parents weekly, while 39% of Scandinavian-Americans visited parents weekly (46). The mutual expectations between generations vary considerably; Scandinavian and German families tend to maintain sharper boundaries between generations than black families (47).

Currently, there is much evidence that the nuclear family is more myth than reality and the American family still contains a significant extended kinship system (48). Extensive and complex emotional and instrumental relationships between family members and significant others are integral to family functioning, and the norm rather than the exception. Family therapy theory and clinical practice initially focused on the nuclear family but has also evolved to include extended family members and other people who participate in a family psychosocial system. This brief review suggests that our fundamental conceptions about the family have deterred investigations of the significance of grandparenthood. Previous emphasis on the nuclear family has conformed well to the judicial system's past conceptions about parental authority and the integrity of the family.

Grandparenthood

Grandparenthood is an ascribed status that has remarkably diverse characteristics rather than a normative pattern. An early study by Neugarten (49) of the perceptions of a middle-class group of grandparents on their roles as grandparents varied from grandparents' viewing grandparenthood as a source of biological renewal, to their being a resource person for the grandchildren. Furthermore, Neugarten identified five styles of grandparenting in this group of grandparents, all of whom lived close but separately from their children:

1) the formal grandparent—clear differentiation between parent and grandparent roles;
2) the fun-seeker—orientation to mutual play and enjoyment;
3) the surrogate parent—cares for grandchild usually due to the mother's employment, usually the grandmother;
4) the reservoir of wisdom subtype—mainly the grandfather; and
5) the distant figure—brief contact.

This study, as well as others, indicates that the role of the surrogate parent is not the most important to grandparents, and when it is important, it is out of necessity rather than choice (50, 51). The style of grandparenting also tends to vary with the age and sex of the grandparent. In general, grandmothers have warmer, closer relationships with grandchildren, and descriptive studies indicate that the grandchild's perceptions of grandparents varies with age and cognitive development (52).

The age of the grandchild also influences the style of grandparenting. Not surprisingly, grandparents are more likely to be more indulgent with gifts with younger children. Younger children easily identify a favorite grandparent on the basis of who is the most nurturing and indulgent. Similar to choosing a favorite parent, school-age children are sensitive to loyalty conflicts in stating their preferences for grandparents (53). This age group also favors shared pleasurable activities with grandparents. Studies of adolescents' attitudes toward grandparents report divergent conclusions. Adolescents either find them very important, especially when teenagers are in conflict with their parents, or they report not feeling close to their grandparents. Hoffman (54) suggests that young adolescents are most likely to report the greatest emotional distance from grandparents. This finding should, of course, be interpreted cautiously since adolescents are usually not forthright about valuing adult relationships. Young adults tend to see grandparents as an important source of influence on them. They expect their grandparents to be bearers of family history and, with older adolescents especially, relish hearing what their parents were like when they were young. Both young adults and grandparents favor activities that promote emotional gratification—"nurturance"—more than any specific instrumental activity.

Kornhaber, in his interview of 300 children, identified three groups of children (55). A small minority of them had close, warm relationships with their grandparents. This group felt that they received unqualified acceptance and affection from their grandparents. The importance of the emotional attachment was strongly emphasized in this group. In addition, these children were thought to make use of their grandparents as models for aging and respect for older persons generally. The second and largest group of grandchildren had sporadic contact with grandparents at some point in their lives. They were still emotionally involved with their grandparents and some tried to make sense out of the grandparents' absence by polarized thinking about their own worth, "I must not be worthy," or by devaluing the grandparents. These children were seen as being less accessible to old people and not wanting their advice. The third group of children, which accounted for about 15%, never had any attachment to grandparents. Some children in this study who did not have grandparents invented them. They did this for example, by adopting an elderly neighborhood person. Kornhaber compared the loss of a grandparent as second only to the loss of a parent.

The preceding discussion has dealt with descriptive studies of the significance of grandparenthood from the perspective of the grandparent and the grandchild. Troll (56) summarizes this literature by saying that grandparenting is peripheral in the lives of both grandchild and grandparent, idiosyncratic and diverse in its characteristics but not unimportant.

In addition to emphasis on the grandparent-grandchild dyad, the significance of grandparenting must also include the influence of interactions between grandparents and the entire family system. We are interested, for example, in knowing what other family factors influence the grandparent-grandchild relationship. For example, Robertson (57) found that parents have a mediating influence on grandparents by regulating visits when the children are young and by conveying attitudes about grandparents and older generations to the children. When contact between grandparents and grandchildren is limited, the grandparents' symbolic importance will be even more contingent upon the mediating parent-child bond.

The influence on a family system of a grandparent living in the same home is also of interest. Kellum (58) found that grandmother-mother families provide the same lower risk of maladaption for their first-grade children as mother-father family subtypes. Even when children were having difficulty in the first grade, there was the same lower risk of maladaption remaining by the third grade in the grandmother-mother families compared to the mother-father families. The mother-grandmother families did a better job with their children than mother-stepfather families, and mother aloneness carried the highest risk in this poor, urban Black community. Kellum found no less than 86 different combinations of adults in the homes of the sixth graders.

Some of the earliest references to grandparents in the psychiatric literature are found in psychoanalytic writings, which mainly dealt with cases in which a grandparent had a detrimental effect on grandchildren (59, 60). Benedek implies that grandparenthood for the grandparent is a different phase of the lifelong process of parenthood in which memories of their own parenting are rekindled by their grandchildren (61). If there is a special intensity or salience in the relationship between a grandparent and grandchild, one might speculate that it comes from this developmental process described by Benedek, namely, the propensity of the child to rekindle memories in the grandparent, not only of his/her own childhood, but also of his/her own parenthood.

CLINICAL EVALUATIONS

It is noteworthy how rarely reference is made to grandparent-grandchild-parent relationships in current guidelines for the clinical court work of child psychiatrists. This lack of attention is particularly striking in cases where the grandparent is not a contestant but has made contributions to a child's welfare. In McDermott's study (62) of court case workers' investigations of custody disputes, it was found that of the several categories of factors considered, the category least often mentioned was that of "alternate caretakers," which includes relatives. It was not thought to be a deciding factor. If family configuration is a variable in the adjustment of children, as Kellum's study suggests, then evaluations should include grandparents more routinely.

Additional guidelines for psychiatric evaluations involving grandparents in visitation, custody, termination of parental rights, and adoption cases can be tentatively offered:

1) What are the ameliorating as well as aggravating effects of grandparents on the parenting of the child? This is especially relevant when a grandparent is closely involved with a parent whose fitness

as a caretaker for a child is being evaluated by the courts. Grand-parents should be identified as one of several factors that may influence a parent's ability to care for a child. A subtle bias against extended family relationships may be revealed by the examiner's readiness to emphasize a grandparent's "overinvolvement," or the parents' "immaturity and dependency" on their own parent. Ethnic variations in family relationships, as well as the stage of develop-ment of the family, need to be considered.

2) Distinguish among various grandparent roles: How do the roles correspond to the developmental needs of the child? It will be useful to help participants clarify whether and how grandparenting differs from parenting. This is especially important in disputes over grandparent visitation, a situation in which the courts may collude with a view that the grandparents are rivals with the parents. The stereotype of the overindulgent, gift-bearing grandmother should not lead to a preemptory dismissal of this role as evidence that the grandparent doesn't appreciate the needs of the child or is merely gratifying the grandparents' need for acceptance. A grand-parent's concern about having his or her name carried on by a grandchild should also not be dismissed as simple self-interest. What, if any, special prerogatives does the grandparent have in the family? How are conflicts around roles worked out?

3) Establish the nature of the grandparent-grandchild relationship by direct observation. Include the grandparents in the interview with the parents.

4) Inquire about a child's preference for custody and visitation with grandparents with tact.

Clinical evaluations that are based on current understanding of family functioning (63) will give the courts the best opportunity to evaluate family law cases. The flexible application of the best interests of the child standard has contributed to at least a tentative redefinition of the family to include extended family members. The competing underlying presumptions of this standard require thorough clinical investigations in order to accommodate this change and to substantiate the influence of various factors in the child's welfare. Certainly, the proliferation of grandparent visitation statutes reflects the weight given to continuing the child's close relationships. However, the unique attributes of the grandparent-grandchild relationship need to be better understood by courts and legislatures as they deal with the effects of high divorce rates, which effectively disrupt and multiply a child's re-lationships.

REFERENCES

1. Foster, H. H., & Freed, D. J. The child's right to visit grandparents. *Trial*, 1984, *21*, 38-41.
2. McGough, R. Coming of age . . . , *Emery Law Journal*, 1978, *27*, 209-245.
3. *Succession of Reiss* 15 Xo:151, 152 (La. 1894).
4. Gault, D. Statutory grandchild visitation. *St. Mary's Law Journal*, 1973, *5*, 474-488.
5. Foster, H. H., Jr., & Freed, D. J. Grandparent visitation: Vagaries and vicissitudes. *St. Louis University Law Journal*, 1979, *23*, 645-675.
6. *O'Dell* v. *Lutz* L&& P. 2d 628, 629-630 (Cal App. 1947).
7. *Williams* v. *Miller* 385 A 2d 277 N.Y. 992 (Pa. Supra Ct. 1978).
8. *Mimkin* v. *Ford* 332 A 2d 199 (N.J. 1975) p. 204.
9. *Benner* v. *Benner* 248 P. 2d 245 (Cal Ct. Appl 1952).
10. *Warren* v. *Warren* 496 S.W. 2d 286 (Mo. App. 1973).
11. Chaloff, M. B. Grandparents statutory visitation rights and the rights of adoptive parents. *Brooklyn Law Review*, 1982, *49*, 149-171.
12. In re *Berman* Cal App. 3d 6876794118 (Cal Rptr. 804 808 1975).
13. *Succession of Reiss*, 1894.
14. Foster, 1984.
15. Derdeyn, A. P. A consideration of legal issues in child custody contests. Implications for change. *Archives of General Psychiatry*, 1976, *33*, 165-171.
16. Goldstein, J., Freud, A., & Solnit, A. J. *Beyond the best interests of the child*. New York: Free Press, 1973.
17. Goldstein, J., Freud, A., & Solnit, A. J. *Before the best interests of the child*. New York: Free Press, 1979.
18. Estate of *Zook* 62 Cal 2d 492, 495, 42 Cal Rptr. 597, 600, 399 P 2d 5356 (1965).
19. Indian Child Welfare Act. P.L. 95-608, 92, Statute 3069, 25, U.S.C. § 5 (1901).
20. Reday, A. M. A comparison between legal visiting rights in France and Switzerland. *International Child Welfare Review*, 1982, *52*, 29-33.
21. Zaharoff, H. G. Access to children: Towards a model statute for third parties. *Family Law Quarterly*, 1981, *15*, 165-203.
22. Chaloff, 1982.
23. *Deweese* v. *Crawford* 520 S.W. 2d 522 (Texas Crt. App. 1975).
24. *Scranton* v. *Hutter* 40 AA 2d at 299 399 N.W. S 2d at 711 (4th Dept. 1973) 98 isc 2d at 332 414 N.Y.S. 2d at 85 (4th Dept. 1973).
25. *Ibid.*
26. *Ibid.*
27. Gault, 1973.
28. Chaloff, 1982.
29. Foster, 1984.
30. Levine, M. Research in law and aging. *The Gerontologist*, 1980, *20*(2), 163-167.
31. Gelfand, D. E., Olsen, J. K., & Block, M. R. Two generations of elderly in the changing American family: Implications for family services. *The Family Coordinator*, 1978, October, 394-403.
32. Levine, 1980.
33. Glick, P. C. The future marital status and living arrangements of the elderly. *The Gerontologist*, 1979, *19*, 301-309.
34. Gelfand, 1978.
35. Glick, 1979.
36. Hess, B. B., & Waring, J. M. Changing patterns of aging and family bonds in later life. *The Family Coordinator*, 1978, October, 204-214.
37. Harris and Associates, Inc. *The myth and reality of aging*. Washington, DC: American Council on Aging, Inc. and National Council on Aging, 1975.
38. Shanas, E. Social myth as hypothesis: The case of the family relations of old people. *The Gerontologist*, 1979, *19*, 3-9.
39. Kahana, B., & Kahana, E. Grandparenthood from the perspective of the developing grandchild. *Developmental Psychology*, 1970, *3*, 98-105.

40. Uzoka, A. F. The myth of the nuclear family. *American Psychologist,* 1979, *34,* 1095-1106.
41. Parsons, T. The kinship system of contemporary United States. *American Anthropologist,* 1943, *45,* 22-38.
42. Goode, W. J. *World revolution and family patterns.* New York: Free Press, 1963.
43. Uzoka, 1979.
44. Shanas, 1979.
45. Woehrer, C. E. Cultural pluralism in American families: The influence of ethnicity on social aspects of aging. *Family Coordinator,* 1978, October, 329.
46. Greeley, A. M. *Why can't they be like us?* New York: Dutton, 1971.
47. Woehrer, 1978.
48. Pattison, E. M., Defrancisco, D., Wood, P., Frazer, H., & Crouder, J. A psychosocial kinship model for family therapy. *American Journal of Psychiatry,* 1975, *132*(12), 1246-1250.
49. Neugarten, B. L., & Weinstein, K. K. The changing American grandparent. *Journal of Marriage and the Family,* 1964, May, 199-204.
50. Lopata, H. *Widowhood in an American city.* Cambridge, MA: Schenkman, 1973.
51. Clavan, S. The impact of social class and social trends on the role of grandparent. *The Family Coordinator,* 1978, October, 351-357.
52. Hoffman, E. Young adults' relations with their grandparents: An exploratory study. *International Journal of Aging and Human Development,* 1979, *10,* 299-308.
53. Kahana, 1970.
54. Hoffman, 1979.
55. Kornhaber, A., & Woodward, K. L. *Grandparents, grandchildren. The vital connection.* Garden City, NY: Anchor Press/Doubleday, 1981.
56. Troll, L. E. Grandparenting. In L. W. Poon (Ed.), *Aging in the 1980s: Psychological issues.* Washington, D.C.: American Psychological Association, 1980.
57. Robertson, J. F. Significance of grandparents, perceptions of young adult grandchildren. *The Gerontologist,* 1976, *16,* 137-140.
58. Kellum, S. G., Ensminger, M. E., & Turner, R. J. Family structure and the mental health of children. *Archives of General Psychiatry,* 1977, *31,* 1012-1022.
59. Rappaport, E. A. The grandparent syndrome. *Psychoanalytic Quarterly,* 1958, *27,* 518-538.
60. Abraham, K., & Abraham, H. C. (Ed.). *Selected papers: Clinical papers and essays in psychoanalysis, Vol. 2.* New York: Basic Books, 1955.
61. Benedek, T. The family as a psychologic field. *Parenthood: Its psychology and psychopathology.* Boston: Little, Brown, 1970.
62. McDermott, J. F., Jr., Tseng, W., Char, W. F., & Fukunaga, C. S. Child custody decision making—the search for improvement. *Journal of the American Academy of Child Psychiatry,* 1978, *17,* 104-116.
63. Fleck, S. A holistic approach to family typology and the axes of DSM-III. *Archives of General Psychiatry,* 1983, *40,* 901-906.

11

Allegations of Sexual Abuse in Child Custody and Visitation Disputes

Elissa P. Benedek and
Diane H. Schetky

REVIEW OF THE LITERATURE

In recent years, the sexual abuse of children has received much attention in both the psychiatric literature (1–4) and the popular media. Children's accusations are no longer assumed to be fantasy, as they were in Freud's time. Rather, most professionals look upon such charges as valid distress signals worthy of careful investigation. In our experience in dealing with many cases of possible sexual abuse, we have found children to be generally truthful in their allegations of sexual abuse. We have, however, recently evaluated several children and families who have made false accusations of sexual abuse. These allegations arose in the context of child custody and visitations disputes. The underlying psychodynamics and family situations in these cases were complex and varied.

In contrast to an abundance of literature on true incest, reports of false accusations of incest are scant. Ferenczi has noted that young children often have difficulty separating reality from fantasy (1). Their feelings of helplessness and need to preserve their image of the good parent may cause them to "forget" what actually transpired. Alternatively, as noted by Katan, they may attribute the sexual abuse to the wrong person (2). Terr (3) has

Presented at the Annual Meeting of American Academy of Psychiatry and the Law, Nassau, Bahamas, October 26, 1984.

elaborated on misperception as a defense to trauma. She also believes that child victims of trauma are not amnesic. Rosenfeld, Nadelson, and Kreiger (4) discuss factors that may aid in determining the validity of a report. They note that in absence of proof of reality, parents may accuse one another of sexual molestation as a means of terminating visitation rights. Kaplan and Kaplan (5) discuss the problem of the custodial parent who coaches the child to make accusations of sexual abuse against the noncustodial parent, but suggest in their case that allegations of abuse arose because the child now felt safe in making them because of geographical separation from the offender. Peters (6), in reviewing 64 cases of alleged sexual abuse, found only four cases where it was concluded that no sexual abuse had occurred. A study out of Tufts University of 100 children alleging sexual abuse found that the abuse was substantiated in all but 5% of the cases (7).

Goodwin, Sahd, and Rada (8) discuss clinical aspects of false accusation and false denial of incest. In their review of 46 families presenting with the complaint of sexual abuse within the family, they found one case of false accusation by a child, two cases of false accusations brought by psychotic mothers, and two cases of false retraction of valid accusations. The false accusations all involved adolescents, who readily admitted that they had lied and who later retracted their accusations when confronted by a psychiatrist. In contrast, false denial of incest occurred in response to threats from the father, infatuation with the father, or out of fear of disrupting the family. These authors concluded that a judgment of false accusation should be made positively, and not by inference or exclusion, i.e., the clinician needs to come forth with a psychodynamic explanation of the hoax.

OVERVIEW

Common questions we are asked to address by referring sources include the credibility of the allegation of sexual abuse, the child's ability to distinguish between fact and fantasy, the nature and extent of the abuse, and the duration of the abuse. We have also been asked to evaluate children's ability to be credible witnesses in court, their ability to withstand cross-examination, and to prepare children for court appearances. We have noted that the number of psychiatric evaluations in our practice prompted by allegations of sexual abuse has increased over the past few years. Coupled with this numerical increase of contested custody evaluations is the current public attention paid to sexual abuse of children.

Allegations of sexual abuse in contested custody cases arise at all stages of determination. Parental separation may be precipitated by the crisis that develops when a child accuses a parent of sexual abuse. Allegations of abuse also emerge at the time of divorce. Such an allegation is used as evidence in regard to a temporary custody determination as, clearly, custody with an abusing parent would not be "in the best interest of the child."

In our experience, allegations of sexual abuse have been most common in child custody disputes that arise after a divorce has been granted and center around issues of visitation. Custodial parents may allege sexual abuse to prevent noncustodial parents from exercising their visitation rights. Conversely, noncustodial parents will allege sexual abuse in an attempt to get the court to change the permanent custody that was awarded at the time of the divorce. In one case, charges arose only after the mother realized that she had unwittingly signed papers agreeing to joint custody.

In an evaluation of alleged sexual abuse in custody cases, it is critical that the child psychiatrist be clear about the questions posed and attempt to answer them. It is important to articulate the facts and observations that form the data base for one's conclusions. Recommendations regarding treatment may also be requested. Validation of sexual abuse rests upon the clinical interview with the child, history of behavioral changes, physical signs of abuse, and, at times, corroborating evidence. This chapter will discuss factors that may facilitate assessment, along with case illustrations, and will review our findings in 18 other cases.

SPECIAL ISSUES

Special problems occur when evaluating the very young child in regard to allegations of sexual abuse. These problems center around the young child's inability to distinguish fact from fantasy, problems with language, and wish to be "good and helpful" or to protect a parent.

Reality Testing

In regard to distinguishing fact from fantasy, three-and-a-half-year-old Yvonne steadfastly denied her mother's allegations that her father's roommates had exposed themselves to her or that her father had molested her. Her mother, however, had tape-recorded a conversation with Yvonne in which Yvonne spoke of her father's friend having a "long body," a term the mother insisted that her daughter used for genitalia, and from this she began to build a case for sexual abuse. The evaluator began to question the child's ability to distinguish fact from fantasy when, during the evaluation, she began to cook a toy mouse for dinner and insisted that she had once eaten a mouse while at her father's. Further questioning revealed that Yvonne was not cognitively mature enough to understand the difference between reality and fantasy. Cognitive ability is not just a function of age and may vary greatly from one child to another. Clear questions to this end, such as "Is that pretend or is that real?", are helpful both in offering an opinion and in subsequent reports or testimony.

Language

The problem of language is a difficult one, but one which can be useful in conducting the evaluation. The language for describing male and female genitalia used by children is often not anatomical. In addition, the language for severe abuse is rarely technical. John, age five, accused his stepbrother of "fellatio." Besides having problems pronouncing fellatio, John could not explain what it meant except to say that his brother had fought with him. Fellatio was in no way consonant with John's more appropriate five-year-old language development and suggested that he might have been coached. On the other hand, precocious sexual vocabulary may also indicate that the child has been sexually overstimulated. In some cases, the vocabulary has been taught by the perpetrator. Obviously, it is also important to find out what sexual terminology parents have used with the child.

In a play interview, it was apparent to the evaluator that above-mentioned Yvonne had no terminology for male genitalia, e.g., she showed much curiosity about the penis of an undressed baby doll and when asked if she knew what it was, giggled and said, "A dinosaur." When asked what she meant by the term "body," she pointed to her own pubic area. She was then asked if the doll had a body and she turned the male doll over and pointed to his buttocks. On questioning she said she had seen her father's body but never his roommate's. In contrast, adolescents, although inhibited about the scientific names of body parts, use age-appropriate language in describing molestation.

Brainwashing

As the child's primary psychological bond may be with the parent who alleges sexual abuse and who has custody of the child, the child may be "brainwashed" by this parent into supporting a series of allegations. It is helpful in such cases to support one's clinical opinion with examples and dynamics that make it possible either to support or refute this possibility. As Green (9) notes, because of defensive operations, children rarely spontaneously talk about sexual abuse, and when they do the story usually emerges gradually accompanied by appropriate affect. For example, Susan, age two and a half, gradually began to talk with the evaluator about ding dongs and bells, then drew pictures of teddy bears with enlarged genitalia, cut out pictures of teddy bears whose bodies were dwarfed by the size of their genitalia, and finally pulled down her pants and told the evaluator that her daddy put his ding dong "right here," pointing to her vagina. The clinical activity, which began with excitement and terminated with a graphic demonstration of the abuse, left little doubt in the mind of the evaluator that there was no possibility of coaching the two and a half year old to sequentially demonstrate her anxiety and preoccupation with the abuse.

In contrast, five-year-old Carla, in automaton fashion, volunteered the same litany of complaints against her father each time she was seen, using identical language. When pressed for specifics, she would change the subject and become evasive. There were no sexual themes evident in her play. Her statement, that "we want Bill out of our lives because we have a new daddy now," raised the suspicion of collusion with her mother. This was further confirmed when she was overheard in the waiting room telling her mother, "I told the doctor all the things you told me to. Aren't I a good girl?" In another case of brainwashing, Kate, age 11, gave a credible and consistent story of her stepfather tickling her private parts but, under pressure from her mother and stepfather's attorney, retracted her story saying she'd been mistaken and that his hand must have "slipped."

FACTORS THAT MAY AID IN ASSESSMENT

Play and Drawing

Many children, especially young ones, will be more comfortable playing out their sexual trauma with dolls and puppets than talking about it. Play, in addition to helping children deal with their feelings about sexual abuse, may provide valuable material for corroborating it. For instance, eight-and-a-half-year-old Maria had been held down in bed by her mother while her mother's boyfriend sexually assaulted her. Maria refused to speak directly of her mother, who was by now incarcerated, but in her play built a fortress around a little boy's bed so he would be "safe from his mother." She later depicted the mother saying to the boy, "I hate your guts," and explained, "That's what my mother said to me once."

Stacey, age three and a half, handled her sexual trauma by compulsively talking about it using a very precocious vocabulary. Upon entering the clinic waiting room with her foster mother, she announced in a loud voice, "Do you know what my daddy did to me? He put his penis in my vagina!" This was said without much affect, in what appeared to be her way of shocking others much the way she had been shocked. Further, by this time it had become a guaranteed way of getting attention. Aware of this, the examiner opted to focus on play and avoid further interrogation. Stacey began inserting marbles inside some hollow dolls and in and out of a kangaroo's pouch. She put some naked dolls in bed together and seemed unduly curious about their buttocks. She then spoke of her father putting his penis in her vagina. When asked if he'd put it anywhere else, she mentioned her mouth, where it "tickled," and her "butt," where it hurt. She then said that the boy doll was feeling very angry, but her own anger remained subdued.

In her second interview, Stacey drew a picture of a man with a very low-slung "belly button." When she was asked to tell a story about him, she turned the man into a gorilla who was about to be eaten by a ghost. She explained, "Him (the gorilla) was mad because he didn't have any fingers or hands," and "If him was angry he would eat the ghost but him wasn't angry, just mad." When asked if she was mad, she replied, "I'm still mad about daddy putting his penis in my butt and vagina." She was then asked if she ever worried about getting eaten up and she said, "If somebody is mad they might eat me up" and she went on to say that that somebody might be her dad. In this case, as with previously mentioned Susan, play and drawings revealed Stacey's trauma-related anxieties and were consistent with verbal accusations.

A contrasting case is that of two-year-old Anna Lisa, whose mother accused her father of spreading ant poison on the floor and forcing his daughter to eat it while he held her face in the poison. The mother also accused Anna Lisa's father of licking Anna Lisa's genitalia while changing her diapers. The mother presented with a detailed list of 49 separate complaints of physical and sexual abuse on the father's part. Yet, in the joint interview, Anna Lisa showed delight in seeing her father, and played freely with him. There was no trace of symbolic or overt sexual play with her father during extensive observation, which was as important to the examiner's conclusion of false allegations as the father's fully age-appropriate interaction with the child.

Direct Questions

In our experience, the clinician should always ask directly, in child-appropriate language, about the alleged sexual activity. Questioning should proceed from the general to the specific. After rapport with the child has been established, the clinician may inquire about the child's relationship with the parent in question and what games they play together. Specific questions should be asked about physical abuse and sexual activity. It may be helpful to frame questions to a young child in the third person. For example, "Sometimes people touch children in private parts, or in ways that make them feel uncomfortable—pause—Do you know any children who have had that happen to them?" And finally, "Has this ever happened to you?" If the clinician fails to ask, the child may feel that his or her thoughts or feelings associated with the abuse are so terrible that the doctor is afraid to ask. A direct admission can be helpful for a child. A denial, however, does not in itself mean that no sexual abuse occurred.

Precocious Sexual Vocabulary and Seductive Behavior

As with precocious vocabulary, a preoccupation with sex and seductive behavior also suggests that a child has been sexually overstimulated. Cassandra, age seven, showed a preoccupation with sex from an early age, spoke freely of sexual activities beyond the domain of most children, and, at six, worried that she might be pregnant. Athena, age five, was reported by her mother to frequently be seen "humping her dollies" and once her brother. In her case, she had been exposed to much adult sexual activity, but there was no evidence that she herself had been sexually abused. Seductive behavior in the child is learned behavior, which is often rewarded by the perpetrator. Thus, it is a mistake and unfair to think in terms of the child seducing the adult.

EVALUATION OF THE FAMILY

Evaluation of Both Parents

As with a standard evaluation, it is important to get past history, current functioning, and a history of the parent-child relationship. Care must be taken to ask about and document allegations against former spouses. It often becomes necessary to structure the interview in such a way as to keep it child-focused, rather than becoming bogged down in areas of spousal conflict. It may be helpful to remind the parents that it is not the clinician's role to decide who did what to whom in regard to the other parent, but rather to evaluate and recommend what is in the best interest of the child.

Parental attitudes toward sex also need to be explored. We have found that in these families, several mothers had a history of sexual problems or were themselves molested as children. The latter often renders them hypervigilant to the possibility that the same fate might befall their daughters. Some, on the other hand, are jealous of any attention their former spouse shows their daughter and allegations of sexual abuse then become a way of gaining control over their daughters and limiting their access to their fathers. One mother, Mrs. F., was totally obsessed with the conviction (in absence of evidence) that her husband, whom she accused of molesting her daughters, was a homosexual. She seemed much more interested in his homosexual tendencies than in what he was purported to have done to her daughters and had great difficulty focusing on her children. In spite of her disapproval of his sexual conduct, she made several efforts at reconciliation in the course of the evaluation. In this case, it was decided that she had an underlying thought disorder with paranoid traits. Obviously, past history of any deviant sexual behavior in the parents is also very relevant.

Psychiatric diagnoses in the parents are important. For instance, hysteria, borderline personality, or thought disorder may contribute to a parent's distorted perceptions of events and tendency to overreact. Substance abuse in the offender may impair judgment and alter inhibitions, thereby contributing to sexual abuse. The presence of thought disorder does not necessarily mean that allegations are delusional. In the case of Cassandra, the mother's thought disorder led to her insistence that the clearly documented sexual abuse of her seven-year-old daughter had not occurred. She insisted that the child's father had not molested her, saying, "I know because I checked her vaginally myself." In another case, involving a schizophrenic mother, the allegations were totally delusional.

Observation of the Child with the Parents

Observation of the child with the parents provides valuable information that might not be picked up in the course of taking a history. For instance, three-and-a-half-year-old Yvonne displayed much sexual curiosity while playing with dolls, which her mother seemed to be at a loss to know how to handle. In contrast, her father, when seen with her, was able to respond to her queries in a simple, matter-of-fact manner. These observations were consistent with the father's comments that the mother had "sexual hangups." He stated that he did not believe in flaunting his sex life before his daughter, but he saw nothing wrong with them observing each other nude or bathing together. His interactions with her, i.e., tickling her, stroking her legs, fondling her hair, had highly seductive overtones about which he seemed totally unaware. In this case, it was concluded that Yvonne had been sexually overstimulated but not abused, and that her mother's anxieties and mistrust of her former husband had caused her to overreact to the situation.

Often a custodial parent will strenuously object to the child being observed with the estranged parent on grounds that it would be too traumatic for the child. While these concerns may, at times, be valid, one should wonder what information that parent might also be trying to suppress or avoid. For instance, Carla's mother insisted that her daughter was terrified of her father and had no relationship with him. When they were observed together, Carla had not seen her father for six months as her mother had failed to comply with visitation orders. Her father, a slight and rather meek man, was extremely anxious. Carla initially totally withdrew from him, opting to sit in the psychiatrist's lap with eyes averted. She then berated her father with allegations of abuse and flaunted the fact that she now had a new daddy and didn't need him anymore. He accepted her anger and gradually was able to engage her in appropriate play. By the end of the hour, she was calling him "Daddy" and attempting to prolong their time together. The ease with which this about-face occurred strongly suggested that there had been a positive bond between them in the past, counter to the mother's insistence that the relationship had been a totally negative one. Brant (10), however, cautions that children can be affectionate and angry at the same time and that affection for the parent per se does not rule out sexual abuse.

Equally informative in Carla's case were observations of the child with her mother. The child seemed totally dependent on her mother's approval of her every move, and even had to confer with her mother as to which color magic markers to use in her drawings. Carla was apprehensive about using them and fearful that her mother would become angry if she made a mess, and indicated that she was not allowed to use them at home. She seemed much more inhibited in her mother's presence than her father's, and later indicated that she was afraid of her mother.

Use of Collateral Information

As in any custody evaluation, credibility of parents is an important issue. Psychiatrists tend to believe patients but must realize that in the adversarial system, each party is putting his or her best foot forward and is likely to be presenting a biased perception of the facts. Collateral information provides a check on this and an outside impression of the child and family. Important sources of information may be siblings, grandparents, babysitters, teachers, medical records, police reports, employers of parents, and the family's clergyman. For instance, Carla's babysitter described her as "a little Sarah Bernhardt." When asked what she meant by this, she said, "She is good at acting out a role when she thinks she is supposed to be that way." She went on to describe the infectious nature of the mother's hysteria prior to the father's visits and how this generated anxiety in Carla and led her to feel that she would not be safe with him.

After the evaluation of Carla was completed, the examiner received in the mail a clipping detailing a one-car accident in which Carla's father had been involved. The article said he was being charged with drunken driving. The mother, at this point, alleged that her husband had abused alcohol during the marriage, a fact she had never brought up during the evaluation. This seemed out of character, given the fact that he held down two jobs with an excellent work record, and said he rarely drank because of a seizure disorder. Hospital records were obtained that verified what the examiner had surmised, namely, that he had had a seizure while driving, and nowhere in the records was there any mention of intoxication.

Formulating Recommendations

It is important to stay with facts and firsthand information and observations. If quoting a parent, it should be clear that this is their perception of events, not the clinician's. Direct quotes from children and adolescents are helpful if available. Drawings and cutouts are also admissible. If allegations are believed to be false, there should be a psychodynamic formulation to explain them, e.g., a borderline mother trying to expunge the "bad" father and replace him with the "good" father, the paranoid mother who projects her own thoughts onto her former husband, or the hysterical mother misperceiving or overreacting to events. In the case of brainwashing, a child's developmental immaturity, extreme dependence on the mother (often fostered by the mother out of her own narcissistic needs), need to please her, and fear of her act as factors in the child's coming to believe everything the mother said about the father. Other less dynamic explanations may focus on parental rage, desire for revenge, or dissatisfaction with custody arrangements.

In many cases, evidence will not be clear-cut, and the psychiatrist must learn to live with irresolution and formulate a plan that offers the child reasonable protection. Several possibilities exist—none of them very satisfactory. These include: supervised visitation by a third party; monitored visitation, whereby the children are periodically seen by the psychiatrist; mediated visits in the presence of the therapist; parental guidance; psychotherapy for the parent; and periodic court review. Parameters may also be placed on visits as to location and duration.

In cases of brainwashing, irrevocable damage may have been done and attempts at reconciliation with the other parent may cause the child to feel disloyal and vulnerable. If the custodial parent remains unyielding, then the therapist may wish to consider recommending change of custody, but must weigh this against the likelihood of further trauma to the child. In our experience, where a clinician is dealing with vindictive parents, who may have character disorders, court-ordered visitation or therapy for the parent is not apt to alter attitudes toward the former spouse. Parents will continue to try to fortify their cases, often interrogating the child after visits in attempts to gather evidence for the next round in court. The child suffers, attorneys' fees mount, and nothing is resolved. The clinician must weigh whether preserving the child's relationship with the noncustodial parent is worth the trauma to the child that surrounds visitation.

SUMMARY OF CASES

In our limited sample of 18 cases, we attempted to discern any features that distinguished the 10 cases of false accusation of sexual abuse from the eight documented ones. Sixteen of the cases involved girls with ages ranging from two to 14 years. Two cases involved boys ages five and 11 years. The alleged offenders were fathers in all but two cases (one stepfather, one boyfriend). The offender suffered from alcoholism in 37% of confirmed cases versus 10% of the unconfirmed cases. In terms of the mothers' diagnoses, there was one case of schizophrenia in each group. Four mothers bringing about false accusations were diagnosed as having paranoia and two as having hysteria, whereas there was only one mother with hysteria and none with paranoia in the confirmed group.

One distinguishing feature in the cases of false accusation of incest was the fact that charges were uniformly brought about by the parents, not the child. In our experience of working with incest cases we have found this to be atypical, i.e., most often it is the child who initiates the charges. Second, in the four unconfirmed families versus the two confirmed, allegations did not arise during the marriage but only after separation or divorce, which raised questions as to possible ulterior motives of the parent. Some of the more common motives we encountered were: 1) the wish to get the former spouse out of the parent's life; 2) vindictiveness; and 3) crying wolf, allegations of sexual abuse as a sure fire way of getting the judge's attention and suspending visitation in situations where a parent was dissatisfied with the custody arrangement. Finally, in confirmed cases, themes of the child's play and drawings were generally consonant with the accusations.

Countertransference feelings pose a particular hazard for the child psychiatrist working with these cases. Such feelings may be directed to the child/victim as the material he or she presents reactivates helpless or incestuous feelings in the therapist. These may be evident when the therapist labels the child as seductive. Countertransference may be directed to the alleged perpetrator, preventing the child psychiatrist from hearing his or her side of the story. In particular, when allegations are false and there is question that the child has been coached, it is important to evaluate the other parent. This evaluation of the other parent has been discussed in evaluating contested child custody cases and is now a clinical axiom. However, countertransference feelings toward the perpetrator may make such an evaluation difficult in these cases.

In summary, in our experience false allegations of sexual abuse by children and their parents are rare. They do, however, occur, particularly in custody cases. Much as in malingering, which is generally rare in psychiatric patients, but can be found in the specialized population of forensic patients where secondary gain from a malingered illness is high, an allegation of sexual abuse may be made for secondary gain on the part of a child or parent. A parent may use such allegations to obtain sole custody, to terminate visitation, to terminate parental rights, or to harass a noncustodial parent. Children may allege sexual abuse falsely because of developmental immaturity, the need to please a parent, anger at a parent, or fantasies and sexual feelings toward a parent. Such allegations need careful evaluation by experienced child psychiatrists as the outcome of such allegations has serious implications for the child's future relations with the parents.

REFERENCES

1. Ferenczi, S. Confusion of tongues between adults and the child. *International Journal of Psychoanalysis*, 1949, *30*, 225-230.
2. Katan, C. Children who were raped. *Psychoanalytic Study of the Child*, 1973, *28*, 208-224.
3. Terr, L. Children of Chowchilla: A study of psychic trauma. *The Psychoanalytic Study of the Child*, 1979, *34*, 552-623.
4. Rosenfeld, A., Nadelson, C., & Kreiger, M. Fantasy and reality in patient's reports of incest. *Journal of Clinical Psychiatry*, 1979, *40*(4), 159-164.
5. Kaplan, S., & Kaplan, S. The child's accusation of sexual abuse during a divorce and custody struggle. *The Hillside Journal of Clinical Psychiatry*, 1981, *3*(1), 81-95.
6. Peters, J. J. Children who are victims of sexual assault and the psychology of offenders. *American Journal of Psychotherapy*, 1976, *30*, 598-642.
7. Horwitz, J., Salt, P., Gomez-Schwartz, Z., & Sanzia, M. Unconfirmed cases of sexual abuse for: *Sexually Exploited Children*: Service and Research Project, Family Crisis Program for Sexually Abused Children. Division of Child Psychiatry. Tufts New England Medical Center, Boston Unpublished 1984.
8. Goodwin, J., Sahd, D., & Rada, R. Incest hoax: False accusations, false denials. *Bulletin of the American Academy of Psychiatry and the Law*, 1978, *6*(3), 269-276.
9. Green, A. Did he or didn't he? True and false allegations of sexual abuse in child custody disputes. Presented at Annual Meeting of the American and Canadian Academies of Child Psychiatry. Toronto, Ontario, October 12, 1984.
10. Brant, R. Dilemmas in court ordered evaluation of sexual abuse charges during custody and visitation proceedings. Presented at Annual Meeting of the American and Canadian Academies of Child Psychiatry. Toronto, Ontario, October 12, 1984.

Part III

THE JUVENILE OFFENDER

12

Commentary:
The Juvenile Justice System

Melvin J. Guyer

But that interest (freedom) must be qualified by the recognition that juveniles, unlike adults, are always in some form of custody. (Justice Rehnquist)(1)

The manner in which children are seen, their role in the family, in work, and in society, reflects historical and cultural perspectives. Across time and societies, the perception of children has taken on a startling degree of variation. They are variously seen as chattel, miniature adults, a cheap labor source, or a most special and protected class of citizens. In our own history, it was not long ago that children worked long hours in mines, factories, and on farms, and were "hired out" for economic gain by their parents. Children in America today are described as a precious commodity and are protected by an array of social values, economic benefits, and special laws. Public education, child labor laws, public health laws, and child protection legislation are all recent innovations reflective of the changing role of children in America.

Along with the changing role has come a certain preoccupation with children. Children are, for example, the subject of considerable behavioral science and medical research and have emerged as a specific constituency attended to by pediatricians, child psychiatrists and psychologists, child development experts, as well as government agencies specifically targeted to address their needs. For example, one of the largest governmental programs in the country, Aid to Families with Dependent Children (AFDC), was enacted into law only 50 years ago and now provides support for several million children and their families.

Accompanying this special treatment of children has been the develop-

159

ment of specialized legal institutions and particular legislation intended to meet the special needs of minors. In particular, there has been the creation of a juvenile court system, a body of juvenile law, and the emergence of a class of professionals trained to specifically address the problems of children, i.e., judges, child advocacy attorneys, social services workers, mental health professionals, and detention and rehabilitation experts. At the root of the concern for children is the notion that children are particularly helpless and vulnerable and so deserve special protection from a variety of dangers, including themselves, their parents, and exploitive social and economic interests. Along with that notion is a certain belief that if we intervene when problems first appear, we can ameliorate later difficulties; by improving the lot of children we hope the next generation of our citizens will be better off than ourselves.

The basis for an elaborate juvenile justice system is not simply a concern about children, but derives from an old and well-established principle of Anglo-American law, the parens patriae doctrine of English law. This doctrine is centuries old and articulates the principle that the state (the Crown) owes a special duty of protection to those who are not fully able to protect themselves. Those coming under this mantle of protection have historically included the aged, the insane, the impoverished, and the young. They receive protection from the state not simply because they deserve it, but because, under the parens patriae doctrine, it is the right and duty of the state to protect them. This distinction becomes important in juvenile law because the state's intervention is founded upon a theory of the *state's* right to do so, not the subject's right to be helped. This same distinction is also important when considering the state's intervention on behalf of the mentally ill. Intervention on a person's behalf may not always be sought and may be unwelcomed by the beneficiary of intervention. However, if the legal right rests with the intervener, rather than the beneficiary, the intervention can be imposed—as it is in the involuntary commitment of the mentally ill or the assertion of juvenile court jurisdiction over a minor.

The juvenile court, whose history is rather brief, began with the legal theory and social ideology that minors should be treated differently than adults. The juvenile justice system has developed on the principle that minors require protection and guidance from the state, not judgment, justice, or punishment. For that reason, since the earliest days of juvenile courts, broad discretion has been given to judges and related judicial agencies to deal with the minors who come under the jurisdiction of the court. An essential legal difference between minors and adults, as bluntly stated in the beginning quote from Justice Rehnquist, is that juveniles are, ordinarily, always "in custody." Usually, parents are the custodians, but assertion of juvenile court jurisdiction shifts some of the custodial power over the minor from the parent to the state. The state, through its juvenile court, assumes parental prerogatives over minors and attempts to deal with minors with a paternalism consistent with the parens patriae doctrine and without the formality of adult proceedings.

The growth in the sheer size and scope of juvenile court activity in recent decades has altered it from a legal entity concerned with and responsive to the specific needs of individual children to a rather large and cumbersome judicial/social bureaucracy with a heavy and expanding case load and a broadening jurisdiction. An example of this expansion is the recent enactment of mandatory reporting laws for suspected child abuse/neglect, which has greatly increased court referrals in the last 10 years.

The flexibility of approach to individual cases, which was a goal of the juvenile court, has been accomplished in part by an absence of the fixed procedural and evidentiary rules that are characteristic of other courts. If judges are to be humane problem-solvers, dealing with minors somewhat as parental surrogates, then strict rules and adversarial trappings would hamper their effectiveness in carrying out the court's objectives: to protect the minor and provide benign intervention when it is decided that help is needed.

Today, the fundamental dilemma of the juvenile court system results from the fact that when intervention, even though intended as benign, is based upon a coercive right of the state, rather than upon the discretion of the beneficiary, there will be inevitable conflicts of interest between those who provide help and those who are the sometimes unwilling recipients of the state's attention. In the adult court system, the tension between the state and the individual's interests is modulated by constitutional due process safeguards and an adversarial process that expressly recognizes the different interests of the state and the individual. Until the landmark Supreme Court decision *In re Gault* (2), it was supposed that the minor needed no such protections because the state, through its juvenile courts, *defined* the child's interests and would act in furtherance of those interests. *Gault* recognized that the juvenile courts did not always serve the minor's interests and that broad discretion sometimes led to arbitrary decisions and harmful results. It was acknowledged that the minor needed to be protected from the state at precisely the point when the state was attempting to protect the minor. What followed from this was the extension to juveniles of some of the same procedural and evidentiary rules that already protected adults.

The emergence of new legal rights for minors is discussed later in this chapter, but suffice it here to note that many child advocates believe that the interests of minors are better served through limiting the flexibility of the juvenile court process and requiring that the state, in its legal dealings with minors, treat them more as adults than as children. This form of advocacy arises from a belief that the juvenile court, acting with broad powers of jurisdiction and intervention over minors and their families, has the potential to do more harm than good; and so there should be a limiting of the scope of juvenile jurisdiction and a strengthening of procedural safeguards.

The juvenile justice system today stands at a watershed; broadreaching proposals to modify the court have been promulgated (3) and they promise to curtail the powers of the court in the jurisdiction, adjudication, and disposition of the cases brought to it. These new modifications acknowledge that the juvenile court system, in its present form, cannot, in fact, carry out the high principles of the parens patriae doctrine. They argue for substantial changes in the court's role in dealing with the problems of minors and their families, and that *less* rather than more intervention serves the minor's and society's interests. Following these introductory comments, the chapter will focus on historical review of the juvenile court, including several important Supreme Court cases which are bellwethers of change.

ORIGINS OF THE JUVENILE COURT

Anglo-American legal history describes the origin of many specialized courts that began to emerge centuries ago in England and are reflected in our current legal system. The array of courts that makes up our judicial structure is based upon such considerations as *subject matter* of the legal issue, for example, civil or criminal matters; degree of seriousness of the matters at issue, i.e., felony or misdemeanor; claims by citizens specifically against a state or its agency, i.e., tax tribunals, etc. Jurisdiction of a court might also depend upon the citizenship or place of residence of the parties to a legal dispute. Matters such as trusts and wills, civil commitments, divorces, and adoptions may also be adjudicated before courts having special jurisdiction for resolving those specific issues.

One such specialized court system is the "juvenile court," although a more accurate description would be "the juvenile court system," since that court often includes a number of ancillary agencies and specialized satellite units that complement its adjudication activity. Surprisingly, the present juvenile court system, unlike most other components of the legal system, does not have extensive origins in English jurisprudence. Those aspects of Old England that are found in our Juvenile Court arise from the long tradition in English law that *children* (or "infants," as those under the age of majority are sometimes called) are to be treated differently than adults in certain legal matters. These circumstances include a child's lack of capacity to form the sort of "intent" necessary to commit certain crimes; or to have the requisite "reasonableness" to be held accountable for negligent behavior in tort actions; or the requisite knowledge to enter into binding legal contracts to perform services, provide goods, or purchase property. These legal differences in the treatment of children owe their origin to a view of children as subject to the total control of their parents—a perception of children as being somewhat like parental property.

A related legal concept, which led to the specialized legal treatment of children, resulted from the parens patriae power exercised by the English Crown. This is the power and duty of the Crown to serve as the special protector of those disabled by age (either too young or too old), poverty, or infirmity (mental or physical), and who are, therefore, unable to adequately provide for and protect their own best interests. In these instances, once it was concluded that the individual either had not yet gained the capacity to adequately look after his own interests (children) or had lost his capacity to look after himself (the aged and infirm, and mentally ill), the Crown would substitute its judgment for that of the disadvantaged individual and, accordingly, plan and provide for the individual what the Crown held to be in his or her best interests. An important historical note is that the Crown administered such special treatment to legally impaired persons in the setting of a general court system and applied the exceptions required by the parens patriae power without creating courts of special jurisdiction to deal particularly with the problems, both social and legal, of children and other disadvantaged persons.

The legal invention of a Juvenile Court was through recent legislative action in the United States, and was not directly inherited from English legal tradition, but instead evolved through legislative enactment at the state level. Courts specifically designated as "juvenile courts" were created at the turn of the century. Illinois is the first state to have enacted such legislation in its 1899 Illinois Juvenile Court Act (4), which created a juvenile court that was essentially noncriminal in nature. These early juvenile courts were designed to provide for abandoned and delinquent children. In dealing with delinquents, the juvenile courts placed emphasis on reform (places of detention were called "reform schools"). Since each child's reform needs differed, juvenile courts could maintain jurisdiction until either "reform" was achieved or the child aged beyond the jurisdiction of the court.

JURISDICTION

As one looks at current practice in the juvenile courts, it is clear that their jurisdiction is over *children*, although obviously, in most instances, parents also come under the jurisdiction of those courts as a necessary consequence of the state's exercise of legal power over children. To have jurisdiction over children in the juvenile court means to have responsibility for solving or dealing with the various problems that children find themselves in. Such problems include two broad classes and one ill-defined middle ground of jurisdiction. First, the juvenile courts have jurisdiction over children who require the *protection* of the state (its parens patriae power) because of parental neglect, abuse, abandonment, or similar situations that require child protection or because of an inadequacy, failure, or absence of private (intrafamily) means for meeting the child's physical and psychological needs. Examples of such unavailability occur, for example, when the parent is incarcerated and cannot provide for private childcare. Similarly, a parent may suffer from a disabling mental illness which so interferes with her capacity to provide for her child's needs that the responsibility to do so shifts to the state through the statutes that bring the child under the jurisdictional provisions of the juvenile court.

Children also come under the jurisdiction of the juvenile court when they are charged with a violation of the criminal code of the state. General laws that define adult criminal acts, i.e., theft, rape, embezzlement, or murder, are (with a few special exceptions) also "criminal" acts when committed by children—at least children above a certain minimum age. However, while adult criminal defendants are brought before certain trial courts depending upon the severity of the crime committed (e.g., misdemeanors may be under the jurisdiction of one court while felonies are brought before another court), any act committed by a juvenile, who is to be tried as a juvenile, will be brought before the juvenile court. Thus, adults are tried by courts having jurisdiction defined by the *laws* that are violated, while the juvenile courts have jurisdictions defined by the *persons* who violated the laws.

Several important differences result from this distinction in jurisdictional basis. Juvenile courts, because their jurisdiction is person-based, are neither civil nor criminal courts, although they are sometimes called upon to adjudicate criminal charges and apply procedures similar to adult courts. Having their own specific procedural rules, a philosophy of rehabilitation rather than deterrence or punishment, and a jurisdiction that ends when the defendant (or convicted minor) reaches the age of majority makes the approach to jurisprudence of minors quite different as compared to adults. The child who commits an act defined as crime by a general criminal code is not adjudicated as a criminal suspect but, instead, in keeping with the philosophy of the juvenile court, is viewed as a child with a problem and in need of the protection of the state, rather than being seen as a person who *is* a problem from whom *society* must be protected. This is an essential difference between general and juvenile courts: The child is viewed as an individual who requires state intervention, for the *child's* benefit and protection, even when the child is found to have committed an act which, if committed by an adult, would constitute a crime.

The special parens patriae obligation of the state to children has created a certain awkwardness in this court's dealings with juvenile delinquency defendants. Acts of delinquency committed by children signal a child who has special problems and who is in need of remedial intervention and the assistance of the state, rather than the imposition of criminal sanctions and societal retribution. The supposedly nonadversarial relationship between the state and the juvenile defendant is reflected in the manner in which cases involving juveniles are captioned: *"In re Doe,"* while with adults it is *"The People* v. *Doe."* Child protection proceedings are captioned in the same way as delinquency cases, i.e., *"In re Doe."* This is due to the underlying legal theory that matters involving children, whether the child is victim or perpetrator, are circumstances in which the state must intercede on behalf of the child who is, for either reason, in trouble.

The most controversial area of juvenile court jurisdiction involves those minors who are designated as "persons in need of supervision" (PINS). This label is given to minors who, in some manner or other, have been troublesome to someone—a parent, a school official, or police personnel. These "troublesome" minors have typically done things that would not be illegal if they were done by adults. For example, a minor who disobeys a parent, or who is truant from school, or who is idling his time away may be brought under the jurisdiction and control of a juvenile court. Obviously, an adult doing these same things would not be subject to judicial action.

What makes the PINS designation controversial is that it is vaguely defined, perhaps unconstitutionally so. This vagueness is an invitation to an arbitrary exercise of the court's power over certain individuals and particular behaviors once the PINS designation is given to the child. Also, the nature and consequences of the subsequent "supervision" that the state provides are also sometimes arbitrary. For example, because the court has continuing jurisdiction over a minor designated as a PINS, supervision may continue indefinitely throughout the individual's period of minority, even though no crime has been committed and there is no risk to the child of parental abuse or neglect. In some situations there is reason to be concerned that a PINS designation may do more harm than good to the "supervised" minor.

Aside from the stigma of coming under court jurisdiction, certain interventions intended to solve a vaguely-defined problem only serve to worsen it or to create new problems. The PINS designation had its parallel in adult law where certain "status offenses" resulted in criminal convictions. Such adult "status offenses" were found unconstitutional some years ago. For example, *being* an alcoholic, or a drug addict, or a vagrant no longer constitutes a crime where adults are concerned; however, for juveniles, such a status constitutes grounds for court jurisdiction. Both socially and legally, minors are seen to be different than adults and so the nature of the legal rights they have remains a question of debate. The juvenile courts are not so much active participants in this debate, but instead mirror how the debate proceeds.

ADJUDICATION

Because of its centralizing function, referrals of children and families to the juvenile court now come from many sources. Police agencies, schools, physicians, hospitals, and the families themselves are common sources of referrals and petitions to the juvenile court. Whatever the referral source, the referral of a problem child also identifies a family with problems. A referral may lead to an adjudication (neglect, delinquency, or PINS) by the court, which may result in the court asserting jurisdiction over the referred child, with other family members also being subject to court intervention. Unlike the adult courts, where adjudication is essentially the end of the court's judicial work (criminal sentencing is often only secondary to adjudication, with probation departments and statutes setting the parameters of sentencing), the juvenile court's primary activity begins *after* adjudication.

The adjudication of a minor in a delinquency matter has the same stated purpose as in a child protection proceeding, namely, to allow a juvenile court to take jurisdiction over a child in trouble and, through that jurisdiction, to allow the court to move on to what is its primary activity: the dispositional process that follows adjudication. This dispositional phase is used to provide those "services" that, in the court's opinion, the child's "best interests" require. In some delinquency adjudications, it may be determined by the juvenile court that a period of detention (i.e., incarceration) may serve the child's interests by allowing the state authorities an opportunity to rehabilitate, restrain, and protect the child, which may include protecting the child from the adverse consequences of the child's own behavior.

Detention for "protection" has become a matter of considerable debate among legal scholars and experts on juvenile law. The "philosophy" of protection of the child was present from the enactment of the first legislation that established juvenile courts in America. Because of the benign mission of the courts, broad leeway and considerable discretion were granted to judges who had jurisdiction over children. However, leeway and discretion to formulate orders affecting children (and their families) were accompanied by a corresponding relaxation of procedures and evidentiary rules, those "due process" requirements that limit the power of the state in criminal proceedings in adult courts. Because juvenile courts were not construed as criminal courts, even when children were brought before the court on petitions alleging violation of criminal codes, the lack of adherence to the due process protections accorded adult defendants was seen as an adjunct to the state's benign intervention on behalf of the child.

Unfortunately, what sounded well in theory could sometimes work against the interests of children. Certain patterns of adjudication occurred in some juvenile courts that resulted in children being treated more harshly than adults for similar offenses, and being brought under the court's jurisdiction under lower and sometimes arbitrary evidentiary thresholds. These patterns also led to the establishment of the power of the court to base its jurisdiction upon the *status* of the defendant rather than the *behavior* of the individual brought before the court. Put another way, juvenile courts have their jurisdiction founded upon the *status* of the persons (minors) brought before them, rather than the *subject matter* of the issues at hand.

Children (minors) are treated differently by the courts because we perceive children to be different than other people. During their minority, children are subject to the legitimate control; custody; and direction of others, typically their parents, and their teachers; and to a greater degree than any other group of citizens except prisoners and mental patients. We accept such treatment of children because our concept of them is that they are persons lacking the full capacities of reason and judgment and, as a class, are in need of special protection. This protection extends through specific laws applicable to children when they have problems and a limitation of their autonomy by a delegation to their parents (or guardians) of the right to make decisions on their behalf and to impose a "best interest" criterion for planning for their welfare, rather than allowing the minor to pursue his own preferences in his conduct and decision making. This is a critical and basic difference in the legal treatment of children versus adults.

DISPOSITION

The dispositional (postadjudication) phase of juvenile court proceedings is the time when an array of social services can be drawn upon to alleviate the problems defined in the adjudicatory phase. Because of this, the juvenile courts often find themselves continuing their jurisdiction in certain cases for months or years, following children through treatment programs, detention centers, or foster care facilities. Regularly scheduled "review hearings" are required for children who come under the court's jurisdiction and who are adjudicated as neglected or delinquent. While these review hearings are sometimes only perfunctory, this continuing review process does underscore the uniqueness of the juvenile court's function as a social rather than a judicial agency.

The enactment of various federal social welfare programs, beginning in the 1930s, simply increased the availability of services that juvenile courts could draw upon. Today, extensive federal-state programs, including Medicaid, Child Protective Services, Departments of Social Services, and drug and alcohol rehabilitation programs, allow the juvenile court to act as a coordinating agency for delivering social services to children and their families.

Because the juvenile court deals with a variety of social problems through the coordination and delivery of social services, one must ask whether it operates in an effective manner or whether the social needs of certain children and their families could be served in a better way. The judicial power of the court allows it to *order* social services, both from the agencies which provide them and for the recipients over whom the court has jurisdiction. Because of the court's power to impose its orders it has become a central coordinator of social services. Unfortunately, the judicial character of the court creates inevitable difficulties in efforts to assure smooth and efficient delivery of services to children and families. The requirements of due process, evidentiary rules, appointment of counsel, and other trappings of jurisprudence slow down, complicate, and sometimes prevent the rapid delivery of assistance, especially in the cases of petitions involving abandoned, neglected, or abused children.

In addition, the adjudication phase in contested petitions, as a prior condition for dispositional intervention, sets an adversarial tone to what is meant to be a benign intervention. Adversarial litigation often sets the stage for defeating the effectiveness of later remedial interventions by putting the parties into opposition. For example, Protective Services workers, who testify against a parent during adjudication, are expected to establish a professional-client relationship with the parent as part of the services provided after the dispositional phase. The difficulties in establishing a helping relationship following participation in an adversarial one are evident.

IN RE GAULT

To briefly summarize, the legal presumption that children lack the capacity for decision making is consistent with the philosophy that there must be a corresponding dilution in their culpability for any criminal acts they might commit. Consequently, since its inception (and until recently), the juvenile court has treated the minors brought before it in an informal manner, dispensing social interventions and providing social services, rather than meting out justice or imposing punishments. Generally, juvenile proceedings are procedurally relaxed and the usual due process safeguards for protecting the constitutional rights accorded adult criminal defendants are not all used.

A landmark Supreme Court case changed all this and focused great public attention on the juvenile justice system. The case, *In re Gault* (5), found that the juvenile court system sometimes treated minors more harshly than criminal defendants were treated in adult courts. The deliberate relaxation and absence of formal procedures in the juvenile courts, which were intended to allow compassionate management of juvenile offenders, had instead led to such practices as indeterminate sentencing of minors to "reform schools" and the imposition of court jurisdiction on weaker evidentiary standards than would be required to convict an adult defendant. The supposedly nonadversarial character of juvenile proceedings made fact-finding casual and made the appointment of counsel for the juvenile seem unnecessary. Similarly, direct and cross-examination of sworn witnesses was seen as unnecessary.

Finding that the informal nature of the juvenile system did not, in fact, protect minors, the *Gault* decision held that in order to truly protect minors in delinquency proceedings, they must be afforded certain fundamental due process rights. The court indicated that the right to notice of charges, the right to legal counsel, the Fifth Amendment privilege against self-incrimination, and the right to call and confront witnesses were the *minimum* procedural protections that were constitutionally required in delinquency proceedings in order to protect minors from the very system of adjudication that was intended to address their special needs. The *Gault* decision was significant for a number of reasons, but perhaps most important was its recognition that juveniles should be entitled to some of the same constitutional rights previously reserved only for adult criminal defendants, and that the extension of procedural due process rights to minors was required to protect them from unfair, arbitrary, and sometimes harsh treatment in the juvenile justice system. Implicit in the *Gault* decision was an acknowledgment that the juvenile court system had somehow failed to provide minors the special protection and gentle treatment that our society felt children deserved. Ironically, the *Gault* Court concluded that minors should be protected from the state's supposedly benign attitude toward them by requiring the state to treat children more as adult defendants and provide them a modicum of due process protections whenever the state exercised its parens patriae power.

BEYOND *GAULT*

The *Gault* decision constitutes a watershed in the legal rights of minors. Having acknowledged that children require certain procedural safeguards when involved with the agency of the state intended to protect their interests, the Court began an era of expansion of the legal rights and protections of children both against the benign intervention of the state and against intervention by their parents. Several notable Supreme Court cases widened the ambit of children's rights, building upon the foundation set down in *Gault*. Included in these right-granting cases were: *In re Winship* (6), which held that the stringent evidentiary standard of "beyond a reasonable doubt" was required in delinquency proceedings; and *Breed* v. *Jones* (7), in which the constitutional protection against double jeopardy was extended to juveniles.

Bellotti v. *Baird* (8) declared the rights of minor females, in certain circumstances, to obtain elective abortions without parental consent and without providing parents with notice of the abortion decision and the medical procedure. It is relevant to note that the more general question of minors' rights to medical treatment (and the complementary right to refuse medical treatment) is an active front line in the struggle over the scope of legal rights that our society will provide to minors.

Especially interesting is the expanding access that minors are obtaining to mental health services without prior parental consent and with some assurance that their medical records will be treated as confidential even when their parents seek access to them. It is sufficient to note that, in certain matters (i.e., minors' abortions and their access to birth control devices and prescriptions), juvenile courts are no longer free to impose the state's "best interests" judgment when evaluating the behavior of children. Instead, they must defer to the informed decision making of the minor. Michigan, for example, modified its mental health code in 1984 in a number of ways which affect minors' rights. In particular, it now provides for minors 14 years and over to receive certain outpatient mental health services without the consent or notification of their parents (9).

Another significant Supreme Court case following *Gault* involved the commitment of minors to mental hospitals. Although the involuntary civil commitment of adults was dealt with in *O'Connor* v. *Donaldson* (10), where the present "dangerousness" to self or others standard was outlined, the civil commitment of minors has typically been left to the discretion of parents in conjunction with the judgment of an admitting physician. In most states there are laws that permit the "voluntary commitment" of minors by their parents (or, in the absence of the parent, a guardian or court designee). Questions concerning children's rights in this area center around the procedures that define the extent to which children can object to "voluntary" civil commitment, and what procedural safeguards must be made available to them if they object to hospitalization, even if it is sought to further the child's best interests. This is so because civil commitment infringes upon the minors's Fifth Amendment "liberty" interest and, therefore, the Constitution requires procedural safeguards.

The constitutional issue of the civil commitment of minors becomes how much process is due? This question was taken up by the Supreme Court in *Parham* v. *J.R.* (11), where the Court set minimum procedural safeguards that must accompany the civil commitment of children. The *Parham* Court balanced the special dependent status of minors and the presumption that their parents would be acting on their behalf against the child's own liberty interests and concluded that although minors were entitled to some due process protections in civil commitments, the amount of process due fell a good bit short of that afforded to adults who similarly objected to hospitalization.

Interestingly, while both *Parham* and *Bellotti* were decided by the Supreme Court in the same year, one appeared to expand the rights of juveniles while the other held that minors were not entitled to the same procedural rights afforded to adults. Both cases involved aspects of medical care (abortion and psychiatric treatment), and in both cases the Court seemed to allow the substitution of impartial medical judgment for the more formal decision-making procedures of the juvenile courts. What these two cases appear to have in common is that they remove from the juvenile courts to the private sphere certain decisions affecting the welfare and well-being of minors. It is open to interpretation as to whether this emerging trend in the appellate courts counts as a tacit acknowledgment that the juvenile courts have not lived up to our expectations that they could effectively oversee important aspects of the lives of minors. The question also emerges of whether narrowing of the juvenile courts' supervisory jurisdiction powers is called for, either through the safeguard protections required by *Gault* and its progeny in delinquency proceedings, or instead through a narrowing of the range of children's problems that can be brought before the juvenile courts.

CURRENT ISSUES

The central issue involving "current practice" in the juvenile courts is the extent to which minors are to be given the legal rights routinely granted to competent adults. This issue has been addressed in several landmark United States Supreme Court decisions. Each decision represents a significant shift in social policy concerning minors. *In re Gault* (12) marked the end of the era of informality and procedural laxity that had characterized the juvenile courts since their origination in the Illinois Juvenile Court Act of 1899. In *Gault*, basic due process protections were made a requirement in certain delinquency proceedings. By this decision, minors were extended a number of the procedural safeguards given to adult defendants. However, the dispositional freedom of the juvenile courts was unaffected by *Gault*.

Another step in giving minors procedural safeguards was taken by *In re Winship* (13), which held that the standard of proof in juvenile delinquency proceedings had to be as stringent as that for adult defendants. A later case, *McKeiver* v. *Pennsylvania* (14), upheld a state rule that denied juvenile defendants the right to a jury trial (a right that is guaranteed to adult defendants). The holding in this case was the result of a judicial balancing of due process requirements for the individual's protection against the parens patriae rights of the state. What is important about this case is what was balanced: It illustrates that in dealing with minors, the courts construe the parens patriae power as one that runs against the due process requirements of the Constitution. The pull between these interests characterizes the effort to draw a line between minority and adulthood, using access to legal rights as the boundary. This tension between individual rights and state paternalism is highlighted in two U.S. Supreme Court cases, one of them only decided in 1984, the other decided in early 1985.

The first of these cases, *Schall* v. *Martin* (15), dealt with a New York law that permitted the pretrial detention of a juvenile accused of being a delinquent when there was a court finding of a "serious risk" that the juvenile might commit a criminal act prior to the time of the initial judicial hearing on the delinquency petition. A due process constitutional challenge was made to this statute in a class action suit which argued that it allowed detention without due process and so resulted in the imposition of punishment for unadjudicated acts. The Supreme Court decision overturned the earlier Court of Appeals decision that the statute was unconstitutional and decided, instead, that preventive detention served the legitimate state interest of protecting the juvenile from the deleterious consequences of any future criminal acts that he might commit while awaiting trial. Thus, the majority accepted preventive detention for juveniles, but not for adults, by construing it as a benign intervention that protected the minor.

A vigorous minority dissent in *Schall* argued on several grounds that the New York law was unconstitutional, but especially that the actual use of preventive detention appeared punitive rather than preventive and also arbitrary, given the inability of magistrates or anyone else to accurately predict the "risk" of someone committing a future criminal or dangerous act. Because preventive detention has been declared an unconstitutional denial of due process when adults are involved, the *Schall* opinion suggests that in the name of protecting minors, the courts will deny minors some of the constitutional protections that were first given them in *Gault* some 17 years earlier and that are generally recognized as rights owed to adult criminal defendants.

The irony of the holding in *Schall* is that it relies upon a parens patriae philosophy of child protection, of the sort which predated *Gault*, to justify a statute that permits juvenile defendants to be treated more harshly than their adult counterparts. Yet, it was precisely harsh and arbitrary treatment that led the *Gault* Court to extend due process safeguards to juvenile offenders as a shield against the sometimes severe consequences of an unfettered parens patriae approach to juvenile justice. *Schall* is significant in that it finds pretrial detention to be a constitutionally permissible infringement upon a juvenile's right to liberty, although this infringement is not permissible with adults. The essential rationale underlying the decision for the holding is stated succinctly by Justice Rehnquist, writing for the majority:

> The juvenile's countervailing interest in freedom from institutional restraints, even for the brief time involved here, is undoubtedly substantial as well. See *In re Gault*, 387 U.S., at 27. But that interest must be qualified by the recognition that juveniles, unlike adults, are always in some form of custody. (16)

A bellwether of the future direction of juvenile justice is found in *New Jersey* v. *T.L.O.*, a case decided by the Supreme Court that deals with the extent to which important constitutional protections given to adults will be extended to minors (17). The central issue in the *T.L.O.* case is the extent to which minors will be given constitutional protections against warrantless searches carried out without "probable cause." This new juvenile law decision deals with whether juveniles should be given the constitutional rights of adult criminal defendants. *Schall* dealt with preventive detention; the *T.L.O.* case deals with warrantless searches of minors and the admissibility in juvenile proceedings of incriminating evidence found through such searches. It appears clear from the facts in T.L.O. that if an adult were the subject of the warrantless search, the search would be illegal and the evidence found would be inadmissible in any criminal proceeding. The simple policy question raised by *T.L.O.* was whether children should be given the same protection from warrantless searches now extended to adults. The decision, by a six-three majority of the Court, is that they are not entitled to "adult" protections. The facts in this new decision are important.

Briefly, a public school official searched a high school student's purse for cigarettes. Cigarettes were found, but the official continued to search and also found some marijuana. Because of this, delinquency proceedings were initiated against the student in a New Jersey Juvenile Court, and the marijuana was offered into evidence. Its admissibility was objected to by the minor's attorney on the grounds that it was found during a warrantless search, one conducted without "probable cause." Such searches generally violate the Fourth Amendment and so the evidence is subject to the "exclusionary rule," which prevents its use in criminal proceedings. Upon appeal, the New Jersey Supreme Court agreed with the minor and found the search of her purse illegal and so held that the evidence found there could not be used in delinquency proceedings against the minor. The State of New Jersey appealed this decision to the U.S. Supreme Court and the U.S. Justice Department filed a brief with the Supreme Court arguing on behalf of New Jersey. The Justice Department's brief urged that school officials be given wider power to conduct searches of minor students than is constitutionally permitted law enforcement officials.

The Justice Department's argument to the Supreme Court for a weakened Fourth Amendment constitutional standard for minors was based upon a stated rationale that such a constitutional narrowing is necessary to reduce crime and disorder in schools. Also advanced in the Justice Department's brief is the legal theory that teachers have parentlike responsibilities and so should be given greater authority to investigate and supervise the conduct of students, including the authority to conduct warrantless searches without "probable cause" of students' persons and property. This is, of course, a parens patriae justification for a restriction of the minor's constitutional rights.

This case is interesting because it illustrates the state's effort to deal with a general social problem—high crime rates—by diluting the constitutional rights of a particular class of persons, namely minors. Although the legal argument of New Jersey and the Justice Department is couched in terms of the parens patriae theory, the result sought is the protection of children through their prosecution in delinquency proceedings. This type of "protection" is obviously not sought by minor defendants. *T.L.O.* epitomizes the dilemma of the juvenile courts. It illustrates that giving special, "protected" status to minors is often accomplished through abridging some of their constitutional rights. Theory and fact concerning juvenile law are often at variance. "Protected" proceedings in juvenile courts often treat minors more harshly than adults for similar offenses. It may be an unavoidable fact that so long as minors are a specially "protected" group, they will also be an especially vulnerable group, since the power given to juvenile courts to protect minors creates the opportunity to overreach. It is not a new observation that benign interventions are sometimes riskier to the protected than benign neglect.

Some of the findings of the United States District Court in a 1982 case in Oregon are quoted below to illustrate the risks. The case concerned the constitutionality of the preadjudication detention of minors (preventive detention), which was struck down by the U.S. District Court in Oregon, but subsequently found constitutional by the United States Supreme Court in the *Schall* case. In its findings, the District Court reported the conditions found in an Oregon juvenile detention facility. The findings are shocking and seem more descriptive of Devil's Island than the American Northwest.

> Toilet facilities are not screened from view and children using these toilet facilities are visible to other children and to corrections officers.
>
> Children are sometimes placed in either of two isolation cells. These are 3' × 8' windowless concrete block rooms, barren of all furniture and furnishings. Sometimes it is very cold in the isolation cells. Near the center of the isolation cell there is a sewer hole, which is the only facility for urination and defecation.
>
> Lighting and the mechanisms for flushing the sewer hole for each isolation cell are controlled outside the cell by the corrections staff. Lights in the isolation cells are sometimes left on or off for long periods of time. Sometimes the sewer hole is not flushed for long periods. When the mechanism for the sewer hole is flushed by a corrections staff officer, water and sewage gushes onto the cell floor.
>
> The isolation cells are located across from a corridor from the adult male dormitory cell, which holds up to 18 prisoners. . . .
>
> There are no written standards for placement of children in isolation. There is no one designated to determine if and when a child should be placed in isolation. There is no absolute limit to the period of time that a child can be held in isolation. Isolation cells have been used when children were intoxicated or under the influence of drugs. Children have also been placed in isolation for perceived offenses or disputes between children held in the same cell. There is no psychological screening of children placed in isolation. No log is maintained when a child is placed in isolation.
>
> No medical screening procedure is used for children admitted other than a visual inspection by an untrained corrections officer.
>
> There is no daily sick call for children. There is no regular program for a doctor or a registered nurse to visit the jail to identify or attend to the medical needs of children held. Emergency medical equipment in the jail consists of a first aid kit and an oxygen tank. Corrections officers determine whether a child needs medical treatment based upon perception, common sense, and experience.
>
> There are no special rules or procedures for the treatment of emotionally disturbed children who panic in a jail setting. There is no emergency medical health service. There are no psychiatrists, psychologists, or counselors on call. Frequently children do not see their juvenile court counselors at all during their incarceration in the jail. There is no written log kept of juvenile court counselor visits to the jail.
>
> There are no educational programs for children. Children are not

allowed to have books or magazines or pencils and paper. This policy is not the jail's policy, but the policy of the Juvenile Department. Corrections officers have been instructed by the Juvenile Department not to give children reading material or pencils and paper.

There are no recreational programs, materials, or activities for children.

There are no facilities or equipment for exercise.

Children are treated considerably differently from adults. Adults have access to books, television, radio, cards, and other recreational materials; children do not. Adults are allowed to have underwear brought to them; children are not. Adults have regular visitation and may visit with friends as well as families; children have no regularly scheduled visitation. Adults are allowed to send and receive mail; children are not allowed to send or receive mail. Adults are provided paper, writing material, envelopes, and stamps. Children are not allowed to have paper, writing material, envelopes, or stamps. Adults are allowed to make one phone call upon admission; children are not allowed to make a phone call upon admission. Adults are allowed to make phone calls during their period of incarceration. Children, prior to the court entering its preliminary injunction dated June 10, 1981, were prohibited from making phone calls without Juvenile Department permission. . . . An inmate manual governs the conduct of adults held. Children are not advised what behavior will result in disciplinary action or sanctions. There are no grievance procedures for children.

The visitation policy for children is not in writing. There are no standards within the Juvenile Department for granting or denying visits with children. No contact visits are allowed. Parents and detained children must talk to one another by means of a telephone and are separated by shatter-proof glass. Jailers sometimes will not tell inquiring parents whether or not their child is, in fact, in jail.

Corrections officers are basically jail staff. They have no training and little time to work with children. For example, if a child locked in a cell is screaming or yelling, the officer may go to the cell and yell, "Quiet down." The personnel are not prepared or trained to treat children in other than a manner consistent with a maximum security lock-up facility. (18)

The judicial management of juveniles has been a topic of debate for almost a century prior to the enactment of the first juvenile court legislation. The body of law that makes up juvenile practice has been primarily a matter of state legislation. Statutes governing delinquency, abuse/neglect, and PINS jurisdiction may vary significantly from state to state and, within states, from court to court. This variability may serve the useful purpose of allowing the state, or a particular judge, to tailor an intervention to meet a particular juvenile's needs. But the variability of legislation and the broad discretion in judicial practice may also result in the arbitrary treatment of juveniles (and their families). Broad legislation invites imprecise and arbitrary guidelines for state intervention. This, in turn, results in minors in similar circumstances being treated quite differently by the courts and related agencies. This lack of consistency erodes our sense of fairness and justice and often leaves juveniles, their families, and the courts somewhat unsure of the court's proper role in dealing with juvenile problems. The disparity between juvenile law theory and juvenile law practice becomes striking by comparing the good intentions of parens patriac detention with the bleak findings that were noted by the Oregon Federal District Court.

JUVENILE JUSTICE STANDARDS

Increasing debate over the role of the juvenile court, fueled by an expanding case load (resulting in part from mandatory child abuse reporting laws), as well as social science research questioning the efficacy of government interventions into family problems, has been the catalyst for a major review of the underlying purpose and philosophy of the juvenile court system. For the first time since its inception, the entire juvenile court system has been the subject of thorough study and review.

The most ambitious effort to study, assess, and reform the juvenile justice system is found in a series of Juvenile Justice Standards that were prepared under the supervision of the Joint Commission on Juvenile Justice Standards. This effort, jointly undertaken by the American Bar Association and the Institute of Judicial Administration, began in 1971 and continued through the decade. All aspects of the Juvenile Justice System were studied and proposed new standards were promulgated to serve as model guidelines for revising state juvenile codes, as well as for promoting thought and discussion on current problems in the juvenile justice system and the existing sociolegal approach to child welfare. A total of 23 volumes have been published since the Juvenile Justice Standards Project began its work. It is impossible to summarize here the monumental effort that the Juvenile Justice Standards represent.

It is important to note that the Standards do propose to significantly curtail the jurisdictional reach of the juvenile justice system in several important respects. The Standards Relating to Abuse and Neglect (19), for example, would allow for court intervention only under much more restrictive circumstances than those permitted by existing child protection statutes. The child abuse and neglect Standards require quite specific types of physical harm or serious risk of harm to exist before state intervention would be permitted. Similarly, the Standards severely restrict the assertion of coercive jurisdiction over minors who come under the presently used

PINS designation. To quote from the Standards Relating to Noncriminal Behaviors:

> These standards posit the elimination of the status offense jurisdiction of the juvenile court and the substitution of services outside the formal justice system, largely voluntarily based, on assumptions that (1) noncriminal misbehavior cases will benefit from the immediate intensive handling that this will allow, rather than the piecemeal investigation, adjudication, and referral that is now more the rule than the exception; (2) the majority of service and helping time should be at the onset of the problem, when the family confronts a crisis, rather than weeks or months later after attitudes and positions have hardened with the passage of time; and (3) such services will be of greater help if they are not coerced. Our experience with the divorce law has demonstrated that the legal system is too blunt an instrument to resolve the complexities of family dysfunction and that the legal system cannot by compulsion order personal relationships.... When a sixteen-year-old girl must petition the juvenile court to declare her incorrigible as the only way out of a home she finds intolerable, the ineptitude of the present mechanisms for resolving the intrafamily conflicts that status offenses represent is apparent. (20)

The publication of the Standards places the juvenile court system at a crossroads. What is proposed by the Standards is nothing less than a bold, if not revolutionary, restructuring of a system, which is motivated by a keen recognition of the harm that can result from overzealous intervention on behalf of children and their families.

Recognizing that the juvenile court system, by bits and pieces, has been transformed from a judicial entity to a hybrid social service agency with coercive power, the Standards conclude that the court cannot perform the required social services as well as alternative agencies that are clearly designated for those purposes. Attempting to provide social services through the judiciary has compromised judicial objectivity. What remains to be seen is whether needed law reform in the juvenile justice system will come about through a systematic and thorough revamping of that system, along the lines recommended by the Standards, a rather ambitious goal in that it demands we revise our thinking concerning the relationship between children, parents, and the state; or whether the juvenile system will continue to function as a broad-reaching intervenor into the lives of children and their families with any reform and modification coming primarily through the present method of slow, cumbersome judicial appellate review where harm might be redressed, but not avoided.

REFERENCES

1. Justice Rehnquist in *Schall* v. *Martin* 104 S.Ct. 2403,81 L.Ed. 2nd 207 (1984).
2. In re *Gault*, 387 U.S. 1 (1967).

3. Institute of Juvenile Justice/American Bar Association. *Juvenile Justice Standards.* Cambridge, MA: Ballinger, 1979-1982.
4. Downs, W. T. *Michigan Juvenile Court: Law and practice.* Ann Arbor, MI: I.C.L.E., 1963.
5. In re *Gault*, 1967.
6. In re *Winship*, 397 U.S. 358 (1970).
7. *Breed* v. *Jones*, 421 U.S. 519 (1975).
8. *Bellotti* v. *Baird*, 443 U.S. 622 (1979).
9. Children's Mental Health Act. Public Act 186 P.A. 1984, Michigan, M.C.L.A. § 330. 1707, 1984.
10. *O'Connor* v. *Donaldson*, 422 U.S. 563 (1975).
11. *Parham* v. *J.R.*, 442 U.S. 584 (1979).
12. In re *Gault*, 1967.
13. In re *Winship*, 1970.
14. *McKeiver* v. *Pennsylvania*, 403 U.S. 528 (1971).
15. *Schall* v. *Martin*, 104 S.Ct. 2403, 81 L.Ed. 2nd 207 (1984).
16. *Schall* v. *Martin*, 1984 at 4684.
17. *New Jersey* v. *T.L.O.*, 105 Sup.Ct. 733, 83 L.Ed. 2nd 720 (1985).
18. *D.P.* v. *Tewksbury*, 545 F. Supp. 896 (Dist. Ct., D. Oreg. 1982).
19. Institute of Juvenile Justice/American Bar Association. Standards Relating to Abuse and Neglect. *Juvenile Justice Standards.* Cambridge, MA: Ballinger, 1981.
20. Institute of Juvenile Justice/American Bar Association. Standards Relating to Noncriminal Behavior. *Juvenile Justice Standards.* Cambridge, MA: Ballinger, 1982.

13

Waiver of Juveniles to Adult Court

Elissa P. Benedek

Drawing distinctions based on age is difficult and necessarily arbitrary. Society has, however, always defined the difference between child and adult on the basis of chronological age. Such a definition has generally been based on a society's needs, not those of a child. For example, in medieval ages, a child became an adult at 21, the age at which he could support himself and his armor on a horse (1).

Differentiating between adult and child is always important as an adult has certain rights and responsibilities in a society that are denied to the child. The distinction is critical in the criminal justice system. After being accused of a crime, the adult faces both the protections and sanctions of the criminal court. Since the early 1900s, the juvenile has had criminal or delinquent behavior addressed in the theoretically more protected haven of the juvenile court.

This chapter will survey and discuss some of the current laws surrounding the waiver process. In addition, it will discuss the American Bar Association's position on the waiver process as addressed in the juvenile justice system. Finally, the role of the mental health professional in the waiver process will be discussed.

SPECIAL PROCEDURES, SANCTIONS, AND DISPOSITIONS

The focus of this chapter is on the legal and clinical issues related to waiver, the process by which the juvenile court releases juveniles from its jurisdiction and transfers them to adult criminal court. In rare instances, reverse waiver may occur, where a juvenile is transferred from the adult court to the juvenile court. However, this chapter will not address that very specialized situation.

The process of waiver is, in some states, as old as the juvenile justice system itself. However, the transfer/waiver issue did not come to national prominence until 1966 when the United States Supreme Court decided the landmark case *Kent* v. *United States* (2). In that case, the Court held that the decision to transfer a child to the criminal courts or to retain him within the juvenile system is "critically important" to the preservation of the accused juvenile's rights and to the outcome of his case. Therefore, the minor is entitled to a hearing in which he is represented by counsel, to counsel's access to all his social records and other reports considered by the juvenile court, and to a statement in the record of the reasons for the court's final decision in regard to waiver.

The term "critical" must be underscored because, in many instances, the process of waiver decides not only the juvenile's punishment for the alleged crime but also his future. For many it also begins a youngster's association with the criminal justice system, which many have alleged does not rehabilitate juveniles but only teaches them to be better criminals. Shornhurst comments:

> There is convincing evidence that most juvenile court personnel and the judges themselves regard the waiver of jurisdiction as the most *severe* sanction that may be imposed by the juvenile court. Not only is the juvenile exposed to the possibility of severe punishment but the confidentiality and individuality of juvenile proceedings is replaced by the publicity and normative concepts of penal law; the child acquires a public arrest record which, even if he is acquitted, will inhibit his rehabilitation because of the approbrium attached thereto by perspective employers; if convicted as an adult, the child may be detained well past his 21st birthday; he may lose certain civil rights and be disqualified from public employment. Moreover, if sent to a typical adult prison, he is likely to be subjected to physical and sexual abuse by older inmates and his chances for rehabilitation are likely to be decreased significantly. (3)

The aims of the juvenile justice system are treatment and rehabilitation. They are not deterrents or punishment, which are the aims of the adult criminal justice system. Society, as a whole, despite conflicting evidence, believes that the juvenile/adolescent is still in the formative stage and that with correction, treatment, and rehabilitation, there is hope for change in criminal behavior patterns. Very few professionals or citizens today believe that the adult criminal justice system has any rehabilitative function. Perhaps it may be a deterrent, and certainly it protects the public, but it is rarely a force for changed behavior.

Minimum Age Requirements

In eight jurisdictions, no minimum age is required for waiver. Theoretically, any child, no matter how young, may be prosecuted as an adult in Alaska, Arizona, Florida, Maine, New Hampshire, Oklahoma, South Carolina, Washington, West Virginia, Wyoming, and Federal Districts. More commonly, however, a minimum age is set that approaches the upper limit of the juvenile court's jurisdiction. The minimum age ranges from 10 in South Dakota, to 10 or older in Indiana for murder, to 13 or more in Georgia, Illinois, and Mississippi, but is most commonly 16 before a waiver can occur. In several states, the minimum age for transfer varies with the offense charged. For example, in New Mexico, a 15 year old can be waived for allegedly committing murder, but a juvenile must be 16 to be waived for other felonies. In Tennessee, 15 year olds can be waived for murder, manslaughter, rape, robbery with a deadly weapon, and kidnapping, but a juvenile must be 16 or more to be waived for other crimes or public offenses. As of 1978, 31 states excluded certain offenses from juvenile court jurisdiction. Twenty states excluded only traffic, watercraft, or game violations. The other 11 states excluded some serious offenses; eight also excluded some minor offenses. In Delaware, Indiana, Nevada, and Pennsylvania, persons of any age charged with a capital offense are prosecuted in adult courts.

A survey in 1977 by Sorrentino and Olsen (4) indicated that nine states amended their minimum age provisions within the past 10 years, increasing the minimum age for a waiver from one to two years, while three states, Connecticut, Hawaii, and Illinois, moved from no minimum age to age requirements of 14 to 16 years. They suggest that the trend toward a higher minimum age may indicate a social policy decision that the transfer process be restricted to or focused on older juveniles who are nearing the age limit of the juvenile court's original jurisdiction and who will automatically face prosecution as adults in a few years.

Increasing the minimal age requirements for waiver may reflect society's heightened concern that juvenile court jurisdictions may be terminated when a youngster reaches age 18, 21, or 24. Thus, youngsters who commit heinous crimes may be under the aegis of the juvenile court for only a brief period, one to three years if they are not transferred. The public may believe that one year is not just desserts for a violent crime. A social policy decision that would allow a longer period of incarceration, as is available in the adult criminal justice system, may be the real reason for increasing age limits and focusing the possibility of waiver on older offenders. Thus, a 13 year old, who commits a murder and is kept in the juvenile court system, may be in the system for five to six years, a reasonable period for attempting rehabilitation. A 16 year old may be in the system for only one or two years.

Thus, a waiver to the adult criminal justice system will allow society to incarcerate a dangerous older youth for a longer period.

The American Bar Association *Juvenile Justice Standards* regarding transfer between courts recommend that the juvenile court have jurisdiction in any proceeding against a person whose alleged conduct would constitute an offense on which a juvenile court adjudication could be based if, *at the time of the offense*, said person was not more than 17 years of age. The Bar Association recommends that no criminal court should have jurisdiction in any proceeding against any person whose alleged conduct would constitute an offense on which a juvenile court adjudication could be based, if, at the time the offense is alleged to have occurred, such person was not more than 14 years of age. Waiver could be considered, according to these standards, if at the time the alleged offense occurred, the defendant was 15, 16, or 17 and juvenile court waived disposition (5).

The various states have not yet agreed whether the age at the time of consideration of waiver ought to be the age at which time the alleged offense took place, or the age at the time the filing of the charges occurs, or the age at the time of the actual waiver proceedings. For example: In Michigan, the minimum age for waiver is 15; a child who is 14 years old at the time of an alleged wrongful act may be waived if his fifteenth birthday occurs before he is apprehended and charged. A prosecutor can circumvent the intent of the juvenile justice system by delaying the filing of charges or motions for waiver until a juvenile has reached the age necessary to become eligible for transfer, a process that became so common in one of our states that it earned the name "Texas-style waiver" after its firm acceptance in the juvenile and appellate courts in that state.

SUBSTANTIVE CRITERIA

Three prototypes of waiver of jurisdiction of a juvenile to a criminal court are the most common in all states: 1) legislative, 2) prosecutorial, and 3) judicial. In approximately 15 jurisdictions, certain serious offenses are excluded from the jurisdiction of the juvenile court by the legislative statute. For example, in Pennsylvania, a youth charged with homicide must be prosecuted in the adult criminal courts.

In eight states, prosecutors have the option of filing charges against the youth in either juvenile or criminal court. Prosecutorial waiver assumes the prosecutors are impartial and that their decisions are not susceptible to political pressure either from the electorate or the police with whom they must maintain cordial working relationships. Such an assumption may be facetious. Prosecutors must run for reelection and their political fate is often determined by how they respond to community pressures. In addition, police and prosecutors are not part of a check and balance system but often have corresponding interests. Severe community pressure may be brought to bear on prosecutors when a juvenile commits a crime that offends a community's sensibilities.

In most states, the decision to transfer is made by the juvenile court judge and is a judicial waiver. Judges may be less immune to public pressure than the prosecutors. The National Association of Juvenile Corrections found, despite the Supreme Court's decision in *Kent* v. *United States*, which held that waiver hearings must incorporate due process safeguards, that barely half the states in the United States had appropriate legal guarantees of probable cause hearings before a judge was allowed to consider waiving jurisdiction (6). In addition, a variety of studies have noted that in making a decision to waive a juvenile, no matter what the state's official legislative waiver criteria are, judges *believe* that the seriousness of the offense and the juvenile's prior record are the most important criteria in regard to waiver. These two criteria are weighted most heavily in judicial decision making (7).

GUIDELINES FOR WAIVER

As a part of the decision in *Kent* v. *United States*, the United States Supreme Court quoted a policy memorandum of the District of Columbia Juvenile Court, which was prepared in 1959 and set forth the guidelines to be considered by the courts in deciding whether to waive jurisdiction of a minor accused of a crime. About half the states in the United States have enacted standards that model upon or are substantially similar to those set forth in *Kent*. In making a decision to waive, the following criteria are most commonly considered either formally or informally. The court makes findings on them before waiver may be granted.

1) *The prior record and character of the child, his physical and mental maturity, and his patterns of living.* This standard suggests that the investigating official should obtain a prior social and family history of the child, a prior criminal history, and a psychiatric/psychological evaluation of the child at minimum. Unfortunately, a realistic determination of these aspects would require extensive psychological, psychiatric, and social evaluations of the child and his family. As juvenile court staff are limited, often untrained, and under great pressure to perform a variety of mandatory tasks, this psychological assessment may be given short shrift as compared to an assessment of the seriousness of the offense.

2) *The seriousness of the offense.* The *Juvenile Justice Standards* suggest two sets of offenses that may be considered on determining the seriousness

of the offense: Class I or Class II juvenile offenses. A Class I juvenile offense is defined in the Juvenile Delinquency and Sanctions volume of the *Juvenile Justice Standards* as "those criminal offenses for which the maximum sentence for adults would be death or imprisonment for life or a term in excess of 20 years" (8). A Class II juvenile offense is defined as an offense that would be punishable by imprisonment for more than five but no more than 20 years. Thirty-six states allow waiver for misdemeanors and it would seem only fair that those offenses that a legislature has elected to punish with severe penalties ought to be considered for waivers. Allegations of lesser criminal acts should be *insufficient* to overcome the presumption in favor of juvenile court jurisdiction.

Unfortunately, in those states which permit waiver for lesser offenses, community pressure is often the basis of the decision for waiver.

3) *Even though less serious, if the offense is part of a repetitive pattern of offenses, it would lead to a determination that the child may be beyond rehabilitation under the regular statutory juvenile procedures.* This criterion suggests that the child's prior record needs to be considered. In a survey of nearly 200 juvenile court judges to determine what considerations ought to be undertaken at the transfer hearing, the juvenile's record and prior contacts with the police, the court, and other official agencies are the second most frequently mentioned criteria, following the seriousness of the offense. Six states have adopted special transfer laws, provisions which are designed to deal severely with the recidivist. In Rhode Island and Delaware, a waiver of jurisdiction is permanent. Once transferred, a child must be prosecuted as an adult for all future offenses, regardless of their nature. The Kansas statute permits the judge to make the original waiver order applicable to any subsequent unlawful act. Unfortunately, this standard allows a child who may be involved in many activities that are not serious or heinous crimes, i.e., joyriding, to be waived if the offense is part of a "repetitive pattern."

Even more difficult is the determination that a child is beyond rehabilitation. It is difficult for professionals to assess which children can be rehabilitated. This determination is often made by probation officers on vague, unspecified criteria.

4) *The suitability of programs and facilities available to the juvenile courts for the child.* Unfortunately, there is a dearth of programs and facilities available to the juvenile offender. In Michigan, a state which is reasonably well endowed with human services, it is difficult to find a suitable mental health placement for a mentally ill juvenile who has been involved in criminal activity. The state has a forensic center for mentally ill adult offenders, but no such facility exists for juveniles. State hospital children's programs will take in an occasional mentally ill juvenile offender. However,

they are reluctant to populate their wards with such children. Private facilities rarely accept such children as they are difficult to manage, require long-term treatment, and more than likely come from impoverished families.

Most states have even fewer facilities available for such children. It is conceivable that a child who is potentially amenable may suffer total deprivation of treatment in rehabilitative programs in the juvenile system due to the state's failure to provide adequate facilities. This problem is illustrated by Sorrentino and Olsen, who note a Minnesota case where a juvenile court found that no programs exist or had been designed that could rehabilitate the child accused of armed robbery, who "is therefore not amenable to treatment as a juvenile and must be referred before prosecution as an adult" (9). Reversing the decision of the juvenile court, the Supreme Court administrator found the present unavailability of programs specifically designed for hard-core, sophisticated delinquents insufficient basis for transfer to adult court. The case was remanded so that the juvenile court could search for alternative existing programs and inquire into the feasibility of constructing an effective program for the juvenile in question and others like him.

In addition to the lack of available resources, juvenile court personnel may not know what facilities are available in their states and in other states. Finally, such facilities are extremely expensive and courts may be reluctant to spend their total budget on one juvenile. It is much easier to waive the child to an adult court, citing the lack of suitable programs for such a child.

5) *Whether the best interest of public welfare and protection of public security generally requires that a juvenile stand trial as an adult offender.* This criterion is the vaguest of all the criteria for waiver. In fact, the criminal justice standards committee recommends that in such a criterion, protection of public security not be considered in transfer decisions. Indeed, the juvenile court was designed to protect the best interests of the child, not the public welfare. Unfortunately, this criterion may be considered the most important by legislatures, courts, and prosecutors in regard to the matter of transfer.

TRANSFER PROCEDURE

It is beyond the scope of this chapter to discuss the procedure for transfer. However, it is important to mention that subsequent to the *Kent* decision, juveniles should have the same procedural due process rights as adults. Such rights include, but are not necessarily limited to, notice of hearing, provision of counsel, access to social records, and probation report. An additional protection suggested by *Kent* was that waiver hearings follow probable cause hearings. Thus, prior to considering transferring a child to adult court, it would seem reasonable that the juvenile court find probable or reasonable cause that the child committed the unlawful act. Unfortunately, many believe the due process rights enumerated are notable more in their breach than in actual practice.

THE ROLE OF THE EXPERT

Mental health experts have a variety of roles in the waiver process including, but not limited to, evaluation of the child and his or her family. Conducting a court-ordered psychiatric examination for purposes of a waiver hearing is probably a familiar role to most mental health personnel.

The evaluation is conducted in much the same manner as all forensic evaluations. That is, prior to the evaluation, it is important to review all pertinent and relevant documents, including police reports, mental health records, medical records, and school reports. Often, the juvenile's attorney has relevant material available and is more than willing to share such material if asked. It is critical to advise the juvenile that the evaluation is being done for the court and that information garnered at the time of the evaluation will not be confidential but part of the court record. Although the waiver of rights is generally given in any forensic evaluation, in this evaluation it is incumbent upon the professional to make certain that the juvenile understands the evaluating professional may not be allied with the juvenile in treatment but may ultimately be part of the adversarial process in the courtroom (10).

The usual areas of interest are covered in the actual psychiatric evaluation. These include: the events of the alleged crime as seen from the juvenile's perspective; the youngster's personal history; family history; school history; social relationships; history of drug and alcohol abuse; prior criminal history; prior mental health treatment; medical treatment; and a more formal mental status evaluation. Juveniles are very often even more frightened of psychiatric evaluations than adults. Their bravado often belies the overwhelming fear that a psychiatrist "can read my mind." In addition, many youngsters are totally unfamiliar with court procedure and processes and have no idea what an evaluation might mean. Thus, the evaluating clinician needs to take into account the juvenile's fear and be patient and careful in explaining the nature and purposes of an evaluation, the results, and the way the evaluation will be used.

Example

John B., a 14-year-old boy accused of murdering a neighborhood girl, seemed cocky, secure, and pseudomature at the beginning of the evaluation.

His rationale for the murder was that the girl called him "pizza face," a slur on his juvenile acne. The evaluating clinician found this an inexplicable reason for a brutal, vicious murder, as did the boy's attorney, who was unable to elicit any more information from the boy than the fact that he resented the girl's name calling. However, the clinician established rapport with the boy by explaining the purposes of the interview, the use to which it would be put, and the fact that he might even be able to help the juvenile if the juvenile's motivation for such a random crime could be understood.

Finally, the young man tearfully explained that the girl was the daughter of his father's girlfriend. He thought his father and his girlfriend would be married in the next several months and he would have to live with this young woman who called him "pizza face," "zit face," "queer," and provoked him with the fact that "no girl will ever want you, faggot." Although it was possible for him to bear her insults when he saw her occasionally, the thought of living with her seemed impossible.

Gradually, through repeated interviews, the clinician was able to form a therapeutic alliance with the boy and understand the dynamic reasons underlying the brutal murder. He was terrified and handled his terror by not sharing any information, concerned that if he told anybody he would be perceived as crazy. John finally revealed a history of anorexia, sleeplessness, weight loss, and anhedonia prior to the murder. The clinician was able to persuade the court that the boy's underlying depression might be amenable to a trial of treatment and that waiving him to adult court with the possibility of long-term incarceration would not be appropriate.

The clinician can also explain appeal processes to attorneys, subsequent to the waiver hearing. In some states, appeal of a waiver is only allowed after a criminal court adjudication. In others, the decision to waive may be appealed immediately. Unfortunately, attorneys unfamiliar with the juvenile justice system often do not fight the issue of waiver in the juvenile court and do not realize that the dispositions available to juveniles are generally much more treatment-oriented than dispositions available in the adult criminal system. Thus, it often is appropriate to suggest to an attorney that the waiver be appealed.

Example

Gary B., a 16-year-old boy with serious tuberous sclerosis, was mildly mentally retarded and the butt of taunts and jeers in his neighborhood. He had only a few friends and had never had a girlfriend. Gary came to the attention of a forensic clinician after he had been waived to adult court. The court-ordered evaluation was for evaluation of criminal responsibility. Gary had been involved in one act of fellatio with a younger neighborhood boy in a middle-class neighborhood. The neighbors had always been concerned about Gary, and his first act of criminal behavior afforded them the opportunity to "get that boy off the streets." The forensic clinician recommended to Gary's attorney that he reopen the issue of waiver, as Gary had mental health problems which centered around his own self-esteem and identity. Gary had never been involved in any criminal behavior before, and there were outpatient treatment programs in the community that might benefit him. Gary's parents had always been supportive and reliable and were hopeful that another disposition could be found for their retarded son.

Forensic clinicians can serve as a resource, affording the courts information about treatment facilities available locally, statewide, and nationally. In small communities, the juvenile courts do not have access to such data because of the limited resources of the court personnel.

Example

Mark was a psychotic youngster who attempted to abduct a school bus during a brief reactive psychosis. The decision to waive was short-circuited when the mental health professional explained the nature of Mark's illness and possible available community treatments to the court at a waiver hearing.

CONCLUSION

This chapter has provided an overview of the statutes governing the transfer of juvenile court jurisdictions to adult court and briefly highlighted the role of the clinician in assisting the courts in performing this duty. The broad impression to be gained from the present state of the waiver statutes is that transfer is as easy to obtain now as it was before *Kent*, and is becoming increasingly easier. There is increased public pressure for such transfer and a belief that "getting them off the streets younger" will achieve safer streets.

There are, on the other hand, those who believe that juvenile courts ought not to be allowed to waive any youngsters at all. These dissenters hold that the vast majority of waiver juveniles are minor offenders and should be treated rather than incarcerated. They believe the few serious offenders who are waived may be acquitted of their crimes in adult courts because of the stricter enforcement of due process standards in the criminal courts. Thus, heinous criminals who are waived are not likely to go free. In addition, those convicted as adults may be treated leniently in regard to sentences as they are first-time offenders. Indeed, Hamperion et al. (11) found that more than 98% of the juvenile waiver cases resulted in guilty verdicts in the adult courts. More than half of these guilty convictions led to fines or probation, not incarceration, thereby further undermining public safety.

Many commentators feel that the decision to waive juveniles is the result of an arbitrary, capricious, and poorly documented process. They believe that waiver abolition may force the juvenile justice system to work with the most difficult youngsters and thus create pressure for the diversion of minor offenders out of the juvenile justice system. The waiver in the juvenile justice system is a controversial area that has always been under evaluation but is increasingly subject to reevaluation as the juvenile justice system's aims, methods, and failings come further under public scrutiny.

REFERENCES

 1. James, T. E. The age of majority. *American Journal of Legal History*, 1960, *4*, 22-33.
 2. *Kent* v. *United States*, 383 U.S. 541 (1966).
 3. Shornhurst, F. T. The waiver of juvenile court jurisdiction: Kent revisited. *Indiana Law Journal*, 1968, *43*, 583, 586-587.
 4. Sorrentino, J. N., & Olsen, G. K. Certification of juveniles. *Pepperdine Law Review*, 1977, *4*, 497-522.
 5. Institute of Judicial Administration/American Bar Association. Standards Relating to Transfer Between Courts. *Juvenile Justice Standards*. Cambridge, MA: Ballinger, 1980.
 6. Sorrentino & Olsen, 1977.
 7. *Ibid.*
 8. Hamperian, D., Schuster, R., Dinitz, S., & Conrad, J. *The violent few*. Lexington, MA: Lexington Books, 1978.
 9. Sorrentino & Olsen, 1977, p. 510.
10. Melton, G. B. *Child advocacy*. New York: Plenum Press, 1983.
11. Hamperian et al., 1978.

14

Treatment Alternatives in Juvenile Justice Programs: A Selected Review

Rosemary C. Sarri

It is frequently asserted today that effective treatment in juvenile corrections is no longer worth attempting because the results from systematic evaluation of many programs have produced such pessimistic outcomes. Those who support this position argue that juveniles who are convicted of violating the law should be committed to programs whose goals are protection of society, deterrence, and retribution (1). At the same time, one finds growth in the numbers of programs and technologies for addressing youths adjudicated as juvenile delinquents. The conflict between these two contending parties remains unresolved, although it is clear that there has been a shift in the proportion of resources allocated to control and custody rather than treatment and rehabilitation. Furthermore, there has been a dramatic reduction in the resources available for prevention, diversion, and other forms of community-based nonresidential programs for juvenile offenders (2).

The attitudes of the past decade reflect a significant change from the values and ideologies that slowly evolved during the twentieth century. From World War II until the 1970s, rehabilitation was acknowledged to be a major goal of corrections, despite the fact that treatment programs were seldom fully implemented or funded. Then, quite abruptly, and for reasons not yet entirely obvious, there was a dramatic shift toward incarceration of adults and a decline in the emphasis on deinstitutionalization of juvenile programs (3, 4). The decline for juveniles was more pronounced in public than private institutions and, in fact, private institutions have had a steady rate of increase between the late 1970s and 1984. Thus, as Lerman suggests, juveniles may have been recycled into private and mental health residential settings and out of public training schools (5).

This chapter reviews selected contemporary literature about the relative effectiveness of various treatment programs for juvenile offenders, placing greater emphasis on those for community-based rather than institutional settings because the latter has been a clear national priority since the Presidential Commission of 1967 (6). The presentation will not be comprehensive or representative of all programs; rather, it will illustrate the types and range of programs that have been designed and actually operated in several locations for one or more years. Where possible, evaluative results will be presented and in so doing a comparative perspective will be maintained.

THE ENVIRONMENTAL CONTEXT

Despite the disenchantment with rehabilitation approaches in juvenile corrections, innovations in programming have continued to grow rapidly, particularly in the area of alternatives to closed institutions (7). The Juvenile Justice and Delinquency Prevention Act of 1974 provided substantial incentives to states for deinstitutionalization of selected classes of offenders, for removal of youths from adult jails, and for the development of community-based alternatives (8). Nearly every state now has at least one example of community alternatives, including: community service and restitution, contracting, group homes, intensive in-home care, home detention, alternative education, work release and vocational training, day treatment, and a variety of highly innovative approaches to case management and residential treatment.

The character of the justice system is critically shaped by the attitudes and behaviors of local communities. They can escalate or alleviate the problems of this system. Community opportunities, resources, and services define basic life conditions and generate motives for deviant behavior. The almost total lack of concern in the United States for the negative consequences associated with extremely high rates of youth unemployment exemplifies such a condition, because, as Freeman indicates, there is ample research evidence documenting the positive relationship between crime and unemployment (9). Community toleration of crime directly affects the rates and volumes of cases presented for formal handling. The responsiveness of community institutions and agencies determines whether individuals in trouble will be isolated within the justice system or will be offered service and assistance toward a conventional life. Localities may lock juvenile offenders in jail and may produce programs, under the guise of community treatment, that rival any maximum security prison. In many areas, local community attitudes have been particularly hostile toward minority urban youths. For example, in the state of New York, 13 year olds may now be tried and sanctioned as adults.

Another facet of the environment that influences universal justice policy is the American proclivity for superficial solutions to problems rather than consistent, long-term rehabilitative service strategies. Decriminalization, diversion, and deinstitutionalization were key program concepts of the 1960s and 1970s, but in the 1980s they appear to have been replaced with concepts such as deterrence, punishment, selective incapacitation, and retribution. Behavior associated with each of the concepts can be observed in programs throughout the country. Patterns are usually haphazard and almost no attention is given to the fundamental contradictions implied by the contrasting paths. Few would doubt that deinstitutionalization is a profound social movement throughout the human services, but in the case of criminal justice, it has progressed very slowly and unevenly (10).

RESIDENTIAL FACILITIES FOR DELINQUENT YOUTHS

Until the 1970s, there were few comparative studies of treatment programs for juvenile offenders that permitted examination of the relative effectiveness of the various types of programs. Passage of the Juvenile Justice and Delinquency Prevention Act of 1974 provided for extensive evaluation, and centers at the Universities of Albany, California at Davis, Chicago, Harvard, Michigan, Pittsburgh, and Southern California, among others, were created to complete systematic assessment of various programs. This research has greatly enhanced our understanding of potentials and outcomes from various intervention approaches. Because it is impossible to deal with a range of juvenile justice treatment in one paper, and because there are excellent reports on nonresidential alternatives available, this chapter will concentrate on residential programs, primarily those in which there is a basic commitment to treatment, rather than custody and control.

There has been a tremendous growth in the number of residential facilities for delinquent youths in the United States since the first national survey was completed by Pappenfort, Kilpatrick, and Kuby (11) in 1966. Their census revealed that there was a total of 441 institutions serving predelinquent and delinquent youths under both public and private auspices. Despite the fact that there has been an 18% decline in the United States' youth population between 10 and 18 years of age since 1966, as of 1979 there were a total of 1,710 public and private residential facilities serving the same population. Of these, 993 were operated under public auspices (12). Table 1 reveals the decline of nearly 12,000 youths in public correctional facilities between 1971 and 1979. Detailed information about private fa-

Table 1. Selected Characteristics of Public Juvenile Custody Residents and Facilities, 1971, 1973, 1974, 1975, 1977, and 1979 in the United States[1]

Characteristic	1971	1973	1974	1975	1977	1979
Number of residents	57,239	47,983	47,268	49,126	45,920	45,251
Juvenile	54,729	45,694	44,922	46,980	44,096	43,089
Male	41,781	35,057	34,783	37,926	36,921	37,063
Female	12,984	10,637	10,139	9,054	7,175	6,026
Adult	2,510	2,289	2,346	2,146	1,824	2,162
Average Age (years)[2]	NA	NA	NA	NA	15.3	15.4
Male	NA	15.2	15.3	15.3	15.4	15.5
Female	NA	14.9	14.9	15.0	15.1	15.1
Number of admissions[3]	616,766	600,960	647,175	641,189	614,385	564,875
Number of facilities	722	794	829	874	992	993
Short-term	338	355	371	387	448	458
Long-term	384	439	458	487	544	535
Number of personnel	43,372	44,845	46,276	52,534	61,060	60,889
Full-time	39,521	39,216	39,391	41,156	43,322	44,234
Part-time	3,851	5,629	6,885	11,378	17,738	16,655
Juveniles per full-time staff member	1.4	1.2	1.1	1.1	1.0	1.0
Expenditures (thousands of dollars)	456,474	483,941	508,630	594,146	707,732	839,895
Per capita operating cost (dollars)[4]	7,002	9,577	10,354	11,469	14,123	16,512

NOTE: Data for 1971-75 are as of June 30 and for 1977 and 1979 as of December 31, except for figures on admissions, expenditures, and operating costs, which are for an annual period, either calendar or fiscal year.

NA   Not available.

[1]   Source: *Children and Custody, Report on the 1979 Census of Public Juvenile Facilities,* U.S. Department of Justice, Office of Juvenile Justice and Delinquency Prevention, October 1982.

[2]   Based on juvenile residents only.

[3]   Based on all residents (juvenile and adult).

[4]   Based on average daily number of residents.

cilities are not as readily available, although Pappenfort completed a re-survey in 1982, the results of which should be forthcoming. Information from a census of private institutions in 1979 indicates that 28,707 youths were held in these facilities at that time (13).

The mean size of programs has dropped substantially over the decade. On any given day, one of four youths in a public facility will be in short-term detention and the remainder in more extended care facilities. In contrast, 97% of those in private facilities are in extended rather than short-term care. Increases in the number of staff and in fiscal resources occurred throughout the 1970s, indicating that there may be more potential for effective programming than had previously existed, although, obviously, resources alone provide no assurance of any effective treatment program. Unfortunately, however, the increases in resources have been allocated more to detention facilities and closed institutions than to community programs. Schwartz (14) recently reported that average annual costs of residential care per youth exceeded $22,000, and went as high as $114,877 in the District of Columbia.

TREATMENT PROGRAMS AND TECHNOLOGIES

To reduce or prevent law violating and other deviant behavior, correctional programs establish various treatment objectives and seek to achieve these through the programs and services provided to the youths committed to their care. The National Assessment of Juvenile Corrections (NAJC) studied a stratified sample of community-based residential and day treatment agencies, institutions, and aftercare services in 16 states (15). These programs were grouped into three categories: 1) "closed" institutions where youths are removed from their usual environment and 80% are confined there all of the time; 2) community residential facilities where youths can interact with the surrounding community; and 3) day treatment programs where youths live at home but are required to participate in a daily program at a specified location. Extensive data were gathered from staff and youths in all of these programs, from parent organizations, and from official records about all major facets of their programs.

Information obtained from staff and youths indicated that these facilities attempted to achieve a large number of treatment objectives, with variable emphases among programs, and differential perceptions within programs about priorities among objectives. Thirteen specific objectives were factor analyzed, and the results produced six factors (identified in Table 2) and presented for the three major types of programs. The presence scores represent the extent to which that factor was present in the specific type of program referred to. Day treatment centers and community residential

Table 2. Treatment Objective Factor Scores in Contrasting Types of Programs

| Factor | Presence Scores | | | | |
	I[a] (N = 15)	G (N = 10)	D (N = 9)	Weighted Mean	Rank
1. Skill development	18.1	18.1	28.6	20.9	2
2. Preparation for community transition	16.7	16.2	18.0	16.9	3
3. Enhancement of youths' psychological states	5.4	10.4	6.0	7.0	6
4. Development or enhancement of youths' problem-solving abilities	13.3	12.2	22.2	15.3	5
5. Behavioral change	10.5	31.6	35.1	23.2	1
6. Development of conducive environment	10.8	24.3	18.0	16.7	4
Mean Score	12.5	18.8	21.3		
Rank of Mean Score	3	2	1		

[a] I = Institutions
   G = Community residential
   D = Day treatment

Source: *Time Out: A National Study of Juvenile Correction Programs.* Ann Arbor: University of Michigan, National Association of Juvenile Corrections. Robert Vinter & Rosemary Sarri Co-Directors, 1976, p. 129.

programs support treatment objectives to a higher degree than do institutions. The most frequently found treatment objective factor among institutions was "skill development"; among both community residential and day treatment programs it was "behavioral change."

The techniques used to bring about attitudinal or behavioral change in young offenders are here referred to as treatment technologies: a series of procedures designed to transform or modify attributes of individuals in a deliberate and predictable manner, through the training of personnel, to perform the necessary tasks. Which treatment technologies are used by correctional programs for young offenders? Do different types of programs tend to use different technologies or sets of them? The data presented in Table 3 indicate that a large number of distinct technologies was reported as being used by this sample of programs. In institutions, the mean number

Table 3. Percentages of Programs Using Specified Treatment
Technologies

	I[a] (N = 15)	G (N = 10)	D (N = 9)	All Programs (N = 34)
Individual counseling	93	80	78	85
Group counseling	87	80	67	79
Reality therapy	80	70	56	71
Behavior modification	73	60	67	68
Family therapy	73	50	44	59
Psychotherapy	67	50	44	56
Guided group interaction	53	30	44	44
Positive peer culture	53	30	33	41
Treatment contracts	40	40	33	41
Religious counseling	80	10	0	38
Transactional analysis	33	30	11	26
Chemotherapy	40	30	0	26
Educateur therapy	7	30	11	15
Other technologies	13	10	0	9
Mean number used	8	6	5	7

[a] I = Institutions
     G = Community residential
     D = Day treatment
Source: *Time Out*, p. 141.

reported was eight, whereas in group homes and day treatment programs
it was slightly fewer: six and five, respectively. Overall, various counseling
technologies were reported as being used most frequently, followed by
several relatively explicit technologies such as reality therapy and behavior
modification. Group techniques were also used in nearly half of the programs. Chemotherapies were, not surprisingly, used most often in institutions. Specialized "educateur" technologies, developed by Piaget in Europe
and Guindon in Canada, were reported infrequently, but these are quite
new in the United States (16).

Merely knowing that a program reports having a certain treatment objective or utilizes a specific treatment technology does not inform us about
the adequacy of the implementation, nor about its effectiveness in the
rehabilitation of youthful offenders. The NAJC study was a cross-sectional
survey; therefore, it is impossible to answer these questions. Because we
do not have large-scale, comparative studies of residential programs that
provide us with detailed program implementation information, this chapter
examines a limited number of specific programs and technologies where

at least some longitudinal information is available. As was indicated earlier, these programs are illustrative of programs actually in operation in a large number of states and communities throughout the United States.

Table 4 presents a summary of key characteristics of the alternative programs being examined in this chapter. Following that is a brief summary of the key elements of each of the programs. A few obvious patterns are revealed in these data:

1) Most youths are referred by the juvenile court or public agency responsible for handling juvenile delinquents;
2) Most programs are small, with few exceeding 30 clients at any given time;
3) Although age range is variable, most tend to be age-homogeneous, with a median of approximately 16 years. Older youths are more often reported as more successful in terms of outcome measures;
4) A few co-ed programs exist, although most continue to serve predominantly males;
5) Programs under public and private auspices exist and outcome data do not suggest that either type of auspice makes a significant difference;
6) Nearly all programs have one or more explicit service technology that they seek to implement; very few have ambiguous or undefined means. Most programs require professionally trained staff, although few specify that only certain professionals are required;
7) Length of stay was highly variable, ranging from a few weeks in most Outward Bound programs to more than a year in many of the group home programs;
8) Outcome criteria and data were less exacting than one would prefer. However, the data that were available indicate that these programs do at least as well as other alternatives and, in the majority of instances, have higher rates of effectiveness.

PROGRAM SUMMARIES

Highfields

Perhaps the first widely utilized model of a contemporary community-based residential program was Highfields, established by Lloyd McKorkle on the Lindberg estate in New Jersey in 1955 (17). Its initial capacity was 20 males who were committed there by juvenile courts from four urban New Jersey counties. They spent approximately four months in the intensive phase of the program. Days were spent working in a variety of service-oriented jobs at a nearby mental hospital and during the evenings intensive peer group counseling took place.

"Guided group interaction" was the service technology developed at Highfields and, as findings in Table 3 indicate, it is a technology still widely used. It was designed as a short-term, informally structured but intensive peer group experience. It was, at least in part, an attempt to operationalize the Sutherland theory of differential association in an intervention modality, but in this instance the group was utilized to inculcate prosocial values and norms. Sutherland had argued that criminal behavior is learned in association with others, particularly peers; therefore, delinquents should be prevented from associating with those who commit crimes. Guided group intervention theory asserted that peer groups could be socialized to prosocial values so that differential association theory could be utilized in effective treatment (18).

Subsequent to the relatively successful experience at Highfields, the model was extended and developed further in Essexfields, Collegefields, Kentfields, Provo, and in S.T.A.R.T. in New York (19). Vinter et al. (20) noted that guided group technology was reported to be one of the most frequently utilized technologies in juvenile justice in the United States. Preliminary findings from the assessment of guided group interaction, or its most recent adaptation, "positive peer culture," in other settings indicate fewer consistently positive results (21).

Achievement Place

Achievement Place (22) has been described as a

> ... community-based, family style, behavior modification home treatment program for delinquent youth. ...
> The goals of Achievement Place are to teach youth appropriate social skills such as study and homework behavior, self-help skills such as meal preparation and personal hygiene and pre-vocational skills that are thought to be necessary for them to be successful in the community. (23)

The family-educational environment was designed to compensate for or overcome the behavioral deficiencies of particular youths in the community. It is a family-type group home where, under the direction of a specially trained male and female, approximately six youths continue to participate in regular community schools and other youth activities. The programs at the home are carried out by the teaching-parents, who are trained in behavior modification, remedial education, juvenile law, and other areas. The adults establish close relationships with teachers, while the youths are en-

Table 4. Characteristics of Alternative Residential Programs for Youth

Program	Size of Client Pop.	Age	Sex	Auspice	Referral Agent	Service Technology	Length of Stay	Outcomes Criteria	Outcomes Change
Achievement Place Lawrence, KS	6-8 (per unit)	14-18	Male	Local Private	Court Social agency School	Social learning Behavior modification	10 mos.	Police record School performance	+ +
PORT Rochester, MN	18	13-50	Male	Local Public	Court	Contracting Guided group interaction Employment	9-12 mos.	Police record Court record Employment	+ +/– +
Highfields Bergen, NJ	15	16-18	Male	Private	Court	Guided group interaction Work	4 mos.	Institutional recidivism Individual change in attitude/ personality	+ 0
Outward Bound Boulder, CO	10-20	15-18	Male Female	Public and private	Court State agency	Physical training Use of environment Stress tolerance Peer group problem solving	20-40 days	No outcome results published	

Program	Size of Client Pop.	Age	Sex	Auspice	Referral Agent	Service Technology	Length of Stay	Criteria	Outcomes Change
UDIS Chicago, IL	Variable	15-18	Male Female	Public and private	Court State agency	Case management Variable services Contracting	6-12 mos.	Intraprogram Postprogram behavior	– +
Group Homes Massachusetts Division of Youth Services Boston, MA	6-15	10-18	Male Female	Public and private	State agency	Variable Family parenting	3-24 mos.	Recidivism School performance	0 +
Educateur	Variable	15-18	Male	Public	Court	Social learning Psychoeducation Group/individual psychotherapy	12-24 mos.	Police Court Individual attitude and personality Drug abuse Delinquent behavior	– – + – +/0
CATC Colorado	26	14-18	20 Male 6 Female	Public/ Private	State training school	Eclectic: Behavior modification Guided group interaction Therapeutic milieu	6-12 mos.	No specific criteria Reduction of violence Recidivism	N/A
Intensive In-home care	30-40 per program	14-18	Co-ed	Public	Court State agency	Family treatment Behavior Contracting	12-24 mos.	Police Court School Community	0 + + +

couraged to do well in school, to develop their capacities for self-government, to change behavior that is problematic, and to cooperate in doing the necessary tasks of running a home and living together.

In order to induce the changes, a token economy is established in which youth can earn or lose points that can be exchanged for conventional rewards. The model assumes that a delinquent youth has not learned the appropriate behaviors that will enable him or her to interact with others in a socially appropriate manner. The program is designed to correct the behavioral deficiencies. Eventually, the point system is faded out to a merit system where no points are given or taken away and all privileges are free. The merit system is the last level a youth must progress through before returning to his own home or being placed permanently in another home.

Youths served by the program have included majority and minority youths, males and females, and youths with various levels of educational disadvantage. Nearly all have had serious behavioral problems in school. All have been adjudicated and committed by the juvenile court—about 55% for relatively serious felonies. Two-thirds of the youths are from single-parent households and more than half of the families have reported receiving some form of public assistance.

There have been several evaluations of Achievement Place and substantial longitudinal data as well. Compared with other conventional group homes and with randomly assigned control groups, Achievement Place has been very successful in producing positive outcomes: improved school performance, less delinquency, fewer court and police contacts, and less subsequent institutionalization. Costs are substantially below comparable institutional programs and consumers (youths, parents, boards of directors, school and court personnel) report higher levels of satisfaction. There have been more than 35 reported replications of the program.

Psychoeducational or Educateur Program

Utilizing a program of activities based on the developmental theories of Piaget and Erikson, this program has been developed most extensively in Quebec in an open institutional setting (24, 25). Criteria for admission are strict and, in addition, each youth must willingly choose to participate in the program. If not, the youth is returned to the court. The model includes a four-stage developmental process of reeducation of the necessary four phases for the actualization of 1) autonomous ego control (surface behavior); 2) production (achievement in activities); 3) personality (discovery and awareness of one's own personal style and identity); and 4) development of self-control and improved self-perception. To realize these goals, the staff stress the role of the educator and the quality of group life.

The role of the educator, who is trained in psychoeducation technologies, is to facilitate the process of reeducation of delinquent youths. They get to know the youths, establish close affectional relationships, help them develop, and resolve daily problems of living. Emphasis is also placed on the therapeutic milieu—the quality of group life. This is a milieu in which life is predictable, organized, with clear expectations on the part of educators, and precise objectives for each youth. The educator influences the youth through support, rather than control, to foster cohesion and a better state of psychosocial health for the individuals in the group.

The Canadian programs have only served male youths between the ages of 16 and 18. Although evaluation of the program indicates positive results in terms of organizational goals and outcomes for those who complete the program, LeBlanc reports that 42% of the youths admitted did not complete the program and usually only remained a short period of time. In addition, a substantial percentage were screened out at admission by the staff or refused to come at all. Approximately 20% were reported to have completed the program to the satisfaction of staff. LeBlanc characterizes the situation as one of natural selection by those who apparently view the program as actually or potentially beneficial to them. The longitudinal evaluation of the program identified limited differences between those who completed the full program and those who remained for shorter periods of time. No comparisons were made with randomly assigned control groups.

More recently, Brendtro and his colleagues (26) have reported on the implementation of the educateur model in the United States. Preliminary results indicate more positive outcomes, but detailed longitudinal information is lacking.

PORT

For a number of years, Minnesota has experimented with a variety of age-heterogeneous, community-based programs in criminal justice, substance abuse, and mental health. One of the most successful of these is PORT (Probational Offenders Rehabilitation and Training Programs) (27). It was initiated in Rochester to serve a three-court area for juvenile and adult offenders—persons adjudicated for both misdemeanant and felony offenses. The program was located adjacent to a community college and on the grounds of a mental hospital where empty cottages were available. It was established for 18 residents and had four full-time staff, plus 15 college students who lived with residents and worked part-time as counselors.

Offenders voluntarily chose the program and were given a three-week probationary period. At the conclusion, each offender completed a contract with the staff about what he would do in order to achieve accepted goals.

All residents were expected to be employed and/or to go to school. A "restitution" element was incorporated for the majority of offenders.

The program was established as a community corporation with a local board representative of important persons in the community, other lay citizens, and members of the law enforcement and judicial systems. Since this was an alternative to prison for convicted adult felons, the board took a very active role in the development of the program and in securing critical community support.

Several evaluations have been completed indicating that PORT is both an effective and efficient alternative to incarceration in prison (28). The counties it served have had very few commitments to state facilities as compared with other comparable counties.

Of particular significance in this program was the fact that it was designed to mix adult and juvenile offenders. The age range of residents was 14-50 and older residents were deliberately invited to counsel and assist younger residents with regard to delinquent behavior. Guided group interaction and other group techniques were used in evening counseling sessions, but not as exclusively as in other programs. Much emphasis was placed on normalizing the program and on using the college students as role models and links to positive community experience for offenders.

UDIS

UDIS (Unified Delinquency Intervention Services) is an experimental public agency in Illinois that serves as a clearing house for a wide variety of community programs for chronic delinquents and/or aggressive youths charged with serious crimes. Participants had a mean arrest rate of 12 and several experiences in detention and on probation. The program incorporated a variety of types of community-based interventions, i.e., group homes, counseling, employment, wilderness trips, and education, all of which were primarily contracted as alternatives to placement in state training schools in Illinois. UDIS began as a demonstration research project in Cook County but has now been extended to 20 other Illinois counties. It was expected to reduce institutional commitments in Cook County by 35% and in the other counties by 50%.

UDIS was established to fulfill four basic premises:

1) Any resources for diversion will be poorly spent without consistent and vigorous effort to identify and correct basic problems in the management of juvenile justice that violate the constitutional, legal, or human rights of youths.

2) To fulfill the purposes of the juvenile court one must have sound community-based treatment readily available.

3) Administrators must accept responsibility for defects in the justice system.
4) The administrative structure of UDIS must be designed to prevent or make difficult administrative capitulation to pressures for self-interest, political interest, or bureaucratic isolation.

In this program much emphasis was placed on public accountability of administration to insure that youths were really served in their respective programs. The service network was monitored carefully to ensure quality control and accountability.

Youths participated voluntarily in UDIS for six to 12 months with termination possible in a variety of ways. The community judge had to approve the plan after a two-week assessment period; judges also approved termination.

UDIS was initiated in 1974, and an evaluation was completed by Murray and his colleagues, but further work is underway because results were controversial. With respect to characteristics of youth, Murray and Cox (29) selected those targeted by the program. Fifty-five percent were adjudicated for major felonies. Most were property offenders (83%), but a substantial proportion had committed serious person crimes (13%). Other results indicate that youths removed from the community and placed in various institutions "did better" as far as intraprogram behavioral measures could determine, but that may have been the result of reduction in opportunity to commit deviant acts. Conclusive evidence on outcomes is not yet available.

UDIS emphasizes the importance of continuous and accountable case management when dealing with youths who have been convicted of serious crimes. It also emphasizes a "brokerage model" for implementation of the case management strategy and active advocacy on behalf of the juvenile. Experience with this program has been enlightening with respect to the requirement for an effective, on-going, individualized case management approach with delinquents who have been adjudicated for serious crimes. A highly dedicated, flexible, and committed staff was one of the variables frequently mentioned by Goins as essential to program effectiveness (30).

Outward Bound Wilderness Programs

Perhaps the most innovative and unusual of all the alternative residential programs are those that could be basically classified as outdoor education and wilderness programs. Some take place in mountainous areas while others have developed in ocean communities. What is characteristic of all the wilderness programs is a deliberate attempt to use the environment as a critical part of the program to provide challenge, stress, and opportunity for youths. Although elements of this approach have been utilized for many decades, the first organized, adventure-based program for delinquents was developed in Colorado in 1964 (31). Since that time, 13 other states have implemented a variety of outward bound wilderness and marine programs.

Although programs vary widely, the standard wilderness experience is built around a 20- to 40-day, carefully planned program. It consists of a series of programmed physical and social problem-solving tasks conducted in a high-impact outdoor environment. Participants are immersed in intense survival exercises that precipitate clear-cut physical, emotional, and interpersonal crises. When problem attitudes and behaviors are identified, trained instructors encourage alternative behavior and provide linkage as to how these behaviors can relate to that youth's community environment. The problem situations are planned to arouse curiosity, to strengthen competence, and to elicit cooperation. Problems, which are introduced incrementally, are concrete and manageable.

Closed Adolescent Treatment Center

Although this chapter primarily examines open residential programs, so much attention is now being focused on violent juvenile crime that it is essential to include a program that specifically purports to treat serious violent offenders. Many of the other programs also treat equally serious offenders, although not exclusively as does the Closed Adolescent Treatment Center (CATC), located in Colorado (32).

CATC is a public, co-ed program designed for emotionally disturbed and violent offenders. It is located in a special unit at the Colorado State Training School and serves approximately 20 boys and six females between the ages of 15 and 18. The overall staff include youth service workers (approximately 16), and eight professionally trained psychologists and social workers.

After being screened by the professional staff, youths are typically transferred from other units of the training school. Thus, it is not clear whether the original commitment offense is the basis for the referral for intensive treatment, or whether the youth is referred because of disruptive behavior within the institution, or a combination of the two. Agee, who is the author of the volume describing the program, is also the program's director. She states that more than half of the youths have been convicted of murder, armed robbery, rape, or serious assault. All were to have been committed for crimes of violence, but systematic information on these offender characteristics was lacking, and external evaluation has not as yet been completed. Without external evaluation one cannot be fully certain that the population actually being served is as described.

The treatment program is eclectic, involving use of the classification based on the "I-level" conceptualization of interpersonal maturity; a token economy behavior modification regimen and guided group interaction therapy, which are presented as a package incorporating concepts from positive peer culture, reality therapy, and therapeutic milieu (33). Situations are deliberately created by staff in which youths are forced into healthy involvement with peers and staff. Each youth participates in highly structured encounter groups in which he explores his interpersonal relationships, life history, and personality. Discussion of the youth's offense behavior and his attitudes toward illegal behavior are essential parts of the program.

The program primarily serves youths who have had considerable experience in the justice system, and considerable emphasis is placed on modification of deviant behaviors learned within that system. Youths are subjected to 24-hour structure and control in a closed setting that provides no opportunity to test the newly learned behavior in the offender's home environment.

There has been no systematic evaluation of this program, nor of most others recently developed to serve violent juvenile offenders, with the exception of Project Pride, a community-based program in Denver that has had positive results in an open setting with similar types of offenders.

Massachusetts Models of Group Homes

Group homes are not a recent innovation in the residential treatment of delinquent youths, but they remain the treatment modality most widely utilized in the largest number of states other than institutions. The most thoroughgoing development of this modality occurred in Massachusetts, where all state public institutions for juvenile delinquents were closed in 1971. Coates, Miller, Ohlin, and their colleagues (34, 35) have studied many facets of the Massachusetts reform, including the group home strategy, and their evaluation provides further insight into this type of program. Of all the community-based programs that they evaluated in Massachusetts, group homes were by far the most prevalent. However, no single design or set of program activities were characteristic of group homes in that state. A variety of approaches were utilized and numerous innovations were designed and tested during the early 1970s, and many were subsequently adopted by other localities throughout the country.

An essential feature of the Massachusetts strategy is that the program is related specifically to the different conditions found in various communities. Group homes are highly variable—some isolated and others thoroughly embedded in their communities. One cannot accept *pro forma* definitions of programs as community-based, but instead has to examine the extent to which they are embedded in community institutions. Some homes use self-help treatment approaches and deliberately avoid close community ties. Others have highly professional staff with a variety of treatment technologies readily available.

Group homes typically serve six to eight youths between the ages of 12 and 18. Males and females are not placed together, but efforts are made to have racially integrated homes, particularly in parts of the state where majority and minority populations are found in the larger environing community. Offenders with all types of offense behavior and criminal justice experience are served in the group homes. Client characteristics are seldom predictive of success or failure during the period of program experience and afterward, with one major exception: Youths who return to social groups that engage in extensive illegal or deviant behavior have high rates of recidivism, regardless of their program experience.

Evaluation of the homes suggests that the extent and quality of relationships between the clients and the people and institutions within the community are critical predictors of success (36). Organizational variables are also of importance in the relative effectiveness of group homes, including auspice, development strategies, conflict resolution, site selection, and community perceptions. In comparing homes that succeeded with those that failed, Coates et al. observed that auspice was not critical, but strategy of approach to the community was important. Low profile entry plus communication with key persons also helped insure success. Those group homes that expected some community resistance and worked on the development of the problem and conflict resolution strategies consistently fared better.

With respect to the outcomes for youths in contrasting homes, those homes that were able to effect changes in the social networks to which the youths were returned were more successful in terms of lower recidivism rates. Youths who had an adult, especially a nonrelative, whom they could look up to, admire, and trust, and who did not break the law, were less likely to be recidivists than those who did not have such relationships. Coping skills taught to youths are important, but, again, more important if they are embedded in normative social support systems.

Considerable emphasis was placed on development of the model of the professional clinician in community-based services. Clinicians were to work interdependently with paraprofessionals and volunteers, and also to train parents and other family members to work more effectively in their respective roles with the youth.

In-Home and Specialized Foster Care

The most recent innovation in juvenile correctional programming has been the development of intensive treatment for the juvenile who remains in his/her own home or in a specialized foster home in the community. In the latter instance, the foster parent is viewed as a paraprofessional, and it is assumed that one individual can handle only two to three youths as a full-time occupation. Such staff are carefully selected, trained, and supervised so that they can serve as effective treatment agents for serious offenders and for multiproblem families from which such youths often come.

Youths referred to the court following adjudication for relatively serious property and/or person offenses are youths who otherwise would have been sent to a closed institution. In some instances, the programs also serve youths who have been in institutions and, in such cases, it is a transition back to the client's usual environment that must be effected.

Detailed contracts are developed jointly with the youth and family by the family worker. These specify behavioral goals, restrictions, and the conditions under which the youth will work with her or his family to achieve the goals. Goals primarily specify concrete behaviors related to the home, community, school, or work placement. Educational coordinators work closely with school personnel because this is the area in which these youths most frequently have the greatest difficulty. The level of educational performance in the Michigan project was extremely poor when youths entered the program. Most had reading scores at least two to four years below that expected for their ages, and math-science scores averaged six years below the expected level.

Because the workers are expected to provide intensive service to the youth and family, caseloads are low—approximately six to eight per family worker and 25-30 per educational coordinator. Family workers maintain several contacts each week with the youth and family in person or by telephone.

As Hazen (37) reports, evaluation of the British program has yielded positive results in terms of recidivism and reintegration. The Michigan project had a tighter research design in that youths were randomly assigned to the program by the court, with youths from the control group assigned to alternative programs provided less intense community treatment. Only preliminary results are available thus far, but these indicate that treatment goals were achieved for more than 70% of the youths. Researchers (38) have observed, however, that long-term service is likely to be necessary because of the nature of the environment in which these families reside. Poverty and unemployment are so widespread that specific programs had to be developed to obtain employment and additional support for parents, the majority of whom experienced long-term unemployment. The cutbacks in welfare programs has aggravated conditions for most of the youths and families.

SUMMARY

This review of selected residential programs for juvenile offenders suggests that there are many viable alternatives to placement in the usual closed institutional facility. Moreover, the evaluation data, while not as complete as would be desired, indicate that relatively positive results have been achieved in these programs at costs that are equal to or less than custodial institutions today. These outcome findings measure not only subsequent delinquent behavior, but also school and work performance and community behavior. In a society where youth unemployment is as high as it is, where educational programs are far less than is considered necessary for a high technology society, where youths are in the most crime-vulnerable age, and where family and community support systems are weak or nonexistent, it is unwise to expect that any single program will be so effective that no further deviant behavior will occur among the youths it has served.

The reports on these programs, as well as results from the NAJC survey, indicate that treatment programs that are designed as alternatives to the traditional custodial institutions face critical survival crises in the current political and social environment. Programs are often initiated on a "shoestring," with a time-limited grant and the hope that more support will be forthcoming. Personnel are expected to design, implement, and successfully operate a program within a 12-month time span. Obviously, such a demand is wholly unrealistic. Experience with UDIS in Illinois, and with a range of alternative programs in Massachusetts, provides useful information for the development of prerequisites for effective management and service delivery (39, 40).

The evaluation reports on these alternative residential programs often fail to provide adequate information about the service technologies and their delivery. Without such knowledge, replication and application often fail. In particular, there is insufficient information available about exact specifications of all aspects of the intervention and about differential staff roles. Also needed are more systematic procedures for the assessment of youths "before" and "after" their program experience so that relationships can be explicitly established between program goals and technologies and individual goals for clients (41).

The lack of effective interorganizational referral and exchange also stands out. Service programs often operate autonomously from the police, courts, and state supervising agencies, despite the fact that each could benefit from close and more frequent interaction. Few programs were observed to involve lay citizens, school personnel, legal services, employment agencies, or other human service personnel. It is not surprising that agencies confront hostile community reaction when they attempt to implement new programs.

Despite the inadequacy of our present knowledge, it is possible to offer several policy and program recommendations based on the information available from this review:

1) Deinstitutionalization and diversion should continue with more resources allocated in all states to the development of alternative services for youths requiring residential treatment.

2) Programs should aim to reduce coercive control, discipline, and punishment because of the negative short-term and long-term consequences. There is ample evidence to indicate that serious offenders can be treated successfully in open programs, provided that staffing is adequate.

3) Youths should only be placed in residential care when they have committed serious felonies and the safety of society is clearly in jeopardy, when they voluntarily elect such a program, or when their age and status are such that they need care and protection. No arbitrary age can be identified, but in most western societies, except the United States, a youth cannot be institutionalized under the age of 15. Younger serious offenders should be treated in intensive in-home and foster care treatment rather than in group residential settings.

4) Programs must be normalized, provide continuing and frequent links to the community, and seek to reconcile the youthful offenders, the victims, and the community.

5) Programs must provide for the adolescent's need for self-direction, growth, and opportunities to resolve his or her identity crisis. Goals must be positive, achievable, and recognized by the clients as in their own interest, not merely in the interest of society at large.

6) Contracting, case management, and voluntary participation are all mechanisms to facilitate more effective receipt of services and more positive orientations toward such services. Specific efforts should be geared to the differential needs and characteristics of youths and communities.

7) Community involvement is essential to successful community-based treatment, but that involvement must be planned for and supported in accord with variable sociocultural characteristics of communities. Evaluation results suggest that there is no single model or approach that is effective for all the variable types of communities.

There are many valid criticisms that can be made about the operation of juvenile justice today because of its costliness and its relative ineffectiveness in achieving positive goals for youths. Society appears to expect organizations in juvenile corrections to solve most of the problems of the youths assigned to them, but they must do so with limited resources, inadequate technologies, and often in social environments that are antithetical to the appropriate delivery of services that are known to be effective. At the same time, society refuses to provide legitimate roles for youths subsequent to their experience in juvenile corrections, so that any progress that is made is quickly undone when youth return to crime-ridden environments without opportunity (42). It is not surprising, therefore, that the response of youths is often further hostility and continuing deviant behavior.

All youth-serving organizations must do far more to facilitate greater implementation of the social policies and priorities necessary for adolescent socialization in legitimate roles in a postindustrial democratic society. Adherence to the law cannot be based solely on the fear of punishment; yet, in many ways, the public school, juvenile court, child welfare, and juvenile correctional agencies operate on this assumption. We speak of the juvenile justice system in a glib manner, as if such really existed, but from the perspective of thousands or perhaps millions of youths in many countries, the system is viewed as one only for control and punishment, not for justice! Nonetheless, the ideal of justice must be fundamental to juvenile corrections in a democratic society, for without it people will not conform to the values and norms that are essential to the viable continuance of that society.

REFERENCES

1. Wilson, J. Q. *Crime and public policy.* San Francisco: Institute for Contemporary Studies, 1983.
2. U.S. Department of Justice, Bureau of Justice Statistics. *Justice expenditures and employment in the U.S., 1971-1979.* Washington: U.S. Government Printing Office, 1983.
3. Krisberg, B., & Schwartz, I. Rethinking juvenile justice. *Crime and Delinquency,* 1983, *29*(3), 333-364.
4. Allen, F. *A modern critique of the rehabilitative ideal.* New Haven, CT: Yale University Press, 1978.
5. Lerman, P. *Deinstitutionalization and the welfare state.* New Brunswick, NJ: Rutgers University Press, 1982.
6. Presidential Commission on Law Enforcement and Crime. *Juvenile Delinquency,* Vol. 4. Washington, D.C.: U.S. Government Printing Office, 1967.
7. Coates, R. Community-based service for juvenile delinquents: Concepts and implications for practice. *Journal of Social Issues,* 1981, *37*(3), 87-101.
8. U.S. Public Law 93-415 (1974); Amended in 1977 and 1980.
9. Freeman, R. Crime and unemployment. In J. Q. Wilson (Ed.), *Crime and public policy.* San Francisco: Institute for Contemporary Studies, 1983.
10. Lerman, 1982.
11. Pappenfort, D., Kilpatrick, D., & Kuby, A. *Institutions for predelinquent and delinquent youth,* Vol. 3. Chicago: University of Chicago Press, 1970.

12. U.S. Bureau of the Census. *Children in custody: Census of juvenile detention and correctional facilities, 1971-1979.* Washington, D.C.: U.S. Department of Justice, Bureau of Justice Statistics, 1982.
13. *Ibid.,* 1982.
14. Schwartz, I. Cost of juvenile incarceration. Unpublished paper, 1984.
15. Vinter, R., Kish, R., & Newcomb, T. *Time out: A study of juvenile correctional programs.* Ann Arbor, MI: University of Michigan Press, 1976.
16. Brendtro, L., & Ness, A. *Re-educating troubled youth.* New York: Aldine, 1983.
17. McKorkle, L. *The Highfields story.* New York: Holt, Rinehart & Winston, 1958.
18. Sutherland, E. H., & Cressey, D. *Principles of criminology* (7th edition). Philadelphia: Lippincott, 1966.
19. Weeks, A. The Highfields project. In R. Giallombardo (Ed.), *Juvenile delinquency: A book of readings.* New York: Wiley, 1976.
20. Vinter et al., 1976.
21. Gendreau, P., & Ross, B. Effective correctional treatment: Bibliotherapy for cynics. *Crime and Delinquency,* 1979, *25,* 463-469.
22. Kirigan, K., Braukmann, C., Atwater, J., & Wolf, M. An evaluation of teaching-family (Achievement Place) group homes of juvenile offenders. *Journal of Applied Behavior Analysis,* 1982, *15,* 1-16.
23. *Ibid.,* p. 3.
24. Tremblay, R. Characteristics of training centers that have a positive influence. In R. Corrado, M. LeBlanc, & J. Trepanier (Eds.), *Current issues in juvenile justice.* Toronto: Butterworths, 1983.
25. LeBlanc, M. A retrospective look at a decade of evaluation: Boscoville. In R. Corrado, M. LeBlanc, & J. Trepanier (Eds.), *Current issues in juvenile justice.* Toronto: Butterworths, 1983.
26. Brendtro & Ness, 1983.
27. Hudson, J., Galway, B., & Lindgren, J. Diversion programming in criminal justice: The case of Minnesota. *Federal Probation,* 1975, *39,* 11-19.
28. Minnesota Community Corrections Program. *A preliminary evaluation summary and recommendations.* St. Paul, MN: Minnesota Commission on Crime Prevention and Control, 1975.
29. Murray, C., & Cox, L. *Beyond probation: Juvenile corrections and the chronic offender.* Beverly Hills, CA: Sage, 1979.
30. Goins, S. Testimony delivered before the Subcommittee to Investigate Juvenile Delinquency in the U.S. Senate Committee on the Judiciary, Washington, April 10, 1978.
31. Krajick, K. Working our way home. *Corrections,* 1978, *4*(2), 32-47.
32. Agee, V. *Treatment of the violent incorrigible adolescent.* Lexington, MA: Lexington Books, 1979.
33. Austin, R. L. I-level and the rehabilitation of delinquents. In N. Johnston, & L. Savitz (Eds.), *Justice and corrections.* New York: Wiley, 1978.
34. Coates, R., Miller, A., & Ohlin, L. *Diversity in a youth correctional system: Handling delinquents in Massachusetts.* Cambridge, MA: Ballinger, 1978.
35. Coates, 1981.
36. Coates, Miller, & Ohlin, 1978, p. 187.
37. Hazen, N. *The bridge to independence.* London: Blackwells, 1982.
38. Creekmore, M. *Intensive in-home care of juvenile delinquents: A preliminary evaluation report.* Ann Arbor, MI: Michigan Human Services, 1984.
39. McEwen, C. *Designing correctional organizations for youth: Dilemmas of subcultural development.* Cambridge, MA: Ballinger, 1978.
40. Wolins, M., & Wozner, Y. *Revitalizing residential settings.* San Francisco: Jossey-Bass, 1982.
41. McSweeny, A., Fremouw, M., & Hawkins, R. *Practical program evaluation in youth treatment.* Springfield, IL: Charles C Thomas, 1982.
42. Rutter, M., & Giller, H. *Juvenile delinquency: Trends and perspectives.* London: Penguin, 1983.

Part IV

SPECIAL ISSUES

15

Legal Issues and the Schools

Kathleen M. Quinn

The law that has had the greatest impact on schools today is the Education for All Handicapped Children Act of 1975, Public Law 94-142 (1). This Act was passed by a clear mandate in Congress in response to the need for increased funding, which was brought about by the widespread recognition by the courts and the state legislatures of the right of handicapped children to an adequate education. No other federal education law has promised so much, been so successful, or sparked such controversy. In tracing its history, we can review the history of schools and the law.

THE ROOTS OF P.L. 94-142

The origins of Public Law 94-142 lie in education, civil rights, and mental health law. As early as the 1930s, the courts recognized that the denial of education was a significant loss to any student (2). The 1954 Supreme Court decision, *Brown* v. *Board of Education*, forbade "separate but equal" school facilities and proclaimed the importance of education.

> Today, education is perhaps the most important function of state and local governments. . . . In these days it is doubtful that any child may reasonably be expected to succeed in life if he is denied the opportunity of an education (3).

The logic of describing the harmful effects of segregation in *Brown* v. *Board of Education* influenced advocates for the handicapped. These early decisions set a pattern; changes in the American education system would be brought about by those previously excluded or inadequately treated by the system—the handicapped and the culturally different (4).

Most handicapped students were excluded from public education in the nineteenth century. In the first half of this century, there were significant advances in the training of teachers and in the development of instructional methodology. Not until after World War II, however, was there a general recognition of the field of special education, which at that time was a generalized approach to all disabilities (5).

By 1957, there were federal monies appropriated for research into the problems of educating retarded children. In 1958, states were allocated federal monies for the training of teachers in mental retardation, a major breakthrough considering the widespread fear of federal influence into the field of education. Three years later, in 1961, President Kennedy established the President's Panel on Mental Retardation, which led to further federal programs and appropriations.

President Johnson and the Eighty-Ninth Congress first documented the dire need for educational services for the handicapped. After extensive negotiation with various education and religious interest groups was accomplished, the legitimacy of an expanded federal role in education, long solely a state function, was recognized. The years 1964–1966 saw the passage of some of the most ambitious programs ever to affect society and the schools: the Civil Rights Act of 1964; the Elementary and Secondary Education Act of 1965; the Higher Education Act of 1965; and in 1966, P.L. 89-750, the first federal education program for handicapped children (6).

In 1966, fewer than one-third of all handicapped children of school age in the United States were provided with an adequate education that was appropriate to their special needs. Public Law 89-750 authorized block-like grants to states to initiate or improve educational programs for handicapped children. Unlike the laws that would be passed in the 1970s, there were no fiscal restrictions for noncompliance with P.L. 89-750.

The passage of Section 504 of P.L. 93-112, the Vocational Act Amendments of 1973, however, profoundly changed the relationship between the federal government and state and local recipients of federal funds. The protection of the civil rights of all handicapped persons had to be guaranteed to ensure the receipt of federal funds. Section 504 states:

> No otherwise qualified handicapped individual in the United States . . . shall, solely by reason of his handicap, be excluded from participation in, be denied the benefits of, or be subjected to discrimination under any program or activity receiving federal financial assistance. (7)

Testimony heard by Congress citing the exclusion of an enormous number of handicapped children of school age, and severe lack of services for the handicapped, prompted the enactment of Section 504 and set the stage for stricter federal education laws for special needs.

Other forces, including a two-year study by the Children's Defense Fund (8) and several landmark court cases, were also preparing the way for P.L. 94-142. The study, entitled *Children Out of School in America*, indicated that over two million school-aged children were out of school. These children were overwhelmingly handicapped, poor, nonwhite or non-English speaking. In the early 1970s, 48 states had statutory exemptions in their compulsory attendance laws for children who were physically, mentally, or emotionally handicapped, or who "could not profit from an education" (9).

This study also demonstrated that those handicapped children who did go to school were segregated into special education tracks without proper assessment of their ability to learn in regular classrooms. Large numbers of black children with learning problems were misclassified as mentally retarded and placed in educable mentally retarded (EMR) classes at a rate three times that of white children (10).

Parents and civil rights advocates increasingly turned to the courts for a response. Two early cases dealt with the exclusion of children from school and their right to an appropriate education. In 1971, the Pennsylvania Association for Retarded Children (PARC) filed suit against the Commonwealth of Pennsylvania, claiming the exclusion of retarded children from school was a denial of equal protection and due process. No ruling was made on constitutional grounds; however, the court ratified a consent agreement that strongly favored the handicapped children. The court gave formal recognition of the right of each retarded child to access to a free public education. Additional requirements of the PARC suit included population and needs surveys, and recognition of the importance of monitoring compliance (11). Commentators described PARC as changing the locus of responsibility from the child to the school system. Now educational programs had to accommodate the child, rather than requiring the child to adapt to the program. Nearly 15,000 previously out-of-school children were admitted to public school in response to PARC. Over 50% were only mildly retarded (12).

A separate but related decision was made in *Mills* v. *Board of Education* (13), which extended the right to publicly supported education to *all* handicapped students. Rights to due process hearings in placement matters, especially where suspension from school was involved, were guaranteed (13). In 1967, *In re Gault* (14) had detailed rights to legal protection for juvenile delinquents. Now, *Mills* detailed a student's rights to both education and due process.

State legislatures began to pass legislation in response to citizen groups representing the handicapped. Vermont passed its education for the handicapped act in 1972, and Massachusetts in 1974. At the national level, the

Council for Exceptional Children drafted a 1972 policy statement advocating that handicapped children be educated whenever possible with children who were not handicapped, but with supplementary special services.

The concept of an educational "least restrictive environment" was also addressed in the PARC case. The court-approved consent decree read:

> It is the Commonwealth's obligation to place each mentally retarded child in a free, public program of education and training appropriate to the child's capacity, within the context of the general educational policy that, among the alternative programs of education and training required by statute to be available, placement in a regular public school is preferable to placement in a special public school class and placement in a special public school class is preferable to placement in any other type of program of education and training. (15)

The major concern of the court, educators, and parents in PARC who began the mainstreaming movement was the widespread practice of "dumping"—the placing of handicapped children into inadequate special classes.

Complementary trends were occurring in the areas of assessment and evaluation. In the late 1960s, public and professional controversy concerning the biases and discriminatory aspects of standard psychological testing of children erupted. A major concern was the false classification of minority students as intellectually subnormal, and their subsequent placement in special classes. This was hypothesized as a major mode of "dumping" minority students into segregated special classes that were overwhelmingly black in composition (16).

Several major cases concern challenges by minority students to the validity and equality of standardized, individually administered intelligence tests. *Diana* v. *State Board of Education* (17) resulted in a court-ratified agreement that children be tested in their native language. *Larry P.* v. *Riles* (18) was a class action suit for the black children in the San Francisco schools in which schools were charged with incorrectly labelling several black youths as mentally retarded, placing them in EMR classes, and thus restricting their educational opportunities.

The 1972 preliminary injunction by the federal district court forbade any future placement of black children in EMR classes on the primary basis of results of intelligence tests. However, the court refused to order reassignment of black students already in EMR classes and upheld the practice of segregating such students. The 1979 final opinion by Judge Peckham permanently enjoined the defendants

> from utilizing, permitting of or approving the use of any standardized tests . . . for the identification of black EMR children or their place-

ment into EMR classes, without first securing prior approval by the court. (19)

Recent action by the California legislature detailed comprehensive modifications of assessment techniques to prevent incorrect labeling and placement. The California Education Code (6902.085) now requires that testing be conducted only with parental consent, that a full developmental and academic history be gathered, and that the child be tested in his native language (20). Public Law 94-142 expanded and guaranteed these safeguards on the national level.

These early legislative and court actions ended the age when schools operated with total authority over children. Increasingly, the schools were becoming accountable to parents, to government, and to the courts.

P.L. 94-142

P.L. 94-142 codifies and expands the broadest procedural rights extended to handicapped children in earlier legislation and court cases. The 1975 Act is unique in both the breadth and detail of its procedural remedies, which are designed to serve the needs of the individual child.

Congress authorized large annual appropriations to aid states that were in compliance with the mandated services of P.L. 94-142. Forty-nine states (New Mexico is the exception) have elected to participate through the receipt of federal funds. The Act required states to provide a "free appropriate public education" to all handicapped children between the ages of three and 18 by September 1, 1978, and to all between three and 21 by September 1, 1980 (21). Handicapped children are defined to include the mentally retarded, learning disabled, physically handicapped, and emotionally disturbed (22).

P.L. 94-142 requires that all handicapped children, regardless of the severity of the handicapping condition, be provided a free, appropriate public education in the least restrictive environment appropriate to the needs of the child. The Act avoids prescribing specific educational programs, but instead outlines the procedure by which a program can be determined for any individual child. This process includes: 1) development of the child's Individualized Educational Program (IEP); 2) procedural safeguards; and 3) parental involvement.

An Individualized Education Program (IEP) is a "written statement for each handicapped child" that is developed at a meeting among the child's parents, teacher, and a qualified school representative (23). Either the school or the child's parents can initiate the individual planning and placement process. Under P.L. 94-142, parents have the right to be notified of any proposed school actions and of their rights under the law. They must be included in the development of the child's Individualized Educational Program through conferences with responsible school personnel.

The first step in developing an IEP is a multidisciplinary and racially nondiscriminatory educational evaluation conducted by school personnel to determine the extent of the child's special education needs. After this evaluation, a meeting is held in which parents and school personnel meet as *equal* partners to write a formal educational plan for the child. This plan must outline short- and long-term goals and the services to be provided to achieve these goals. If agreed upon by both parents and the school district, the IEP becomes a binding contract that can be enforced through either administrative hearings or civil litigation. If the parties do not agree, parents are entitled to an "impartial due process hearing" before a hearing officer who is not an employee of the agency involved in the education of the child (24). The issue may be appealed up from the local level to the state agency for review and then to civil action in a state or federal court. The legal burden of proof is based on the preponderance of the evidence.

The IEP is the key to obtaining needed services. Even if a district does not have the program specified in an IEP, it must arrange for such a program from other public or private agencies. These services are provided at no cost to the parent and must be in the least restrictive setting appropriate to the child's needs. P.L. 94-142's goal of "full educational opportunity" for all handicapped children and the provision of "a free appropriate public education" includes the provision of both special educational instruction and "related services." These related services, which are all specified in the IEP, may include transportation, speech therapy, psychological services, physical and occupational therapy, recreation, and diagnostic medical services. Other key provisions in P.L. 94-142 include monitoring procedures and population surveys of handicapped children in need of services.

P.L. 94-142 has had a profound effect on all its participants—children, parents, and educators included. The limits of P.L. 94-142 continue to be defined by the developing educational case law.

THE PERSONAL IMPACT OF P.L. 94-142

Impact on Parents

The greatest impact of P.L. 94-142 appears to have been on parents. P.L. 94-142 was demonstrated to be an impetus for parents to become more involved in the school life of their children. A 1980 study states:

By their own report, these parents have acted more and believed themselves to have accomplished more on behalf of their disabled children, than was ever the case for most prior to the legislation. In addition, as a result of the legislative responsibilities newly assumed, parents report having begun to think more optimistically about their children, about their children's potential in the larger society, and more broadly about their own possibilities as parents to help realize that potential. (25)

The impact on parents was not, however, totally positive. Many recounted bitter parent/professional confrontations over IEP's or the delivery of promised services. The vast majority of parents espoused the emphasis on mainstreaming their children whenever possible. The only organized opposition to integration come from parents of children already in separate placements (26). Overall, consumer satisfaction paralleled the individual school system's compliance with the due process safeguards detailed in P.L. 94-142, and the parents' agreement with their child's placement (27).

Impact on Children

The direct impact of P.L. 94-142 on children is more equivocal. There is no current evidence to suggest that students learn better in integrated versus segregated settings. Ongoing research on the impact of P.L. 94-142 may challenge this statement in the future (28).

Mainstreaming does offer children, teachers, and parents the single most effective way to combat prejudice about handicaps. Integration is also resulting in curriculum development to enhance the social interactions of all students in mainstreamed classrooms. One such example is an increased emphasis on group projects that include handicapped and nonhandicapped children, who share both the process of doing the project and the resulting grade (29, 30).

Factors are beginning to be identified that are associated with successful mainstreaming programs. Some of these factors include:

1) strong administrative and teacher support for an integrated program;
2) students grouped by chronological and not developmental age;
3) parents of both disabled and nondisabled students having a voice in school decision-making;
4) adequate staffing; and
5) a school with high expectations for achievement for both the disabled and nondisabled students (31).

Impact on Educators

The impact of P.L. 94-142 on educators has been profound. For all types of teachers, diagnoses and assessments are considered highly stressful activities. For resource room and special classroom teachers, pupil load and teaching responsibilities are major stresses. Surprisingly, in one study, writing IEP's and due process paperwork, two major P.L. 94-142 compliance issues, were rated low in terms of producing stress. High compliance with P.L. 94-142, which assisted in role clarity, alleviated stress (32).

Mainstreaming has confronted regular classroom teachers with their own biases. Studies show that regular classroom teachers' attitudes toward mainstreaming become less positive as grade level increases. The most negative attitudes toward mainstreaming are shown by junior high school teachers. Classroom size and type of school have little impact on teacher attitude. Variables such as the teacher's perception of his or her success with the handicapped students, the level of administrative support received, and the availability of supportive services have significant impact on teacher attitude (33).

These findings, and the persistent finding that children are most often placed on the basis of negative behaviors, not developmental level (34), strongly emphasize the need for effective in-service training of all school personnel active in implementing P.L. 94-142. Training must be intensive (e.g., weekly) to effect change in teachers' attitudes toward the handicapped and their own perceived ability to teach special needs children (35).

Impact on Physicians

Physician participation has traditionally been limited in school placement decisions. However, two separate trends may increase their role. The increasing emphasis in many pediatric training programs on behavioral pediatrics, family assessment, neurodevelopmental evaluation, and child advocacy may pave the way for some increase in the role of the pediatrician in the development and clinical monitoring of IEP's (36).

The publication of the American Psychiatric Association's *Diagnostic and Statistical Manual of Mental Disorders* (Third edition) (37) permits improved diagnosis and description of childhood disorders. Many public school districts have begun to require psychiatrists' reports as part of their diagnostic procedures. This is an outgrowth of the recognition by educators of the ambiguity in many special education classifications, especially in the area of severe emotional disturbance as defined in P.L. 94-142 (38).

RECENT CASE LAW

P.L. 94-142 has spurred rapid case law development to more fully define the Act's scope and limitations. Several trends evident in the origins of P.L.

94-142 continue. For example, in *Plyer* v. *Doe* (39), the Supreme Court reaffirmed that although education is not a fundamental right subject to the strictest judicial scrutiny, it is, without question, considerably more important than other forms of social welfare legislation. The Court stated that before education can be denied, the state must show the existence of a substantial countervailing state interest that outweighs the national benefits of educating children. Although *Plyer* v. *Doe* concerned children whose parents were illegal aliens, the arguments for concluding that the education of handicapped children is also of special importance is compelling.

In another major decision, the Supreme Court, in *Board of Education* v. *Rowley* (40), further defined "a free appropriate public education," stating that it required the state to provide personalized instruction and adequate supportive services to ensure that each child actually benefits from his or her planned education. An appropriate education for the handicapped is less than the best education possible, but more than the same education that nonhandicapped students receive. In the regular classroom, which is the preferred placement under the Act, the test is whether the IEP is reasonably calculated to enable the child to be promoted to the next grade level. What is "appropriate" allows for a wide range of alternatives to be tailored to each individual child.

The second general ruling of *Rowley* states that the scope of the Act's provisions for judicial review of the state's actions is circumscribed to include two situations: 1) whether there has been compliance with statutory procedures; and 2) whether the IEP is reasonably calculated to provide the child with educational benefits. Courts are to review procedures while educational methodology is left to local and state agencies. Many commentators see *Rowley* as a reentrenchment from the newly won right of the handicapped envisioned in the original drafting of P.L. 94-142.

Several other cases and budgetary proposals by the Reagan administration have also heralded such a backlash. These include a new federal district court opinion (*PASE* v. *Hannon* [41]) that concludes that intelligence tests, when supplemented by other data, are not racially biased when applied to the placement of black children into specialized classes for the mentally retarded. In 1981 and 1982, the Reagan administration pushed to return to the model of educational block grants, as well as a prohibition of federal regulations governing education. These proposals have been set forward, despite the poor history of compliance by states in the 1960s and early 1970s under similar fiscal conditions.

More expansive interpretations of P.L. 94-142 have arisen in other cases. In *Tatro* v. *Texas* (42), a federal court ruled on an ongoing suit brought by the parents of a five-year-old handicapped child in need of urinary catheterization as a "related educational service." The court ordered the provision of catheterization services by the local school district. Most importantly, it ordered, under Section 504, attorneys' fees and expenses. The awarding of attorneys' fees has become a major issue in many educational cases due to the expense of pursuing litigation. Recent cases on the appellate level are nearly equally divided on this question of awarding attorneys' fees.

Financial issues around placement have been more consistently handled by the courts. Numerous cases have stated that the child must remain in the current placement during the pendency of administrative and judicial proceedings unless the parents and the school officials agree to a change. Unilateral special placements by parents will not be reimbursed (43).

In a continuing effort to individualize educational plans, the Third Circuit upheld the *Armstrong* v. *Kline* (44) district court decision that voided the 180-day educational year limit in Pennsylvania. The compelling argument to the court was the description of a regression/recoupment cycle suffered by the plaintiffs that was caused by breaks in their education program.

Finally, one of the most difficult and controversial areas concerning P.L. 94-142 has been the procedures necessary to expel students who argue that their behavior is a result of a handicap. The majority of recent cases state that expulsion constitutes a change in educational placement that requires the procedural protection of P.L. 94-142, and that expulsion never justifies a complete cessation of educational services (45, 46).

CONCLUSION

P.L. 94-142 has been described as the Magna Carta of education (47). Its origins are entwined with the civil rights movement of the 1950s and 1960s. As the most important piece of educational legislation in this country's history, it presents a continuing challenge to educators, mental health professionals, and the courts as standards are established by individual cases (48). Particular emphasis should continue to be placed on the continuously underserved, such as the handicapped adolescent (49), and unique populations, such as migrant children (50).

REFERENCES

1. Pub. L. No. 94-142, 89 Stat. 773 (1975) (codified at 20 U.S.C. §§ 1401-1461 [1976]).
2. *Sioux Tribe* v. *United States*, 84 Ct. Cl. 16 (1936), cert. denied 302 U.S. 740 (1937).
3. 347 U.S. 483, 493 (1954).
4. Keogh, B. K., & Barkett, C. J. Children's rights in assessment and school placement. *Journal of Social Issues*, 1978, *34*, 87-111.
5. Dybwad, G. Avoiding misconceptions of mainstreaming, the least restrictive environment, and normalization. *Exceptional Children*, 1980, *47*, 85.
6. Hamilton, B. E., & Yohalem, D. The effects of federal deregulation. The case of handicapped children. *Education and Urban Society*, 1982, *14*, 399-423.

7. 29 U.S.C. §§ 794.
8. Children's Defense Fund. *Children out of school in America.* Cambridge, MA: Children's Defense Fund, 1974.
9. *Ibid.*
10. *Ibid.*
11. *Pennsylvania Association for Retarded Children* v. *Commonwealth of Pennsylvania*, 343 F. Supp. 279 (E.D. Pa., 1972).
12. Gilhool, T. K. Changing public policies: Roots and forces. In Special Learning Corporations, *Mainstreaming: Origins and implications*, Vol. 20. Minneapolis, MN: University of Minnesota, 1976, p. 9.
13. *Mills* v. *Board of Education*, 348 F. Supp. 886 (D.D.C., 1972).
14. In re *Gault*, 387 U.S. 1, 87 S.C.E. 1428, 18 L.E.D., 2d. 527, (1967).
15. 334 F. Supp. at 1260.
16. Hobbs, N. (Ed.). *Issues in the classification of children (Vol. 2).* San Francisco: Jossey-Bass, 1975.
17. *Diana* v. *State Board of Education*, No. C-70-37 (N.D. Cal. 1970).
18. *Larry P.* v. *Riles*, 343 F. Supp., 1306 (N.D. Cal. 1972).
19. *Ibid.*, p. 989.
20. Keogh & Barkett, 1978, p. 91.
21. 20 U.S.C. § 1412(2)(B)(1976).
22. 20 U.S.C. § 1401(1)(1976).
23. 20 U.S.C. § 1401(19).
24. 20 U.S.C. § 1415(b)(2).
25. Biklen, D. The least restrictive environment: Its application to education. In G. B. Melton (Ed.), *Legal reforms affecting child and youth services.* New York: Haworth Press, 1982, p. 22.
26. *Ibid.*
27. Polifka, J. C. Compliance with Public Law 94-142 and consumer satisfaction. *Exceptional Children*, 1981, *48*, 250-253.
28. Biklen, 1982, p. 131.
29. Dunlop, K. H., Stoneman, Z., & Cantrell, M. L. Social interaction of exceptional and other children in a mainstreamed preschool classroom. *Exceptional Children*, 1980, *47*, 132–141.
30. Johnson, D. W., & Johnson, R. T. Integrating handicapped students into the mainstream. *Exceptional Children*, 1980, *47*, 90-98.
31. Biklen, 1982, p. 136.
32. Bensky, J. M., Shaw, S. F., Gouse, A. S., Bates, H., et al. Public Law 94-142 and Stress: A Problem for Educators. *Exceptional Children*, 1980, *47*, 24-29.
33. Larrivee, B., & Cook, L. Mainstreaming: A study of the variables affecting teacher attitude. *The Journal of Special Education*, 1979, *13*, 315-324.
34. Voeltz, L. M., Evans, I. M., Freedland, K., & Donellon, S. Teacher decision-making in the selection of educational programming priorities for severely handicapped children. *The Journal of Special Education*, 1982, *16*, 179-198.
35. Larrivee, B. Effect of inservice training intensity on teachers' attitudes toward mainstreaming. *Exceptional Children*, 1981, *48*, 34-39.
36. Levine, M. The child with school problems: An analysis of physician participation. *Exceptional Children*, 1982, *48*, 296-304.
37. American Psychiatric Association. *Diagnostic and Statistical Manual* (Third ed.). Washington, D.C.: American Psychiatric Association, 1980.
38. Forness, S. R., & Cantwell, D. P. DSM III psychiatric diganoses and special education categories. *The Journal of Special Education*, 1982, *16*, 49-63.
39. *Plyer* v. *Doe*, 50 U.S.L.W. 4650 (U.S. June 15, 1982).
40. *Board of Education of the Hendrick Hudson Central School District* v. *Rowley*, 50 U.S.L.W. 4925 (U.S. June 28, 1982).
41. *Parents in Action on Special Education* v. *Hannon*, NO. 74C 3586, (N.D. Ill. July 7, 1980).
42. *Tatro* v. *Texas*, No. CA-3-79-1281-6 (N.D. Tex. May 26, 1981).

43. Reimbursement pending education appeal denied by three U.S. circuits. *Mental Disability Law Reporter*, 1983, 7, 77-79.
44. *Armstrong* v. *Kline*, No. 79-2158 (3rd Cir., July 15, 1980).
45. *S-1* v. *Turlington*, 635 F. 2d 342 (5th Cir., 1981).
46. *Kaelin* v. *Grubbs*, No. 81-5101 (6th Cir., July 9, 1982).
47. Corrigan, D. C. Political and moral contexts that produced P.L. 94-142. *Journal of Teacher Education*, 1978, 29, 10-14.
48. Note, Enforcing the right to an "appropriate" education: The Education for All Handicapped Children Act of 1975. *Harvard Law Review*, 1979, 92, 1103-1127.
49. Miller, S. R. A crisis in appropriate education: The dearth of data on programs for secondary handicapped adolescents. *The Journal of Special Education*, 1981, 15, 351-360.
50. Pyecha, J. N., & Ward, L. A. A study of the implementation of Public Law 94-142 for handicapped migrant children. *Exceptional Children*, 1982, 48, 490-495.

16

Psychiatric Commitment of Children and Adolescents: Issues, Current Practices, and Clinical Impact

W. V. Burlingame and Marc Amaya

HISTORICAL PERSPECTIVE

Until the past several decades, any attempt to discern a "children's rights" movement would have constituted an empty exercise inasmuch as the American legal traditions, which descend from 18th century English common law, tended to view children as chattel or property of their parents and household. In this context, children were construed as indebted to their parents, and the latter as holding near total responsibility and authority regarding the care, management, and placement of their children. Only comparatively recently has a body of law emerged that enunciates the constitutional rights possessed by children vis-à-vis their caretakers, including schools, public agencies, health care facilities, correctional institutions, and societal authorities in general, as well as parents and guardians. Originally, the doctrine of *parens patriae* established a philosophical basis for the state to intervene on behalf of dependent, handicapped, and defenseless individuals, specifically children, mental patients, and the retarded. *Parens patriae* theory was applied in its earliest years to conspicuous instances of dependency, neglect, and abuse. Intrusions into parental authority were balanced against the nature of a particular situation, but did include the most extreme of remedies which was the termination of all parental rights.

Perhaps the grandest embodiment of *parens patriae* was the establishment of the juvenile justice system in this country, in which "the best interest of the child" standard provided enormous latitude and discretion to courts in their dispositions of matters relating to children. Conventional courtroom procedures, standards of proof, and due process protections were abridged and relinquished, and the newly established child mental health disciplines were embraced, thereby creating a social welfare model espousing treatment and rehabilitation to guide judges in their dispositions. Unfortunately, the newly prescribed remedies—child guidance clinics, juvenile correctional facilities, foster placements, detention centers, and assorted children's institutions—were all too often grossly underfinanced, understaffed, and overcrowded. As a result, familial editions of neglect and abuse were supplanted with those perpetrated by the state and its agencies. Generations of children who failed to respond to the ministrations of the mental health disciplines or who appeared to deteriorate in response to multiple foster placements and inadequate institutional care led to a growing disenchantment with the social welfare and rehabilitation model, and, in some quarters, for a yearning to return to due process principles with a lesser reliance on the ambiguous "best interest" standard.

The pivotal event in contemporary children's rights occurred in 1967, when the Supreme Court ruled that the then common juvenile court procedures permitted infringements on the constitutional rights of children. Several years before, in Arizona, 15-year-old Gerald Gault was charged with making an obscene telephone call consisting of sexually charged questions directed at a neighbor. This alleged act fell on an already existing probation (having been in the company of another boy who had stolen from a woman's purse), and he was committed to his state's industrial training school for a period not to exceed his minority (six years). These juvenile court transactions were, of course, considerably out of keeping with what might have occurred had Gault been an adult: If convicted as an adult, he would have been issued the maximum fine under Arizona statute—$50 or a jail sentence of 60 days. The Supreme Court ultimately reversed the conviction and required sweeping procedural and due process protections, which fell somewhat short of those enjoyed by adults in criminal proceedings, but did include the right to written notice of charges, the right to counsel, the privilege against self-incrimination, and the rights to confrontation and sworn testimony of witnesses (1). Included in the decision was a ringing assault on the "best interest" standard and the social welfare model for juvenile justice, in keeping with a slightly earlier decision in which a federal court observed "...that the child receives the worst of both worlds: that he gets neither the protection accorded to adults nor the solicitous care and regenerative treatment postulated for children" (2). In noting the discrepancies in sentencing and the multiple limitations of the juvenile court, the Supreme Court held that:

... it would be extraordinary if our Constitution did not require the procedural regularity and the exercise of care implied in the phrase "due process." Under our Constitution, the condition of being a boy does not justify a kangaroo court.(3)

Eight years were to elapse before the principles established in the *Gault* decision were successfully transferred from juvenile justice proceedings to psychiatric hospitalization. The transference occurred in North Carolina when Michael Long, a 15-year-old, was admitted to Dorothea Dix Hospital on the signature of his mother. The admission was consistent with that state's voluntary admission statute, which permitted a parent, guardian, or person standing *in loco parentis* to admit a minor for psychiatric treatment in a public or private facility, with or without his concurrence and without further administrative, judicial, or clinical review, aside from that of the admitting physician. This particular procedure was by far the most common practice and was honored in nearly all states, as a result of either direct statutory provision or derivative policy, in the same fashion as an admission of a minor to a general hospital might occur. Irrespective of Michael Long's psychiatric condition, a superior court released him on the basis of a finding of deprivation of freedom without due process protections guaranteed by the Fourteenth Amendment. The North Carolina Court of Appeals later upheld the lower court's decision, citing the possibility of error in judgment of admitting psychiatrists, and applying the principles of *Gault*.

So, in 1975, psychiatric hospitalization in North Carolina was deemed to constitute a loss of liberty for a child admitted by a parent, and such children were seen as at risk in view of a potential for diagnostic error and an inherent conflict of interest between parent and child (4). Due process protections were mandated and, in order to avoid the precipitous release of several hundred children and adolescents, the North Carolina legislature hastily enacted a statute that established adversarial hearings within 10 days following the admission of a minor by his parent. Guaranteed to the child or adolescent were representation by counsel, the right to notice, the right to confront and cross-examine witnesses, and a mechanism for review consisting of periodic rehearings at which treatment personnel must demonstrate continuing evidence of mental illness and a need for additional treatment.

Independent of the North Carolina case, two additional cases were advancing through the courts from Pennsylvania and Georgia. The essential issues were identical: whether parents may secure psychiatric hospitalization for a minor child on the recommendation of mental health personnel without additional independent judicial or administrative review. Other circumstances, however, made these latter cases considerably more complex. North Carolina hospitalized relatively few children in state psychiatric facilities, and most of these were in comparatively well-funded child and adolescent specialty units. Larger numbers of children resided in the Georgia and Pennsylvania institutions, a significant number of whom were in the custody of state agencies and had no residence or placement beyond the facility. In Georgia, state authorities acknowledged that more than half of the children no longer required hospitalization but remained in the institution due to the absence of other placements, particularly foster care. These circumstances were telling and apparently weighed heavily in lower court decisions that ordered due process protections.

In 1979, a divided Supreme Court ruled in a most controversial decision to uphold parental authority for psychiatric admission when accompanied by concurring clinical opinion and periodic review. Chief Justice Burger, writing for the majority, described the case as a balancing of the child's liberty interest in not being unnecessarily confined, the parents' interest in maintaining the mental and physical health of the child, and the State's interest in "confining the use of its costly mental health facilities to cases of genuine need" (5). In speaking directly to the issue of the child's constitutional rights, he wrote:

> We conclude that the risk of error inherent in the parental decision to have a child institutionalized for mental health care is sufficiently great that some kind of inquiry should be made by a "neutral fact-finder" to determine whether the statutory requirements for admission are satisfied. [Citations omitted] That inquiry must carefully probe the child's background using all available sources, including, but not limited to, parents, schools and other social agencies. Of course, the review must also include an interview with the child. It is necessary that the decisionmaker have the authority to refuse to admit any child who does not satisfy the medical standards for admission. Finally it is necessary that the child's continuing need for commitment be reviewed periodically by a similarly independent procedure. (6)

The Supreme Court thus preserved the admissions procedures in some 30 states, and prescribed a constitutional minimum in terms of clinical and administrative safeguards of the child's liberty interest. It also spoke, somewhat ambiguously, to the need for periodic review of the commitment and, in so doing, appeared to set the stage for another round of litigation. In establishing a minimum, it did not, of course, prohibit states from enacting additional due process, as had North Carolina and, later, California, which found the traditional admission procedure to be violative of that state's constitution.

The *Parham* decision was perceived in many quarters as a stunning defeat ("a hell of a way to celebrate the year of the child" [7]). Some considered it to be a definitive statement that would resolve issues regarding the balance of parent-child-state authority relative to psychiatric admissions. For example, Judge Patricia Wald, writing shortly after the decision, stated:

> The *Parham* decision represented a resounding victory for parental authority. It is difficult to envision very many—if any—situations short of abuse or neglect, where courts will now intervene to monitor family decisions about the medical or psychiatric treatment of children if professional support is present. Legislative changes are still possible but, in light of the political strength of family-rightists, not likely. (8)

Others considered the decision to be sufficiently narrow and restricted that additional tests were likely, while some, perhaps wishfully, felt that the decision was so out of keeping with the times, as well as empirical data regarding diagnostic and placement errors in the admissions process in some states, that it would eventually be overturned. Still others observed, probably quite accurately, that the pace of providing additional due process protections would certainly be slowed by *Parham*, but that the next round would be fought out in the states.

In a larger sense, the *Parham* decision needs to be viewed in the context of an array of items over which the relative power and interests of children, their parents, and the State is being vigorously contested and forged. While broad parental authority over minor children was reaffirmed in keeping with our family centered society, courts have gradually tailored additional rights to children and adolescents, but with increasing restraint and less willingness to provide the complete adult panoply. Thus, juveniles have since been denied the right to a jury trial in juvenile justice proceedings, although *Gault* forced many additional due process procedures previously enjoyed by adults in criminal proceedings. Increasingly, children have been able to secure medical and psychiatric treatment in their own right, and parents have been prohibited from exercising a veto over a girl's decision to secure an abortion. Limited due process rights have also been secured relative to school disciplinary measures. In spite of the setback for children's rights advocates in *Parham*, the impetus for further definition will surely be maintained, and litigation is certain to continue on many fronts. David Ferleger, who was counsel for the plaintiffs in the Pennsylvania case, even suggests items for future suits, although the following statement was written before the final *Parham* decision:

> The declaration of a right to a hearing prior to a stigmatizing deprivation of liberty raises tantalizing questions about children's rights to object to boarding schools for "problem" children, summer camps for the handicapped, and parental consent for psychotropic medication.

A more general sensitivity of the freedom of people in childhood may lead to a questioning of issues in our national lifestyle that now go unnoticed. Does a child have a right to an advocate to protect against an unnecessary tonsillectomy? Can a daycare student object to placement in one play group when he prefers another? Under what circumstances can a child choose to leave the protection of his or her parents for a life with other loving adults? And more. (9)

CURRENT PRACTICES AND ISSUES

As previously noted, the 1979 *Parham* decision protected statutes and policies existing in a majority of states that established parental authority relative to the psychiatric admissions of minors. In a summary of state statute prepared the year before, the movement for judicial review and procedural protections was only barely discernible (10). In 37 states, the statutes, as of 1978, provided for unilateral parental consent until age 18 (or with variant procedures in some states between 13 and 18); in an additional seven states, no mention of minors occurred, presumably leaving authority to parents or to state agencies to develop additional policies. Judicial oversight was provided for in only five instances. Several more states recognized the developing competencies of minors to make decisions on their own behalf by permitting those over 14 or 16 to admit and discharge themselves, while others attempted to balance the matter by requiring the consent of both parents and their minor children. All states, of course, provided for involuntary hospitalization based on a "dangerousness" standard for both adults and minors, while a few states provided for initial parental admission of a minor according to the voluntary statute that, if opposed by the child, could be continued only if the minor met the standards for involuntary commitment.

Within five years, practices changed significantly (11) (see Table 1). Distinct shifts toward establishing procedural due process relative to voluntary psychiatric admission of minors by their parents (and to their continued hospitalization), toward permitting youths to admit and discharge themselves, and toward sharing the authority with parents, occurred. *Parham* itself, of course, could have better served to reverse the trend, and it would appear that the shift was set in motion by the lower court decisions in the Georgia and Pennsylvania cases occurring in concert with vigorous advocacy on the part of children's rights advocates.

Thus, the years surrounding *Parham* led to an even greater diversification of practice among the various states—with several maintaining parental control over admission and discharge up to age 18, and with North Carolina alone requiring formal adversarial hearings for all admissions and at specified intervals thereafter if treatment is to continue. The following is a more

Table 1. Voluntary Admissions Statutes for Minors in 1982.

Number of States	Statutory Provision for Voluntary Admission
22	Unilaterial parental consent is authorized for minors up to at least age 12, with some states providing varying procedures for minors between 13 and 18; no statutory provision for appeal or objection exists.
4	No mention of minors or younger minors occurs or is implied in statute, presumably leaving authority to parents (as in other medical care), or to state agencies to develop additional policies.
12	Consent of both parents and minors (usually adolescents) was required for admission.
14	Children and adolescents (16 and 17 year olds in six states, 14 and 15 year olds in five states, and 12 year olds and younger in three states) may apply for admission unilaterally.
5	In five additional states, adolescents may admit themselves voluntarily, but parents may then seek discharge via a hearing or hospital decision.
19	Judicial or administrative review is or may be mandated prior to or subsequent to parental admission of minors, as follows: screening by external mental health authorities is required (California, Delaware); "voluntariness" of the minor's unilateral consent for treatment is reviewed (New Jersey, Florida); child, older adolescent, or other person may petition for or secure a judicial review potentially leading to release or transfer to another setting (Colorado, Connecticut, Hawaii, Iowa, Michigan, New Mexico, Ohio, Pennsylvania, Texas); children 12 and older may object to continued hospitalization and, if not discharged, are reviewed by court (Illinois); courts review all admissions under age 14 and conduct hearings if the child objects (Wisconsin); courts review all admissions of minors in formal, adversarial hearings (North Carolina); objection to continuing hospitalization triggers an administrative review by external mental health board (South Dakota); any patient may appear before a review board at six month intervals (Minnesota); an independent admissions review committee must approve all hospitalization lasting beyond six months (Tennessee).
2	Voluntary admissions of minors or younger children are essentially prohibited.

detailed description of specific state policies that serves to illustrate both overall patterns as well as innovative approaches (12, 13).

South Carolina: In South Carolina, the traditional admissions process for juveniles has been retained. For children under 16, a parent may apply for admission "on behalf" of the child. However, those 16 and over may apply for psychiatric admission in their own right and without regard to parental wishes (as is permitted in 12 other states). There is no statutory provision for the appeal of, or challenge to a parental decision to admit, and there is no provision establishing a right to counsel or other advocate; the statutes do not speak to the issue of review of continued treatment. The provisions in South Carolina are similar to the practices of approximately half the states. However, in 1983, a legislative committee recommended the enactment of a judicial review procedure, modelled after that of North Carolina, that would result in dramatic changes and, if adopted, would place this state among the handful that has chosen the adversarial hearing as the vehicle for ensuring procedural due process.

District of Columbia: As a federal facility, St. Elizabeth's Hospital could be bound only to the minimum standards established by *Parham*. In a post-*Parham* consent order, which settled a suit contesting the same constitutional issues, the parental right to admit a child up to age 18 was retained. However, there was recognition of the vulnerability of one particular group of children, those in agency custody. St. Elizabeth's agreed not to admit children in the Department of Human Resources's custody without a hearing in which guardianship is assigned to the Department, or unless another legal guardian makes voluntary application for admission. Thus, some form of additional due process would be provided for wards of the District in many instances. Consistent with the Supreme Court's opinion that independent review of the child's continuing treatment was required, the consent decree calls for a review every 60 days in which there would be assessment of the correctness of diagnosis, the appropriateness of treatment, and whether St. Elizabeth's constituted the least restrictive alternative. The reviews are to be conducted by a two-person multidisciplinary team of child experts that is clinically and administratively independent of the child's treatment unit.

Tennessee: This state has enacted an administrative review that is both unique and innovative, and may represent a potential for compromise that could be adopted or modified by other states. Children under 16 continue to be admitted to state facilities by their parents, and as of the most recent interpretation of statute, are not permitted to discharge themselves. If a child is to remain beyond an initial six month period of treatment, then his treatment must be reviewed by the facility's admissions review committee, which is empowered to secure discharge. The committee is comprised of child mental health professionals, two of whom are appointed by the facility superintendent and two of whom are appointed by the Tennessee Association of Mental Health Centers. A vote of at least three of the four members is required in order to approve additional hospitalization. The statute is apparently limited in that it does not extend to private facilities and does not specify standards, criteria, or procedures to be followed.

New Mexico: In 1978, this state established an elaborate, complex, and perhaps cumbersome admissions statute that leaned heavily in the direction of ensuring due process protections and shifting greater authority for admission to the minor child. Minors 12 and older may voluntarily admit themselves for treatment without parental consent after completing various documents prior to admission. They may also discharge themselves at any point, unless the hospital initiates and secures an involuntary commitment. An attorney who has no conflict of interest meets with the child to assess the voluntariness of his admission within seven days of admission. For those under 12, dual consent for admission is required, and the child is entitled to a court hearing if he objects to continuing hospitalization. The statute is weighted with much procedural detail (e.g., the initialling of documents, certifications of voluntariness, notifications to concerned parties).

North Carolina: This state has enacted statutes representing the most rigorous of due process protections currently in existence. The voluntary admission of a minor by his parents, guardian, or person standing *in loco parentis* requires a closed hearing in district court within 10 days, in which a three-pronged standard must be met if hospitalization is to continue: that the minor is "mentally ill," i.e., impaired in the development or exercise of age-appropriate or age-adequate self-control, judgment, or initiative (as determined by affidavits and/or testimony); that the person is in need of further treatment; and that lesser treatment measures will be insufficient. The minor is represented by counsel, and the hearing is adversarial in nature if the patient chooses to contest. In an uncontested hearing, the presence of the patient may be waived by counsel. The parents' interests are not represented unless they opt to retain private counsel, although an Assistant Attorney General represents the state and hospital's interests which are often those of the parents if both are seeking continued hospitalization. Upon presentation of testimony and other evidence, the court may approve 90 days of maximum treatment at the initial hearing, and must conduct rehearings periodically if treatment is to continue. North Carolina's judicial review is required for both public and private psychiatric facilities, and has been recently extended to other, nonpsychiatric forms of closed or restrictive residential care; this expansion of due process in North Carolina is as unprecedented as the initial judicial review of psychiatric admissions. There is also provision for a 30-day admission for evaluation in which less rigorous standard must be met.

Quite apart from constitutional matters relating to the child's liberty interests and the rights of parents, a host of related issues have generated intense discussion. In North Carolina, for example, the initial establishment of judicial review did not result in the release of any of the hundreds of minor patients, suggesting to some that there was essentially no one who needed or required that state's new safeguards.

As untrained judges rendered decisions and as attorneys of varying quality were assigned to represent minors, a body of lore emerged to the effect that judicial error was more devastating than clinical error, and that the manipulations of occasional attorneys provided additional unsavory models for delinquent adolescents. The process itself was found to be cumbersome, expensive, time-consuming, and intrusive into the staff time that might otherwise have gone to patient care; the preparation for court appearances, the provision of affidavits, and the maintenance of support to parents, minor patients, and community personnel, all of whom might testify in a contested hearing, might consume weeks of clinical time.

It also seemed probable that certain youths were essentially deprived of treatment because some psychiatric inpatient units, which were comfortable in dealing with voluntary adult patients, were unwilling to endure the process of judicial review or would discharge a youth rather than be subjected to a contested hearing. On infrequent occasions, patients were released whom mental health professionals deemed as meeting statutory criteria for admission and treatment. Occasionally, attorneys for the patients resorted to utilizing an unintentional technical error committed in the admitting process as grounds for securing release.

In general, however, in those states that provide for formal adversarial hearings, the most vociferous objections come from mental health professionals who cite unfortunate clinical outcomes resulting from a significant number of the hearings (14, 15, 16). For some children, personality defenses and self-esteem are further threatened by the disclosure of diagnoses and psychiatric findings in court, while the adversarial proceeding itself creates an additional forum in which the disturbed relationship between the parents and child may deteriorate further as the former press for hospitalization against the child's wishes and recite once again the litany of the child's difficulties and offenses. By the same token, the all-important relationship between the child and his therapist, who must also testify in favor of hospitalization, may be taxed in an unfortunate fashion, and the therapist may need to warp and distort his techniques in order to secure data in preparation for a hearing.

At least as distressing for many clinicians has been the finding that delinquently-oriented adolescents who, as a group tend to deny, rationalize, and project responsibility for their acting out, find the adversarial hearing made to order for legalistic maneuvering and manipulation—thus continuing their refusal to assume personal responsibility for their dilemma while essentially prolonging treatment as a function of enhanced resistance. The very nature of the proceeding suggests to the delinquent what he craves to hear: The crux of the issue is that others may infringe on his rights and that he is entitled to resist in order to continue in his narcissistic, omnipotent, and antisocial activities.

For younger children, and for those who are fragile, the challenge to the authority of parents and treament personnel may inordinately and unfortunately threaten their security by implying that the adults upon whom they must rely are fallible, in error, or, perhaps, duplicitous. Some clinicians have called attention to adolescents' ambivalence and conflicts regarding authority, dependency, and autonomy and have interpreted adversarial hearings as unfortunate events that may aggravate these issues:

The first court hearing within ten days of admission focuses largely on the youth's past life, and the reasons for hospitalization are usually readily apparent. For some youths, this is another part of the admission process which is confusing but not paramount. For others, an adversarial tone is immediately set. The youth finds external support for the longstanding defense of trying to stir adults to battle in order to avoid inner feelings. These often are the adolescents who yearn most to have reliable adults set limits on their impulses. They are threatened by the fact that the adults they long for are held as needing scrutiny and to being overruled by an outside authority whose full fighting force they can mobilize by even capriciously saying they do not want the longed for adults. The ambivalence is acted out in the courtroom rather than being examined in therapy. Additionally, a tone of punishment is set because of the societal context of the court and "rights" issues. The common phrase after a court hearing is "I got" so many days. Unmistakably, the implication is a sentence and the youth's attention is directed toward what the judge rules rather than progress in treatment in order to be ready for discharge. On some level, regressive defenses of looking for magical answers for problems are rekindled. For some adolescents this theme persists and greatly interferes with investment in the difficult treatment process. The youth remains convinced that instead of doing the hard work the Program stands for, the judge can magically pronounce an end to the problems and that persistance will lead the judge to "give in," since Program staff who are tested daily have shown the needed stamina to resist defensive attempts at shortcuts to true progress. (17)

In at least one instance, however, clinicians cited a beneficial outcome resulting from a contested hearing, in which an experienced juvenile court judge admonished an acting-out adolescent girl and urged her to make use of the opportunity for treatment (18). But, on the whole, clinicians tend to be much more dubious regarding the overall impact of judicial incursion on what was previously the domain of parents and clinicians. In states and programs where children are placed appropriately in psychiatric facilities, clinicians are able to respond directly to what they perceive as the deleterious impact on treatment:

> clinicians are likely to see their jobs made needlessly more complicated by the legal system. Since the system offers one more avenue of escape from the internal changes necessary for these adolescents to have a chance of succeeding in society, it does a great disservice to those it is designed to protect. By questioning and challenging the authority and wisdom of the recommended treatment, the system endangers the legitimacy of the teenager working with the treatment team. The teenager's investment must partly reside outside of treatment, focused instead on what a judge may do or think. The court hearings, if they operate in a true adversary fashion, are hardly benign affairs and are considered by clinicians to be a cruel charade. Instead of protecting the adolescent, the legal system serves as one more institution insensitive to the adolescent's actual needs, and provides one more set of adults to be used and manipulated. (19)

VIGNETTES AND DISCUSSION

In the absence of empirical data regarding the actual outcomes and side effects of the various procedures employed in the psychiatric admissions of minors, there must be continued reliance on anecdotal accounts. The following vignettes are disguised events and are offered without any certain knowledge of their frequency. Although clinicians are troubled by both the outcomes and the by-products of courtroom encounters, most would agree that the larger proportion of admissions in those states providing judicial review go uncontested. Similarly, most children's rights advocates would agree that psychiatric admission is certainly useful and necessary in many instances. Thus, much of the controversy must surround those few cases in which there is damage or loss to the child for whatever reason, together with those measures—legal, clinical, and administrative—that will protect the most and damage the fewest at the least cost.

Indefensible Institutionalization

Joey L., one of the two plaintiffs in the Georgia suit, is probably an archetypal representative of that class of children for whom the original purposes of hospitalization were achieved, but who remain within a facility due to the lack of an alternative placement. Joey, as well as the other plaintiff (J.R.), were both in the custody of the Department of Family and Children's Services, which was unsuccessful in securing a foster placement with "a warm, supportive, truly involved couple" as had been recommended by Central State Regional Hospital professionals following some four years of hospitalization (20). Joey was admitted at age six, with uncontrollable aggression, which led to school expulsion, and did not respond to outpatient treatment. His mother and stepfather participated in family therapy, permitted visits, and eventually attempted to have Joey reside with them while attending school at the hospital. Their inability to control him led to his readmission to the hospital after two months, and they ultimately relinquished parental rights to the county when he was 10. He remained at Central State, and in the following year, the *Parham* suit was filed.

Joey's co-plaintiff, J.R., was deemed neglected and was removed from his parents at three months of age. At age seven, he was admitted to the hospital due to severe aggression and the failure of seven foster placements. During his stay at the hospital, there were additional unsuccessful attempts at foster care prior to the inception of the suit, which sought less restrictive placement.

Joey and J.R., and the plaintiff group in the Pennsylvania suit, are representative of the larger group of agency children. To the extent that such exist in residential or group care—including public and private hospitals, centers for the retarded, wilderness settings, schools, and residential treatment settings—there need to be mechanisms to protect their liberty interests, as well as their treatment and developmental needs.

The Supreme Court held that the independent admission evaluation was sufficient for psychiatric hospitals, but did not consider those children in less obvious or conspicuous forms of care. For those other settings, the most extreme of remedies, mandatory judicial review, would be burdensome beyond belief to all concerned. However, it would appear that administrative or clinical review, perhaps as a continuing condition of licensure, may be in order for other forms of group care of dependent, disturbed, or retarded children. In public facilities, the inability to force discharge or release, not institutional unwillingness or a failure to recognize need, constitutes the major factor contributing to the presence of these groups. The absence of reliable data regarding the numbers of these youths in particular states makes it additionally difficult to propose solutions. In a tragic and ironic footnote to the Joey L. case, it was dramatically demonstrated that a less restrictive, noninstitutional placement is no guarantee of relief. Joey hanged himself at age 12, shortly after his natural father secured custody and took Joey to live with him. The father was convicted of abuse six months later following testimony that Joey had been tied to a bed, forced to sit in one place for up to 15 hours, and had suffered other similar disciplinary and control measures.

There are other comparatively rarer instances of psychiatric hospitalization that are of dubious merit. Melanie was the 17-year-old daughter of the board chairman of a major corporation. After a childhood of material comfort, but with a father who was largely absent and a depressed, remote mother, she was sent to boarding school at age 13. Although bright and capable, she did poorly and rather quickly became involved in drug usage, running away, and life on the streets. On the advice of consulting professionals, Melanie was hospitalized in a costly but conservative, closed, private psychiatric facility, from which she immediately attempted to escape. What ensued was a three year struggle between Melanie, her family, and hospital authorities, with Melanie vigorously resisting treatment, running away, and being returned by private detectives.

Melanie sought legal advice and obtained an alternative psychiatric opinion to the effect that there was no convincing evidence of disabling psychopathology requiring hospitalization, but rather, a marked value clash between her and her upper-middle-class parents. It was also argued that her father's willingness to hospitalize was more in the service of preserving his authority and avoiding the embarrassment of his runaway daughter, and that his affluence was a determining factor in the hospital's willingness to continue to hold her. A writ of habeas corpus was filed, but the hospital discharged her in preference to participating in a public court encounter.

There are other similar cases, in which, for example, a 17-year-old girl was hospitalized to prevent an elopement, as was a boy whose companions were objectionable to his suspicious, controlling parents. It seems doubtful that an adversarial court proceeding, which may well include contradictory psychiatric testimony, could sort out the complexities and the competing interests. An administrative tribunal composed of independent mental health professionals might well be the more desirable mechanism for protecting the child's interests in such cases.

Judicial Error and Attorney Malfeasance

Little has been written considering the potential for judicial error, although a body of anecdotal account has emerged in those states utilizing judicial review and determination. The dangers inherent in parental and professional authority have been well documented and extensively debated, but, of late, it is apparent that lodging the decision with a court establishes new avenues for error and bias. By way of example, a North Carolina district court judge abruptly released four children from a long-term psychiatric facility by inappropriately applying the dangerousness standard utilized for involuntary proceedings. During the course of the hearings, the unit director was summoned and read the statute and its definition of mental illness to the newly appointed judge. Nothing would prevail, and parents and agency personnel came from the far corners of the state to retrieve the children, who were prohibited from spending another night in the facility. A week later, the children were readmitted after intercession by the Attorney General and the chief district court judge.

There are other instances in which caprice operates, as in the occasional instance of a judge who whimsically insists, in essence, that his definition of mental disturbance supercedes that of statute. The most common error of this sort is the lay presumption that mental illness is comprised exclusively of delusional or hallucinatory activity, thus excluding the conduct and personality disorders. The upshot is that many clinicians and not a few judges are convinced that the experience with judicial review to date offers little evidence that judicial wisdom is inherently greater, that the adversarial proceeding is best geared to disclose "the truth," or that judges or attorneys can discern a proper course given competing evidence offered by differing clinicians. They are thus unable to reduce an admission or retention error because, insofar as the substantive issues are concerned, the "screen" provided by the court is simply too crude or too gross. Minute technical or procedural flaws may be observed, and errors which are so major as to be apparent to all parties may be rectified, but the legal enterprise lacks the technical expertise to render finely tuned judgments in complex, contested cases.

In this regard, James M. was a highly intelligent but increasingly reclusive 16-year-old boy who was admitted to a psychiatric unit for evaluation following massive anxiety attacks, coupled with inability and unwillingness to attend public school. Psychological testing and psychiatric evaluation both suggested the emergence of paranoid schizophrenia, but of greatest concern was the discovery by his parents of narratives in his diary suggestive of fantasy or intent to assassinate a public figure. At the initial hearing, after having reconstituted himself somewhat in response to medication and the structure of the unit, James argued convincingly and eloquently that although he had written those paragraphs, he was indulging only in fantasy and was totally capable of making distinctions and choices between fantasy and deed. Obviously much taken by the cogency of his presentation, the judge terminated James's evaluation, essentially dismissing a preponderance of testimony to the presence of severe mental illness, incapacitation, and the need for the completion of the evaluation.

The role of counsel to the minor patient who opposes hospitalization is even less well defined, and provides unfortunate opportunities for manipulation and the use of technical error to overturn an otherwise justified admission. For example, in the stress surrounding an admission, proper procedure is occasionally slighted, as in those instances where the proper custodian or guardian fails to sign the admitting document. Such errors are often easily corrected in the light of day. They may also, however, be employed to force the release of a minor, particularly when they are sprung without warning in a proceeding that appeared to be routine and in which the proper guardian is not present. Aside from the termination of psychiatric treatment or evaluation, there are other losses: The inherent message to an opportunistic, exploitive, omnipotent adolescent may be that "wheeling and dealing" and legalistic maneuvering are acceptable techniques in matters of principle and conscience, or that what one does does not matter if the consequences can be avoided.

In general, attorneys representing the child are provided with enormous latitude in the assumption of their role. Some presume that their responsibility is the most concrete manifestation of legal canon, that is, to represent their client's wishes, even if "by hook and by crook" as described above. Others feel free to oppose their client's wishes in private but represent them in a courtroom. Still others choose to ensure that data damaging to the child's wish for release is heard, although they are on record as defending the child's professed desires. Finally, some attorneys view their role as providing a penultimate review mechanism in the total process of psychiatric admission and continuing treatment, and are quite comfortable in presenting what they believe to be the child's need, as well as the child's wish, when the two are in conflict. That the latter choice undercuts the adversarial proceeding is clear, but it also recognizes that such a strictly constituted hearing may not be the best model or forum for ensuring that the child's treatment needs are squared with his need for due process.

A number of states that provide for challenges in the courts to voluntary admission by a parent provide counsel for the child patient but not for the parent. There are recent proposals to the effect that the appointed counsel should present the interests of both parents and child—a proposal that would essentially abolish the adversarial relationship and force counsel into rendering a useful, reasoned, and balanced judgment. The psychological impact of this arrangement seems preferable, and would place the attorney in the role of "neutral fact finder," to use the terminology of the Supreme Court (21), while eliminating, to some extent, the incentive to utilize less than direct means to secure release of the child.

The Effects on Treatment

Each of the several models for psychiatric admission of minors has its own peculiar impact. The traditional approach, that of unilateral parental consent, may well trigger once again the rebellious machinations of the acting-out adolescent. Even an adolescent who holds relatively little conflict in this dimension may react with sensitivity to the presumption that only his parents can make the responsible decision to pursue (or terminate) inpatient psychiatric treatment. Unfortunately, under this paternalistic arrangement, the adolescent's energy may be nearly totally consumed in the struggle for power as he resists, runs away, and attempts to defeat his parents and their surrogates on the treatment unit. If the struggle continues, little progress can occur, and the underlying pathology, usually depression and difficulties with intimacy, goes unaddressed. Experienced and sensitive clinicians, who are themselves comfortable in giving up authority when necessary, have developed methods of working through these issues with power conscious adolescents and their parents.

Another model, that of reducing the age of consent to as young as 12, may well place authority in the hands of the person who has the least experience, judgment, and perspective to exercise it wisely. The age of consent in most other matters is seldom below age 16, and so the younger adolescent may be in the peculiar predicament of being able to refuse hospitalization but unable to consent to any other alternative. This is surely an empty victory. The enormous discrepancies in competency between adolescents of the same chronological age, discrepancies which are additionally amplified in cases of psychological disorder, suggest that attempts to tailor consent based on fine distinctions in chronological age may not ultimately be very useful. Instead, it would seem most provident to permit older adolescents to admit themselves over the objections of their parents, and then to establish some form of guardianship to transfer authority to one who could stand *in loco parentis,* while also permitting parents to admit unilaterally.

As a group, clinicians are most seriously troubled by procedures in those states that provide for the full-blown adversarial proceeding. There is a limited body of literature (22, 23, 24) that attests to the numerous damaging by-products of contested hearings, including: psychotic decompensation of the child or adolescent; further deterioration of the already troubled relationship between parent and child; damage to the relationship between the patient and therapist as the latter testifies in opposition to the patient's release; assaults on the adolescent's already shaky self-esteem due to the disclosure of diagnoses and other results of personality appraisal; anxiety and resistance in response to the premature revelation of personality dy-

246 Emerging Issues in Child Psychiatry and the Law

namics or unconscious content; the reinforcement of pathological defenses among delinquently-oriented and narcissistic youths who seek to avoid responsibility for their plights; and a myriad of undesirable effects on the milieux of child and adolescent units.

Many of the outcomes are less obvious than those cited and, although not totally devastating to the treatment process, may operate in subtle ways to delay and deter a more complete enlistment of the youth in the treatment effort. Ginny G., a 16 year old, is a case in point. At the initial hearing, and with several previous psychiatric hospitalizations, she was well aware that her recent history of substance abuse, reckless risk-taking, and running away would suffice for the judge to concur with her parent's decision to seek admission. At the 90-day hearing, however, she could present several months of relatively well-controlled behavior within the structured milieu of the treatment unit. She then utilized the hearing as a forum to display the dynamics of her borderline personality disorder and its accompanying hysterical features. Given her depression and inner emptiness, and a propensity to utilize the "splitting" mechanism, she had to some extent met dependency needs and distracted herself from her depression by pitting the adults in her life against each other. In the therapy hours preceding the hearing, she regaled her therapist with various versions of testimony and the mechanisms she would use to influence, if not seduce, the judge. On the day of the hearing, she was immaculately dressed and made up (having dieted and lost 10 pounds for her appearance). Her therapist chose not to testify personally in order to reduce the "pay-off" of the splitting, and relied on an affidavit that presented the basic findings and recommended that the court approve six months of additional treatment. The judge took the course of least resistance, approving three months in an apparent attempt to please everyone while ensuring that further treatment could be requested.

Ginny determined to interpret his concession as a triumph, and used the outcome as a means of threatening her parents and attempting to further the struggle with her therapist. Always one to capitalize on the full range of possibilities inherent in every situation, she began to coach other girls for their court appearances and to prepare herself for the next hearing. Although her strategies were surely "grist for the mill," and in keeping with her pathology, all personnel regretted the unfortunate medium provided by the mandatory hearings. While most observers have been disturbed by the due process mechanisms, the present authors have also cited an instance in which a contested hearing provided the catalyst for significant change within a resistive patient (25).

The Court and the Treatment Unit as Allies

In a few circumstances, mandatory judicial review, whether triggered by the patient, another party, or as a routine function of hospitalization, may provide a vehicle by which beleaguered clinicians and administrators can initiate the release of children who are inappropriately placed on psychiatric treatment units. In the case of Ronnie C., given the inevitable scarcity of beds, community mental health authorities attempted to force this severely retarded, seizure-disordered, speechless, early adolescent into a regional adolescent psychiatric unit using an involuntary commitment. The commitment occurred in the middle of the night with, on complete inspection, only a minor behavioral episode as an indication of dangerousness. In the morning, however, the unit director was presented with a *fait accompli*, with political support already well in place for keeping Ronnie at the hospital, and with an explosive situation on Ronnie's ward. The boy's primitive qualities were frightening to the other aggressive older males on the ward. He had already achieved scapegoat status, and it seemed only a matter of time until this relatively defenseless, severely handicapped boy would be assaulted. The administrator's threat to present the full circumstances of his admission at the 10-day hearing and to recommend that the court discharge Ronnie set the stage for negotiations in which a more suitable placement was found.

In the case of Daniel, the matter was additionally complicated by the fact that he was named as a plaintiff in a major class action suit against his state on behalf of highly aggressive youths. In point of fact, Daniel was much too aggressive to be contained on his open adolescent unit, and he had to be transferred to the behavioral control unit, which had as residents the 15 or so most aggressive adult males in the 600-bed psychiatric hospital. His presence there was intolerable to the plaintiff's attorneys, but there was no facility at the regional or community level that was suitable.

Caught with no options, and not wishing to offend state officials by a precipitous discharge, the hospital appealed to the court at its routine judicial review of Daniel's case. They stated that Daniel was no longer in need of treatment at their facility, particularly in view of the absence of an adequate, age-appropriate program. Community officials also appeared and presented the hapless judge with essentially the same opinion relative to their resources. Hanging the onus on a judge, who in the course of the hearing discovered that he could not order expensive, out of state treatment but could only discharge, seemed somewhat unfair. It reflected, however, the increasing tendency to utilize the court to render unpopular decisions and to accept some degree of responsibility for unpleasant outcomes. This judge continued Daniel's stay on the behavioral control unit for 30 days, and issued an unenforceable order that an appropriate alternative program be located within that time.

In some quarters, there would be applause for the utilization of the court to release Ronnie C. or Daniel, since these cases have some similarities to the children on whose behalf the Georgia and Pennsylvania cases were undertaken. Others would argue, however, that the authority of the court was useful in securing a release, but that it would be much more effective if that authority were tied to an administrative panel of child specialists that might better render decisions in clinically complex and contested cases.

SUMMARY

An analysis of state practices regarding the psychiatric admission of minors reveals a distinct shift over the past six to eight years toward providing an array of due process protections to youths. Although approximately half of the states maintain the traditional pattern of unilateral parental consent, others have provided judicial or administrative review, selected some form of sharing autority between parents and children, or placed greater authority with the child by lowering the age of consent. During this same period, the Supreme Court in *Parham* emphatically endorsed parental authority for admission when accompanied by a concurring clinical opinion. This most controversial decision has perhaps slowed but not reversed the trend, as states have been left to their own devices to provide the constitutional minimum or to develop additional safeguards. Presently, the largest group of children at risk appear to be those for whom the original purpose of hospitalization has been accomplished and who now wait indefinitely for foster placement or less restrictive environments. There may well be even larger numbers of these children in private psychiatric and nonpsychiatric residential and group care.

From the point of view of clinicians and others, little has been found to support the most rigorous of remedies, the mandatory adversarial hearing in which child, parent, and treatment personnel may unfortunately be pitted against each other if hospitalization is contested. The children at risk could be protected at least as effectively by administrative panels of child specialists who are empowered to order release. In the multitude of far more complex cases, in which the issue of mental illness or disturbance must be weighed against conflicting clinical opinions, nothing less than such a panel would seem to suffice. All things considered, in a significant number of cases the courts introduce new sources of error and generate noxious clinical by-products, while constituting a crude and ineffective screen in less than obvious instances. For those states that choose to retain some version of the adversarial hearing, consideration should be given to modification of its more damaging aspects, including excusing the child, and providing counsel for the parent and treatment facility. Perhaps the greatest need at the present is for accurate data on a state-by-state, facility-by-facility basis regarding the numbers of children at risk, and for additional research regarding the clinical impact of the several models of psychiatric admission.

REFERENCES

1. In re.*Gault,* 387 U.S. 1, 1967.
2. *Kent* v. *U.S.,* 383, U.S. 541, 1966, ab p. 556.
3. In re. *Gault,* 387 U.S.1, 1967, pp. 27-28.
4. In re. *Long,* 25 N.C. App. 702, 1975.
5. *Parham* v. *J. L. and J. R.,* 47 LW 4740, 1979, p. 4745.
6. *Ibid.,* pp. 4745-4746.
7. American Psychological Association. *Monitor,* July, 1979, *10*(7). p. 2.
8. Wald, P. Introduction to the juvenile justice process: The rights of children and the rites of passage. In D. Schetky, & E. Benedek (Eds.), *Child psychiatry and the law.* New York: Brunner/Mazel, 1980, p. 18.
9. Ferleger, D. *Kremens.* v. *Bartley:* The right to be free. *Hospital and Community Psychiatry,* 1976, *27,* p. 712.
10. Wilson, J. *The rights of adolescents in the mental health system.* Lexington, Ma.: DC Heath, 1978, pp. 302-308.
11. Knitzer, J. *Unclaimed children.* Washington, D.C.: Children's Defense Fund, 1982, pp. 113-129.
12. *Ibid.*
13. Wilson, 1982.
14. Amaya, M. & Burlingame, W. Judicial review of psychiatric admissions. *Journal of the American Academy of Child Psychiatry,* 1981, *20.* 761-776.
15. Planavsky, G., Ritchie, V., & Silverstein, E. Intensive residential treatment for adolescents in North Carolina and the present legal system: A review and proposed changes. *North Carolina Journal of Mental Health, 1978, 8,* 4: 1-15.
16. Silverstein, E. Civil commitment of minors: Due and undue process. *North Carolina Law Review, 58,*1981, 1133-1159.
17. Planavsky et al., 1978, p. 12.
18. Amaya & Burlingame, 1981, pp. 772-773.
19. Silverstein, 1981, p. 1156.
20. *Parham* v. *J.L. and J.R.,* 1979, p. 4741.
21. *Ibid,* p. 4746.
22. Amaya & Burlingame, 1981.
23. Planavsky et al., 1978.
24. Silverstein, 1981.
25. Amaya & Burlingame, 1981, pp. 772-773.

17

Psychiatric Approaches to Cults: Therapeutic and Legal Parameters

David A. Halperin

In working with cult members and their families, the psychiatrist undertakes a complex and demanding task. It requires not only a personal commitment to work with an extremely diverse, needy, and, at times, provocative group of patients, but also developing a familiarity with the *modus operandi* of the more than 3,000 cult and cult-like groups currently active in the United States. Moreover, the psychiatrist's task is complicated by the reality that each cult imposes its uniquely individual demands on its members and their relationships to their families. In addition, the question of the First Amendment rights subjects the very question of psychiatric concern to an intense legal scrutiny, which hangs over this area like a backdrop, and both obscures and confuses the legitimate role of the psychiatrist. This chapter examines the therapeutic and legal parameters that define the psychiatrist's role and the unique problems experienced in working within this novel but important area.

It is notoriously difficult to precisely define the differences between religions, sects, and cults. Historically, cults have appeared during transitional periods in which the consensual religions of the broader society have appeared to lose their validity. The growth of new religions appears to be fueled by their ability to offer their communicants a sense of freedom from constraints that are experienced as stifling and anachronistic (1). New religious movements are often the product of a single inspired leader. But, it is extremely difficult to present clear-cut criteria differentiating between religious leaders of authenticity, genius, and charisma such as Moses or Luther, and charlatans such as Simon Magus or Sabbatai Zevi. Moreover, cults may reflect other constructive trends within their time and may transform leaders of dubious motivation and uncertain conviction into constructive figures (2). The following criteria are useful but not rigid determinants of what makes up a cult (not all cult-like groups necessarily meet these criteria):

1) A leader who claims divinity or a special relationship with God.
2) A leader who is the sole judge of a member's actions of faith.
3) Totalitarian governance.
4) Total control over the member's daily lives.
5) Exclusivity and isolation.
6) Development of deep emotional dependence.
7) Prohibition of critical analylsis and independent thinking.
8) Utilization of methods of ego destruction and mind control.
9) Exploitation of a member's finances.
10) Underemployment and exploitive working conditions. (3)

Obviously, the conditions in many hierarchical organizations could be construed as meeting many of these criteria. However, there is a quantum leap between the conditions present within conventional organizations and those in a group whose leader declares:

> If you are not thinking of the Supreme or of me, if you are thinking of somebody else, some other human being, then unless it is absolutely a mundane thought about telling that person something totally unimportant that is your destruction. If you think of someone even with softness or tenderness be careful: danger is approaching you.... I warn all of you with no exception, whatever you cannot do right in front of my eyes, you will not do in my absence. If you want to become my most perfect instrument.... (4)

A primary consideration in defining the role of the psychiatrist in this area is the presence of three related but distinct populations seeking psychiatric assistance and deserving psychiatric concern. Their relationship with the psychiatrist occurs in disparate legal contexts that delineate the course and goals of any psychiatric intervention. Numerically, the primary population seeking psychiatric assistance is the families of cult members. Indeed, initially, the psychiatrist may work almost exclusively with this population. A second population is the cult members themselves. These may include individuals whose current cult affiliation has become tenuous, or those who have recently left a cult. Finally, there are children of cult members. The needs of all these populations are distinct and the demands they place on the psychiatrist quite different.

THE FAMILIES OF CULT MEMBERS

Cult affiliation inevitably entails major changes in the preexisting familial relationships. The rigidity of the demands that the cult imposes on its members inevitably alters the focus of the individual's life and his relationship to his family, irrespective of any ostensible cult openness or flexibility. Nonetheless, despite these rigidities, the actual relationship between the individual cult member and his family is often subject to considerable variation (particularly if the individual achieves a position of responsibility within the group) (5). Cult affiliation is often experienced by the cult member's family as an act of total separation. It may be seen as an implicit criticism of either the family's value system or religious identification. Cult affiliation alters the bonds within families, even when the group ostensibly provides instruction in self-help techniques and is "nonreligious." Thus, the parental attitudes presented to the psychiatrist during the initial consultation may include elements of angry dependence combined with the fantasy of the omnipotent psychiatrist whose magic will dispel the evil spells that have ensnared the child and restore an idyll of family unity and continuity.

The resurrection of the lost child and the restoration of family unity form the parental agenda. This agenda frequently includes the denial of any past intrafamilial difficulties or emotional problems within the child. Thus, the psychiatrist's first task is to take a very thorough individual and family history. During the course of consultation, the family may ruminate about their own previous religious disengagement as a factor leading toward cult affiliation. Or, the family may obsess about their inattention to their child's religious interest, which is now approached as having foreshadowed cult affiliation. At this stage, the psychiatrist can be particularly helpful to concerned parents by pointing out that prior religious training does not provide an inoculation against cult affiliation, and that some religious preoccupation often forms part of the separation process of early adolescence (6). It should be noted that the parental burden of guilt is often particularly heavy in those families in which the parents' *own* religious disengagement formed part of their struggle to separate from their families. Here, the child's cult affiliation is experienced as both a rebuke and a vindication of the parents' admonitions. This is particularly true in families where the child has joined a rigidly orthodox or fundamentalist version of the parents' religion.

The importance of a careful preaffiliation history is illustrated in the following with its complex intermeshing of therapeutic and legal issues.

Case 1

Joan Z. sought an emergency psychiatric consultation because her son, Ian, left her home to hitchhike to Mexico to commune with a prominent disciple of the guru of an Eastern-style religious group. Ian left without money, food, or clothing—convinced that God would support him on his pilgrimage. Joan obtained an all-states' alert for her son. Indeed, Ian was found by the police in Kentucky, but released after he convinced the psychiatrist at a hospital emergency room that although his actions appeared bizarre and disorganized, they were the product of his religious convictions. Joan sought assistance to hospitalize Ian if another opportunity presented itself.

Ian's history is revealing. An only son, he showed promise during his early high-school years. While religiously preoccupied during puberty, his concerns had apparently subsided. (Joan ruminated about her lack of concern at that time.) The family was Jewish, but unobservant. Ian withdrew in his junior year and developed friendships with a drug-oriented crowd that expressed interest in Eastern religion. His school performance declined dramatically but, despite this, he was accepted at any Ivy League college. Academic and social difficulties forced him to withdraw during his first year. After a brief stay at home, he entered the ashram of an Eastern group. At the ashram, his behavior was disruptive. He was summarily expelled at the direction of the group's leader. Returning home, he continued in the observance of the group's practices. His unexpected departure was prompted by his hope that a meeting with the guru's disciple might gain him readmission into the ashram.

In retrospect, Ian was unable to function academically and socially. He became increasingly involved in the drug subculture. The separation entailed by his departure for college exacerbated his difficulties. The normal difficulties experienced by college freshmen were exaggerated because Ian's previous relationship with his controlling and intrusive mother had not prepared him for the transition from the symbiotic and structured setting of his home to the individualistic maelstrom of college. At college, Ian sought out the support of another structured setting. His cult affiliation may be seen as his attempt to develop structure after losing the holding environment of his home.

Ian's history raises the question of the extent to which cult members have significant preexisting pathology. His story is similar to those of many other adolescents whose severe borderline pathology leaves them open to experiencing severe depression on separation from home. They are vulnerable to the promise of fusion that accompanies the blandishments offered by groups who promise to provide a "new family" and structure to replace the old. Moreover, the traditional crises of the freshman year—the breakdown of significant preexisting relationships or the threat to career plans created by examinations—provide a context in which many will be tempted to seek support from groups that deny the importance of worldly career plans or sexual activity. Experience at both the Cult Hotline and Clinic (in New York City) and the Cult Information and Treatment Program (in Westchester County, New York) suggest that like Ian, a significant percentage of those who become cult members have severe preexisting illness.

Ian's experience demonstrates that cults are not therapeutic communities. Life in the ashram, with its long periods of meditation and isolation, may well have exacerbated his preexisting pathology. While the structured setting of the group may have provided some initial relief, cults by their very nature tend to be arbitrary—subordinating individual to group needs. Certainly, the group's response to Ian's apparent decompensation was to disavow any responsibility and to assume that his illness was evidence of his lack of commitment (entailing more meditation, etc.). Ian's expulsion from the group appears to have precipitated his acute disorganization and subsequent flight.

Psychiatric intervention was inhibited by the therapeutic realities of Ian's absence and by legal constraints even if he were present. Ian's distraught and histrionic mother described him as being in extremis—involved in a self-destructive project. The psychiatrist recognized that Ian, like many late adolescents, presented with identity diffusion and academic and/or vocation confusion, but that these factors do not necessarily justify hospitalization. Nonetheless, Ian's pilgrimage appeared to be part of a scenario that could eventuate in suicide, particularly if the guru's disciple were absent and Ian were disappointed in his quest. But his mother's efforts to have Ian hospitalized on an involuntary basis were frustrated, in large measure, because the psychiatrists who saw Ian considered his bizarre behavior and quixotic actions to be the product of his religious philosophy. Thus, a specious variety of cultural relativism prevented mental health professionals from either diagnosing severe pathology or recognizing the potential consequences of overtly self-destructive behavior when it is undertaken with the cover of intense religiosity.

Involuntary Deprogramming, i.e., coercively sequestering an individual and exposing him or her to anticult material has received a great deal (and perhaps an undeserved amount) of attention and aroused continuing concern among civil libertarians and mental health professionals. This disproportionate emphasis on "deprogramming" has elevated it to the status of a "magic bullet," particularly among parents who have been unsuccessful in attempting to convince their children to leave cults (7). However, the existence of this magic bullet may serve to draw attention away from the more conventional therapeutic approaches to the cult member and his family. It may even serve as a resistance during the progress of therapeutic activity with the cult member and his family (8). Indeed, during the early therapeutic work with the cult member's family, the psychiatrist's main task may be to point out that deprogramming, with its aggressive and coercive style, is an extraordinarily expensive approach that is frequently futile, potentially counterproductive, and may ultimately have extensive legal repercussions. Nonetheless, despite the psychiatrist's most explicit caveats, the families of cult members may persist in attempting a deprogramming. Indeed, the families of cult members may regard it as the treatment of choice, or as the only effective treatment modality, as the following illustrates.

Case 2

Jacob G. was the middle son of Holocaust survivors. He was unable to find a vocation after graduation from college. Eventually, he started to work for his father in the family appliance business. During the course of his trips to the warehouse, he met members of an Eastern-style group. He met with them secretly—concealing his new religious orientation from his parents. His parents learned of his change after he refused to participate in family activities because of the demands of his meditation schedule. They sought psychiatric consultation.

During the course of the consultation, they were advised that their son's cult affiliation appeared to be part of his attempt to create some distance between himself and his very enmeshed family. They were specifically counseled against involuntary deprogramming. Nonetheless, they sought out deprogramming. Jacob underwent an involuntary (but not physically coercive) deprogramming. Despite the advice of the deprogrammer (a responsible individual who often works in concert with mental health professionals), the family did not obtain any rehabilitation or follow-up care for their son. Within a month, he left his home, his job, and his family to return to the group's headquarters in California.

Jacob's family denied that there was any preexisting pathology. They saw Jacob's problem simply as an outgrowth of his cult affiliation and of cult practices (his temporary periods of confusion may well have been the product of excessive meditation). They refused to recognize that his inability to pursue a career and his social isolation indicated any emotional difficulties. The possibility that Jacob's difficulties reflected preexisting emotional problems was rejected because it threatened the family's enmeshed style of interaction. Thus, Jacob's family pursued a course of involuntary deprogramming, despite sound clinical advice, because more conventional psychotherapeutic approaches were experienced as too threatening to their symbiotic relationship with their son. Their subsequent failure to provide any rehabilitation was part and parcel of this pattern of denial.

This case dramatically illustrates that the psychiatrist's role in working with the cult member's family may simply be to help contain the parents' anxiety. While the psychiatrist can appreciate and empathize with the profound human dilemma that leads parents to consider involuntary deprogramming, he must help them confront the reality that it is a procedure whose legality is suspect and that it carries the very real risk of a countersuit for unlawful imprisonment if it fails (9). The psychiatrist plays a very constructive role when he helps parents to appreciate that weighty constitutional questions cannot simply be dismissed with the retort, "If the cult brainwashes him to keep him in, I can brainwash him to take him out."

The possibility that "mind-altering" techniques can interfere with or eliminate the individual's ability to make a free and unrestrained decision to remain in a cult has received continuing attention. West and Delgado noted:

The cult-joining process is often not fully consensual. It is not consensual because "knowledge" and "capacity"—the essential elements of legally adequate consent—are not simultaneously present.

They add:

In fact, few, if any, social institutions claiming First Amendment protection use conditioning techniques as tense, deceptive or pervasive as those employed by many contemporary cults. A decision to intervene and prevent abuses of cult proselytizing and indoctrinating does not by its logic alone dictate intervention in other areas where the abuses are milder and more easily controlled. (10)

The rights granted in the Bill of Rights are not absolute and, as Justice Jackson once ironically observed, "the Constitution is not a suicide compact." It may be that the continuing abuses perpetrated under the cover of the First Amendment, particularly because of the question of limitation on consensuality in either affiliating with a cult or leaving one, will lead the courts to create a remedy (11). But the psychiatrist has an obligation to point out to the parents considering coercive deprogramming that this is an exceedingly dubious premise on which to proceed.

After having obtained a careful preaffiliation history, the psychiatrist should obtain a careful precis of the individual's behavior after affiliation (including details of the group's practices, etc.). In many cases, the psychiatrist will be familiar with the group and its activities. In some instances, he will be able to reassure parents that the group is eccentric, but not a cult. If the group is obscure, recourse to either the Jewish Community

Relations Council of New York City or the American Family Foundation of Boston, who have extensive libraries on the more than 3,000 cults active in the United States, may be helpful. If the individual has recently joined a group (particularly in the absence of severe preaffiliation pathology), the prognosis for exiting is good. Recent surveys note that a significant percentage of new members of the Unification Church, for example, leave within the first year (12).

In this acute situation, the psychiatrist's role often defines itself into one of helping the family resolve any intrafamilial conflicts that will interfere with their ability to communicate directly with the cult member. The family's ability to knit itself together, contact the cult member with unity, and maintain an open and respectful dialogue is crucial. The family's resolution and ability to fashion a plan for exit counseling (the voluntary counseling of a cult member) is often decisive in this early period.

The psychiatrist's role changes when the period of cult affiliation has been prolonged. If the individual remains in the cult, then the decision to leave becomes a more personally complex action. It involves severing ties with fellow cult members. Moreover, the routine work performed within a cult encourages regression and the loss of vocational and academic skills (although if the individual reaches a position of responsibility within the group, then he may gain useful work experience), which raises realistic problems in rehabilitation. Thus, the psychiatrist and the cult member's family must deal with the reality that in a credential-oriented world, the college dropout attempting to return to mainstream society faces realistic handicaps. In addition, if the long-term cult member has achieved a position of status within the group, exiting involves the loss of status and authority, which adds to the burden of transition.

If the cult member married within the group, the decision to leave obviously becomes more complex—particularly if there are children. In this context, exiting may involve loss of contact with children and/or lengthy and problematic legal efforts to obtain visitation and/or custody. These issues will be considered, at length, later in this chapter. Ultimately, the psychiatrist may have the onerous responsibility of helping parents to respect the new ties their children have made and the responsibilities they have assumed, and to limit their efforts primarily to supporting their children's efforts toward autonomy within the cult context. (Parenthetically, as the individual becomes more autonomous he may not need the cult's support.) In the context of helping the long-term cult member, coercive deprogramming seems a particularly questionable enterprise.

The self-help group has been particularly useful to the families of long-term cult members (13). These groups allow participation without stigmatization. Within them parents can share the burden of relating to the long-term cult member without being afflicted by self-critical ruminations about their presumed failures in parenting. The psychiatrist's primary role in working with the self-help group is as a group facilitator to help the members exchange their feelings, rather than to help them explore their feelings psychodynamically as in group psychotherapy. Resistances and transference develop even in this context. But the role of the psychiatrist is to promote the development of an environment in which emotional interchange occurs, as opposed to the development of insight regarding underlying intrapsychic or intrafamilial dynamics.

As the self-help group evolves, the members may demand that the psychiatrist become the omnipotent agent who will resurrect their "dead" child. These demands can be explored as a resistance that deflects scrutiny away from an examination of what members can do in the "here and now" to help their children and one another. Members may also use a meeting to discuss recent developments regarding various movements. Finally, the demand for a magical solution can be explored as an example of the process that led to the cult member's initial interest in cults, and communication between parents and children can be facilitated as parents develop a heightened appreciation of the need for magical solutions to personal problems.

Parental communication with cult members is often clouded by the legal and financial consequences of cult affiliation. Since cult members often spend much of their time working in "volunteer" activities, their income may be minimal. Wages, when they are paid, are often nominal (ex-members have started action to obtain even these pittances) (14). Requests for parental financial assistance are common, particularly as tuition for "courses" which groups seemingly create on an as-needed basis. Demands may extend to asking parents to pay for hospital or medical insurance. Cults may even encourage their members to attend school primarily to take advantage of generous student loans, which are then donated to the group while the member-student is forced to live on public assistance (15). The pressure of these demands is often intensified by the inherent threat of the members to break off contact with the parents if these demands are not met. Not surprisingly, parents are torn between their desire to help their children and their recognition that whatever monies are given may rapidly disappear into the cult. Comparable problems arise in arranging for disposition of estates. In this context, psychiatric consultation can be extremely helpful in enabling the parents to establish reasonable limits. Finally, the psychiatrist may be called upon to establish either the competency of an individual who has donated monies to a cult or the possibility of coercion as a factor altering long-established testamentary dispositions.

CULT MEMBERS

The second population seeking psychiatric assistance is the (ex-) cult members themselves. These contacts may arise during affiliation as the individual becomes disenchanted with the movement and questions the increasing demands and limitations imposed by the cult. Or, these contacts may develop during the course of affiliation as the individual starts to question the gaps between the cult's idealistic pretensions and the reality of the cult exploitation. The following cases are illustrative:

Case 3

Zev, a 19-year-old Israeli, was in placement because of his difficulties in living with his conflict-ridden family. Despite his personal problems, he worked and attended night school. He started attending the meetings of an Eastern-style group. Soon, he noted that he was spending an increasing amount of time chanting a phrase repetitiously in order to reach his goals. Academic disaster loomed.

During the course of psychiatric consultation, Zev discussed his fear of failure and his dissatisfaction with his slow rate of progress at school. He discussed his need for magical solutions and the reassurance magic provided. As a greater sense of self-competence developed, Zev stopped attending the meetings of the group.

Case 4

A more aggressive program of outreach may be required as the following case illustrates.

Toby, an 18-year-old college freshman, precipitously left college and hitchhiked to the headquarters of an Eastern-style group in Oregon. He called his parents to announce that he was taking his final vows to become a member of the community. After intensive psychiatric consultation, his parents were able to persuade him to return home. In the ensuing psychiatric consultations, Toby was able to discuss his fears of failing in his premedical program and his resentment toward his parents—particularly their exaggerated expectations of academic achievement. Toby was able to leave the group.

As these cases illustrate, crucial periods for psychiatric intervention are prior to full cult affiliation (Zev), or during the period that the individual is considering increasing the intensity of his commitment (Toby). Prevention is possible, particularly when the groups do not overtly interfere in contacts between the new member and his family. Moreover, many vulnerable youths are "fellow travellers," using the group primarily for social purposes. In these circumstances, the potential cult member is readily available for consultation. Psychiatric consultation can be particularly effective as it helps the individual explore the needs for certainty or the support that cult groups provide during periods of transition.

Cult groups do provide a modicum of support for some severely damaged individuals. In these cases, the psychiatrist may be of assistance in helping the individual to place appropriate limits on his investment in the group, i.e., forestalling the decompensation that may arise through excessive indulgence in meditation, etc. While many cult groups are exceedingly skeptical about psychiatry, some groups are less rigid in their opposition. In these instances, psychiatric consultation may be sought either by a committed cult member or by the friends and family of a cult member (who retains his or her commitment to the group) when it appears that a cult member is becoming psychotic. However, as was noted in the case of Ian Z., many groups have a tendency to disavow any responsibility for the potentially psychotic member. Finally, it should be noted that cults may approve of otherwise bizarre behavior such as glossolalia, extended periods of dissociation/trances, intense quasimanic activity and/or euphoria, as well as auditory and visual hallucinations. Indeed, they may be viewed as signs of grace.

Psychiatric consultation is obviously facilitated when the cult member has made a definitive decision to leave the group. While many are able to leave a group without significant sequelae, the Atypical Dissociative Disorder (DSM-III Diagnostic criterion 300.15) (16)—"floating"—may be present, particularly if the group's practices included excessive meditation, chanting, or other consciousness-altering techniques. During the Atypical Dissociative Disorder, the individual's ability to focus on his external environment is sharply decreased (17). If this external reality includes a psychiatrist attempting to establish a therapeutic relationship or contact, floating obviously interposes a formidable resistance. Floating is not under conscious control. It is an extremely seductive derivative of mind-altering practices because it enables the individual to withdraw from any intense or uncomfortable experience, e.g., psychiatric consultation. In this potentially frustrating circumstance, the psychiatrist must adopt an active, nonconfrontational, nonjudgmental, and reality-oriented approach. Above all, the psychiatrist should appreciate that the resort to mind-altering techniques reflects the problems that many group members have with the overt expression of anger, and may parallel their exercise of extensive denial of any anger/hostility (18). Indeed, a therapeutic impasse may develop if the psychiatrist pursues this issue of denial of anger, single-mindedly.

During psychotherapy, the ex-cult member's anxiety over the overt expression of anger may display itself in the ambivalence that the ex-cult member may feel toward "his" cult. To be sure, anyone will feel some ambivalence toward the cause to which he may have devoted so much time and energy (despite the individual's current misgivings and his recognition of the exploitive nature of cult practices). In this regard, the greater ease that ex-cult members experience in expressing anger toward the cult after an involuntary deprogramming, affect which has been considered an artifact of involuntary deprogramming (19), should simply be regarded as a reflection of the ability of deprogramming to confer on otherwise inhibited individuals the right to experience and express an appropriate anger after having been exploited. Nonetheless, the psychiatrist should avoid joining with the ex-cult member in participating in a process of splitting and polarization. By helping the ex-cult member to recognize that the cult experience had both positive and negative aspects to it, the psychiatrist helps the ex-cult member to develop a less polarized and apocalyptic view of the world. In this manner, the psychiatrist is able to provide the ex-cult member with a more integrated picture of reality that enables the ex-cult member to mature out of the polarization inherent in the cultic weltanschauung (which parenthetically resembles the style of the borderline personality).

The relationship between the psychiatrist and the ex-cult member should allow the individual to reach his own conclusions about his past involvement and former associates. While the ex-cult member may intellectually appreciate that the period of affiliation was one spent in pursuit of a spiritual fools' gold and accompanied by exploitation, the act of cult affiliation *did,* after all, represent a move toward personal independence. The psychiatrist must respect this aspect of what may otherwise have been a misguided venture. Above all, the psychiatrist should communicate to the ex-cult member that he shares his human concerns, respects his spiritual quest, and reserves his criticism only for the totalism inherent in cult life that often precludes genuine individual spiritual growth.

During the course of treatment, the ex-cult member often presents the psychiatrist with a new and confusing array of jargon: lighted, clear, decreed, witness, centering, etc. Obviously, familiarity with these terms, their eccentric usage, and the nuances they convey is very useful. These idiosyncratic (unique to the particular cult) terms often convey the existential character of the individual's experiences within the group. Thus, the patient describing his group's preoccupation with "controlling tantric lines of energy" may also be talking about his sense of being controlled by the group *and* his own sense of being unable to control himself without the group's support. An understanding of this elliptical mode of communication is extremely useful in establishing a constructive therapeutic alliance.

THE CHILDREN OF CULT MEMBERS

The third population of concern is the children of cult members. One third of the victims at Jonestown were children—many of whom were in foster care under the auspices of the People's Temple (20). Rudin vividly described the pattern of child abuse and neglect within many cults or eccentric religious groups (21). While the hecatomb at Jonestown is unique, the following individual tragedy is not:

> Sixty-six children were removed from a religious camp and placed in temporary court custody yesterday in an order prompted by the beating death of a 12-year-old boy who refused to do his chores. . . . The camp is headed by cult figure William A. Lewis who bases his punishment teaching on a literal interpretation of the Bible. (22)

The basis for legal intervention in these cases is quite different from those cases involving adult cult members. It has been succinctly stated that:

> The right to practice religion freely does not include liberty to expose the community or the child to communicable disease or the latter to ill health or death. (23)

Child abuse within cults falls into four broad categories: (1) the resort to excessive discipline; (2) the denial of conventional medical care; (3) the resort to unusual educational practices and/or the absence of an appropriate nurturing environment; and (4) the denial of visitation to concerned family members (24). All of these abuses may coexist.

Many cults and cult-like groups (primarily, but not exclusively, of a fundamentalist Christian orientation, e.g., the House of Judah [25], or the Northeast Kingdom Community Church [26] practice excessive discipline. The ostensible basis for the brutality lies in a rigid interpretation of Biblical precepts. Within these communities, children may be punished for trivial infractions of rules in an unrelenting and ultimately fatal manner because these infractions are viewed as satanically inspired. The recent events in Vermont and their ultimately inconclusive denouement illustrate the complex problems involved in the attempt by public authorities to ensure that children are treated with a modicum of appropriateness (27).

This harsh view of childlike behavior is a product of the group's viewing the world as being rigidly divided into the "pure" (the group leader's view) and the "impure" (the satanic or noncult world's view). Psychiatric consultation has been sought by concerned family members who are appropriately disillusioned by the group's resort to brutality, and by the courts as part of legal proceedings. Not surprisingly, grandparents and/or other family members are often very reluctant to challenge the discipline provided within a group that cloaks physical abuse in highsounding religious/philosophical principles. The psychiatrist can provide significant support to the concerned family members who seek to modify eccentric and brutal modes of discipline within the group, or who hope to modify custody and visitation in a manner that will ameliorate childrearing conditions.

Psychiatric testimony has also been sought by the courts because eccentric childrearing practices and excessive discipline have resulted in physical injury up to and including the death of a child. In this context, the issue of "mind control" is raised with particular cogency. Psychiatrists are often asked to help the courts decide whether or not the perpetrators of child abuse were acting in an independent manner when violent acts were committed. Moreover, the question of the responsibility of the group leader as a conspirator in the abusive acts has been raised (the leader of the House of Judah was eventually found not guilty, but comparable issues have been and are being raised in other cases). Finally, the question of custody of the other children within the cult presents very real challenges—particularly when the perpetrators of the acts of child abuse regard themselves as acting under Divine sanction (28).

Cults may relegate conventional medical care and conventional educational experiences to the satanic realm. Preventive medical care may be extremely haphazard. The child's diet may be extremely limited. There may be an emphasis on prolonged periods of meditation and sleep deprivation. In addition, groups may prescribe that children undergo prolonged separation from their parents in order to strengthen their attachment to the group. In some groups, education is rigidly restricted to eliminate the temptations of the outside world (although this is hardly restricted to cults). The education that is provided may have a very pronounced sexist bias with severe restrictions being placed on educational opportunities for women, e.g., ISKON/Hare Krishna. The solution to these problematic practices may lie either in the realm of legal action by concerned family members or in the political realm of demanding adherence to appropriate child care standards. But there are formidable obstacles present as the following case indicates.

Case 5

Lillie N. contacted a psychiatrist for assistance in helping her granddaughter, Evelyn, receive psychiatric care. The granddaughter had repeatedly run away from her parents because voices kept telling her to hitchhike to California. The child's parents refused to take her for any psychiatric assistance because they felt that the solution to their daughter's problems lay in continued prayer. The parents were members of an Eastern-style group that believes in "natural" medicine. The grandmother's description of her granddaughter's state left little doubt that the child was actively psychotic and acting under direction from auditory hallucinations.

During the course of brief psychiatric consultation, the child's grandmother was supported in her efforts to contact the child's parents. However, the child's father was unremitting in his opposition to conventional psychiatric treatment. Faced with a complex and uncertain legal process, Lillie decided to continue to work with her daughter (the child's mother) in the effort to convince her to protect Evelyn.

In other cases, grandparents have successfully adopted a more confrontational approach and the threat of legal action has forced cults to adopt more appropriate child rearing practices. In these cases, the psychiatrist is able to provide support for the concerned family member by validating their fundamental perception of their children as individuals who have surrendered their independence of judgment and autonomy to the cult and the cult leader. Unfortunately, in many cases, the appropriate concerns of concerned family members (particularly grandparents) are not treated with the respect they deserve, and constructive action is inhibited.

Children are born to cult members. And, as cults persist, their childrearing practices may well become a matter of increasing concern. Fortunately, in this area, the potential for intervention is grounded in a longstanding body of law (29). The psychiatrist has a responsibility to alert his colleagues and the broader public to cults' potential for child abuse. Psychiatric testimony has been of signal value in altering visitation rights, custody arrangements, and protecting the rights of children to receive adequate nurturing and medical care and to reach their potentiality for mature development.

SUMMARY

Cult affiliation is an area of increasing concern to psychiatrists and other mental health professionals. This chapter delineates the role of the psychiatrist in working with three different but related populations: the cult member, his family, and his children. The problems that arise in therapeutic activity with these diverse groups are described and the complex legal ramifications of cult affiliation, including its effect on the therapeutic process, are examined. This is a rapidly changing area. Recent decisions awarding substantial damages to former cult members for abuses suffered during the period of cult affiliation, as well as attempts to recover pay for services performed during the period of cult affiliation, suggest that the simplistic recourse to the First Amendment is being increasingly recognized as an insufficient answer to the real problems posed by cult affiliation.

REFERENCES

1. Pagels, E.H. Born again. *New York Review of Books,* 1983, *30*(11), 41-43.
2. Halperin, D. Cults: Their psychiatric aspects and legal implications. Presented at the 13th

annual meeting of the American Academy of Child Psychiatry and the Law, New York, October 23, 1982.
3. West, L.J., & Singer, M. Cults, quacks and nonprofessional psychotherapies. In H. Kaplan, A. Freedman, & B. Sadock (Eds.), *Comprehensive textbook of psychiatry III*. Baltimore: Williams and Wilkins, 1980.
4. Sri Chinmoy. *Writings*. New York: Agni, 1978, p. 3.
5. Halperin, D. Selfhelp groups for the parents of cult members: Agenda, issues and the role of the group leader. In D.A. Halperin (Ed.), *Psychodynamic perspectives on religion, sect and cult*. Littleton, MA: John Wright-PSG, 1983.
6. Blos, P. *The adolescent passage*. New York: International Universities Press, 1966.
7. Maleson, F.G. Dilemmas in evaluation and management of religious cultists. *American Journal of Psychiatry*, 1981, *136*, 925-929.
8. Spero, M.H. Individual psychodynamic intervention with the cult devotee: Diagnostic and treatment procedure. In D.A. Halperin (Ed.), *Psychodynamic perspectives on religion, sect and cult*. Littleton, MA: John Wright-PSG, 1983.
9. *Mental Disability Law Review*, 1983, *7*(1), 36-37.
10. West, L.J., & Delgado, R. Psyching out the cults' collective mania. *Los Angeles Times*, November 26, 1978, Section D, p. 3.
11. Frakt, A. Legal aspects of dealing with the new religions. In D.A. Halperin (Ed.), *Psychodynamic perspectives in religion, sect and cult*. Littleton, MA: John Wright-PSG, 1983.
12. Galanter, M. Psychological induction into the large-group: Findings from a modern religious sect. *American Journal of Psychiatry*, 1980, *137*(12), 1574-1579.
13. Halperin, 1983.
14. Rosedale, H. Commentary on Halperin, 1982.
15. Kleinman, C., & Halperin, D.A. Ethical issues in working with cult members. Prepared for presentation at the 3rd International Congress of Psychiatry, Law and Ethics, Haifa, Israel, February, 1983.
16. American Psychiatric Association. *Diagnostic and statistical manual of mental disorders* (Third edition). Washington, DC: American Psychiatric Association, 1980.
17. Conway, F. & Siegelman, J. *Snapping*. New York: Delta, 1978.
18. Deutsch, A., & Miller, M. A clinical study of four Unification Church members. *American Journal of Psychiatry*, 1983, *140*(6), 767-770.
19. Galanter, M. Unification Church dropout: Psychological readjustment after leaving a charismatic religious group. *American Journal of Psychiatry*, 1983, *140*(8), 984-989.
20. Wooden, K. *The children of Jonestown*. New York: McGraw-Hill, 1981.
21. Rudin, M. Women, elderly and children in religious cults. Presented at the annual conference of the Citizens Freedom Foundation, Arlington, VA, October 23, 1982.
22. Court takes 66 kids from cult's horror camp. *New York Post*, July 8, 1983, p. 8.
23. *Prince* v. *Massachusetts*. 321 U.S. 158, 166-167. 1944.
24. Halperin, D.A., & Markowitz, A. Cults and children: The abuse of the young. Presented at the annual meetng of the American Association of Psychiatric Services for Children, Houston, TX, February 5, 1983.
25. Court takes 66 kids from cult's horror camp, 1983.
26. Starr, M., & Sabarsky, M. The Kingdom of Island Pond. *Newsweek*, November 29, 1982, p. 52.
27. Child beatings: Questions of abuse or discipline. *New York Times*, July 1, 1984, Section I, p. 14.
28. Discipline and a boy's death. *Washington Post*, October 26, 1982.
29. Rubinstein, I. H. *Law on cults*. Chicago, Ordain, 1981.

18

Role Models for Violence

Diane H. Schetky

He who resorts to violence has lost the argument.—Chinese proverb

Violence is nearly as popular a topic with health professionals as death. Though not quite as inevitable, violence is closely related to death and murder, and is now the fastest growing cause of death in the U.S.A. (1). One's chances of becoming a victim of a violent crime are greater than the risk of divorce, being injured in an auto accident, or death from cancer (2). Statistics on violence, as the reader will soon learn, are alarming, yet it is easy to relate to statistics as mere numbers rather than people. Often it is not until one has had a personal encounter with violence that one becomes motivated to do anything about the problem.

This chapter will focus on specific role models for violence—domestic violence, television, handguns, and examples of institutionalized violence—and will explore how they affect the attitudes and behavior of children. It is the hope of the author not just to inform but to explore with the reader ways in which we might as individuals have some influence, no matter how small, on the growing problem of violence.

Lorenz (3) has noted that aggression in animals is an innate drive, which is usually adaptive in that it serves to control population and food supplies, and permits only the fittest to survive. Prohibitions, against infanticide exist in all species and are usually violated only in conditions of extreme crowding (4). Among monkeys who live in the wild, quarreling is rare and violence almost nonexistent, although it becomes appreciable under the stressful conditions of zoo living (5). However, recent reports by Goodall (6) on chimpanzees counter these findings. Regarding the nature versus nurture controversy, Dixon (7) has shown that artificial stimulation of the amygdala can induce aggression in animals, yet the question of to whom the aggression is directed is determined by the animal's social experience with colony mates. Thus, Dixon argues that "among primates social experiences can override hormonal and neurological status." Lorenz hypothesizes that inhibitions controlling aggression occur in heavily armored carnivores in order to prevent self-destruction of the species. He speculates that man's troubles may arise from the fact that he is lacking any natural weapons and is, therefore, devoid of built-in safety devices that prevent "professional" carnivores from abusing their killing power to destroy members of their own species (8).

Violence has been with us since early mankind. Anthropologist Louis Leaky reported fossil finds that include manlike forms with holes or fractures in their skulls thought to have been inflicted by our ancestors (9). Moving forward a few million years, we find that ours is a country that tends to glorify violence, which, as Silberman (10) observes, is one of the most durable aspects of the American experience. He refers to the "Frontier ethos" of self-reliance, taking what is there, and winning at all costs that has encouraged people to violate rules that get in the way. Guns have always been a part of our cultural heritage. Often misquoted is the Second Amendment of the U.S. Constitution, which refers to the right to bear arms, not as individuals, as the National Rifle Association would lead us to believe, but rather as a collective right.

Our American fascination with guns continues. A small bank in Illinois began giving Colt pistols to its customers in lieu of interest in hopes of luring new customers, and was soon deluged with 1,500 depositors. The bank's senior vice president commented that "most people still believe in God, guns, and guts as what made the U.S. what it is today" (11). Pistol ads have appeared in such unlikely places as Vogue magazine and American Express advertising, suggesting that some may view them as fashionable or even sexy. American Express recently offered its members a re-creation of Wyatt Earp's .44 revolver "to display and enjoy for only $325." This highly seductive, glossy, full-color ad invited card holders to

> hold it in your hand. Feel the satisfying weight. Pull back the hammer with your thumb . . . hear the double click as the cylinder revolves . . . then press the trigger and gauge for yourself the ease of its quick even "pull." And there is more to the experience. With the hammer at half-cock, you can "break" the gun open just as Earp did to reload. First you thumb up the latch, then, as you swing the frame down on its hinge, the shell extractor glides out from the cylinder . . . automatically retracting again when the gun is fully open (12).

The author responded to this mailing with a letter of protest reminding the promoters that guns were lethal weapons and that their ad was promoting gun ownership. American Express sent a reply that sidestepped the issue of social conscience and stated, "We at American Express recognize the needs and demands of the buying public must be met in order to be successful in today's competitive market."

VIOLENCE IN THE FAMILY

Violence in the family will be defined as "any mode of behavior involving the direct use of physical force against another family member" (13). Two major theories have been put forth to explain this phenomena. Gil, a proponent of the culture of violence theory, assumes that "violence in families is rooted in societal violence and can therefore not be understood nor overcome apart from it" (14). He views violence in the family as mirroring cultural values, and favors a broad definition of violence extending to "acts or conditions which violate the process of human development." He recommends a sociological approach to the problem that would focus on issues such as poverty, unemployment, and social class, all of which contribute to abuse. Proponents of the structural theory of violence believe that violence breeds violence and that the family, through acts of violence or condoning violence, becomes the training ground for violence (15-22). The studies to be discussed here lend support to the latter theory, though the two are certainly not mutually exclusive.

Strauss, Gelles, and Steinmetz (22) note that physical violence occurs between family members more often than it does between any other individuals, and that "most violent acts which occur in the family are so much a part of the way the family relates that they are not even thought of as violent." Violence in the family may take many forms. While child abuse has received the most attention in the literature, we are becoming increasingly aware of spouse abuse, parent abuse, and sibling abuse. Prevalence figures can be arrived at either through individual reports in which case there is likely to be underreporting, or through surveys of "normal" populations wherein results are then extrapolated. Violence is less likely to be reported among the middle and upper classes but, according to some surveys, it is equal among all income groups and educational levels and may even be more common among the middle class than the lower class (23). Similarly, in regard to the use of corporal punishment, Erlanger disagrees with Bronfenbrenner's earlier claims that working-class parents use physical punishment more frequently than upper-class parents, and finds a relatively weak relationship between social class and the use of spanking (24, 25). Supporting this finding is the survey by the National Commission on Prevention of Violence, which found that poorly educated whites have the highest rates of outright rejection of corporal punishment and that those most likely to score high on spanking were college graduates (26).

Child Abuse

Most people associate child abuse with young children, whereas in fact over 75% of victims are over age two and 20% are teenagers. However, children under age two remain at greatest risk (65%) for severe injury (27). Strauss et al. (28) conducted a nationwide survey of violence in 2,143 families and found that every other home was the scene of violence at least once a year. Among their findings are the following: In the year previous to the study three in five parents hit a child; 70% viewed spanking and slapping a 12 year old as necessary, and 77% as normal; 73% reported using violence at some point on their children; and 63% mentioned at least one episode of violence occurring in the previous year. For 58% this consisted of slapping, but 3% kicked or pummeled and .1% actually used a gun or knife (3% in the child's lifetime). If one extrapolates these figures 3.1–4 million children have been kicked, bitten, or punched by a parent at some point in their lives, and 900,000–1.8 million have had a parent use a gun or knife on them. The same study showed that mothers were more likely than fathers to use violence against a child presumably because they have more contact with their children, and that male children were almost twice as likely as females to be victims of parental violence. Consistent with Gil's findings, Strauss et al. found that 8% of college students received injuries at the hands of their parents in the last year they lived at home.

The likelihood of a parent abusing a child increases with the number of children in the family until five, whereafter it decreases. According to Strauss et al., the more a parent hits a child the more likely the child will severely attack a sibling. They found sibling abuse to be prevalent, occurring in 82% of children in the previous year. Sixteen percent of siblings had beaten up a sibling in the previous year and 20% in a lifetime.

Feshbach (29) comments on the irony that "man and woman, the only species which has the most advanced communication system must rely on non-verbal means of training their young." She speculates that the use of corporal punishment may lead to a loss of empathy between parent and child, and that low empathy is associated with high aggression. She decries the deliberate infliction of pain as an uncivilized practice and believes the young should not be subjected to it. Weisberger (30) speaks to the inequity of corporal punishment and the obvious contradiction apparently unnoticed by many. She offers the example of a father who boasted of having thrashed his eight-year-old son to within an inch of his life saying, "I'll teach him to pick on someone smaller." She speculates that the efficacy of spanking may lie not so much in the infliction of pain as in the fact that the child comes to realize that parents mean what they say.

Spouse Abuse

Nearly six million women are abused by their husbands per year and 2-4,000 are beaten to death annually. Battery constitutes the major cause of injury to women (31). Strauss et al. found that every year one in six couples commits a violent act against his or her spouse and that the more punishment one received as a child the greater the rate of having a violent marriage. In spite of the publicity given to wife abuse, figures were almost equally divided with 12% of husbands and 11.6% of wives doing the abusing. They estimate that if married, one has a one-in-three chance of being abused by one's spouse, and comment that "the marriage license is a hitting license for a large part of the population" (32). In contrast to most authors, Strauss et al. found more husbands (4.6% vs. 3.8%) had actually been beaten than wives, though violence inflicted by husbands was likely to be more severe. Wives were particularly vulnerable to attack while pregnant. One fourth of spouses felt that slapping each other was necessary, normal, or good. A similar acceptance of slapping was found by the National Commission on the Causes and Prevention of Violence (33). While spouse abuse is condoned by many, it is also a reason for seeking divorce for 20% of middle-class and 40% of working-class couples (34).

One study of psychiatric inpatients reported that 48% had a history of battering with an intimate relationship (35). Carmen, Rieker, and Mills (36) found that almost half of the psychiatric inpatients they studied had been victims of physical (22%) or sexual abuse or both and that 90% had been abused by family members. They observed that abused males become more aggressive, while abused females become more passive. Another study found that 50% of women referred for psychiatric evaluation from a rural health clinic reported to be victims of domestic violence (37). Rounsaville and Weissman's study of battered women seen in an emergency room found abuse to be of long standing in 64% of cases, and that it occurred on an average of 6.7 times per year. All of the women reported that their children had seen them abused. Their partners had also abused their children in 23% of cases and 5% of the women admitted that they also had (38). A study of husbands who abused their wives found that as children 71% had witnessed physical violence between parents and 49% had been victims of child abuse (39).

Parent Abuse

Parent abuse may take the form of children, adolescents, or adults attacking their parents and has been estimated to occur in 10% of families

(40). A common scenario is the enmeshed family where the parents have abdicated authority and the violent adolescent is parentified. Parents in these families are likely to deny the problem out of a need to cling to the myth of a happy family (41).

Abuse may also involve the aged parent, a problem that has largely been ignored by the medical profession and may affect as many as 2% of the elderly. Victims of this type of abuse are often former abusers of their own children and "the violence comes full circle as the abusers become the abused" (42).

T.V. AND VIOLENCE

T.V. both reflects and shapes the values of our society. As noted by the National Commission on the Causes and Prevention of Violence, "In a fundamental way, television helps to create what children expect of themselves and of others and what constitutes the standards of civilized society" (43). Regarding the T.V. dramas viewed by children, a 1982 GAP report states:

Because the dramas evoke strong identifications and intense emotional responses in the viewer, they have great possibilities for facilitating human growth, as well as for doing damage (44).

The potential impact of T.V. on children is staggering considering how ubiquitous it is and how indiscriminate most viewers are. For instance, more Americans have T.V.'s than have refrigerators or indoor plumbing (45).

The average child watches 27 hours of T.V. per week and some estimate that preschoolers watch up to 54 hours per week (46). According to a 1983 Nielson survey, the average household watches seven hours and two minutes of T.V. per day, a significant increase from the early fifties when the average was four-and-a-half hours per day (47). High frequency of T.V. viewing is associated with being female, of minority and low socioeconomic status, and poorly educated (48). Statistics indicate that adult fare is hardly restricted to adults with 40% of T.V. viewing by first graders consisting of adult programs (49). Twenty million children ages two-17 are still watching T.V. at 9 P.M. and 5.3 million children at 11 P.M. (50). By the time the child graduates from high school he will have witnessed 13,000 real or simulated violent deaths, 101,000 violent episodes, and between 350,000 and 640,000 commercials. He will spend more time watching T.V. than in school or with his parents (51, 52). He will also have seen alcohol consumed 75,000 times before he is of drinking age. Drinking scenes, 99% of the time, are portrayed as neutral or favorable, and T.V. manages to ignore the link between alcohol and violence. Whereas 50% of real life violence is associated with alcohol consumption, only 10% of T.V. violence is presented that way (53).

Kenniston notes:

> the difference between T.V. and a human companion is striking. One can reprimand or even fire a baby-sitter who constantly talks of murder, mayhem and violence or how wonderful the latest toys, cereal and candies are, but it is impossible for an individual parent to influence programs and advertisements that do the same thing. If what is broadcast is consistently in conflict with the parents' values, they have virtually no recourse short of smashing or locking up the set and if parents did that what would they watch? The result again is a sense of uneasiness about the handy but uncontrollable electronic baby-sitter that seems to play so large a role in raising children (54).

Concerns about T.V. violence first arose in the 1950s and have led to monitoring the situation but not much action, and the public, for the most part, has remained apathetic about the matter. Studies done in the 1960s showed cartoons to be more violent than prime-time shows: two thirds of leading cartoon characters were violent, most male characters were violent, and retribution by violence was common (55). During the 1970s, Action for Children's T.V. emerged and the F.C.C. attempted to establish family viewing hours. The courts, however, sided with the networks who argued that restraints against portraying violence violated the First Amendment and infringed on the right of trade. Citizens, the A.M.A., and the P.T.A. expressed mounting concern about T.V. violence, and the House Committee on Interstate and Foreign Commerce held several hearings indicating its dissatisfaction but stopped short of blaming the broadcasters or demanding a change.

At present, T.V. violence continues much as before with children's programs being even more violent than prime time. On prime-time weapons appear at an average of nine per hour, but most shots fired are missed so the lethality of guns is not accurately portrayed (56). Rarely is pain or suffering depicted in association with violence, nor is the anguish of the bereaved. The objects of violence are often dehumanized, which may further impair the child's capacity for empathy. The repeated message that comes across is that violence is an accepted, quick, and effective means of resolving conflict.

With the advent of cable T.V., children now have the opportunity to view explicit and sadomasochistic sexual acts that combine rock music with images. MTV, Warner Communications' music cable channel, features 18 instances of violent or hostile acts in each hour, 35% of which are of a sexual nature (57). Cable T.V. is said to offer three times as much violence as other channels during prime time and, according to HBO, viewers are not complaining (58). There is also the booming video cassette industry and, as noted by one purveyor, "The best renters are blood and guts and violence. The kids talk their parents into getting 'The Exorcist' and 'Creepshow' " (59). Periodically we read of tragic cases of deaths resulting from viewers emulating violent acts of characters seen on T.V. or in movies. After the film "Deer Hunter" was shown on cable T.V. 35 men shot themselves, 31 fatally, while imitating a scene of Russian roulette in the movie (60). Such occurrences are examples of the difficulty some viewers have in differentiating fantasy from reality on T.V.

Studies done on T.V. violence show overwhelming evidence that it is positively correlated with aggression in children (61-67). According to the National Coalition on Television Violence there are now over 850 scientific studies and reports from 20 nations that conclusively show the harm of T.V. and movie violence.* Specific effects noted include increase in anger, irritability, verbal aggression, loss of temper, and desensitization toward violence. Also noted are increased fighting, distrust, dishonesty, less sharing and cooperation, and increased willingness to rape and commit criminal behavior. Further studies associate conflict with parents, fighting, and delinquency with total amount of time spent viewing T.V., not just violent programs (68).

The T.V. industry has taken issue with these findings and recently issued their own longitudinal study which concluded that over the three-year period of the study, there was no evidence that T.V. was causally related to the development of aggressive behavior in children and adolescents. The study did not attempt to look at short-term arousal or modeling effects, nor the effect of specific depictions triggering arousal or rare acts of violence. It did find a correlation between aggression and being exposed to neighborhoods or families where violence is common. Violence was also correlated with maternal rejection and low socioeconomic status (69). One problem with the study concerns the fact that subjects studied were likely to include the more aggressive boys who reported more exposure to violent T.V.

Theories that attempt to explain the link between T.V. and violence as noted in the NIMH report "Television and Behavior" (70) include:

1) Observational learning theory, which postulates that if a child sees a T.V. character rewarded for aggressive behavior, then he will probably imitate that behavior. However, the persistence of that behavior will be contingent upon whether or not it is rewarded or punished (71).

---

*See NCTV News T.V. Film Biography, 1933-1983, and Cartoon and Hostile Humor, Annotated Bibliography, 1984, 5(9).

2) Disinhibition theory, which holds that when aggression is sanctioned, children's inhibitions against violence may be slowly and unconsciously eroded (72).

3) Attitude change, which holds that watching T.V. affects viewers' attitudes. For instance, people who view a lot of T.V. tend to be more suspicious and distrustful of others and are more likely to view the world as a dangerous place than those who are not heavy viewers (73, 74). Indeed, a person is 200 times more likely to be attacked on T.V. than in real life (75).

4) Arousal process theory, which holds that children who watch a lot of violence show less arousal. It postulates that people may seek an optimal level of arousal and may act aggressively to raise that level of arousal. Conversely, some believe that T.V. increases the level of arousal, which then leads to an increase in aggression (76).

One must also consider what activities children who are heavy viewers miss. Passive T.V. viewing may become a substitute for more active solving of conflicts, initiating activities, and interacting with peers and families, thereby depriving the child of opportunities for emotional growth. It is important to remember that some children may be more vulnerable to T.V. violence than others. For instance, the child who enjoys watching violence may be more affected by it because of his involvement with the program. Likewise, the child with a vivid fantasy life and poor reality testing may be more affected by T.V. violence than a more mature child with good ego strengths. Thus, as Maccoby reminds us, we must ask what kind of children are affected, under what circumstances, and by how much T.V. (77).

The T.V. industry has responded to arguments that T.V. violence breeds violence with denial and rationalizations, much in the same way the tobacco industry has managed to ignore facts linking smoking with cancer and heart disease. Typical rejoinders are either that T.V. content merely reflects what is out there, or that violence is what viewers want. Radecki concludes, "as long as violent T.V. is profitable, T.V. will be violent" (78). Some advertisers claim they have no control over the program that will appear in the space they purchase, whereas others express confidence in the ability of viewers to censor what they watch. Some even rationalize that they are actually providing a service to children (79). It should be noted that 25% of the T.V. industry's profit comes from 7% of its programming directed toward children (80). Miller, a communications specialist, points out that "advertisers perceive kids the same way they perceive adults as not vulnerable and not to be protected." He characterizes commericals aimed at children as being unfair freemarket transactions, i.e., "When you have an advertising executive with $50,000 in his pocket on one end of a string and a kid with a nickel in his pocket at the other end, who will end up with the nickel?" (81). In response to a massive campaign by Action for Children's T.V., 40% fewer ads are now appearing on children's T.V. and T.V. star hosts no longer sell products to children on the air, which lends a ray of hope regarding the ability of consumers to have some influence on what is broadcast.

HANDGUNS

There are presently 45-60 million handguns in circulation in the U.S.A., 2.5 million of which will eventually be used in 600,000 acts of violent crime. Another 2.5 million handguns are produced every year, and one is sold every 13 seconds (82). Because of their availability and lethality, they are, in contrast to other weapons, much more likely to cause death. In 1981, 11,258 people were murdered by handguns and about the same number committed suicide by handguns (83% of all firearm suicides) (83). Homicide rates have risen from 1.2 per 100,000 in 1900, to 11 per 100,000 in 1980; and half of all homicides are committed with handguns (84). Homicide is now the leading cause of death for nonwhite males between the ages of 25-34 years (85). Homicide and suicide account for over 40% of deaths in the 15-44 year age group (86), and 10% of all deaths among adolescents and young adults (87). The rate of suicide by handguns has risen from 4.9 to 7.1 per 100,000 over the past 25 years, whereas the rate for nonfirearm suicide has remained constant (88).

Violence by handguns receives frequent, but usually isolated, publicity in the headlines as when an important leader is assassinated. (There have been 17 assassination attempts on presidents, all but one of which were by handguns.) We have had public protest over killings in Vietnam, yet during the peak years of war in Vietnam, more Americans (52,000) were killed by handguns than were killed (42,300) in combat. Similarly, the number of persons killed in Northern Ireland in 1972 invoked the outrage of the press and public, yet almost twice as many, 751, homicide victims in Detroit (which has a population of approximately the same size) went almost unnoticed during the same period (89). Any disease that produced such an alarming number of deaths would be responded to with prompt attention from the government and health professions, as occurred in the recent outbreaks of Legionnaire's disease, Toxic Shock Syndrome, and AIDS, whose numbers of victims have been miniscule compared to the toll taken by handguns. The government has responded to handgun violence with apathy or rationalizations that the problem is multifaceted and beyond control. In spite of the fact that an estimated 500 million dollars (90) is spent annually in treating gunshot injuries, the medical profession has tended to turn a deaf ear to the problem.

Prior to 1970, violence was not even listed as a topic in *The Cumulative Index Medicus*. Of those articles on violence and handguns appearing in recent years, few have been in the psychiatric literature, yet psychiatrists are probably the specialists most likely to deal with the emotional aftermath of suicide and homicide.

Increasingly, we must also deal with the fear of violence. It is estimated that one in 17 persons has been threatened with a gun or shot at, and an equal number have used a gun or knife to defend themselves (91). In response to the fear of becoming a victim of crime, many Americans have taken to owning firearms, and approximately half of American homes now have one or more firearms (92). However, as several studies have demonstrated, gun ownership leads to a false sense of security and a gun in the home is much more likely to cause accidental deaths or be used in domestic homicide than used to deter a burglar (93, 94, 95). In keeping with this, it should be noted that 55% of murders in 1981 were carried out by relatives or persons acquainted with their victims, and 42% of murders ensued from arguments (96).

A gun in the vicinity of children becomes particularly lethal as young children do not distinguish between real and pretend, nor do they understand the concept of death. Gun accidents are now the leading cause of accidental death among children (97). Newspaper stories of a youngster firing a loaded gun at a sibling or friend in imitation of his favorite T.V. hero are legion. In a day care center in Tennessee a three-and-a-half year old found a loaded pistol in an employee's handbag that had been left in a toy cabinet. While playing with it, it discharged killing the school director (98). Children are not the only ones who have difficulty distinguishing between real and make believe. A California police officer killed a five-year-old boy who pointed a gun at him when he attempted to enter the apartment where the child had been left alone while his mother was at work (99).

Toy guns are now a 72 million dollar industry and their sales doubled between 1979 and 1982 (100). Also on the rise are the number of injuries they cause, with 1,756 children treated for injuries from toy guns in 1981 (101). A second cause for concern regarding their prevalence has to do with the fact that toy guns have been shown to lead to more aggressive behavior in children (102-105). Finally, we must ask why killing people should be considered play, and why we must raise little boys to feel as if a gun is a necessary appendage to their masculine identity?

Ours is the only developed nation that has no restrictions on handgun availability, despite the fact that most Americans favor strict controls on them (106, 107). Those countries that have enacted strict controls on handguns show negligible deaths from handguns, e.g., in 1980, there were eight in Great Britain, eight in Canada, 43 in Australia, and 18 in Sweden

(108). The U.S. government has had five presidential commissions on violence in the past 12 years that have stressed the gravity of the situation, yet their recommendations have been ignored. What legislation has passed has been considerably weakened by effective lobbying on the part of the National Rifle Association, the biggest spending lobby in the U.S.A., which has 1.85 million members, a budget of 30 million dollars, and five full-time lobbyists (109). The NRA contributed generously to President Reagan's campaign and Reagan, an NRA member, sympathizes with their objectives. President Reagan observed that gun control did not prevent John Hinckley from making an attempt on his life, but failed to mention that Hinckley's gun was purchased, not in Washington D.C., which has gun control legislation, but in Texas, which has none and has one of the highest homicide rates in the nation (110).

INSTITUTIONALIZED VIOLENCE

Let us consider very briefly some models of violence presented to children that are condoned in schools, government, and organized sports. The spare-the-rod and spoil-the-child philosophy of childrearing appears to be ingrained in our school systems. A 1970 Gallup poll found 62% of responders approved of spanking in grade school. Equal support for corporal punishment came from grade school teachers with 65% of elementary school teachers and 55% of secondary school teachers favoring judicious use of violent bodily punishments (111). Further, half of all American adults approve of teachers striking students given proper cause (112). But, Gil noted, "rarely if ever is corporal punishment administered for the benefit of an attacked child, for usually it serves the immediate needs of the attacking adult who is seeking relief from his uncontrollable anger and stress" (113).

Americans are also supportive of capital punishment with approval going up to 68% in a 1983 Gallup poll from 59% in 1973 (114). The deterrent value of the death penalty has never been established and West speculates that it may actually increase the number of murders as many people consciously kill in order to get themselves killed (115). He notes that one-third of murderers end up killing themselves. Meanwhile, the publicity that surrounds capital punishment must surely be confusing to children, who see the state repaying violence with violence in a talion type mentality, and condoning what they have been led to believe is morally wrong.

Finally, we need to look at violence in organized sports. The extreme, of course, is boxing where winning is based upon cumulative damage inflicted and crowds take pleasure in seeing opponents inflict brain damage upon each other. Children are often privy to close up T.V. coverage of this carnage, and the popularity of this sport among the young has been documented by the success of the Rocky movies. In 1983, the World Medical Association demanded a ban on boxing because it endangers participants' health. Indeed, 350 boxers have been killed in fights since 1945 (116). Violence in contact sports such as football, lacrosse, and ice hockey is common both on and off the field or arena, and once again television hones in on these episodes, bringing vivid displays of violence into the living room. It used to be assumed that violence in sports was cathartic for fans, however, several studies have found that observing sports violence actually increases spectators' hostility (117, 118, 119). It has also been demonstrated that people behave more aggressively as a result of viewing violence that is realistic, sanctioned by society, and when the viewer is identified with the aggressive character (120).

Children may become active participants in sports violence. Some parents pressure young children into playing contact sports unaware of the potential for battering and serious injury, especially among prepubertal children. Others consciously encourage their child's aggression in hopes of either "making a man out of him," or out of their own need to win. Parents on the sidelines screaming "kill him" and coaches chanting "no pain, no gain" are an all-too-common phenomenon, and the net effect is enormous pressure on children to win at all costs.

CONCLUSION

Violence is both endemic and epidemic in our society. The evidence presented here supports the view that violence breeds violence. To summarize, some of the mechanisms by which children learn violence include: identification with the aggressor; turning passive into active, as with the victim who later becomes the abuser; imitation of behavior that is rewarded; the effect of repeated exposure to violence on attitudes and one's view of the world; desensitization with gradual erosion of inhibitions against violence; and the theory that exposure to violence leads to increased levels of arousal and aggression.

The question is not one of shielding children from all violence but rather trying to keep it to proportions that they can handle. Massive amounts of violence at one time or continuous daily infusions that risk overwhelming their psyches or inuring them should be avoided. Further, we need to balance the steady diet of violence that our society serves our children with more models of prosocial behavior that demonstrate more civilized means of resolving conflicts. How do we as individuals begin to combat the problem of violence in our society? Should we even bother to try? A passive approach to the problem amounts to condoning it, which we cannot afford to do as the problem only becomes bigger and will not go away. What follows are some suggested responses to the problem:

1) Examine your own family lifestyle, the frequency of violence or exposure to it, and consider the implications and alternatives. Is there a handgun in your home and are the risks of keeping it worth taking? Do your children have toy guns or are there guns in your office playroom? If so, what sort of message are you conveying? Providing a child with a gun amounts to an endorsement for the use of guns.

2) Be alert to possible signs of abuse in your patients.

3) Don't be afraid to ask clients or patients about violence. If you are not getting histories of violence, then you may not be asking the right questions. As noted by Lion, "In our experience, the problem is not so much a matter of whether violence is syntonic or dystonic to the patient; rather, the problem lies in whether or not the clinician dares to ask about violent propensities in the first place. Denial plays a very great role. Psychiatrists often avoid asking frightening questions about past violence and criminal acts or ownership of weapons" (121). Perhaps one reason we hesitate to ask is because we are not sure how to handle the answers.

4) Promote services for violent families such as shelters, day care, crisis nurseries, and medical, psychiatric, social, and legal services that may help break the cycle of violence from one generation to the next.

5) Educate families regarding corporal punishment, T.V., and handguns. Offer them alternate means of discipline and limit setting and help them find other ways of feeling effective as parents. Teach them to view T.V. with what Action for Children's Television terms TLC: Talk about it, look at it with children, and choose programs. Solnit reminds us that "every young child in front of an unsupervised T.V. is at risk" (122). Learn to turn the T.V. off and teach children to watch selectively and critically. Limit the number of hours they may watch and don't be afraid to say no. For determined viewers, there are T.V. locks available. Try a week without T.V. to learn how dependent family members have become upon it. Discover alternatives to T.V.

6) Become aware of sexual stereotypes and how they may encourage aggression in boys. Help them find other ways of developing masculine identity without guns. We can stop glorifying violence at an early age by looking at the type of play we encourage or discourage in young children.

7) Make your opinion known. Write to sponsors of T.V. programs that are violent, encourage those programs that are prosocial. Encourage both commercial and cable T.V. to serve children and develop programs aimed at helping parents; i.e., instead of afternoon soaps or game shows that underscore the discrepancies between what the viewers have and the winners win, programs could be developed that are aimed at improving parenting or overcoming a sense of social isolation.

8) Contact legislators and make your views known about issues such as handguns, T.V. violence, corporal punishment in schools, and capital punishment. Be willing to testify on bills. Support pending legislation such as the Kennedy Rodino bill that would end the manufacturing of "Saturday night specials" and regulate handguns, and the Children's Television Education Act of 1983 that mandates an hour a day of educational programming on commercial stations.

9) Support organizations that reflect your views and are trying to combat violence such as Action for Children's Television, the National Coalition on Television Violence, Handgun Control, and the Medical Council on Handgun Violence.*

10) Encourage research into the area of violence and the need for government support in this endeavor.

REFERENCES

1. Klebba, A.J. Homicide in the United States, 1900-1974. *Public Health Report,* 1975, *90,* 195-204.
2. U.S. Department of Justice Statistics. *Report to the Nation on crime and justice.* Oct. 1983.
3. Lorenz, K. *On aggression.* New York: Bantam Books, 1963, p. 233.
4. Hardy, S.B. Infanticide among animals: A review, classification and examination of the implications for reproductive strategies of females. *Ethnology and Sociobiology,* 1979, *1*(13), 40.
5. Russell, C., & Russell, W.M.S. The natural history of violence. *Journal of Medical Ethics,* 1979, *5,* 108-117.
6. Goodall, J. Infant killing and cannibalism in free living chimpanzees. *Folie Primatol,* 1977, *28,* 259-282.
7. Dixon, A.F. Androgens and aggressive behavior in primates. *Aggressive Behavior,* 1980, *6,* 37-67.
8. Lorenz, 1963.
9. Sagan, C. *Dragons of Eden.* New York: Random House, 1972, pp. 91-92.
10. Silberman, C. *Criminal violence, criminal justice.* New York: Random House, 1978, pp. 22, 37-38.

*ACT, 46 Austin Street, Newtonville, MA 02160; NCTV, P.O. Box 12038, Washington, D.C. 20005; Handgun Control, 1400 K Street, N.W., Suite 500, Washington, D.C. 20005; MCHV, 109 North Dearborn Street, Suite 701, Chicago, IL 60602.

11. Tiny bank in Illinois welcomes armed customers. *The New York Times,* January, 26, 1983, p. 16.
12. American Express Mailing, July 1983.
13. Lystad, M.H. Violence at home: A review of the literature. *American Journal of Orthopsychiatry,* 1975, *45*(3), 328-345.
14. Gil, D. (Ed.). *Child abuse and violence.* New York: AMS Press, 1979, pp. 357-358.
15. Owens, D., & Strauss, M. The social structure of violence in childhood and approval of violence as an adult. *Aggressive Behavior,* 1975, *1*(3), 193-213.
16. Lewis, D. Letter to the Editor. *American Journal of Psychiatry,* 1983, *140*(8), 1107.
17. Steele, B.F., & Pollock, C.B. A psychiatric study of parents who abuse infants and small children. In L.H. Kempe, & R.I. Helfer (Eds.), *The battered child.* Chicago: University of Chicago Press, 1968.
18. Bakan, D. *Slaughter of the innocents: A study of the battered child phenomena.* Boston: Beacon Press, 1971.
19. Kempe, C.H., & Helfer, R.I. *The battered child.* Chicago: University of Chicago Press, 1968.
20. Bandura, A., & Walter, R. H. *Social learning and personality development.* New York: Holt, Rinehart & Winston, 1963.
21. Bandura, A., & Walters, R.H. *Adolescent aggression.* New York: Ronald, 1959.
22. Strauss, M., Gelles, R., & Steinmetz, S. *Behind closed doors: Violence in the American family.* Garden City, NY: Anchor Books-Doubleday, 1980.
23. Stark, R., & McEvoy, J. Middle class violence. *Psychology Today,* 1970, *4,* 52-65.
24. Bronfenbrenner, U. Socialization and social class through time and space. In E. Maccoby, J.M., Newcomb, & E.L. Hartley (Eds.), *Readings in social psychology* (3rd ed.), New York: Holt, Rinehart, & Winston, 1958.
25. Erlanger, H. Social class and corporal punishment in child rearing. In D. Gil (Ed.), *Child abuse and violence.* New York: AMS Press, 1979.
26. Baker, R.K., & Ball, S. Mass media and violence. Report of the National Commission on Causes and Prevention of Violence. Washington, D.C.: U.S. Government Printing Office, 1969.
27. Gil, 1979, p. 180.
28. Strauss et al., 1980.
29. Feshbach, N. Effects of violence in childhood. In D. Gil (Ed.), *Child abuse and violence.* New York: AMS Press, 1979, p. 571.
30. Weisberger, E. *Your young child and you.* New York: Dutton, 1975, p. 361.
31. Wife beating: The silent crime. *Time,* September 5, 1983, p. 23.
32. Strauss et al., 1980, p.48.
33. Baker & Ball, 1969.
34. Levinger, A. Sources of marital dissatisfaction among applicants for divorce. *American Journal of Orthopsychiatry,* 1969, *26,* 803-807.
35. Post, R.D., Willet, A.B., Franks, R.D., House, M.H., et al. A preliminary report on the prevalance of domestic violence among psychiatric inpatients. *American Journal of Psychiatry,* 1980, *137*(8), 974-975.
36. Carmen, E., Rieker, P., & Mills, T. Victims of violence and psychiatric illness. *American Journal of Psychiatry,* 1984, *141*(3), 378-383.
37. Hilberman, E., & Munson, K. Sixty battered women. *Victimology,* 1978, *2,* 460-470.
38. Rounsaville, B., & Weissman, M. Battered women: A medical problem requiring detection. *Journal of Psychiatry in Medicine,* 1978, *8,* 191-202.
39. Fitch, F., & Papantonio, A. Men who batter: Some pertinent characteristics. *Journal of Nervous and Mental Disease,* 1983, *171,* 190-192.
40. Strauss et al., 1980.
41. Harbin, J., & Madden, D. Battered parents: A new syndrome. *American Journal of Psychiatry,* 1979, *136*(10), 1288-1291.
42. Abuse of aged is often ignored. *The New York Times,* July 13, 1983, Section C, p. 9.
43. Adler, R.P., Lesser, G.S., Merringoff, L.K., Robertson, T.S., et al. *The effects of television advertising on children.* Lexington, MA: Lexington Books, 1980.

44. Group for the Advancement of Psychiatry (GAP). *The child and television drama: The psychosocial impact of cumulative viewing* (Report #112). New York: Mental Health Materials Center, 1982, p. 2.

45. *Television and behavior: Ten years of scientific progress and implications for the eighties,* Vol. 1. Summary Report, U.S. Department of Health and Human Sciences, 1982.

46. Adler et al., 1980.

47. T.V. Notes. *The New York Times,* January 28, 1984, p. 47.

48. *Television and behavior,* 1982.

49. Adler et al., 1980.

50. Hickey, D. Does America want family viewing time? *T.V. Guide,* December 6-12, 1975.

51. Adler et al., 1980.

52. Steinfield, J.L. T.V. violence is harmful. *Reader's Digest,* April 1979, pp. 37-45.

53. Radecki, T. Press release. National Coalition on T.V. Violence, July 11, 1983.

54. Kenniston, K. *All our children.* New York: Harcourt Brace Jovanovich, 1977, p. 7.

55. *Television and behavior,* 1982.

56. Higgins, P.B., & Ray, M.W. *Televisions action arsenal: Weapon use in prime time.* Washington, D.C.: U.S. Conference of Mayors, 1978.

57. NCTV Press Release, Jan. 10, 1984.

58. Price, F.J. Cable T.V. said to top networks in movie violence. *The New York Times,* January 22, 1983, p. 46.

59. Cassettes are changing movie audience habits. *The New York Times,* July 11, 1983, Section C, p. 11.

60. *NCTV News,* Deerhunter continues to kill, 35th victim, 31 dead. 1984, Vol. 5 (3 & 4), p. 3.

61. Belson, W. *Television violence and the adolescent boy.* London: Saxton House, 1972.

62. Singer, J.L., & Singer, D.G. *Television imagination and aggression: A study of preschoolers play.* Hillsdale, NJ: Erlbaum, 1980.

63. Williams, T.M. Differential impact of T.V. on children. A natural experiment in communities with and without T.V. Paper presented at a meeting of the International Society for Research and Aggression, Washington, D.C., 1978.

64. Eron, L.D. & Huesmann, L.R. Adolescent aggression and T.V. *Annals of the New York Academy of Sciences,* 1980, *347,* 319-333.

65. Hartnagel, T.F., Teevan, J.J., Jr., & McIntyre, J.J. Television violence and violent behavior. *Social Forces,* 1975, *54,* 341-351.

66. Greenberg, B.S. British children and television violence. *Public Opinion Quarterly,* 1975, *38,* 531-547.

67. Lefkowitz, M.M., Eron, L.K., Walder, L.G., & Heusmann, L.R. *Growing up to be violent: A longitudinal study of the development of aggression.* New York: Pergamon Press, 1977, pp. 115-116.

68. *Television and behavior,* 1982.

69. Milavsky, J.R., Kessler, R., Stipp, H., & Rubens, W.S. *Television and aggression: A panel study.* New York: Academic Press, 1982.

70. *Television and behavior,* 1982.

71. Bandura, A. Behavior theory and models of man. *American Journal of Psychology,* 1974, *29,* 859-869.

72. Belson, 1972.

73. Gerbner, G., & Gron, L. Living with television: The violence profile. *Journal of Communication,* 1976, *26*(2), 173-199.

74. Gross, L. The scary world of T.V.'s heavy viewer. *Psychology Today,* 1976, *9*(12), 41-45.

75. Radecki, T. Mailing from National Coalition on Television P.O. Box 647, Decatur, Illinois 62521.

76. Stein, A.H., & Friedrich, L.K. Television content and young children's behavior. In J.P. Murray, E.A. Rubinstein, & G.A. Comstock (Eds.), *Television and social behavior, Vol. 2. Television and social learning.* Washington, D.C.: U.S. Government Printing Office, 1972.

77. Maccoby, S. Effect of mass media. In M. Hoffman, & A.W. Hoffman (Eds.), *Review of child development research,* Vol. 1. New York: Russell Sage Foundation, 1964.

78. Radecki, 1983.
79. Feingold, M., & Johnson, G.T. Television violence: Reactions from physicians, advertisers and the networks. *New England Journal of Medicine*, 1977, *296*(8), 424-427.
80. Rothenberg, M. Effect of television violence on children and youth. *New England Journal of Medicine*, 1975, *234*(10), 1043-1046.
81. Miller, N. T.V. and children not a happy combination. *Psychiatric News*, 1982, *XVII*(22).
82. Shields, P. *Guns don't die people do*. New York: Arbor House, 1981.
83. *Handgun facts*. Washington, D.C.: Handgun Control Inc., 1981.
84. Report to the Nation on Crime and Justice. U.S. Dept. of Justice Statistics, Oct. 1983.
85. Rushforth, N., Ford, A., Hirsch, C., Rushforth, N., & Adelson, L. Violent death in a metropolitan county. *New England Journal of Medicine*, 1977, *297*(10), 531-538.
86. Weiss, N. Recent trends in violent deaths among young adults in the U.S. *American Journal of Epidemiology*, 1976, *103*(4), 416-422.
87. Better health for our children: A national strategy. The report of the select panel for the promotion of Child Health to the U.S. Congress and Secretary of Health and Human Service, Vol. 1, 1981.
88. Boyd, J. The increasing role of suicide by firearms. *New England Journal of Medicine*, 1983, *308*(15), 872-874.
89. Shields, 1981.
90. *Handgun facts*, 1981.
91. Stark & McEvoy, 1970.
92. Newton, C.D., & Zimring, F.E. Firearms annd violence in American life. A staff report submitted to the National Commission on the Causes and Prevention of Violence. Washington, D.C.: U.S. Government Printing Office, 1969.
93. Shields, 1981.
94. Newton & Zimring, 1969.
95. Alviani, J.D., & Drake, W.F. Handgun control: Issues and alternatives, Washington, D.C.: U.S. Conference of Mayors, Unpublished manuscript.
96. *Handgun facts*, 1981.
97. *Better health for our children*, 1981.
98. 3½ year old kills day care director. *The Stamford Advocate*, January 14, 1983, p. A8.
99. Photos of toy gun shown in shooting of boy 6. *The New York Times*, March 8, 1983, Section A, p. 11.
100. War toys boom. *NCTV News*. September-October, 1983, *6*(5,6), 6.
101. National Electronic Injury Surveillance. National Injury Information Clearing House. Washington, DC: U.S. Consumer Product Safety Commission.
102. Feshbach, S. The catharsis hypothesis and some consequences of interaction with aggressive and neutral play objects. *Journal of Personality*, 1956, *24*, 449-462.
103. Turner, C., Simons, L.S., Berkowitz, F., & Frodi, A. The stimulating and aggressive effects of weapons on aggressive behavior. *Aggressive Behavior*, 1977, *3*, 355-378.
104. Yarrons, S. Should children play with guns? *Parents Magazine*, Jan. 1983, 50-55.
105. Turner, C.W., & Goldsmith, D. Effect of toy guns and airplanes on children's antisocial free play behavior. *Journal of Experimental Child Psychology*, 1976, *21*, 303-315.
106. *Handgun facts, 1981*.
107. Controls on guns supported in poll. *The New York Times*, June 20, 1983, Section A, p. 16.
108. *Handgun facts*, 1981.
109. Shields, 1981.
110. King, W. Seven Texas cities are top in 20 in murder per capita. *The New York Times*, May 7, 1983.
111. Gallup Poll in Phi Delta Kappa, October, 1970, *1*(2), 101.
112. Stark & McEvoy, 1970.
113. Gil, 1979.
114. *Christian Science Monitor*, May 11, 1983.
115. West, J. The epidemiology of violence. Annual Meeting of the American Psychiatric Association, New York, NY, May 2, 1983.

116. Boyle, R.H., & Ames, W. Too many punches, too little concern. *Sports Illustrated,* April 11, 1983.
117. Martin, D. Sports violence seen as ritual amid chaos. *The New York Times,* October 26, 1982, Section C, p. 1.
118. Sports violence. *NCTV News,* July-August 1983, *4,* p. 9.
119. Sports violence annotated bibliography. *NCTV News,* January-February 1984, *5,* p. 6.
120. Eron & Huesmann, 1980.
121. Lion, J.R. Are clinicians afraid to ask about violence? Letters to the Editor. *American Journal of Psychiatry,* 1978, *35,* 757.
122. Solnit, A. Are we exaggerating the impact of T.V. on children? T.V. Debate. Annual Meeting of The American Psychiatric Association, New York, May 3, 1983.

19

Psychiatric Interventions with Children Traumatized by Violence

Spencer Eth and
Robert S. Pynoos

The condition of man . . . is a condition of war of everyone against everyone.—Thomas Hobbes, 1651

Violence is necessary; it is as American as cherry pie.—Rap Brown, 1966

For over 300 years social critics have noted that violence seems endemic to our species. The extent to which this phenomenon represents the expression of a basic aggressive drive or is an aberrant response to psychosocial pathology has been widely debated. Regardless of which view one accepts, the sad fact remains that people are continuously killing, maiming, and abusing themselves, their families, and others. This chapter presents the methods that the authors have developed to assist children who have been exposed to such violence.

VIOLENCE AND ITS EFFECTS

Each year in the United States over 20,000 homicides and 80,000 rapes are committed. Of those rapes, about a quarter involve women under the age of 18 years. Further, about one million cases of child abuse and neglect are reported, and it has been established that 4% of all children aged three to 17 years are subjected to severe violence every year (1). Children are affected by this climate of violence in at least two ways: They are the direct victims of abusive injury, including brain damage; and they are indirectly exposed to violence perpetrated against other family members. In a survey of adult emergency room patients, 22% identified themselves as domestic violence victims (2). Evidence indicates the majority of abused wives have children who have observed the sight of aggression directed against the mother (3). Over 40% of all deaths in the 15- to 44-year-old, child-bearing age group are due to homicidal and suicidal acts, often in the presence of dependent children.

The potential consequences of being victim of or witness to violence are legion. Self-destructive behavior is commonly exhibited by abused children (4). Victims of violence also "have extreme difficulties with anger and aggression, self-image, and trust"(5). About 50% of adult psychiatric in-patients have a history of battering within an intimate relationship (6). Intergenerational transmission, with battered children becoming abusive parents, demonstrates that violence does indeed breed violence.

Although many factors are implicated in the cycle of violence, one in particular may be especially responsive to therapeutic intervention. Our work has focused on the traumatic component of children's exposure to violence. Psychic trauma may occur when children are victims of or wit-nesses to violence, and it may result in psychological harm through the development of Post-traumatic Stress Disorder (PTSD) or other pathological mechanisms, such as identification with the aggressor.

The available reports on children's traumatic reactions to incidents of violence are filled with poignant accounts of the impact of these events on emotional and behavioral function. Psychic trauma occurs when an indi-vidual is exposed to an overwhelming situation resulting in helplessness in the face of intolerable danger, anxiety, and autonomic and instinctual arousal. The threat, viewing, or experience of major violence is painful, frightening, and distressing, and often constitutes a trauma. The suscepti-bility of any child to psychic trauma is a function of several parameters, including: genetic, constitutional, and personality makeup; past life expe-riences; the state of mind and phase of development; the content and in-tensity of the event; and the family circumstances (7).

Several case reports suggest that the DSM-III criteria for PTSD can be applied directly to children who have been physically abused, kidnapped, or bitten by a dog (8,9,10). The DSM-III diagnostic symptoms of PTSD involve: recurrent and intrusive recollections of the event; anxiety dreams; psychic numbing with markedly diminished interest in activities; feelings of detachment and constricted affect; fear of repeated trauma and renewed anxiety resulting in hypervigilant or avoidant behavior; decline in cognitive performance; startle reactions; and persistant feelings of guilt out of proportion to personal responsibility (11).

Some authors have stressed the common traumatic elements that can be found across all age groups, or have emphasized the continuum of the response to trauma from the infantile to the adult form. For instance, after studying the children of Chowchilla, who were abducted in their schoolbus, Terr comments: "There was an amazing similarity of response across the entire age range [five–14 years]"(12). However, Eth and Pynoos, based on their own research and analysis of the literature, have clarified distinct, phase-specific features of PTSD in children (13).

Other general characteristics of PTSD identified as common in children include: increased misperception of the duration and sequencing of time and events; premonition formation; traumatic play and reenactments; pessimistic expectations for the future; and marked, enduring personality changes (14). More than any other age group, preschool children can initially present as withdrawn, subdued, or even mute. This attitude should not be mistaken for traumatic amnesia, which has not been reported in studies of childhood psychic trauma. Young children are also prone to react with anxious attachment behavior and other regressive symptomatology. School-age children are more likely to react to traumatic violence with aggressive or inhibited behavior and psychosomatic complaints. All too often adolescents embark upon a period of post-traumatic acting-out behavior expressed by school truancy, precocious sexual activity, substance abuse, and delinquency. In summary, psychic trauma causes deleterious effects on cognition (including memory, school performance, and learning), affect, interpersonal relations, impulse control and behavior, neurovegetative function, and the formation of symptoms.

All children exposed to major violence, and especially those suffering from PTSD, are in need of psychiatric assistance. Unfortunately, for a variety of reasons few actually receive professional help. The child's family may themselves be so preoccupied with their own reactions to the violence that the child's special needs are overlooked. In other families, well-intentioned adults may seek to shield the child from any potentially upsetting reference to the violence (15). Their efforts to encourage the child to forget may involve a prohibition against discussing the incident with anyone, including a therapist. A few parents become focused on litigation instead of treatment. A common obstacle for families and communities to overcome is the scarcity of financial and treatment resources. Victims of violence are seldom a priority concern in the competition for mental health care. Even those children who are in the public social service system may not be evaluated specifically for violence-related symptoms.

CLINICAL RESEARCH

During the past four years the authors have been investigating the consequences for children of witnessing a violent event of high personal impact.

Our interest in this area began when we were referred a few children who had observed the murder of a parent, thereby suffering an unforgettable tragedy. We embarked upon a clinical study of a series of children and adolescents, all of whom were present during a parent's homicide. The success of this endeavor depended on the cooperation of several Los Angeles agencies. We were gratified to discover that we were able to reach the target children without encountering significant resistance.

We began by contacting the police and sheriff's departments, since all homicides are reported to law enforcement. The officers and detectives specializing in homicide were receptive to our overtures, and several meetings were scheduled. Eventually, we were invited to lecture at the police academy about the importance of our work and the critical role the police play for the child exposed to violence. We then approached the District Attorney's office. Prosecutors tended to be more wary of psychiatric involvement, in part because of their fear that we might unduly influence, and thereby contaminate, criminal witnesses. However, they soon came to recognize that our therapeutic interventions produced a less traumatized, more verbal, and potentially more effective child witness.

We were most successful in forging an affiliative relationship with the Victim-Witness Assistance Programs operated from the District Attorney's office. The Victim-Witness Assistance counselors were active in notifying us of appropriate children, securing parental consent, and bringing the child for sessions. In addition, these programs will often fund treatment of eligible children. We have also worked closely with the county child protective service. Child victims of violence will frequently require immediate placement and other concrete services. The child's caseworker will continue to be a critical person in arranging for care.

Our ability to influence the Los Angeles rape response network has developed more slowly. We know that sexual assault commonly occurs in the home. Although the rape victim often receives counseling, no inquiry is routinely made about whether any children were present during the attack. Hence, an important opportunity for intervention with the victim's children is lost. However, as our reputation has grown, we have been called by many clinicians seeking to discuss their violence-affected patients. We believe a formal violence victim psychiatric program would meet an important, though still largely unacknowledged need. In the next sections we will outline three separate components of our own work with children traumatized by violence.

INTERVIEW TECHNIQUE

The child recently exposed to major violence may present as numb or mute, and direct inquiry about the traumatic event may be unproductive, leaving the clinician feeling stymied and the child more detached. We have found it necessary to develop a generic interview technique to be used in the first session with such a child (16). This three-stage, semi-structured interview protocol facilitates a spontaneous and complete exploration of the child's subjective experiences, and allows for support and closure within a 90-minute time frame. The format has been revised as our work with many types of trauma has grown and as we have learned from the children's own comments about their interviews. Before meeting with the child, it is crucial to obtain information from the referring source and family about the circumstances of the event and the child's emotional and behavioral responses. The clinician can then be alert to significant references or omissions in the child's account during the session.

Opening Stage

In the opening stage we begin by establishing the focus of the interview. After greeting the child in our usual way, we state that we have spoken with other children who have "gone through what you have." Less experienced therapists might say that they would like to understand what it was like to go through what the child has been through. By so doing the child is informed that he is not alone in his predicament and that someone is willing to share with him what has occurred. The child is then immediately asked to draw and tell a story about a picture of his choice. The child is given art materials and reassured that the quality of the drawing is unimportant. Younger children tend to engage in play along with their scribbling and are similarly instructed to "make up a story." Most children readily participate in this assignment even hours after witnessing violence. The product varies enormously in style and projective content, from sparse recounting of the event to imaginative fantasies. This activity initiates the therapeutic process of countering the passive, helpless stance of the traumatized victim.

It is our assumption that the violent incident will become an intrusive element somewhere in the child's drawing or story. This traumatic reference must be identified by the interviewer, even though the child may seek to suppress associations to the violence. In fact, the drawing and story's details can provide clues to the sources of the child's anxiety and current means of coping. For example, a child may devise a happy ending to a frightening story by reversing some consequence of the action. One five-year-old girl, who witnessed a parent's murder, told of a clown who was pushed off a highwire, but was suddenly rescued by the appearance of a safety net. Another five-year-old drew a snowman who melted every day only to be repaired every night by the neighborhood children. A second-grade boy, who witnessed a schoolmate's kidnapping, drew the getaway car but explained that the car couldn't start. All of these children are employing the defense mechanism of denial in fantasy to undo the traumatic outcome. Another common coping strategy is omission of some salient feature of the drawing or the story. For example, one eight year old, who saw his mother stabbed, failed to mention a knife he had clearly drawn. This boy displayed an interruption in his fantasy elaboration in order to avoid being reminded of the trauma.

Trauma Stage

The second or trauma stage is marked by the transition from the child's drawing and story to an explicit discussion of the actual event. The therapist links an aspect of the child's production directly to the violence. For instance, a therapist could say to the first girl: "You probably wish that your father could have been saved at the end like the clown." Or one might add to the second child, ". . . your mother could be put back together like the snowman," and to the second grader, ". . . the car didn't start so the kidnappers didn't take away your friend." What often follows is a profound emotional outcry by the child. The child needs to be comforted and protected from being overwhelmed by the intensity or prolongation of the emotional release, and the interviewer must be prepared to share in the horror and to offer physical comfort.

After there has been an adequate release, the therapist can suggest that "now is a good time to tell me what happened." The child may respond by reenacting in play or by drawing the violent scene. Eventually the child is encouraged to express the event in words. The child is directed to maintain a focus on the central action of the violence. Although a marked increase in anxiety may precede these details, afterwards the child appears strengthened in his resolve to continue. Following a description of the action, the child's sensory experience is addressed. Violence involves the sight and sound of gunfire, screams and sudden silences, etc. This can be elicited by a statement such as, "I wonder if blood got on your clothes." Whenever a child speaks of his perceptions, we ask about concomitant autonomic and physical sensations. When one child said "it felt awful," we asked where he felt it. The child answered, "My heart hurt, it was beating so loud."

The role of the therapist during this second stage of the interview is to promote a full description, despite a rising level of anxiety. The child may need to be questioned carefully to ensure that the circumstances and aftermath are fully reviewed. This work is particularly exhausting for both the child and the therapist, and the child may need a brief period of rest or some snacks to feel adequately cared for during the emotional challenge.

Children will frequently invest a particular detail with special traumatic meaning, which may have the psychodynamic importance of pointing toward the child's initial identification. We have seen children identify with the assailant, the victim, and a protector such as the police or therapist. One 10-year-old boy bitterly recalled having been forced to wear the belt his father used to beat his mother in order to hide the weapon. The therapist can use this material to assist the child in distinguishing his fate from that of the person with whom he is identifying.

The interviewer should at some point ask what was the worst moment for the child. Even young children are able to consider the event before articulating a uniquely painful moment. It may involve a memory from earlier in the day, from the event itself, or from the aftermath. One 14 year old described her intolerable anger when, at the police station, her father yelled to her, "I'm sorry!" after having shotgunned her mother. This question presents an opportunity for the child to feel especially close to and understood by the therapist. The impact of the violence can then be approached. Witnessing actual physical injuries can result in recurrent, intrusive memories that seem difficult to unburden. We have been impressed by the child's desire to restore an image of a wounded or slain parent as intact. We might look with the child at a photograph if one is available. In cases of parental death, this aids grief work and helps the child retain earlier, happier recollections of parental interactions to counter the more recent violent images. However, the confirmation of the reality of death is critical for successful mourning.

Violence, unlike natural disasters, inevitably raises the issue of human accountability. Although the child may prefer to refer to the event as an accident, there remains an awareness and conflict over who is responsible. The interviewer may wonder aloud, "How come it happened?" or "What would make someone do something like that?" If the perpetrator is a stranger, it may be easy for the child to assign blame. However, family violence can propel the child into a conflict of loyalty, which may be expressed in the drawing or story. A seven year old saw her mother shoot her father as he wrestled with her brothers, who were trying to protect their mother from further wifebeating. Although nearly everyone involved held the abusive, alcoholic father at fault, his daughter, in her story, told of two evil boys who come to make trouble. Sorely missing her father and depending on her mother, she resorted to shifting the blame to her brothers. The assignment of responsibility may vary during the session and may also include the child. Children may be preoccupied with feelings of self-reproach for not having done more to prevent the violence, when in reality nothing could possibly have been done. One child berated herself for not having treated her mother's lethal stab wounds.

The discussion of responsibility naturally leads to issues of punishment and retaliation. Some children may be terrified either by their own revenge fantasies or by fear of counterretaliation by the assailant. We allow the children to express these feelings and permit them to imagine all the dreadful tortures they have reserved for the criminal, often by requesting a picture of "what you'd like to see done to him." We might comment on how good it feels to get back at the bad man now, even though it was impossible to have stopped him then. If the assailant has been captured, then we actively reassure the child that there is no further danger. Children are frequently confused about what actually has happened to the suspect, and whether he will eventually be released. We are concerned about how unusual it seems to be for police or prosecutors to reassure a worried child about these concerns.

Any discussion of violence implicitly calls into question the child's own impulse control. It is appropriate to ask the child what he used to do when angry and if the violent episode has produced any change. Viewing an open display of aggression may erode the child's trust in adult restraint and cause fear of his own ability to handle angry feelings. Problems in this area may be readily apparent in the school-age group. Normally exuberant children can turn passive, inhibited, and unspontaneous. Otherwise well-behaved youngsters can become irritable, rude, and argumentative. For example, an eight year old confided that he became nauseated and ran to the lavatory when a fight erupted in the schoolyard. This incident occurred two weeks after he watched his father stabbed by a stranger.

We usually inquire about recent dreams, and often learn of traumatic dreams and other sleep disturbances. A child may also dream of his own death. This can serve as a bridge to questions about the child's future plans. Immediately after violence, the child may crystallize a restrictive view of the future, which may be reinforced by the stigma of the crime. Several children swore that they would never become parents because of their belief that tragedy would repeat itself.

During the second stage of the interview, it is common for a child to mention a past episode of violence. In this stage we have learned previously unrevealed histories of child abuse, suicidal behavior, and local crimes. Rather than immunize the child against violence, these experiences more often sensitize the child to traumatic symptoms. Some of the most severely disabled children come from the war-torn countries of Central America. For them, each discrete bombing, execution, or terrorist attack seems to blend into a montage of violence. A goal of the initial session is to help the child sequence the events and thereby achieve some distance from the violent milieu.

Closure Stage

The closure stage centers on the sensitive, critical process of terminating the interview. We elicit the child's cooperation in reviewing and summarizing the session. By emphasizing how understandable, realistic, and universal the child's responses are, he comes to feel less alienated and more willing to accept support from others. We repeat that it is all right to have felt helpless or afraid during the violence and then sad or angry later on. We may return to the original drawing or story to underscore a point. For instance, in one case it was pointed out how far away the child placed himself in his drawing when in fact he was close enough to have been shot. We routinely compliment children on their bravery during the violence and their courage in dealing with their experiences in session. These children's beleaguered self-esteem needs support, and they usually swell with pride upon hearing these words.

We always ask about the child's present life concerns. Violence can result in changes in home or school, notoriety from media coverage, ongoing involvement in legal proceedings, and disruptions in family relationships. All of these issues can augment the child's distress. These children need to be in contact with a variety of social service agencies, and networking is an important component of any therapeutic intervention. Further, with enhanced trauma mastery the child will be better able to function as his own advocate to ensure that his needs and interests become known.

Before ending the session, we request that the child tell us what had been helpful or disturbing about the interview. The children appreciate our interest, and they have been our wisest teachers. As we end the session, we express respect for the child and for the privilege of having shared the interview experience. We might alert the child to what is expectable as he progresses through a traumatic reaction. For instance, "You may feel uncomfortable using a knife, but that will diminish over time." If we are not planning to meet with the child again, we give assurance that we can be reached, and give the child our professional card with our telephone number. We anticipate that a child may wish to call during a reactivation of the trauma, such as on an anniversary. In those instances in which a child is later seen for psychiatric treatment, we have noted that the interview with proper closure facilitates the child's entry into psychotherapy.

This step-by-step detailing of the interview technique is not intended to imply a rigid structure. Rather, we are suggesting that there is an inherent logic and flow to the format. The sessions generally follow the child's lead and rarely seem stifling or arbitrary. It should be understood that the interview is designed for use within weeks following the violent act. With the passage of time the method becomes problematic as the traumatic reference grows obscure, memories are repressed, and the child becomes increasingly reluctant to face renewed traumatic anxiety. However, even years later, a child may be relieved to have a chance to finally unburden himself, and the therapist may find these principles helpful.

Our experience confirms that the open discussion of a violent episode offers immediate relief and not further distress to the child. Some colleagues have been apprehensive, as we first were, that the focus on violence would be unduly upsetting. For example, Lebovici states, in referring to his sessions with children who witnessed the violent death of a parent, that "obviously, I was very cautious in my investigations, and made no attempt to encourage the child to talk about the murder" (17). We have learned from the children's own reviews, and their clear improvement in spontaneity and hopefulness, to press on despite initial resistance.

It is a mistake to underestimate the capacity of even the youngest child to confront the anxiety and grief associated with violence. Perhaps it is our own countertransference difficulties that prompt therapists to avoid the horror and tragedy of this material. Therapists working with victims of violence find it beneficial to be able to discuss the difficulty of the work with colleagues. We are impressed with the resemblance between our technique and that adopted long ago by military psychiatrists for the treatment of shell shock during war (18). We share the view that exposure to violence can cause psychic trauma, and that an early intervention aimed at reexperiencing the event fosters mastery. In many other respects, however, this interview and the procedures of military psychiatrists diverge.

GROUP CONSULTATION TECHNIQUE

During the course of our work with children who have been directly exposed to acts of violence, we recognized that siblings and other family members not present during the event will also be adversely affected. In fact, violence can have a noticeable impact on friends, neighbors, and, in particular, local schools. The intrusion of violence into a school community can precipitate anxiety in students and teachers, prompt disturbing behaviors, and disrupt the educational process. Fortunately, the structure of a school renders it highly amenable to outside therapeutic influence. Over the past several years, we and our colleagues have developed a group consultation technique for use in elementary and preschool classrooms touched by violence (19). This widely applicable intervention may assist students and teachers to cope with stress following a violent occurrence. Further, this technique permits the identification of at-risk children and serves to reverse the erosion of classroom function. Sadly, we have had many occasions to perfect this skill.

Consultation Following Family Violence

For illustration purposes a school consultation arising from an episode of catastrophic family violence will be described. Michael, eight years old,

Eddie, five years old, and their infant brother lived with their natural parents who were experiencing serious marital discord. Following an angry confrontation between the parents, the father proceeded to knife his three sons and then slash his own throat. Eddie managed to flee to a neighbor who summoned the police. The infant was found dead, and the older boys were hospitalized for treatment of their cuts. Father was admitted to the prison ward, where he claimed to have no recollection of his attack. The child psychiatry consultation service interviewed both children within a day. Michael drew a picture of their residential hotel and related a story in elaborate detail of an older male friend who lived in the same hotel and who had been killed by some neighbors. Arrangements were made for outpatient psychiatric follow-up after their discharge later the same week.

Contact was immediately made with the principal of the boys' elementary school. She was extremely receptive to the offer of a violence-focused consultation. The on-site technique began when the team of therapists met with the principal and other key administrators to plan the intervention. We jointly identified several groups of children as being particularly likely to be affected by the widely publicized violence. These groups included Eddie's kindergarten classmates, Michael's second-grade classmates, and the children who regularly rode the schoolbus with Eddie and Michael. This last population primarily consisted of children residing in the neighboring residential hotels, and they were subdivided into three groups according to grade level (kindergarten, first through third grades, and fourth through sixth grades). In this initial meeting, the school staff took the opportunity to share their own reactions to the event. Frequently, additional work is needed to help the staff deal with their personal associations to violence.

The group consultation sessions start when the therapists, usually three or four in number, enter the classroom and introduce themselves. The students were encouraged to speculate about the reason for the team's presence, and eventually a focus on the violent event emerged. The therapists elicited the children's fantasies about what happened to Michael and Eddie, thereby giving permission for them to speak about the unspeakable.

For example, the kindergarten-bus children said that a father got drunk and killed a baby, that there was a lot of blood, that the mother wasn't there, that the father became crazy, and that the police took him to jail. Not all of the information offered was accurate, as one boy volunteered that the father killed himself too. One girl explained, "It's better in my apartment because we go to church," illustrating her desire to delineate her family's destiny from the other family's fate. In Eddie's class, several children denied that he had been absent or insisted that he was out with a cold. The older children were, in general, less anxious and more depressed during the discussion. A few blamed the boys' mother for failing to protect them and excused the father because he was drunk. Some wondered whether the injured boys had been bad and therefore deserving of their punishment. As one child observed, "We'll have to take care of Michael and forgive him for anything he did." This expressed the common sentiment that the boys were hurting and should be protected from further harm.

The team calmly shared the truth about the violence. The aim was to dispel the wild rumors and fantasies and to refocus the discussion on the actual event. The therapists sought to demonstrate that there are adults who will tolerate hearing and talking openly about violence, because of the sense that so many parents and teachers are unable to do so. They characterized what the father had done as sick and terrible behavior, and related it to whatever violence the children had mentioned they had experienced. For instance, one girl confided that her own father was once drunk and had threatened to kill her teenage brother.

Paper and markers were distributed, and all of the children were instructed to draw whatever they liked. This structured activity tends to bind the anxiety evoked by the group discussion. While the children were busy with their free-drawing task, the therapists circulated throughout the group. In face-to-face interactions, the children were individually questioned about their drawings, with special attention given to aggressive themes, identifications, and conspicuous anxiety, depression, or denial. The projective use of an art technique provided the child with an opportunity to safely share his concerns with a therapist who will offer appropriate clarifications and interpretations. Often a child will then create another drawing illustrating the progression of the therapeutic interaction.

Although the artwork from the groups displayed differences according to developmental level and individual concerns, several themes recurred frequently. Many children drew the scene of the violence. In some pictures the violence escalates to the point where there is so much blood that it collects in a pool on the sidewalk. Another child drew, in addition to the knifing, a small child falling to her death from a window. Some children displaced the source of the threat away from people and onto witches and imaginary creatures. A few drew idyllic scenes of a beautiful house in the country. To that type of picture a therapist might say, "Wouldn't it be nice if you lived far away from all the trouble here?" One child composed a picture of a very sad, small dog. Depressive elements appeared in pictures of cemeteries and funerals. In one picture a camper truck crashes into a car, killing all of the passengers and causing great sadness. The boy who drew this told of how he had witnessed an accident on the highway some months earlier. He thought he had completely forgotten the incident, but ever since the stabbings he had become obsessed with his memory of that crash.

With the emphasis on violence and death, some children sought divine assistance. A popular film at that time was *ET.* In several drawings ET symbolized hope, redemption, and reunion. However, a few children were fixated on real violence that had intruded into their lives, such as shootings and gang activities. Those children whose anxiety or depression could not be relieved by the face-to-face conversation were identified as candidates for formal psychiatric evaluation.

The group consultation technique entered a closing phase with the children reassembling to summarize common issues. The team members recapitulated the violent event and the work of the consultation. They explored what it would be like for Michael and Eddie to return to school and how each child might facilitate the process. One child proudly told the group that he had given toys to the boys because he was so upset about them. The focus was then placed on the learning tasks that had been disrupted by the violent episode and its aftermath. The classroom teachers and aides, who were in attendance throughout to offer security and to observe for their own training, then proceeded with the scheduled activities of the day. The intervention ended with the team debriefing the administrative staff and planning for follow-up sessions and referrals, as indicated.

Because of the widespread interest in the consultation, the senior therapist was invited to attend the next faculty meeting. The consultation methodology was reviewed for all of the teachers, since the majority had not participated in the class sessions. The feedback indicated that the team had achieved the goals of relieving anxiety in the affected students, easing Michael and Eddie's return, and lifting the responsibility from the teachers of discussing the distressing topic of violence. Almost without exception, the children who had been in the sessions were not "stirred up" and had performed well during the rest of the day. One teacher asked whether innocent children should be exposed to the details of family violence. Other teachers quickly responded that the children in the school were already quite knowledgeable about the threat of violence in their lives. Subsequent requests for consultations from that school testifies to the accepted value of the intervention.

This model of group consultation derives both from the theory of crisis intervention and from our interview technique. The approach is designed to be effective when a group of children has been recently exposed to some aspect of a violent occurrence. It is well documented that children will respond symptomatically to a violent tragedy involving a person known to them, from a President to a classmate's parent (20, 21). When that happens, the classroom may be the ideal location for a group consultation. It has been noted that since children can readily discuss their feelings during structured school activities, this setting offers an opportunity for enhancing coping skills (22). The group consultation economically addresses both the primary symptom of anxiety in the children and the secondary loss of school function. The breakdown of classroom cohesion exacerbates stress and, in another context, has been termed a loss of communality (23). Although not conceptualized as formal psychiatric treatment, the team did observe that following the consultation, the children and teachers seemed somewhat stronger in their resolve to face a violent and unpredictable world.

Consultation Following School Violence

When catastrophic violence erupts in the school itself, the psychiatric team must be prepared for a large-scale project. Danto has described his involvement with an elementary school in the wake of the murder of a teacher in her classroom (24). He recognized how that event traumatized the student witnesses and severely stressed many other students, staff members, and parents. Although Danto's meetings with school staff and parents were valuable, no attempt was made to reach all of the affected children. We believe our techniques are an appropriate response to violence on the school grounds, although the domain of services must be greatly expanded. For example, a sniper fired into the playground of an inner-city elementary school, killing two and injuring many students and staff. As a result, the number of children who were physically injured or in direct danger numbered over 100. The majority of these children suffered psychic trauma. Further, many of the other 1,000 students attending the school, as well as most of the staff, became severely anxious. These indirect victims could be found in every class in the school. Exacerbating the crisis was the stressed condition of the teachers and administrators, who, while trying to cope with their own reactions to the violence, were forced to contend with the children's responses, worried parents, intrusive district personnel, and media stigma.

The intervention following catastrophic violence on the school premises must be comprehensive. School adminstrators need to be met with early and often in order to bolster their confidence and foster the recovery of their leadership abilities. We believe that every classroom deserves a group consultation. It is an efficient means to identify those children who were direct victims and to screen for those indirectly, but nonetheless severely affected. All of the direct victims and the symptomatic indirect victims are then seen for an individual interview. The group technique also has a therapeutic function. The drawings, one-to-one interactions, and open discussions bind the children's anxiety and reverse their sense of passive helplessness. Importantly, the consultants can help construct a "trauma membrane" around the class, repairing the ruptured institutional protective shield (25). Ongoing teacher groups and sessions with parents are also needed. Teachers and parents are always concerned about the violent event, about their personal associations, and about their estrangement from the children. All of these issues can be raised in group sessions. If the assailant survives, which was not the case with the sniper, then liaison with the police and judicial system is also important. A mental health team should be prepared to remain involved with a school for as long as a year after an episode of catastrophic violence.

LIAISON WITH THE JUDICIAL SYSTEM

Children who are exposed to violence, especially those who are victims or witnesses of crimes, routinely become involved with the judicial system. The significance of the child's involvement has become apparent to child psychiatists, especially when they become enmeshed in the same proceedings (26). For the child, the various stresses associated with judicial encounters may cause distress, exacerbate traumatic symptoms, and complicate psychiatric treatment. For the child psychiatrist, the stresses associated with the nonclinical roles of advisor to the judiciary and of expert witness in criminal and civil action may produce anxiety or result in avoidance of these critical tasks. This next section will follow the child participant through a sequence of judicial phases and indicate appropriate liaison activities for the child psychiatrist.

Investigation Phase

The police are responsible for the timely investigation and arrest of the criminal suspect. The police seek to accumulate and protect the available evidence in order to substantiate the state's case. In their effort to collect evidence, the police may follow procedures that exacerbate the child's distress. For instance, during the police interrogation the child may be suddenly separated from parents or other family members. Children will complain of being sequestered alone while awaiting their interview in a strange and foreboding police station. According to police lore, a tired witness offers less guarded responses during the interview. Although this rule may prove useful with adults, it is counterproductive with children who have been traumatized by violence. The police are well advised to allow the child witness to crime to rest and be comforted by family after the ordeal. Although a few hours may be lost in the process, the child is then much better prepared to articulate a clear description of what was seen. In fact, some children are reassured by the presence of the police, who are perceived as safeguarding the child from further danger.

The highly structured police interview is intended to elicit information about the crime. The average detective has received little training in work with children and pays scant attention to the developmental capacities or emotional needs of the child witness. The officer usually begins by re-questing identifying data from the child (i.e., name, age, address, etc.). A young child may misinterpret these initial questions as implying that he is under investigation or faces arrest. The interview then focuses on the chron-ological details of the crime, without concern for the child's subjective experience at the time of the violence or while being interviewed. This interview method contrasts markedly from our own technique previously described. We believe that the child and the law are better served by applying some of the principles of a trauma-oriented interview—that is, allowing children to recount the events in their own way, at their own pace, and with their own emphasis.

When confronted with a withdrawn, silent preschool-age child, most police will feel defeated and reject the child as a potential source of infor-mation. The police are generally unaware that even a young child can process, remember, and reenact the central action of a violent crime. It may be necessary to elicit the cooperation of the custodial adult, who can then notify the detective when the child seems ready to cooperate with an interview. Although a delay in describing the crime will erode the child's credibility, it may nonetheless be a unique source of information.

School-age children are subject to being forced into an accomplice role, especially by a parent or other adult relative. They may be coerced into lying, playing "dumb," or being otherwise uncooperative with the police. This situation commonly arises in instances of family violence. However, children usually feel conflicted in this role and may unconsciously reveal the truth. One eight-year-old boy told the police a rehearsed story of his father's efforts to shake and awaken his drunken wife. The police, having conferred with us, asked the boy to draw a picture and tell a story. The boy drew a man being arrested for killing an unprotected woman—an account consistent with his mother's fatal beating. Adolescents tend to be quite aware of the implications of their answers to police questions. They un-derstand how, without overtly lying, they can influence critical issues, such as motivation, premeditation, etc. In those cases, psychiatric consultation by the police could be valuable as well.

Trial Phase

Many questions have been raised about the wisdom of having children testify in criminal trials. Some feel that the child may be burdened with the intolerable responsibility of convicting a person of a crime, while others wonder whether a child's testimony ought to be sufficient to convince a judge or jury. We appreciate these opinions, but find compelling counter-arguments for the use of children as criminal witnesses. It is crucial to remain cognizant of the fact that it is the defendant, not the child, who is on trial. The child must be helped to accept that his only responsibility as a witness is to report truthfully whatever was seen and heard. It was the adult, not the child, who committed the crime and faces the punishment. On occasion the child may be implicated in the crime by some family member or in his own imagination. Especially in family violence, the child may have unarticulated ambivalence about being called as a witness. It would seem that testifying "against" a close relative would place the child in an untenable position. However, from what children and adults have told us about their testimony, sometimes years later, the opportunity to speak aloud was of overriding importance. Several children who were not called to the stand felt that they had failed to assist the victim in that way.

There has been an historic reluctance to have children testify in criminal trials. This has been true despite the fact that children tend to be excellent witnesses in criminal cases where the observed violence has had a major impact. As one deputy district attorney confided, there is always the lingering fear that the child will "turn against us" by introducing entirely new and discrediting testimony. Child psychiatrists may be able to offer appropriate reassurance in that regard. In jury trials, the jury determines the credibility of each witness by reconciling any discrepancies in the evidence and assigning weight to the relevance of the testimony. The jury, having heard all relevant testimony, deliberates the question of guilt. It serves neither the child nor society to deprive the jury of the child's account.

In order to qualify for testifying, most children under the age of 10 years will need to be interviewed to establish their competence (the "voir dire"). Legal competence refers primarily to the mental capacity to observe the occurrence, remember the facts, and communicate them in court. Children need to demonstrate that they understand the difference between the truth and a lie and that they feel compelled to tell the truth. Some appellate decisions suggest that judges are obliged to examine child witnesses regardless of age, and, if qualified, a child must be allowed to testify. The voir dire is the critical test for the potential child witness. Failure to qualify will leave the child feeling incompetent and demoralized. Successful qualification depends on the child's developmental abilities and state of mind that day and on the judge's sensitivity to psychological considerations. Child psychiatrists will be particularly helpful when they familiarize court personnel with these issues.

The qualification examination is often conducted in a manner that is developmentally inappropriate to the child. Questions should be directed to the child's real world experience, rather than relying on inquiries about abstract concepts such as truth. Objects from the child's life, including toys, books, and pictures, can be properly introduced to establish competence. The young child should not be asked to reason from assumption; for instance, by asking "what if" questions. It is not required by law, nor should it be demanded in the courtroom, to describe specific punishments for lying to the child. To do so in the presence of the uniformed bailiffs and a black-robed judge can unduly inhibit the young witness. As long as the child is able to relate the material facts of the event, he is competent without necessarily knowing his birthdate, address, school, the number of days in a week, or other immaterial facts. Very young children can be qualified on this basis.

The child's state on the day of testimony is an important variable determining performance. The judge should pay attention to such details as health, hunger, sleeplessness, fatigue, and toileting needs. It is common for other family members to be excluded from the courtroom because they may be called as witnesses. In such a situation the child may be left without the presence of a trusted adult, feeling abandoned and threatened. The child may have an intense and idiosyncratic reaction to the court milieu or to one of the participants or spectators. Every child witness should have an opportunity to explore the courtroom prior to being called to the stand. The judge has the authority to ensure that the child is placed at ease. He can, if needed, exclude the public, allow the child to sit on a parent's lap, and hold the voir dire in chambers.

Even the very young and legally incompetent child may play a vital role in the judicial process. The district attorney has the discretionary power to file charges and pursue prosecution of a suspect. A very young child may dramatize the crime in play, indicating to the district attorney's satisfaction the identity of the assailant. This may convince the district attorney of the suspect's guilt and the necessity of bringing the case to court, even if the child cannot be used as a witness. A child psychiatrist's belief in the validity of reenactment behavior may contribute to the district attorney's decision.

Once qualified, the child will begin direct testimony, usually conducted by the district attorney. Testifying in court is always stressful for the child witness, as well as for the psychiatric expert. However, for the child suffering from traumatic symptoms, the experience of being forced to remain in the presence of the defendant while being questioned about the violence can add immeasurably to the distress. The constitutional rights of the defendant clearly require that the child witness be subjected to direct and cross-examination. The judge does have the discretionary power to clear the courtroom of spectators. Of greater potential impact is the possibility of utilizing innovative technology to spare the child the burden of directly facing the defendant. Two-way, closed-circuit television can provide a mechanism by which the child can be sequestered from the courtroom and yet the defendant, counsel, and child can simultaneously see and hear each other. One of the authors (SE) testified as an expert witness in support of this procedure as a means to limit the potential terror to a sexually abused child of physical confrontation by the defendant. Ultimately, the legislature and appellate courts will precisely define the acceptability of these alternatives to traditional court proceedings. Psychiatric input may well prove instrumental in their deliberations.

Unlike being interviewed by a therapist, testifying on the witness stand often leads to distress rather than relief for the child. Although counsel conducting the direct examination seeks to establish a trusting and secure relationship with the child, the adversarial structure of the courtroom setting is an inevitable source of stress. The critical task for any witness is to report what was personally seen, heard, and experienced. The child's cognitive capacity is a limiting factor in the performance of this task. For example, young children may be able to testify that someone was struck, but may be unable to count the precise number of blows. If properly given the opportunity to supplement their verbal account with a reenactment, these young children may prove to be convincing witnesses despite developmental limitations.

Of utmost importance is that the child's testimony reflect a thread of consistency. Especially with a long delay between the violence and the court appearance, the child may waver in recollecting details or may introduce retrospective distortions. Trauma itself has been shown to have deleterious effects on memory. However, the child's testimony can bear some degree of confusion, uncertainty, or even error, if the description of the central action of violence is clear, accurate, and compelling. Child psychiatrists can assist counsel in perfecting skill in eliciting such an account from the child witness.

After completing direct testimony, the child witness must face the rigors of cross-examination. Common goals of cross-examination are to discount the evidence and to discredit the witness. The child must be able to withstand thorough questioning, because if he "freezes" on the stand then the judge must dismiss the child and strike the entire testimony. Preschool-age children will have their very capacity to perceive, recall, and test reality challenged. Counsel may ask questions out of chronological sequence or exaggerate minor inconsistencies in order to confuse the young child's understanding of the material facts. Without proper preparation, often requiring psychiatric assistance before, during, and after the trial, the child can easily become uncertain about whether what he saw really occurred. It appears that with the passage of time, most children become less willing to reexplore a frightening event and less able to remember the details. The unprepared or vulnerable child may leave the stand feeling anxious, demoralized, and helpless. For such a child, the experience of testifying represents retraumatization. However, with appropriate psychiatric input, successful testifying can offer an opportunity for trauma mastery through the active performance of a relevant and vital task.

Older children will be challenged more intensely over their specific recollections of the violence. A standard device during cross-examination is to ask questions about peripheral details, such as the furniture in an unfamiliar room. Incomplete memories for these unessential "facts" tend to discredit other, better preserved core memories of the central action. Should the child begin to fill in the gaps by making up those details, then counsel will confront this presumed "confabulation" of evidence. Likewise, the child who employs unconscious fantasy elaboration will be similarly impeached as a creditable witness. School-age children are at risk of feeling stupid and humiliated if their testimony wavers and is challenged. Child psychiatrists can be of value in alerting the district attorney to these dangers and distinguishing this variety of error production from intentional lying. As during the violence itself, the child is susceptible to feeling ineffectual, and the therapist can provide comforting reassurance to the child about facing adversity on the stand.

Adolescents are apt to be questioned at length concerning motive and circumstance, and about their own biases in the testimony presented. They can be placed in the untenable position of presenting evidence supporting the assailant's claim of mitigating circumstances. For example, one girl unwittingly corroborated her stepfather's alibi by honestly reporting his statements to her about "accidentally" killing her mother. Adolescents' own love or ambivalence for a parent can be turned against them. Not infrequently, teenagers become acutely self-conscious while testifying. Although adolescents are older and more mature, they are not immune to stress in court. We know of two adolescents who developed a psychotic decompensation on the witness stand during cross-examination. Neither received sufficient preparation from the prosecutor, consistent support from their family, or the benefit of psychiatric consultation around the time of testifying about violence.

The judge's discretionary power can be especially helpful to the child witness during direct and cross-examination. A critical point is at the beginning of direct testimony. The judge should be alert to the child's level of anxiety. The judge can interrupt the proceedings to inquire whether the child is afraid, and if so to guarantee the child protection. The judge can also call frequent recesses to prevent exhaustion. It is the judge's prerogative to intercede at any time to ensure that the questioning of the child is developmentally appropriate and, if not, to rephrase the question to assist the child. If the child falters during cross-examination, the judge can intercede to determine the source of the child's difficulty. The judge can refuse to permit an antagonistic or hostile attitude by counsel. The judge may comment to the jury on the value of the child's testimony. We heard one judge say: "Don't believe him just because he is cute, but you may seriously consider his statements in your deliberations." However, the judge should refrain from such observations while the child is still in court. Because of the nature of their role, we believe that judges should seek out consultation with psychiatrists whenever a child witness is called. Unfortunately, criminal court judges seem rarely to avail themselves of this service.

Sentencing Phase

The final phase to be considered here is sentencing following conviction. Punishment has serious practical, ethical, and psychological implications and elicits the strongest reactions. Punishment confers retribution, protection, deterrence, and rehabilitation. Whether the assailant is a stranger or a threatening known adult, the child and society unite in demands for incarceration for an act of violence. However, when a parent is the perpetrator, the desire for justice may oppose the need to preserve family stability and parental attachment. Even in these instances, however, children will need to recognize the parent's crime in order to validate their own experience. The subsequent development of the child's superego, capacity for impulse control, and primary identifications will be greatly influenced by the judicial outcome.

When the convicted assailant is a stranger and is incarcerated, the child's fantasies of punishment as revenge may be intense, persistent, and frightening. Young children may imagine that what they fantasize will actually happen to the assailant in prison. These children need an explicit explanation of what it means to be imprisoned. If a parent is sentenced to prison, this explanation is particularly important and may be followed by visits to prison to correct lingering misconceptions and to confront any denial of where the parent is actually residing. We believe all child witnesses deserve to be informed of the verdict and, if guilty, the sentence. Sadly, many children are left in doubt about the outcome, and may be too anxious or inhibited to attempt to find out. The therapist may serve as an advocate in helping to secure this information and interpret its significance for the child.

Civil Proceedings

In addition to participating in criminal proceedings, children may become involved in civil actions as well. Although also adversarial, these judicial encounters have their own psychological agenda for the child and the child psychiatrist. Terr has written about civil suits claiming psychic injury to children (27). In such cases, the child victim may have been physically injured with concomitant psychic injury, or the damage may be entirely emotional. With increasing frequency we have been requested to evaluate children who have developed PTSD after observing violence of high personal impact.

As Terr notes, these psychiatric evaluations tend to be requested long after the traumatic event and in the context of considerable financial incentive for the family. The child may be subjected to psychiatric examination by the defendant's expert, who may be seeking to limit the estimate of damage to the child. The child psychiatrist is called upon to determine psychiatric morbidity, and estimate with reasonable certainty any future suffering and the cost of treatment. To the consultant's dismay, urgent treatment recommendations often go unheeded. These are intrinsically difficult tasks, and the psychiatric consultant must then be willing to defend his opinions in court. If the child psychiatrist is called to testify as an expert witness, then he should be thoroughly knowledgeable about both the facts of the case and the subtleties of PTSD. Only thus forearmed will cross-examination be experienced by the psychiatrist as an opportunity for demonstrating clinical wisdom, rather than an exercise in frustration.

Many children affected by violence, especially those who have been victims of abuse and those who have had a parent killed, enter custody proceedings. Reported abuse propels the child into a system designed to protect him from further injury. Often this priority necessitates removing the child from the home. If the suspected abuse is confirmed, a legal decision will need to be made about whether the child can be safely returned home or whether prolonged placement is indicated. Child psychiatrists may be in a position to offer pertinent information about the child's psychological function and adaptation to the placement situation.

In cases where the caretaking parent is killed, the child requires immediate placement in a new home. This emergent decision will have long-term implications, and the grief-stricken child should be assured of object constancy and residential stability. These and other considerations will complicate the ultimate resolution of custody proceedings. For example, a girl of two-and-a-half years witnessed her father shotgun her mother to death. Father was convicted of voluntary homicide and sentenced to a maximum of eight years in prison. Both sets of grandparents petitioned the court for custody. The paternal grandparents clearly indicated their intent to care for the child until her father's release, at which time he planned to reassert his parental right of custody. The maternal grandparents were determined to have the court rule that their daughter's murderer would never gain custody of their granddaughter. The age of this child was such that her principal connection to her father was her traumatic memory of his brutal assault on her mother. This fact, along with the child's marked preference for her maternal grandparents, greatly influenced the child psychiatrist's recommendation.

In another custody case, an eight-year-old boy was present during his parents' and sister's horrifying murders. During this child's hospitalization for treatment of his own serious injuries, the parents' will was read and their request that their son be placed with a paternal uncle was honored. Unfortunately, the uncle and his family lived in another state and were virtual strangers to the child. Instead, the boy begged to go "home" with his beloved maternal grandmother who lived in the same area. Again, child psychiatric input was critical in advising the judge that the psychological evidence favored the grandmother's request for custody. Grandmother was awarded temporary custody, with vacation visitation with the uncle, despite the parents' wishes to the contrary. The judge also followed the psychiatric recommendation by ordering psychotherapy for the child. Final disposition will await follow-up reports. As illustrated, child psychiatrists may be forceful advocates to ensure that the best interest of the child is the deciding factor.

FUTURE DIRECTIONS

Our work to date suggests that there are therapeutic interventions available to assist children exposed to violence. We are optimistic that further studies in this area will produce significant progress. Clearly, there is a need for long-term, controlled investigations to characterize the course of children affected by violence. The next stage of our own clinical research involves comparison groups in order to control for proximity to violence (i.e., victim, witness, nonwitness), and lethality of outcome (i.e., homicide, rape). Other pertinent variables to be evaluated include developmental phase, temperament and defensive constellation, preexisting psychopathology, and familial reaction. With this information, identification of vulnerable children will be based on firm scientific evidence.

Children exposed to violence are susceptible to a variety of morbid responses. PTSD is common following an extreme or catastrophic psychosocial stressor. Our single-session technique has proven helpful, but these children often require further treatment. Additional work is needed to adapt existing focal, brief psychotherapy models for use with traumatized children. Other youngsters develop behavioral syndromes following exposure to violence. These children are candidates for a range of current psychiatric modalities, including group and family techniques, though adequate attention must be directed to the experience of violence and its effects.

We have become alert to the impact of violence on a child's emerging pattern of identifications. Prominent identification with a victim or aggressor may profoundly alter a child's life trajectory. Long-term psychodynamic-oriented therapy may be necessary to free the child from the disabling legacy of violence. Although clinical work with this population of children frequently proves difficult and personally painful, the rewards are great. Our civilization's destiny might well depend on the interruption of the escalating cycle of violence. Child psychiatrists have an important role to play in this struggle.

REFERENCES

1. Heins, M. The "battered child" revisited. *Journal of the American Medical Association*, 1984, *251*, 3295-3300.
2. Goldberg, W.G., & Tomlanovich, M.C. Domestic violence victims in the emergency department. *Journal of the American Medical Association*, 1984, *251*, 3259-3264.
3. Rounsaville, B., & Weissman, M. Battered women: A medical problem requiring detection. *Journal of Psychiatry in Medicine*, 1978, *8*, 191-202.
4. Green, A.H. Self-destructive behavior in battered children. *American Journal of Psychiatry*, 1978, *135*, 579-582.
5. Carmen, E.H., Rieker, P.P., & Mills, T. Victims of violence and psychiatric illness. *American Journal of Psychiatry*, 1984, *141*, 378-383.
6. Post, R.D., Willet, A.B., Franks, R.D., et al. A preliminary report on the prevalence of domestic violence among psychiatric inpatients. *American Journal of Psychiatry*, 1980, *137*, 974-975.
7. Furst, S.S. A survey. In Furst, S.S. (Ed.), *Psychic trauma*. New York: Basic Books, 1967.
8. Green, A.H. Dimension of psychological trauma in abused children. *Journal of the American Academy of Child Psychiatry*, 1983, *22*, 231-237.
9. Senior, N., Gladstone, T., & Nurcombe, B. Child snatching: A case report. *Journal of the American Academy of Child Psychiatry*, 1983, *22*, 579-583.
10. Gisalason, I.L., & Call, J. Dog bite in infancy: Trauma and personality development. *Journal of the American Academy of Child Psychiatry*, 1982, 21, 203-207.
11. American Psychiatric Association. *Diagnostic and statistical manual of mental disorders* (Third edition). Washington, D.C.: American Psychiatric Association, 1980.
12. Terr, L.C. Children of Chowchilla: Study of psychic trauma. *Psychoanalytic Study of the Child*, 1979, *34*, 547-623.
13. Eth, S., & Pynoos, R.S. Developmental perspective on psychic trauma in childhood. In C.R. Figley (Ed.), *Trauma and its wake*. New York: Brunner/Mazel, 1985.
14. Terr, L.C. Chowchilla revisited: The effects of trauma five years after a school bus kidnapping. *American Journal of Psychiatry*, 1983, *140*, 1543-1550.
15. Schetky, D.H. Preschooler's response to murder of their mothers by their fathers: A study of 4 cases. *Bulletin of the American Academy of Psychiatry and the Law*, 1973, *6*, 45-57.
16. Pynoos, R.S., & Eth, S. Witness to violence: The child interview. *Journal of the American Academy of Child Psychiatry*, in press.
17. Lebovici, S. Observations on children who have witnessed the violent death of one of their parents: A contribution to the study of traumatization. *International Review of Psychoanalysis*, 1974, *1*, 117-123.
18. Grinker, R.R., & Spiegel, J.P. *War neuroses in North Africa: The Tunisian Campaign*. New York: Josiah Macy, Jr. Foundation, 1943.
19. Eth, S., Silverstein, S., & Pynoos, R.S. Mental health consultation to a preschool following the murder of a mother and child. *Hospital and Community Psychiatry*, 1985, *36*, 73-76.

20. Harrison, S.I., Davenport, C.W., & McDermott, J.F. Children's reactions to bereavement. *Archives of General Psychiatry,* 1967, *17,* 593-597.
21. McDonald, M. Children's reactions to the death of a mother. *Psychoanalytic Study of the Child,* 1964, *19,* 358-376.
22. Bloch, D.A., Silber, E., & Perry, S.E. Some factors in the emotional reactions of children to disaster. *American Journal of Psychiatry,* 1956, *113,* 416-422.
23. Erikson, K.T. Loss of communality at Buffalo Creek. *American Journal of Psychiatry,* 1976, *133,* 302-305.
24. Danto, B.L. A man came and killed our teacher. In J.E. Schowalter, P.R. Patterson, M. Tallmer, A.H. Kutscher, et al. (Eds.), *The child and death.* New York: Columbia University Press, 1983.
25. Lindy, J.D., Green, B.L., Grace, M., & Titchener, J. Psychotherapy with survivors of the Beverly Hills Supper Club fire. *American Journal of Psychotherapy,* 1983, 37, 593-610.
26. Pynoos, R.S., & Eth, S. The child as witness to homicide. *Journal of Social Issues,* 1984, *40,* 87-108.
27. Terr, L.C. Personal injury to children: The court suit claiming psychic trauma. In D.H. Schetky, & E.P. Benedek (Eds.), *Child psychiatry and the law.* New York: Brunner/Mazel, 1980.

Part V

EMERGING ISSUES

20

The Baby as a Witness

Lenore C. Terr

In the volume *Child Psychiatry and the Law*, the chapter "The Child as a Witness" (1) presented the first attempt to psychiatrically characterize what frightened, traumatized, or neglected children could offer in the courtroom. Since that chapter was published, considerable interest has focused upon child witnesses. Pynoos and Eth have studied youngsters who observed parental homicides or suicides (2,3), Goodman has organized an issue of the *Journal of Social Issues* to focus on the reliability of youngsters' memories (4), and the psychologist, Elizabeth Loftus, reported several impressive experiments on how normal children remember what they have seen (5). Early as it may seem in the process of establishing psychiatric criteria and methods of treatment for child witnesses, I will delve further into unexplored territory by considering how the most immature, nonverbal youngsters may function as witnesses.

This chapter includes sections on the use of evidence directly obtained from the baby, the use of statements and testimony from lay witnesses, the use of expert child psychiatric testimony, and the appearance of the baby as a witness. The premise that the infant psychiatrist will oversee these presentations of evidence underlies all of these sections. Most lawyers will not be in the position to understand infant development well enough to set up what type of evidence they will need for a baby-related case. Unless the attorney shows unusual expertise in psychiatric matters, the child psychiatrist will be needed to help the lawyer "orchestrate" the case.

Up to the present time, the topic of infants as witnesses has been handled in a confused and inconsistent way by U.S. Courts. In 1897, the Supreme Court stated, "No one would think of calling as a witness an infant only two or three years old" (6). American judges of the 1940s and 1950s, however, brought illegitimate infants directly into their courtrooms to help determine their paternity (7,8,9). Now reading a little like a Woody Allen satire, these appellate level decisions considered whether "the child is old enough to have well defined features and thus to make a comparison of his appearance with the defendant ['father'] meaningful" (10), or whether counsel has a right to bring a baby into court stating that "his purpose is only [to] identify the baby" and then later to argue "that there was a resemblance in certain physical traits of the child and the appellant ['father']" (11). These cases wryly amuse us today because current blood and tissue-typing techniques have removed much of the guesswork from paternity suits. But the precedent these cases established of bringing infants into court must be taken seriously in newer contexts.

Infants, more than older witnesses, experience abuse, neglect, abandonment, relinquishment, adoption, and argument regarding their parentage. The baby, because of his vulnerability and helplessness, may be very seriously harmed by only one instant of adult ire or just a few weeks of parental despair. The nonverbal youngster, therefore, has a future lifetime and his current well-being at stake when an issue regarding custody or his protection comes to court. As such a crucially involved participant, the baby certainly must be granted a "voice" in the legal decision-making process.

DIRECT EVIDENCE FROM THE BABY

Speed is the key to psychiatric planning for legal proceedings affecting the infant. Time will not be perceived by an infant as it is sensed by adults in the court system (12). A few days' waiting may seem like an eternity for a youngster. Furthermore, an infant's extraordinary resiliency sometimes works against him if he is required to take part in a legal process several weeks after an emergency. What seemed at one time to be a life-saving medical action on the baby's behalf may appear to be a tempest in a teapot by the time the matter slowly wends its way through the legal system. The medical answer to this, of course, is the immediate collection of direct evidence from the baby by pediatricians, surgeons, and child psychiatrists. In far too many cases of harm to infants, immediate graphic, convincing evidence taken directly from the baby is not collected in time by the medical team. Even when bodily harm is not the issue, carefully written records, immediate photos, or tapes of behaviors prior to treatment can be tremendously effective in creating data that will later establish the baby as an effective "witness."

Two cases—one involving harm to the baby and one a dispute in parentage—may demonstrate why the immediate collection of direct evidence from the infant proves so effective legally. Both of these cases are negative examples, unfortunately; they are cases in which the doctors failed to collect the medical data needed early enough for courtroom use.

Case 1

Joella was three months old, malnourished, and dehydrated when she was abandoned—close to death—by her mother. One night the unfortunate woman left Joella in a brown paper bag in the doorway of an urban grocery store. The medical emergency team warmed the baby, fed her intravenously, corrected her skewed blood chemistries, and gave her oxygen until her lungs could function more effectively. After two weeks, the mother redis-covered some hidden interest in Joella, came for the first time to visit the baby at the hospital, and demanded to take her young charge home.

What evidence did the hospital have to counter the mother's unexpected demand? The physicians had no photos, no old brown paper sack filled with feces, urine, and vomitus (that, of course, had been disposed of), and no tapes of a youngster in an Isolette fighting for life with each breath. The hospital simply owned a sheet of blood chemistry numbers, virtually un-translatable by the medically untrained judiciary. Joella was literally brought back to life in two weeks by the hospital nurses and doctors—she gurgled, played, and smiled. Her cheeks filled out—dimples highlighted places where sunken, dusky skin once prevailed.

The hospital was powerless in the face of Joella's mother's demand. A hospital social worker worked out a discharge plan for the baby to return to the mother. Mother was advised to seek psychiatric help and visiting nurses were alerted. Joella went home. She returned two months later to the hospital, again battling with death.

The problem in the case of Joella was a lack of immediate documentation and prompt, effective legal action on the baby's behalf. Joella came to the Emergency Room loaded with evidence: her appearance, her paper sack, and the horrified grocery clerk who found her. But no one on the medical team collected Joella's evidence. Too busy treating the baby's immediate physical problems, the medical personnel inadvertently discarded crucial materials. In this case they needed: 1) polaroid photos of the baby's initial appearance, her feeding apparatus, and the Isolette (every emergency room needs a polaroid-type camera); 2) the paper bag itself; and 3) a statement, sworn and notarized, by the grocery clerk. The social worker who arrived on the scene much later was in no position to arrange for child protective actions on behalf of the now appealing, happily gurgling infant.

Case 2

Fred, a 38-year-old, unmarried computer programmer, sought help to claim his paternal rights to a yet unborn fetus. The expectant mother, upon discovering she was pregnant, talked a previous lover into marrying her.

Fred indicated that he desperately wanted a relationship with this baby and that he would willingly pay child support for the next 18 years. Fred's attorney filed a motion claiming paternal rights to the fetus, but the mother's attorney countered that tissue typing would not be possible for at least six months. By the time the infant would be testable, psychological attachment would be well underway. I investigated myself, learning that simple blood tests could be done at the time of the child's birth, solving in any but the most difficult cases the question of paternity. But the child was born in secret, and the mother's lawyers successfully fended off immediate blood tests.

Months passed, and Fred, now living far away, stayed silent. He appeared to have lost interest in the youngster. Fred's lawyer had not heard from him.

When the disputed baby would have been about eight months old, I received a hand-delivered letter at my office.

> I wanted to let you know that I learned last week that the blood tests I compelled established that I was not the father of the child born last January in San Juan Bautista. After months of wrangling (and after months of being told by the child's mother that the blood typing was ambiguous)...I was excluded both by the HLA and ABO procedures.

There it was. The ABO at birth indeed would have concluded the matter. The "father," Fred, could have rested his mind and the baby might have been brought up with less maternal tension. Fred went on to say in his letter what the eight-month wait did to him:

> I am in San Francisco for a few days, hoping to get the legal matters tidied up ... obviously the emotional aspects won't be so neat—not that I suggest a hell of a lot of neatness in the law, mind you. I recall what you said about a certain amount of grief which may be present if I discover that the child is not mine. True enough. I also worry about the anger that has been generated by the way I was treated. I'm not going to kick in the door of that happy home out in San Juan Bautista as I figure the child would suffer, but I am aware that I'm going to have to do something about this residual rage and sense of betrayal.

Here is a case in which immediate procurement of evidence directly from the baby—his blood at birth—would have saved all parties, adults and infant, much grief and tension. In issues of paternity, the baby is his own best witness. He must be allowed to donate his direct evidence, his blood, in order to get on with the business of "psychological attachment" (13).

Videotape documentation of pathological parent-child interaction would be important early evidence for situations involving emotional disturbances rather than physical disabilities in infants. Videotapes, movies, or photographs should be produced only with parental consent or by order of the court. But court orders for gathering possible evidence are relatively easy to obtain in American courts. Again, early action is the key to this type of intervention on behalf of babies.

EVIDENCE FROM BYSTANDERS

On-the-spot lay witnesses may contribute particularly crucial bits of information about a baby's plight. The child psychiatrist must listen to, read, or record such statements, and retain the names and addresses of bystanders. Lay observations can be astute and accurate. When nonverbal infants are involved, such bystander reports may take on the role of convincing courtroom evidence.

Case 3

Lex Luthor Jones was the infant son of two narcotics-addicted parents. He, along with two older siblings, came daily to a charity-sponsored urban day care unit. Once, Lex's mother told the child care worker that she had named her baby after the villain of the Superman story because she knew prior to his birth that he would be "evil." Lex's mother also strongly hinted that her infant had a different father than did her other youngsters. Much of Lex's mother's pregnancy with Lex had taken place in prison, while the mother served a narcotics-related sentence.

The day care staff could tell that Lex was an infant at risk. His name alone spelled trouble. One day the social worker came outside and found the nine-month-old baby lying on the sidewalk screaming. His arm was limp, oddly held. Several three- and four-year-old children, who had been standing there at the time, reported to the social worker that Mrs. J, Lex's mother, had twisted Lex's arm. An adult helper, who was collecting children at the sidewalk, had not seen the incident. The social worker rushed the infant to the hospital. His arm was broken. The children dispersed, and the staff assumed that since no adults in the immediate vicinity had seen the incident, no witnesses were available. No battered child complaints were ever filed.

Over the next two years Lex suffered a string of "mysterious" illnesses and small physical damages. As the agency became more and more suspicious, the mother began, in turn, to suspect the social workers. She threatened that she would remove herself from their caseload should they report her care of Lex to officials. Each time Lex was injured, there was less available documentation of the causality.

In this case, several preschool "witnesses" were shocked to see the twist-ing of a small baby's arm. Perhaps one worker could have rushed Lex to the hospital while another staff member took names, addresses, and state-ments from the preschool "witnesses." Needless to say, the newly discov-ered fact that small children *can* serve as reliable witnesses could not possibly have reached these day care workers prior to their moment of decision regarding Lex. Hopefully, in the near future, this kind of information will reach the legal profession and to the public-at-large in time to prevent further tragedies like the Lex Luthor Jones story.

If Lex's case had ever gone to the courts, the most convincing evidence would have been the naive testimonies of the little nursery-age lay witnesses. They would have had to be prepared in advance by their social worker for the courtroom, the judge, and the questioning process. Perhaps the social worker could have taken them to the court ahead of time to look and to "practice" answering some nonthreatening questions. The young children would have had to know in advance that they could not lie and that they must say "I don't understand" or "I don't remember" if something very difficult was asked. But perhaps a couple years of misery could have been saved for Lex if such small bystanders could have come to court. Further-more, several of the preschoolers might have felt a little more effective as people if they had been given the chance to help stop or to aid in punishing such obvious maltreatment of a baby.

EXPERT TESTIMONY

According to the rules of evidence in British or U.S. courts, medical witnesses, because of training and experience, are allowed to give opinions and to explain the reasons for reaching these opinions. Hearsay rules are set aside for these experts because they often rely upon communications from others to develop medical opinions. Infant specialists, more than other psychiatric experts, utilize these outside "hearsay" communications, de-pending upon indirect sources of information, because the baby cannot speak for himself. The child psychiatrist must put the baby's behaviors into words so that the laymen at the court can "see" what the baby conveys.

Case 4

From ages 15 to 18 months, Sarah stayed five days a week at a married couple's home while her mother worked. When Sarah was three, the police found her picture in a batch of child pornography materials confiscated by U.S. customs agents. It appeared that the "father of the house" at the ba-bysitter's, a much older man, had posed naked with tiny Sarah. He was sentenced in criminal court, but a civil suit was also filed on Sarah's behalf. There was no question that the child in the photographs was Sarah. Her birthmark was highly distinctive.

In her second year, her parents had noted that Sarah would not stay still while they changed her diapers. She would not sit on her grandfather's lap. She had become quite modest and rather quiet. A child psychiatrist expert would have to interpret this and any other data the little girl presented. The facts themselves would not be enough to prove psychiatric harm.

When the parents gave Sarah's history, one peculiar slip of the tongue of the father's arrested my attention. As he described the child in the pornographic photo, he said "the woman in the picture," referring to his own tiny infant. This slip demonstrated what kind of damage the pornographer and his wife had effected to the father-daughter relationship. It would have to be explained in court in my "expert testimony."

On psychiatric examination, the five year old could still remember the the babysitters. "Every time we haded to go to Mary Beth's house, I would cry. She was soooooo mean." Sarah could not remember Leroy H. taking pictures of her, nor could she remember undressing, but she *did* know she felt afraid.

> I used to be scared of a cow. I never saw one. Mooooo. I thought *that* part [the udder] was REAL scary too. It looked like some kind of monster to me when I was little. I also remember we went on a boat in Disneyland—an animal boat. Some have stripes. We saw lots of animals and little Indians with spears. I'm scared of *that*! Somebody scared me with a finger part. I can't remember. *I'm afraid of a finger part on my stomach.* I'm afraid of sharp finger nails. I like ladies better than men.

Up to this point in the evaluation, I had not asked the father exactly what the pornography pictures showed. (The mother and children had never seen the pictures, which were the property of the police.) But from the child's nonverbal memories from ages 15 to 18 months, it seemed that she had been exposed to a male "finger part," on or near her stomach. She was afraid of spears, udders, fingers, fingernails, and men.

After my session with Sarah I now asked the father what the photos which the police showed him actually depicted. He said they showed Leroy H.'s penis on Sarah's abdomen. Four years after the assault, the little girl's fears exactly duplicated her past plight. As an expert witness, I would be able to tie together current research on children's reactions to psychic trauma (14,15,16), observations that the parents made, evidence from the police, and Sarah's own account. The evidence would be impressive. Sarah, through the expert psychiatric witness, could be granted an indirect but very distinct voice in the courtroom.

In cases of infantile psychic trauma, particularly where there is clear reenactment, trauma-specific fear, or post-traumatic play (17,18), expert psychiatric testimony may entirely bypass the child's own appearance in court. This is particularly helpful in sexual abuse cases where the child feels extremely ashamed and can barely find the words to describe his sexual anatomy, let alone his past sexual activity.

In California, for instance, where rape victims are protected by statute from insinuating cross-examinations in criminal trials, no such protections to sexually assaulted witnesses are afforded in civil suits. Children are not protected by any special statutes when they appear as witnesses in sexually-tinged civil cases or when they are bystander-witnesses to the criminal rapes of others. In such cases, the child psychiatrist can take over for the child, sparing him the mortification of cross-examination. Whenever the expert witness's history, observations, examination, and supporting information concerning the baby are strong and complete enough to bypass the infant's own testimony, such a substitution is to be encouraged.

THE BABY IN COURT

Nondramatic but crucial psychological attachment issues in adoption, custody, and infant visitation may require direct observations of the baby in court. Cases of infant-parent connectedness—or lack thereof—are often too subtle for the expert to explain convincingly. These cases, so very difficult for courts to settle, may be concluded, unfortunately, based upon the judge's personal prejudices and misinformation.

In these cases bringing the baby to court, or better yet to the judge's chambers, might settle difficult controversies. In disputes about who is the "psychological parent," the emotionally connected parent should be demonstrably preferred by the baby by the time he is six or seven months old. The baby relaxes in the psychological parent's arms and feeds most naturally with him or her. The consistent caretaker usually is more relaxed with the baby than would be those adults with whom the child has no ties. If the parent-claimant were to feed, diaper, or hold the "infant witness" in the presence of the judge—particularly if a child psychiatrist were also present to explain the infant's behaviors—many cases might automatically resolve themselves.

As mental health professionals, we can rely fairly heavily upon the "repetition compulsion" (19). What a judge observes under stressful conditions in chambers will most likely be a pretty fair duplication of what happens at home under stress. Of course, videotapes may accomplish the same result without bringing the baby to court at all, but the judge might prefer to see the parent-child interaction for himself.

Demonstrating the baby and "parent(s)" to the judge may help resolve disputes in which natural mothers try to claim adopted infants months to years after the original relinquishment. Such demonstrations could also solve some mysteries about which parent *really* took care of a baby prior to the breakup of a marriage. Bringing a baby to court might also help clarify whether a negligent mother still has or ever had a psychological tie with an infant.

One takes a chance, of course, in bringing a baby to court. Perhaps on this one particular occasion, the infant will fuss or squirm miserably in an excellent parent's arms. Or a cold, awkward parent might perform marvelously well just one time. A family attorney told me that he had instructed an inadequate mother years ago to pinch her baby while passing it to the father, so the judge would think the baby was displeased to go to its strongly preferred parent. To counteract this trickery, judges could carry the baby themselves to the opposite party, or the infant expert might hold the infant between "demonstrations." Despite unprincipled tricks or bad days, the repetition compulsion is really quite reliable. Almost always, the infant witness will behave predictably. The infant's demonstration of parent preference or of pathological development is at least as convincing as any other evidence that might be brought to the court on the baby's behalf.

Case 5

Will, 41, sought psychotherapy when he and his 20-year-old girlfriend, Emily, broke up. Will wished to figure out why he had chosen a life companion so badly. Emily had given birth to Domino, a baby girl. She and the infant moved out when the youngster was four months old. At first Will reported that his short, semiweekly visits with the infant were progressing smoothly. The court had preliminarily "heard" the couple's separation matters, ordered temporary physical custody to the mother who was not working, ordered the father to pay child support, and allowed the father two short visits per week. I saw the baby at age nine months, and although quiet vocally, she was very adept physically.

When Domino was 10-11 months old, however, everything changed. She developed a nasty diaper rash that Will photographed and began treating. She stopped walking, and clung piteously to her father. When she fell—more frequently than previously—she cried inconsolably. Will investigated, and discovered that Emily went back to work and began dating on her days off, leaving the baby with sitters six days a week. Furthermore, the five-day babysitter was in acute mourning for a dead husband and the one-day babysitter was an alcoholic. Both babysitters kept the infant "resting" without toys or adequate room to play for hours at a time.

I asked Will to bring the baby to my office on one of his short visitations. This time the child vocalized very poorly, cried much of the time, screamed whenever she fell down, and followed Will desperately—crawling toward him whenever he moved in his chair.

At my urging, Will's lawyer brought a motion for an immediate hearing. I testified and also suggested bringing Domino along to court. There was no question that the judge would recognize how pathological the baby's behaviors had become. Furthermore, I would be there to explain.

Will's attorney refused. He was afraid that the baby might not behave predictably. I appeared alone as an expert witness, and Will won three-and-a-half days' custody. Emily promised not to work on her three-and-a-half days.

After the temporary hearing, Emily continued to work. Domino improved remarkably as she adjusted to playing and running about in her father's house. But she still suffered under her mother's care. For example, each time her mother picked her up from Will's house, Emily plugged in her Walkman earphones and appeared as if she would ignore the child during the entire 90-minute drive to her home. Contrary to the judge's orders, Emily kept Domino in the alcoholic sitter's home at least one day a week.

I believe that if the judge had seen Domino in severe distress at 11 months old, she would have ordered the baby into the father's full physical custody. As it turned out, the father received half custody and the promise of a full hearing in the future. But Will's case would be far more subtle once the baby improved. There was a good chance that when Domino began school, the court would change the custody-visitation arrangements, giving the mother far more of the child's care. Unfortunately, in the long run for both the father and the little girl, the moment of "infant demonstration" came and went.

SUMMARY

From Biblical times on, it was recognized that a mute witness could plainly point the way to truth. King Solomon established this fact more than 2,000 years ago (20), when he brought a disputed baby into his court so he could determine its parentage. Our American courts must begin to act upon the same truth today. Watching babies in chambers may become essential for fair judicial outcomes.

The child psychiatric expert witness is essential to this process. He must set up the baby's medical-legal case and make sure that the most crucial evidence is gathered early. He must testify about his expert opinions and interpret the baby's behaviors to the judge or jury. It is important for child psychiatrists to come to court willingly and well-prepared in matters involving babies. Without expert child psychiatric testimony, infants may forever remain mute.

REFERENCES

1. Terr, L. The child as a witness. In D. Schetky, & E. Benedek (Eds.), *Child psychiatry and the law*, New York: Brunner/Mazel, 1980.
2. Pynoos, R., & Eth, S. The child as criminal witness to homicide. *Journal of Social Issues*, 1984, *40*, 87-108.
3. Pynoos, R., & Eth, S. Witness to violence: The child interview. *Journal of the American Academy of Child Psychiatry*, in press.
4. Goodman, G. (Issue Ed.). The child witness. *Journal of Social Issues*, 1984, *40*, 175.
5. Loftus, E. *Memory*. Reading, MA: Addison Wesley, 1980.
6. *Wheeler* v. *United States*, 159 U.S. 523, 40 L Ed 244, 16 SCt 93 (1897).
7. *Green* v. *Commonwealth ex rel.* Helms, 297 Ky. 675, 180 S.W. 2d 865 (1944).
8. *State ex rel. Fitch* v. *Powers*, 75 S.D. 209, 62 N.W. 2nd 764 (1954).
9. *Thomas* v. *U.S.*, 121 F. 2d 905 (D. C. Cir. 1941).
10. Clark, H., Jr. *The law of domestic relations*. St. Paul, MN: West Publishing Co., 1968.
11. *State ex rel. Fitch* v. *Powers*, 1954.
12. Solnit, A. Child placement—On whose time? *Journal of the American Academy of Child Psychiatry*, 1973, *12*, 385-392.
13. Goldstein, J., Freud, A., & Solnit, A. *Beyond the best interests of the child*. New York: Free Press, 1973.
14. Terr, L. Children of Chowchilla: A study of psychic trauma. *The Psychoanalytic Study of the Child*, 1979, *34*, 552-623.
15. Terr, L. Time sense following psychic trauma: A clinical study of ten adults and twenty children. *American Journal of Orthopsychiatry*, 1983a, *53*, 244-261.
16. Terr, L. Chowchilla revisited: The effects of psychic trauma four years after a schoolbus kidnapping. *American Journal of Psychiatry*, 1983b, *40*, 1543-1550.
17. Terr, L. "Forbidden games": Post-traumatic child's play. *Journal of the American Academy of Child Psychiatry*, 1981, *20*, 741-760.
18. Terr, L. Play therapy and psychic trauma: A preliminary report. In C. Schaefer, & K. O'Connor (Eds.), *Handbook of play therapy*. New York: Wiley-Interscience, 1983c.
19. Freud, S. (1920). Beyond the pleasure principle. In J. Strachey (Ed.), *The Complete Psychological Works of Sigmund Freud*, *18*, 1-64. London: Hogarth Press, 1955.
20. First Kings 3:16-28. *The Holy Scriptures*. Philadelphia: Jewish Publication Society of America, 1955, pp. 452-453.

21

New Areas in Litigation for Children

Gilbert W. Kliman

A psychoanalytic clinician's identity usually involves much discipline and containment, especially of aggressive energies. Many psychoanalysts, this author included, find a constructively restrained passivity the ideal mode for enhancing patient communication and evoking transference phenomena.

The opposite is true when a psychoanalyst functions in litigation for children. Seldom will an analytically-oriented psychiatrist find more adventure available than at the legal frontier. Aggressive application of psychoanalytic and related developmental concepts to questions of children's rights and welfare continues to break new ground. It is the effectiveness of creative professional assertiveness in the good cause of a child's well-being that makes the combat so intellectually and emotionally rewarding for the psychiatric expert.

Illustrative areas of activity, based on my experience in litigation, are given throughout the chapter.

COMPENSATION FOR LOSS OF PARENTAL SERVICES

The Center for Preventive Psychiatry, located in White Plains, New York, is a nonprofit community mental health agency serving over 1,000 persons per year. It operates under a contract with the State of New York, which permits it to provide preventively-oriented psychotherapy to persons of all economic classes. As a result of its special purpose and identity, the Center is able to focus on areas of experience not ordinarily the subject of psychiatric intervention. In particular, it specializes in the prevention of pathologic consequences of severe situational crises such as bereavement and divorce.

Of particular relevance to this chapter is the stress of violent or wrongful death of a parent during a patient's childhood. Over the past 17 years, this author has worked personally with hundreds of father- or mother-bereaved children (1-7). Many of the children and surviving spouses suffered their grief as a result of a murder or other form of wrongful death. Yet, as analytically-oriented clinicians, it escaped our attention until recently that potential existed for a legal precedent on the children's behalf. In 1981, however, an alert attorney, Robert Conason, raised the legal question, should a court financially compensate children for the psychological, moral, and educational damages due to loss of parental services (8)?

In 1981 loss of parental services with consequent psychological damage to a surviving child had seldom or never been a successful basis for a wrongful death action. Yet, enough was known about childhood bereavement to indicate that some forms of loss of parental services may lead to serious damage (9,10). Surviving children commonly exhibit learning inhibitions, antisocial behavior, chronic depressive reactions, and gender identity disturbances, as well as an increased incidence of neurotic and psychotic disorders. A prospective study of 10,000 Minnesota school children by Gregory (11) showed that the death of a parent was associated with marked increase of truancy, multiple arrests, failure of one or more grades, and school drop out. Kohut's views that parents serve as ego-auxiliary or self-objects are thus well substantiated (12). The loss of these auxiliary functions of parental service can be profoundly damaging to many children.

Eth and Pynoos (13) reported on a series of 40 children who witnessed a parent's homicide. The additive demands of mastering such a pathogenic experience, as well as doing the work of mourning, gripped these investigators' attention. They note the children experienced "continued intrusion ... of the central action when the lethal physical harm was inflicted...." The children underwent intense perceptual reexperiences, involving multiple sensory modalities, and autonomic arousal. There is frequently a

> post-traumatic stress disorder [with] ... intrusive memories, unconscious reenactments, startle reactions, recurrent nightmares, fears of repeated trauma, and avoidant or other symptomatic behaviors.... These expectable reactions to trauma are superimposed on the child's grief.

It is apparent that the combination impairs the work of mourning and that prominent memories of the perceptions of the particulars of the death contaminate any pleasant recall of parental interaction.

At present, the legal status of compensation for psychiatric and psychological aspects of loss of parental services is still being debated and court responses are difficult to predict. A jury award of six million dollars mainly for psychiatric aspects was recently overturned on appeal. The appeal of the case—in which the author testified on behalf of two double-orphaned children—dealt solely with technical liability rather than damage aspects (14). However, the law has recently changed to the advantage of the bereaved and even the traumatized witness, including children. Broadened attitudes governing compensation for psychologically-damaged witnesses to a death are inherent within recent decisions in New York and a new code in Ohio.

In New York the relevant cases of *Bovsun* v. *Sanperi* (17) and *Kugel* v. *Mid-Westchester Industrial Park* (18) were appealed. The appeal was decided in favor of the plaintiffs in both cases. It was the decision of the court that

> a plaintiff may recover damages for injuries suffered in consequence of shock or fright resulting from the contemporaneous observation of the serious physical injury or death of a member of his or her immediate family, where the defendant's conduct negligently exposed the plaintiff to an unreasonable risk of bodily injury or death and the same conduct by defendant was a substantial factor bringing about the injury or death of plaintiff's immediate family member.

As a direct result of the above decisions, the author is already reviewing two cases of children who witnessed the death of a close family member. In each case there are allegations of psychological damage. The children were not themselves seriously injured, but they are claiming permanent mental disorder consequential to the accident, as a result of being within the zone of danger. An even broader case law has evolved in Ohio, permitting compensation for children who have lost parents and the services of those parents through wrongful death.

During 1982, a bill was passed by the Ohio state legislature and recently signed into law by the Governor, allowing for compensation in cases where a wrongful death produces psychological harm (19). The conditions under which a jury or court may award damages in such a case are of great relevance to the child psychoanalyst or child psychiatrist whose special knowledge may be more appropriate than any other professional's. The range of compensable losses includes:

> The loss of support from the reasonably expected earning capacity of the decedent;
> The loss of services of the decedent;
> The loss of the society of the decedent, including loss of companionship, consortium, care, assistance, attention, protection, advice, guid-

ance, counsel, instruction, training and education, suffered by the
surviving spouse, minor children, parents, or next of kin; and
the mental anguish incurred by the surviving spouse, minor children,
parents, or next of kin. (20)

Such cases will also open new avenues of compensation for family survivors
of medical malpractice who, in the past, have had a narrow scope of causes
for awardable damages.

USE OF VIDEOTAPED CHILD PSYCHIATRIC INTERVIEWS

The current, widespread tendency to keep children from testifying in the
courtroom may often be based on false premises. It is unrealistic to believe
that children may, by this simple means, be protected from conflict, future
regrets, anxiety, and adversarial abuse. All of these problems frequently
occur outside the courtroom. Furthermore, in the courtroom there is better
control over the etiological agents than outside circumstances permit.
Judges can protect children better than many other caregivers in the adversarial system. It might even be postulated that one or another plaintiff
or defendant objects to the testimony of a child because of the compelling
power of the child's presence and testimony, rather than because of the
child's frailty and vulnerability to stress in the courtroom.

In the belief that many children may be accurate as well as powerful
sources of information, I have made it my custom to videotape forensic
consultations, after obtaining consent from both the child and the adult
who brings the child for consultation. This is essentially an extension of
the practice of many psychiatrists who routinely videotape initial diagnostic
interviews. In one case, the videotape proved a valuable supplement to
judicial interviews in chambers. And, in several recent custody disputes,
the viewing of videotapes by the adversarial attorneys, as well as by the
children's attorneys, led to prompt out-of-court settlements.

An example of such an out-of-court settlement occurred almost immediately following a videotaping in my office a few years ago. Two children,
ages nine and 14, were involved in a custody dispute in which the father
claimed the mother was abusing the children and threatening their lives.
Several interviews of the parents were fruitless, and the children were kept
away. The author insisted on and received permission from both parents,
their attorneys, and the children to videotape the children's interviews.
While on camera, the children separately and convincingly described not
only their mother's homicidal behavior, but her serious suicidal threats and
heavy alcohol intake. One child pleaded that the mother not be allowed to
see the tape, a request that was honored, but allowed the attorneys to see

the tape. This viewing produced a meeting of minds and a prompt transfer of the children to their father's care. To everyone's surprise, including my own, the mother asked to become my patient, and is now much improved by a combination of chemical and psychodynamic treatment. She is now grateful for the videotaping, and to have been confronted by an unequivocal means that required her to deal with her illness and behavior. Her children remain with their father in another city and are more respectful and affectionate with their mother, whom they visit regularly.

Precedent may have been set in one visitation case, in which the judge requested that a court-appointed child psychiatrist study videotapes that were part of the author's medical records. After reviewing the videotapes, the reviewing psychiatrist agreed that the two little girls in question believed they had been repeatedly sexually molested by their father. The judge decided against the father—who had been demanding visitation rights—according to the court-appointed psychiatrist's recommendations. I now strongly recommend that as part of medical records, videotapes be kept whenever a child's testimony is likely to be required.

In this same case, two other novel uses of psychiatric expertise were utilized. The first was the use of hypnosis to challenge allegations. Since the daughters, ages eight and 10, were the only witnesses to the alleged sexual activities, I had to consider that they might be fabricating or in collusion with a fabrication of an adult party to the dispute. Therefore, the children's and mother's consents were gained to use hypnosis for additional interviewing by me. The children's accounts remained unchanged in a hypnotic state, despite challenges. These hypnotic inductions and interviews were also videorecorded and later viewed by the children's attorney, both parents' attorneys, and the court-appointed psychiatrist.

As a guard against tampering with the videotapes, the operator of the equipment was an independent attorney. Certification was made of the tapes in the same fashion as videotaped depositions. An electronic chronograph device was used within the video apparatus to further secure it against tampering. From the time of its recording to the time of its viewing under court direction, the tape remained in the possession of the independent attorney, who also testified in court concerning the security of the procedure.

Still another, somewhat unusual use of an expert in this case was that of courtroom assistant to the attorney. Together, the attorney and I observed an altercation between the allegedly abusive father and a witness, and noted the father's varying degrees of impulsivity and agitation. My testimony was utilized on both direct examination and, later, rebuttal. During rebuttal, portions of the transcript were read and each relevant section presented as part of a hypothetical question for expert opinion.

USE OF HYPNOSIS WITH CHILDREN IN LITIGATION

My own work with hypnosis began in testing psychoanalytic hypotheses (21). Hypnosis allows for the suspension of a particular defense, perceptual avoidance, in hypnotized subjects. This is related to the use of hypnosis to assist memory in cases where memory is avoided or otherwise defended against. Psychoanalytic points of view also produce an understanding of how much caution must be brought to bear in the use of hypnotic testimony. Transference and countertransference processes tend to be rapid, intense, and magnified in hypnotic relationships. As part of this ebb and flow of emotion, there can be unwitting distortions and fabrications introduced by both the witness and the hypnotist.

Since children are particularly open to suggestion and hypnosis (22), the risk of contaminating testimony is especially real for the inexperienced interviewer. This risk of contamination with hypnotic interviewing at any age, but even more with children, makes it necessary to use objective recordings such as videotapes provide. Some courts, as Orne (23) points out, have excluded the use of testimony that has been refreshed in recall through the use of hypnosis, so that the forensic expert using such techniques in some jurisdictions now risks his work being counterproductive.

Earlier in this chapter a case was described in which two sisters independently corroborated each other's testimony concerning sexual abuse by their father. Separate hypnotic state interviews of each child did not change or differentiate their accounts, leading to an increased credibility of the children's testimony. It is my belief that hypnotic techniques are best reserved for such assessments and for another purpose—the development of clues that will lead to other evidence. It is other evidence that will corroborate the hypnotic recall, a recall that should not, in my opinion, be the sole subject of testimony.

ALLEGATIONS OF SEXUAL ABUSE OF CHILDREN

The occurrence of sexual abuse of children is becoming increasingly known. However, a cautionary note must be introduced here. Most of the cases in which I have examined children have been convincing cases of sexual abuse. But the very sensational and highly publicized numbers of recent cases, some of them on a mass scale, have created special burdens for child psychiatric experts. Certainly, childhood sexuality in general is an area that can benefit from psychoanalytic understanding of developmental processes. These include the multifarious roles of childhood fantasy and the ease with which childish behavior can be interpreted as complying with the fears and expectations of interviewers.

A psychoanalytically-informed clinician has a special skill he or she can bring to bear on children who, it is suspected or alleged, have been sexually abused. The inexperienced examiner may have his perceptions biased so that he unwittingly and unwarrantedly reads a history of abuse or incest into the child's play. The puppet and doll play of preschool children is often erotic if there is the slightest encouragement or permission for such expressions. Thus, some widely occurring themes can be mistakenly interpreted as evidence of sexual abuse, including incestuous experience.

I recently examined a mother, father, and preschool boy in a case where the mother was accused of incestuous activities with her son. She brought the child to a clinic when her then three year old complained of wanting to be a girl and told her that he thought, if he cut his penis off, he could be like his sister. The clinic personnel were alarmed by his doll play. It included some frankly erotic scenes and the child expressed clear conflict about his own gender.

History revealed causes that were strong enough from a psychoanalytic point of view to account for his preoccupation with sexual identity and for his genital anxieties. He had a new sister whose genitals he often observed when she was being changed. He himself had recently had a hernia repair, near his testicles, a common source of genital anxiety. His sister was then hospitalized for hip dysplasia and he envied the attention she was getting for wearing a large bandage. Adding to these stresses was major surgery on two other family members, marital tensions, and his mother's reactive depression. Clearly there was an ample etiologic explanation of his presenting problems. There was no scientifically persuasive evidence for incest, and the child never reported any abuse. Indeed, he denied having any contact with his mother's nude body, or she with his except while being cleaned.

In spite of all this evidence, this child was removed by a protective service organization from the family home, and it took over two months to return him to his distraught family. During that period his psychological condition deteriorated. This is an example of clinical weaknesses within the legal system dealing with children's evidence. Such difficulties can best be prevented or resolved by careful psychoanalytic supervision or self-observation by the observers. Only the most powerful measures to support objectivity can reliably avoid the contagion of biases that are produced by epidemics of child sexual abuse reports.

CONCLUSION

In conclusion, psychoanalytic orientation and the informing of forensic activities by psychoanalytic experience and theory are very productive.

They lead the forensic psychiatrist to appreciate the impact of the loss of a parent. This approach also produces an appreciation of the power of the child as a witness, and an openminded approach to allegations of sexual abuse, not all of which are true. The author recommends that psychoanalytic clinicians should increasingly endeavor to contribute to the field of litigation for children, where they will cast new light and find new directions.

REFERENCES

1. Kliman, G. Oedipal themes in children's reactions to the assassination of a president. In M. Wolfenstein, & G. Kliman (Eds.), *Children and the death of a president.* New York: Doubleday, 1965.
2. Kliman, G., *Psychological emergencies of childhood.* Grune & Stratton, New York, 1968.
3. Kliman, G. Facilitation of mourning during childhood. In I. Gerber, A. Wiener, A. Kutscher, et al., *Perspectives on bereavement.* New York: MSS Information Corporation, 1979.
4. Kliman, G., & Rosenfeld, A. *Responsible parenthood: The child's psyche through the six-year pregnancy.* New York: Holt, Rinehart, & Winston, 1980.
5. Kliman, G., Schaeffer, M.H., & Friedman, M. *Preventive mental health services for children entering foster home care/and assessment.* White Plains, NY: The Center for Preventive Psychiatry, 1982.
6. Kliman, G. Cruel Experiments of Nature: General Remarks on Childhood. Bereavement and Developmental Pathology, presented at the American Psychoanalytic Association, Vulnerable Child Workshop, Chicago, IL, April 10, 1983.
7. Kliman, G. Experiences and Problems in Research Concerning Childhood Bereavement, presented at the University of Ottawa, Department of Psychiatry, Int. Res. Meeting, Ottawa, Canada, November 10, 1983.
8. Kliman, G., & Schaeffer, M.H. Summary of two psychoanalytically based service and research projects: Preventive treatments for foster children. *The Journal of Preventive Psychiatry,* 1984, *2*(1), 117-121.
9. Kliman, 1968.
10. Kliman, 1980.
11. Gregory, I. Anterospective data following childhood loss of a parent. Part I. *Archives of General Psychiatry,* 1965, *13.*
12. Kohut, H. Forms and transformation of narcissism. *Journal of the American Psychoanalytic Association,* 1966, *14.*
13. Eth, S., & Pynoos, R. Children of homicide victims. Presented at meeting of the American Psychiatric Association, Los Angeles, CA, May 16, 1984.
14. *Martens v. City of New York,* 1982. Cited in Conason, R. *Providing and defending against damages in catastrophic injury cases.* New York: Practicing Law Institute, 1984.
15. Case Notes and OAJ, Ohio Code Supplement § 2125.02.
16. *Ibid.*
17. *Bovsun v. Sanperi,* 61 N.Y. 2d 219 (1984).
18. *Kugel v. Mid-Westchester Industrial Park, Inc.,* 90 AD 2d 196, (Second Dept., 1982)
19. Case Notes and OAJ Proceedings. Ohio Code Supplement Par. § 2125.02.
20. *Ibid.*
21. Kliman, G., & Goldberg, E. Improved visual recognition during hypnosis. *Archives of General Psychiatry,* 1962, *7,* 155-162.
22. Bernheim, H. *Suggestive therapeutics (1887).* Westport, CT: Associated Booksellers, 1957.
23. Orne, M.T., Soskis, D.A., & Dinges, D.F. Hypnotically induced testimony. In G. Wells, & E. Loftus (Eds.), *Eyewitness testimony—Psychological perspectives.* New York: Cambridge University Press, 1984.

Emerging Issues at the Interface of Law and Medicine Concerning Children of the 1980s

Judianne Densen-Gerber and Jean Lothian

By the 1980s, America has, through medical technology and its "sexual revolution," outdistanced itself. Our legal systems, public awareness, and societal ability to respond to change are far behind medical knowledge and practices, which have a profound effect upon children and, therefore, all future generations.

This chapter will address sexual abuse of children, including child pornography, female circumcision, and satanism. It will discuss legislative revisions that are necessary to expand protection of children, and will identify emerging issues which have yet to be addressed by current legal systems such as surrogate mothering, handicapped infants, the right to be well born, and gay adoptions.

OVERVIEW: INCIDENCE AND PREVALENCE OF ABUSE

The last decade has made great strides in the recognition of child sexual abuse as the significant problem it is. While in 1953 Kinsey reported that 25% of the adult women in America had experienced molestation as minors (1), widespread awareness of the prevalence of child sexual abuse did not come until the late 1970s. The Child Abuse Prevention and Treatment Act of 1973, and the establishment of the first federal agency to address child abuse, the National Center on Child Abuse and Neglect, stimulated increased research and treatment for sexual abuse victims and their families. Media attention also expanded.

This chapter is respectfully dedicated to Mr. Justice Byron White.

By 1982, at the University of New Hampshire Family Violence Center, Finkelhor reported that 93% of parents he interviewed in a random survey had been exposed to a discussion of child sexual abuse in the previous year, primarily through television and newspapers (2). Today, every state in the country has either direct or indirect services for child sexual abuse victims through government child protection agencies, private family counseling centers, and/or women's groups that also treat adult victims of rape.

Finkelhor's study is the first to call upon a random sample population to predict the incidence of child sexual abuse. His survey showed:

1) 9% of the parents stated their own children had been victims of sexual abuse or attempted abuse;
2) 47% knew of a child who had been molested; in 37% of these cases, the child was six years old or younger; and
3) 50% of the parents still believed the abuser is usually a stranger, in spite of the fact that it has been shown that 60%–75% of child sexual abuse is committed by relatives, neighbors, or acquaintances. In other words, most often the perpetrator is someone known to the child and family.

The authors, as well as Finkelhor, believe that secrecy still works to keep the true levels of child sexual abuse hidden. In earlier studies, Finkelhor found that 19.6% of college girls and 8.9% of college boys had been molested in childhood (3). Giarretto, Founder of Parents United, estimates that some 300,000 children are molested each year (4).

CHILD PORNOGRAPHY

In July 1982, the United States Supreme Court distinguished child pornography from adult pornography (5). Obscenity is not the test, but rather the danger to children. By definition, since children cannot consent, the pornographic activity is abusive. The First Amendment protections are not absolute; they do not permit us to yell "Fire" in a theater, nor do they allow the filming of a gang rape of a 10 year old.

Not only is child pornography destructive to the child involved, but it also gives consensual validation to the very people who are sufficiently deviant to have sought out such material in the first place. It libidinizes these pedophiles, and encourages them to act out both within their families and with children in the community. Child pornography is clearly a threat to the children who are used, to the children who are in potentially incestuous family constellations, and to the children in the community at large. Regardless of where the pornography is produced, it is where the material is bought that children are at risk from the purchaser. The pedophile who buys Danish or Thai material advocating sex with children commits his crimes in the local park—common sense tells us that he doesn't book a ticket to a distant place.

Current tolerance of hard-core adult pornography is partly a reflection of the "sexual revolution," the lessening of family values, and a generally permissive attitude. Tolerance of hard-core child pornography indicates our inability to distinguish freedom from license, and criminal activities from freedoms provided under the First Amendment. Of particular concern in this area are groups like the North American Man/Boy Love Association, which works to abolish all age-of-consent laws; the Renee Guyon Society, which advocates lowering the age of consent for sexual relations to the age of eight; and the Pedophilic Information Exchange, which works to lower the age to four (6). Such groups promote sex with children and have as their stated purpose the removal of laws that deny adults sexual access to children.

THE NEED FOR INTOLERANCE

In the next decade, professionals of all disciplines must redefine the limits of tolerance, articulate the unacceptable, and mediate the competing priorities between the best interests of America's children and many of our social freedoms. Legislation must be clearly intolerant of child abuse. As Baden, one of the nation's leading forensic pathologists who has autopsied hundreds of children killed by guardians, writes, "Mercy to the lion is death to the lamb" (7). In our commitment to preservation of the family, we cannot afford to endanger our children. Our first priority must always be the protection of life and limb.

MULTIPLE PERSONALITY

Twenty years ago, medical students learned during training that they would rarely, if ever, see a true multiple personality. Today, a growing number of psychiatrists are pursuing research related to the diagnosis, treatment, and consequences of the disorder. Most agree that this severe dissociative reaction results from brutalizing experiences in childhood (8). Some assert that such a diagnosis is found only in patients who have been severely sexually abused at young ages (9). While debate surrounds the process by which the child creates a series of separate personalities within one body, the legal implications, such as issues of legal sanity and criminal responsibility, under such circumstances have as yet not been addressed (10). For the patient whose multiple personality diagnosis has been confirmed, the legal ramifications are challenging. Putnam, at the National Institute of Mental Health, has shown through a series of neurological tests that the individual with this diagnosis often exhibits separate and distinct physiological results for each personality (11). Usually there is little co-consciousness and it is impossible to expect or require consequential thinking. Since a primary function of the disorder is to defend the personality against the trauma of severe sexual or physical abuse, to escape an emotional familial Auschwitz, the victim usually is amnesic to the existence of the other personalities and they to each other.

In most cases both a homicidal and suicidal personality are present. A series of "negative" personalities functions to release the hostility and rage of the victim against the abuse. When the negative personalities commit crimes, the other personalities within the body have no knowledge of said activities. Furthermore, since the others serve very different purposes (such as being acquiescent, or nurturing the injured child, or carrying pain without complaint, etc.), they in fact are incapable of committing the acts that the negative ones carry out.

A court and jury are often hard-pressed to determine guilt in such instances or even to find the diagnosis or facts credible. For example, in the Ohio case of Billy Milligan (12), a female personality within a male body raped several college females. In such a case the law must decide whether to assign guilt to the unknowing, innocent personalities, and whether or not to incarcerate the common body that houses both the innocent and guilty personalities. Issues of punishing the innocent along with the guilty must be considered along with long-term protection of society. Furthermore, what role does treatment play, who should pay for it, and what should happen once the individual is merged and no longer a danger to society?

Early diagnosis and intervention prior to commission of crimes should prevent many of these problems. The role of child abuse should not be overlooked and the weight it should have in later court interventions must be assessed. Should courts give weight to prior child abuse victimization when faced with criminal sentencing, particularly in juvenile delinquency cases? Recent studies (13) have explored these concerns in depth; these researchers have definitely advocated a treatment approach combined with protecting society in most of these reaction-formation cases to severe child abuse and/or neglect.

HOMICIDE

In yet other instances, children who have at some point experienced severe long-term abuse may break by murdering the abuser. As in most crimes of passion or justification, such children will never murder anyone else. In most instances the judicial system should expand the definition of justifiable homicide to cover these deaths (14). Our system should intervene to protect abused children before the only solution to self-preservation perceived by the victim is murderous rage.

SATANISM

An area of child sexual, physical, and emotional abuse that has not yet been sufficiently explored involves the ritualistic torture and killing of children by Satanic or other cult worshippers (15). Seven autopsies of children in the Northeast area in 1983 revealed that the youngsters were ritualistically killed; their bodies carried markings known to be used by Satanic cults (16). Several reliable sources have indicated such practices in the Atlanta child murders. Most of these children are given over by their parents either because of belief or for money. *Cults in America: Programmed for Paradise*, by Willa Appel (17), shows that many such groups have integral doctrines embodying hatred for and abuse of children such as, but not limited to, Jonestown, the most infamous example. The protection of children from such dangerous cult practices of their parents must be addressed, as well as the concerns when the parents' religious beliefs interfere with maintaining the health or life of the child.

There is also a rising incidence of abducted children being used in Satanic practice. The authors strongly advise the fingerprinting and the retention of these records by parents of all minor children. Autopsies of children are increasing each year; many are buried annually in unmarked or communal graves because identification was impossible, particularly in mass disasters. Fingerprints can help prevent this, as well as help to identify abducted children.

With the passage of the Missing Children's Act of 1982, mechanisms have been developed to collect statistics regarding numbers, conditions of disappearance, and experiences of missing children (18). The number increases annually. We suggest that many will be children who have fallen prey to Satanic cults and to pedophilic groups. A mandatory tracking system for children needs to be developed.

First, however, a campaign to fingerprint all children is immediately needed. To avoid fears of "Big Brotherism," such fingerprinting should be done by voluntary agencies and parents should keep the fingerprints. They should be advised to maintain the prints as they do other important documents, such as the child's birth certificate or health immunization records.

FEMALE CIRCUMCISION

Another area that involves religious practices that are abusive is the mutilation of female genitalia to insure virginity and, later, fidelity. Female circumcision has been practiced for centuries by certain religious groups in the Middle East and Africa. Only recently has the migration of such peoples made the practice a reality in the United States, Australia, and England. The authors estimate that in the U.S. perhaps as many as 300 young girls, at about nine years of age, are being circumcised annually, often without antiseptic or surgical equipment. Child protection legislation must be immediately amended to include such practices under the definitions of child physical abuse, and to prohibit them from occurring. All involved (physicians, clergy, as well as parents) must be held criminally responsible. No confusion with freedom of religion can be allowed to protect this mutilation. Psychiatrists must reach out to teach these foreign parents other ways to live with the threatening circumstances caused by the freedom of their first generation daughters (19).

A reevaluation of both the religious and health basis for male circumcision must be considered, although the male counterpart operation is in no way as mutilating. However, the child cannot be considered to have consented. Just as we must be willing to challenge the religious validity of the potential sacrifice of Isaac by Abraham, so must we be willing to question here.

Clearly, additional difficulties are encountered in protecting female children from such procedures that are also justified on religious grounds in states that have ERA statutes. Since male circumcision is so widely practiced in almost all cultures in our society, we wonder if female circumcision were banned, would the practice also be banned for males? The authors wish to clearly state that while we are raising questions concerning emerging issues, we are not yet prepared to suggest answers. Much work remains to be done.

In Third World countries, without the benefit of a constitution or bill of rights, the World Health Organization (WHO), as well as many concerned feminist groups, are working to educate villagers as to why this practice pertaining to female children is abusive and should be forbidden. In the West, as the problem emerges, various Parliaments have acted; yet our Congress remains strangely silent.

SURROGATE MOTHERING

The 1980s have brought medical advances that raise legal and ethical concerns regarding the status of children. The ability now to rent one's uterus and/or rent or donate one's ovum presents many more problems than artificial insemination ever has. While America's initial reaction is to want to help everyone who wants to have a child, there are some very real and complex issues concerning the reproductive rights of parents versus the best interests of the child. A few, but far from all, of the emerging considerations are:

1) The surrogate mother's rights to the child versus breach of contract if she doesn't wish to release it for adoption after birth;

2) Product guarantees, i.e., warranties—who pays for the child if defective;

3) Responsibilities of the contractors;

4) Windfall profits, tax and income averaging;

5) Disability compensation, workmen's compensation for thrombophlebitis, etc.;

6) Child protection if both parties cancel the contract after birth; and

7) If women are prohibited from being surrogate mothers, will artificial insemination be outlawed so that men cannot be donors of sperm?

SPECIAL CONCERNS OF THE HANDICAPPED CHILD

Much publicity has surrounded the case of Baby Jane Doe, a severely handicapped child whose Catholic parents, in consultation with their family priest, decided not to permit any extraordinary surgical or other procedures that would prolong life to any significant degree without remedying the basic handicap. Furthermore, the procedures contemplated were predicted to increase pain and suffering of the child. It was the expressed wish of the parents that the child at all times be kept as comfortable as was humanly possible. Under the new Federal equality for the handicapped legislation, the Department of Justice intervened and the parents agreed to allow the child to receive treatment.

Medical advances and the inalienable right of the handicapped to life have raised some serious questions for our legal system. For example, a pregnant woman can abort by right. However, if, because of fetal indications, she elects to have amniocentesis (to diagnose Down's syndrome, hemophilia, etc.) and the baby is proved to be abnormal, then she can no longer abort. If the baby is found to be normal, however, then she still has the right to terminate the pregnancy. The absurdity of this situation illustrates that in the cases where children's rights and parents' decisions conflict, solutions should be made by national legislation and model codes on the total picture rather than by the piecemeal approach of case law in each state.

THE RIGHT TO BE WELL BORN

The right to be well born, which is the right of the fetus to be drug-, alcohol- and nicotine-free, to receive good nutrition and prenatal care, and to live in a safe environment, comes into being as soon as the mother decides to bear a living child. From that moment in time the mother should not act in a way that might reasonably be expected to negatively affect the child once born. Such acts, for example, include the drinking of excessive amounts of alcohol, which may cause neonatal fetal alcohol syndrome; the taking of heroin, which may cause addiction of the newborn; or Thalidomide ingestion, which causes phocomelia. The authors strongly believe that the lifetime of a child weighs out much heavier on the scale of choices than the limitations for nine months of the civil liberties of the mother. The right to be well born does not involve the abortion debate. The right to be well born does not vest in the fetus until his or her mother decides to bear the child.

In two recent cases, the courts have ruled in favor of the fetus and against the mother when her behavior was deemed damaging to the child (20,21). The overall magnitude and far-reaching effect of the establishment of the right to be well born cannot be underestimated. If accepted as a social policy decision, it might follow that if a woman could not provide adequate food for her child, it would be incumbent upon society to do so. Since the most important factor in the delivery of a healthy baby is, in the long run, prenatal nutrition, the production of a thriving next generation would not only be most humane but also the most cost effective. The authors believe this is the bottom-line direction of the end of this century.

GAY ADOPTIONS

The distinction between "right of sexual preference" and activities that constitute child sexual abuse and/or neglect has not yet been clearly made. Pedophilia is not a gay issue any more than rape is a heterosexual one. Indeed, much of child sexual abuse is heterosexual in nature.

A more difficult issue, however, is gay adoption without any evidence of contemplated sexual activity. Should lesbians and homosexuals be allowed to adopt? (Removing naturally born children from homosexual homes is an entirely different issue. In adoption, the state is called upon to approve and condone the home as fit rather than to declare a home unfit because of the sexual preference.) The authors strongly believe that children need parenting and role modeling from both sexes. Family, whenever possible, should consist of at least one adult person of each sex. An extended family may serve this purpose as children need both a mother and a father figure. In cases of homosexual adoptions, the court must assure, as in the cases of heterosexual adoptions, that:

1) adequate exposure to opposite sex role models will occur;

2) children raised in a homosexual atmosphere will receive attention for any emotionally troubled condition that may arise from the home situation; and

3) neither parent will be abusive.

LEGISLATIVE PROCESS

Age of Consent

In order to effectively invoke the power of the court to protect children, laws covering child sexual abuse need to be realistic, clear, consistent, comprehensive, and workable. At present, child protection laws regarding sexual abuse are inconsistent and vary widely from state to state. While 46 states require that sexual abuse and/or molestation be reported under their child protection laws (22), legal definitions of activities that constitute abuse need revision. Many states protect female children more than males of comparable age. For example, the District of Columbia has no sexual protection statutes for boys. Some states afford greater protections for the mouth or anus than they do the vagina. Some permit consensual sex for certain acts at 11, others protect until age 18 (23). There should be a uniform, codified age-of-consent law throughout all states. An American boy or girl should be equally protected from Maine to Florida, from Alaska to Hawaii. In the authors' experiences with victims, most states do not include in their protection statutes many activities that children have been forced to engage in such as acts of urination, defecation, and instrumentation performed for the sexual arousal of the offender.

In summary, our studies of the age-of-consent laws nationwide have revealed the following trends:

1) Often states do not recognize the male minor as a potential victim and assume that sex is something done to women by men;

2) the age of consent varies widely from state to state and in respect to the sex of the victim and the sex of the offender;

3) age discrepancies or parity between the offender and victim are often omitted, i.e., the larger the age differentiation, the less control available to the child, the less valid is any consent;

4) certain body parts (such as the vagina) are protected while other body parts (such as the anus and mouth) are not.

The authors urge the following legislative reforms:

1) The age of consent be set at 16, nationwide.

2) Male and female minors receive equal protection under the law.

3) Sex crimes be ranked by severity in terms of relationship of the offender to the child (the more the child has a right to expect protection from the adult, the more severe the crime), and in terms of probable, prolonged, and traumatic torture.

4) Particularly odious, deviant acts, such as urine drinking or feces eating, should be separately addressed.

5) Each state governor should establish a task force to review age of consent legislation and draft legislation as close to a proposed model law as possible (24).

6) The President should establish a national task force of state governors to develop and review model legislation in order to develop a national standard and definition of abuse and treatment programs for victims.

7) Local citizens' groups must organize to see that at both a state and national level the appropriate political and legislative action is forthcoming.

8) All terms for offenses should be standardized and well-defined nationally and punishments uniform to minimize abductions of victimized children to states with more lenient laws.

9) Opposition to groups that lobby for the abolition of child sexual protections should be strengthened.

Statute of Limitation Issues—Legislative Response

The state of Washington allows adults to sue for damages incurred as children as long as legal action is taken within two years after they have reached the age of 18 (25). We strongly recommend that more states implement such legislation but that the Statute of Limitations not begin to be filled until that point in time when the adult victim realizes that damages occurred in childhood. This type of legislation is very similar to that already in existence in medical malpractice suits. The Statute of Limitations in medical suits does not begin to run until the victim is aware of the negligence, i.e., a sponge left in an abdomen. This certainly should be the case with incest victims, particularly where civil damages are involved. Normally, incest victim children are adults before they can face the trauma, at which time they are usually in need of therapy. Clearly the abuser should be held responsible, both criminally and civilly.

Many victims (66% according to Finkelhor [26]) never disclose the abuse; they suffer years of painful, undiagnosed emotional disorders. They do not know what compensation is possible. The opportunity for compensation would not only allow the adult victimized as a child to be able to obtain funds necessary for psychiatric treatment, but also at least partially right the wrong by having the adult pay, financially, for the child's trauma. Restitution, retribution monies are becoming more and more common in our system. When the perpetrators cannot pay, the establishment of a state fund, as we have for other victims of violent crime, might very well be in order. Incest and child sexual abuse flourish in secrecy and it is well known that the consequences for the offender will be small. Such Statute of Limitations issues are now clearly before the courts and legislators, as is evident in the cases of the D.E.S. babies.

Conspiracy

Groups that promote child sexual activity with adults who meet regularly throughout the United States, in Canada, and on the other major continents are also of concern. Members exchange information, pornographic photographs, and even share children for sexual activity. The authors are working with legislators in New York, Michigan, and New Hampshire to pass legislation that makes it a crime to conspire to commit child sexual abuse. Debate over these proposals as violative of civil rights is expected; however, we strongly believe that such legislation is necessary to limit the ability of groups to organize for the covert purpose of abusing minors.

Child Safety as a Priority

In 1983, the state of New Hampshire moved to change the priority of its child protective laws to put the safety of the child first and the maintenance of the family second (27). Such a change represents an important step toward making laws responsive first to children and secondarily to the best interests of adults. Such clear statements of priorities will provide important leverage when deciding issues where the best interests of children come into conflict with adult social freedoms. No child should remain at risk because we cannot prove perpetration beyond a reasonable doubt. True, all children have an inalienable right to family. Family is necessary to a child to grow to be a full-functioning, self-actualized adult. But biological families too often fall "life-threateningly" short; it is then that we must intervene. There are three basic functions that parents or guardians must fulfill for their children: 1) They must provide a minimum amount of love and security; 2) they must negotiate the system on behalf of the child; and 3) they must be role models (28).

Judicial Process

Many social service workers hesitate to bring court action on behalf of the child sexual abuse victim because they justifiably believe the court process often further traumatizes the already troubled child. However, it has been shown by many other legal systems, such as the Israeli one, that in many instances the court and supportive adults who work with the child can offer a very strong and positive demonstration of protection and authority. In Israel, the child victim or perpetrator is, on initial contact, provided with a trained worker who alone interacts with the child and acts as a surrogate whenever the legal system is involved. Modifications of this technique to meet the requirements of the adversary system, with its right to cross-examination, have been developed in the United States. For instance, in some states the trained worker does the questioning (questions are submitted by counsel from both sides) through a one-way mirror; in others evidentiary videotapes are made in carefully controlled settings so that the victimized child does not have a face-to-face confrontation with the offender. Such protections also serve to counter the power differentiation between the adult abuser and the child.

To allow court action to become helpful rather than damaging, all involved in the process must become aware of special factors at work in such cases. We suggest the following:

1) Multidisciplinary professional workshops and seminars are needed about: the impact of premature sexual stimulation on child development; professionals must become more attuned to the cognitive and maturational development patterns of children. They must understand how such growth stages make child testimony and the courtroom experience very different for children than for adults. Children's testimony is less concrete as to time, place, and/or events, but not necessarily less credible than the adults' in the same situation. Indeed, a child's information may be more credible since he or she has less of a sexual data base upon which to draw and is not amnesic in most cases. Interviewing the child witness requires special skills (29). Evaluation of child testimony must be made within a framework that understands ages at which children are able to symbolize, use language, name body parts, differentiate right from wrong, recall painful material with accuracy, etc. It must take into account children's natural fear of, and deference to, adults, and the difference in role definition and appreciation of power.

2) The courts must consider accepting videotaped testimony as evidence. This process protects the child from the fear and stress of the courtroom, fear of confrontation with the offender, the possible emotional damage of a merciless cross-examination, the pressure of family requests not to testify against the perpetrator, and the fatigue and trauma of repetition of anxiety-laden material; it also protects testimony details that may be forgotten with the inevitable passage of time.

3) A reconsideration of the Tender Years Common Law Doctrine, a form of which was in effect in Michigan until 1982 (but then deemed inadmissible), needs to be addressed. This rule of law allows an exception to the hearsay rule by permitting the person to whom the child reveals the abuse to appear as witness to the facts. An adequate, admissible substitute form must be found.

4) In cases where custody or divorce proceedings undermine the credibility of the abuse report, a guardian ad litem must be appointed to independently review the case to report findings and recommendations in the best interest of the child.

5) When minors are themselves charged with having sexually abused other children, service agencies should be mandated by the court to explore the possibility that previously the offender might have been a victim. Few youngsters act abusively unless once abused themselves. To prevent repetition of the crime, the juvenile offender will need evaluation and treatment (30).

6) When either the child victim or the juvenile offender is removed from the home because of sexual abuse by a family member, both the institutions and/or foster care parents who receive the child should be trained in how to best work and live with that child. For example, a child who has been prematurely sexually stimulated usually sexualizes all future relationships unless guided and redirected. While child protection agencies and group home staff receive some education in this area, juvenile institutions and foster care families most often remain uninformed about the dynamics and treatment of the child sexual abuse victim.

7) Legal professionals should be educated to distinguish appropriate roles when adults become sexually involved with children. There are still cases in which the child is deemed "seductive" and, therefore, responsible for the molestation. Seductiveness is a learned behavior that is selectively reinforced by the offender. For an adult to misinterpret a child's need for attention (often due to previous inappropriate sexualization) as an invitation is to apply adult concepts and symbols to an age group too young to understand them. We label inappropriate interpretations of a child's behavior, seen in adult terms, as "adultomorphisation." Just as a court would not accept adult claims of having stolen at the behest of a child, neither should a court accept that an adult can be seduced by a child. In addition, it must be recognized that most pedophilic behavior is driven behavior, obsessive-compulsive in nature, and repetitive. At present there is no known cure (including, but not limited to, castration) for this sexual perversion. More than one pedophile we have personally evaluated has admitted to over 1,000 victims. Indeed, one confessed to abusing more than 3,000 boys. These ruminative perpetrators must be controlled indefinitely for the sake

of potential child victims. Children must be seen to be a sacred trust and, because of their minority, unable to consent to such activities. Both these concepts, *age of consent* and *sacred trust*, are key elements in establishing valid protective systems.

SACRED TRUST—CONCLUSIONS

In the July 1982 United States Supreme Court decision, *New York* v. *Ferber* (31), Mr. Justice Byron White allowed states to ban the sale of child pornography under a doctrine that declared America's children to be a sacred trust. This opinion moved our children from being the chattels or property of their parents to being protected by their communities or societies at large. Now, under American law, children have become as important as the corpus in a trust or a deposit in a bank; parents are fiduciaries for, not owners of, their children. At long last the law has officially recognized that children, not parents, have rights and the latter have clearly defined and circumscribed responsibilities.

This recognition necessitates a whole new body of law. Previous legal thinking about children has been closely tied to the common law concepts of property and protection of property. New attitudes are already developing and the authors are proud to be part of the emerging traditions. We trust that by the 21st century, children will no longer be our last slaves but will be cherished and loved. It is our only hope for the continuation of our species.

REFERENCES

1. Kinsey, A.C., et. al. *Sexual behavior in the human female.* Philadelphia: Saunders, 1953.
2. Collins, G. Child sexual abuse prevalent—Study finds. *The New York Times,* February 2, 1983, pp. C1 & C10.
3. Finkelhor, D. *Sexually victimized children.* New York: Free Press, 1979.
4. Giarretto, H. A comprehensive child sexual abuse treatment program. In C. Henry Kempe (Ed.), *Sexually abused children and their families.* Oxford, England: Pergamon Press, 1982.
5. *New York* v. *Paul Ira Ferber. The United States Law Week,* July 29, 1982, 50(50), pp. 5077-5087.
6. O'Carroll, T. *Paedophilia: The radical case.* London: Peter Owen, 1980.
7. Baden, M. Homicide, suicide and accidental deaths among narcotics addicts. *Human Pathology,* 1972, 3, 91-95.
8. Elliott, D. State intervention and childhood multiple personality disorder. *The Journal of Psychiatry and Law.* Winter, 1982, 441-456.
9. Braun, B., & Braun, R. Clinical aspects of multiple personality. Unpublished paper, 1981, p. 8.
10. Lasky, R. *Evaluation of criminal responsibility in multiple personality and the related dissociative disorders.* Springfield, IL.: Charles C Thomas, 1982.
11. Hale, E. Inside the divided mind. *The New York Times Sunday Magazine* April 17, 1983, p. 100.
12. Keyes, D. *Minds of Billy Milligan.* New York: Random House, 1981.

13. Sandberg, D. Testimony submitted to the United States Senate Subcommittee on Juvenile Justice on the relationship between child abuse and juvenile delinquency. Boston: Boston University School of Law, October 19, 1983, p. 3.
14. Mewshaw, M. *Life for death.* New York: Doubleday, 1980.
15. Smith, M. & Pazder, L. *Michelle remembers.* New York: Pocket Books, 1981.
16. Private conversations with various medical examiners across the United States.
17. Appel, W. *Cults in America; Programmed for paradise.* New York: Holt, Rinehart & Winston, 1983.
18. Potter, J. Kidnapped kids: Home safe but how sound? *Woman's Day,* July 5, 1983, pp. 110-124.
19. Barnen, R. *Female circumcision.* Stockholm, Sweden: Radda Barnen Headquarters, 1983.
20. A Baltimore (Maryland) physician requested the court to restrain a woman in her last trimester of pregnancy from taking drugs and the court complied. *New York Times,* April 28, 1983, p. 18.
21. *Margaret Blunston* v. *Chicago Rush Presbyterian St. Luke's Medical Center. Orthopsychiatric Association Newsletter.* Winter, 1983, p. 51.
22. Magri, M. State action on key issues. In M. Magri (Ed.) *Legislators guide to youth services.* Denver, CO: National Conference of State Legislators, 1982.
23. Odyssey Institute, Law/Medicine Division. *Age of consent statutes in the United States: An overview of the present laws and a proposal for reform.* Bridgeport, CT: Odyssey Institute Corporation, 1983.
24. *Ibid.*
25. Dad pays 30G in sex abuse. *The Daily News,* April 22, 1982.
26. Finkelhor, 1979.
27. Legislature, State of New Hampshire: "An Act Relative to the Child Care Act and Termination of Parental Rights." *Laws of New Hampshire,* Chapter 331, Concord, N.H., 1983.
28. Densen-Gerber, J. *Child abuse and neglect as related to parental drug abuse and other anti-social behavior.* New York: Odyssey Institute, 1978.
29. Bulkey, J. *Child sexual abuse and the law.* Washington, D.C.: American Bar Association, 1981.
30. Magri, M. The link between child abuse, neglect and delinquency. In M. Magri (Ed.), *Legislators guide to youth services.* Denver: National Conference of State Legislators, 1982, p. 20.
31. *New York* v. *Paul Ira Ferber,* 1982.

Index

Abandonment of babies, 315
Abarbanel, A., 88
Abortion, 24, 170, 338
Abuse, 23
    of babies, children as witnesses to, 317-18
    of children, 269-70
    children traumatized by, 285-308
    in cults, 262
    female circumcision as, 336-37
    homicide by victims of, 335-36
    juvenile Justice Standard on, 177
    of parents, 270-71
    in refusal of treatment cases, 41-42
    by Satanic cults, 336
    of spouses, 270
    statutes of limitations for compensation
        for, 341-42
    videotape interviews as evidence of, 327-
        28
    see also Sexual abuse
Accidents, involving guns, 276
Achievement Place (Colorado), 199-202
Adjudication
    in cases with child witnesses, 305
    in juvenile justice system, 166-67
Adolescents
    abuse of parents by, 271
    autonomy for, 14-16
    consent and confidentiality in care of, 13
    grandparents and, 139-40
    homicide and suicide among, 275
    in joint custody cases, 93, 96
    police interviews of, 300
    post-traumatic stress disorder in, 287
    psychiatric commitment of, 229-48
    therapeutic decision-making by, 29-30
    violence against, 269
    as witnesses in trials, 304
Adoption
    by homosexuals, 339-40
    natural family and, 132
    visitation rights of biological grandparents
        in, 134-35

Advertising
    of guns, 267-68
    on television, 274-75
Age
    of children in custody of fathers, 110
    of children in divorces, 82
    of consent for sexual relations, 334, 340-
        41
    for consent to organ donations, 45, 46
    in distinguishing adults from children,
        180
    in joint custody cases, 96
    in psychiatric hospitalization admissions,
        245
    for waiver of juveniles to adult courts,
        182-83
Agee, V., 206
Aggression
    in animals, 266-67
    See also Abuse; Violence
Ahrons, C., 87-88
Alcohol, 271-72, 339
Alexander, J., 88
Alternative juvenile justice treatment
        programs, 191-212
American Academy of Child Psychiatry
        Code of Ethics of, 9-13, 16-18
    on training in forensic child psychiatry,
        xix-xx
American Academy of Pediatrics, 13
American Association for Mediated Divorce
        (AAMD), 76, 77, 80, 83
American Bar Association, 177, 183
American Family Foundation, 257
Animals
    aggression in, 266-67
    parental behavior in, 103
Appel, Willa, 336
Armstrong v. Kline (1980), 226
Assassinations, 275
Assent, 24, 55
    for organ transplants, 44-46

347

Attorneys
  in cases of juveniles for waived to adult
    courts, 188
  in custody disputes, 62, 69-70, 72, 74, 75
  in divorce mediation, 76, 77
  father custody and, 101
  fees for, under Education for All
    Handicapped Children Act, 226
  malfeasance of, in contested psychiatric
    hospitalization cases, 242-44
  in psychiatric hospitalization cases, 238
Atypical dissociative disorder, 260
Autonomy, 25
  of children, 27
  of family, state intervention in, 23-24
  paternalism versus, 14-16

Babies (infants)
  in custody of fathers, 110
  social interaction by, 104-5
  as witnesses, 313-23
  See also Children
Baby Jane Doe case, 338
Baden, M., 334
Battering, *see* Abuse
Battery (assault), 270
Behavior
  biological basis of, in parenthood, 103-4
  of homosexuals, parental, 119-21
  of homosexuals, stereotypes of, 117
  programs to change, 196
  seductive, 151, 344
Behavior modification, 199-202
Bell, A., 118
Bellotti v.*Baird* (1979), 170
Benedek, T., 141
Benefits, indicated on consent forms, 50-51
Benner v. *Benner* (1952), 130
Berry, K., 107-8
Bettelheim, Bruno, 102
Biology, of parenthood, 103-4
Blacks, incorrectly labelled "mentally
    retarded," 219-21
Blom, G.E., 8
Blood tests, 316
Board of Education v. *Rowley* (1982), 225
Bosvun v. *Sanperi* (1984), 326
Boxing, 277-78
Boys
  circumcision of, 337
  sexual protection statutes for, 340
  sexual stereotyping and, 279
  toy guns and, 276
  See also Sons
Brainwashing, in sexual abuse allegations,
    148-49

Brant, R., 153
Breed v. *Jones* (1975), 170
Brendtro, L., 203
Bronfenbrenner, U., 268
Brown, Rap, 285
Brown v. *Board of Education* (1954), 217
Burger, Warren E., 28, 232
Bystanders, evidence from, 317-18

Cable television, 272-73
Campbell, S.B., 29
Cancer, in children, refusal of treatment for,
    37-43
Capital punishment, 277
Carmen, E., 270
Center for Preventive Psychiatry, 324
Child abuse, *see* Abuse; Sexual abuse
Child Abuse Prevention and Treatment Act
    (1973), 332
Childcare, by fathers, 108
Child custody, *see* Custody
Child pornography, 318-19, 333-34, 345
Child protection laws
  priority of children under, 342
  sexual abuse under, 340
  see also Abuse; Legislation
Childrearing
  in cults, 262-64
  in joint custody, 89
Children Out of School in America
    (Children's Defense Fund), 219
Children's Bureau, 8
Children's Defense Fund, 219
Children's Television Education Act (1983),
    280
Child support, 81
Circumcision of females, 336-37
Civil commitment, 170-71
Civil trials, 305-7
  babies as witnesses at, 320
  statutes of limitations on, 341-42
Clinical issues
  in children's capacities for treatment
    decision-making, 26-28
  in psychiatric hospitalization cases, 238-
    39
Closed Adolescent Treatment Center
    (CATC; Colorado), 206-7
Coates, R., 207, 208
Code of Ethics (American Academy of Child
    Psychiatry), 9-13
  on consent and confidentiality, 16-18
Codes of ethics, 18-19
Co-ed programs, 206-7
Cognitive development
  consent decisions and, 28, 29

for consent to organ donations, 45
impact of fathers on, 106
in sexual abuse allegations, 147-48
testimony by children and, 343
Collateral information, in cases of alleged
sexual abuse, 153-54
Common law
grandparent visitation rights in, 128-31
tender years doctrine in, 344
Community-based programs for juvenile
offenders, 192, 210-12
Community property statutes, 78-79
Compensation
for loss of parental services, 324-27
statutes of limitations on, 341-42
Competency
of children as trial witnesses, 301-2
to consent, by children, 28-30
impact of psychological and psychiatric
illness on, 30-32
of psychiatric patients, 25-26
Conason, Robert, 325
Conciliation Court, 76-77, 79
Confidentiality, 12-13, 16-18
in custody disputes, 64
erosion of, 6
in examinations of juveniles for waivers
to adult courts, 187
indicated on consent forms, 51-52
Consent, 12-14, 16, 18
age of, for sexual relations, 334, 340-41
for cancer treatment, refusal of, 37-43
children's decision-making capacities for,
22-33
to circumcision, 337
in joining cults, 256
for organ transplants, 44-55
for photographic evidence, 317
to psychiatric hospitalization, 245
for videotape interviews, 327
Consent forms, 48-54
Conspiracy, legislation on, 342
Co-parenting, 80-81
tasks of, 90-91
see also Joint custody
Corporal punishment, 268-70
in schools, 277
Council for Exceptional Children, 220
Counseling, in correction programs, 197
Countertransference, 155
Cox, L., 205
Crime
committed by persons with multiple
personalities, 335
guns used in, 275
unemployment and, 192

violent, 266
see also Abuse; Murder; Sexual abuse
Criminal justice system
waiver of juveniles to, 180-90
Criminal law, juvenile justice system and,
164-65
Cross-examination, of children, 303-4
Cults, 250-52
children of members of, 261-64
families of members of, 252-58
members of, 258-61
Satanic, 336
Custody, 59-60
assisting families in reaching agreements
on, 70-71
awarded to grandparents, 131
of children experiencing violence, 306-7
in divorce mediation, 79
ethical issues in, 17
evaluation in, 62-70
by fathers, 100-12
grandparent visitation rights and, 128,
129
by homosexual parents, 115-18
joint, 85-99
legal standards for, 61
mediation over, 80-81
model evaluation program for, 72-75
points of legal involvement in, 60-61
sexual abuse allegations in, 145-56
testimony by babies in, 321-22
videotape interviews as evidence in, 327-
28

Danto, B.L., 298
Death
by handgun, 275, 276
loss of parental services from, 324-27
by murder, 266, 335-36
by murder and suicide, 286
resulting from spouse abuse, 270
Death penalty, 277
Decision-making
by children, 22-33
in joint custody, 90
Deinstitutionalization, 193
Delgado, R., 256
Delinquents
adjudication in juvenile justice system for,
166
alternative treatment programs for, 191-
212
in juvenile justice system, 163, 165
pretrial detention of, 172-73
waiver to adult courts of, 180-90
Dependency, 10

in consent to organ donation, 45
Deprogramming, 254-56, 261
Detention
    by juvenile justice system, 166
    of juveniles, preventive, 172-76
Deweese v. _Crawford_ (1975), 134
_Diagnostic and Statistical Manual of Mental
    Disorders_ (American Psychiatric
    Association), 119, 224, 286-87
Diana v. _State Board of Education_ (1970),
    220
Disclosure
    in divorce mediation, 77
    indicated on consent forms, 51-52
    see also Confidentiality
Disposition, in juvenile justice system, 167-
    68
District of Columbia, psychiatric
    hospitalization of children in, 236
Divorce
    allegations of sexual abuse in, 146-47
    child custody disputes in, 59-75
    custody awarded to grandparents in, 131
    custody by fathers in, 107
    grandparents and, 137
    joint custody in, 85-99
    mediation in, 76-84
    spouse abuse as cause of, 270
Divorce trials, 60
Dixon, A.F., 267
Douglas, William O., 28
Drawing
    in assessment of sexual abuse, 150
    in treatment of children exposed to
        violence, 289, 296-297
Dreams, of children exposed to violence,
    292
Drinking
    by pregnant women, 339
    on television, 271-72
Due process
    for juveniles, in civil commitments, 171
    for juveniles, _In re Gault_ decision on, 169
    for juveniles, Supreme Court decisions
        on, 172-73
    in psychiatric commitments, 231
    in waiver of juveniles to adult courts,
        184, 186-87

Educable mentally retarded (EMR) classes,
    219-21
Educateur (psychoeducational) programs,
    197, 202-3
Education
    for children of cult members, 263

    legal issues in, 217-26
    of retarded, 219-21
    see also Schools
Education for All Handicapped Children Act
    (P.L. 94-142; 1975), 221-22
    impact of, 222-24
    origins of, 217-21
    recent case law on, 224-26
Educators, _see_ Teachers
Emergencies
    abandoned babies as, 315
    family violence resulting in, 286
    procedures for, indicated on consent
        forms, 50
Erikson, Erik H., 202
Erlanger, H., 268
Ethics
    in child psychiatry, 3-20
    children's treatment decision-making
        capacities and, 22-33
    of issues involving handicapped children,
        338
    in organ transplantations, 44-55
    of refusal of treatment in childhood
        cancer, 37-43
    of surrogate mothering, 337-38
Evaluations
    clinical, grandparent-grandchild
        relationships in, 141-42
    in custody disputes, 62-70, 72-75
    of family, in allegations of sexual abuse,
        151-54
    in transfers of juveniles to adult courts,
        187-89
Evidence
    from babies, 314-17
    from bystanders, 317-18
    hearsay, Tender Years Common Law
        Doctrine on, 344
Expert testimony
    by child psychiatrists at civil proceedings,
        306
    in custody cases involving homosexual
        parents, 117-18
    by infant specialists, 318-20
    by psychiatrists, in custody cases, 70
    in transfers of juveniles to adult courts,
        187-89
Explusions from schools, as result of
    handicaps, 226
Extended family, 138

Family
    changing roles in, 104
    of cult members, 252-58

custody agreements for, 70-71
evaluation of, in allegations of sexual
    abuse, 151-54
evaluation of, in custody disputes, 63-69
grandparents and grandchildren in, 137-41
legal priority for children over, 342
state intervention in, 23-24
treatment decision-making in, 32
violence in, 268-71, 286
violence in, treatment of, 294-98
Fathers
childcare by, 83
custody by, 100-12
gay men as, 115-24
joint custody by, 87
in paternity cases, 315-16
Fees
for attorneys, under Education for All
    Handicapped Children Act, 226
in custody disputes, 62
for divorce mediation, 77
Female circumcision, 336-37
Ferenczi, S., 145
Ferleger, David, 233-34
Feshbach, N., 269
Fetuses, rights of, 338-39
Fingerprinting of children, 336
Finkelhor, D., 333, 341
Foster, H.H., Jr., 102
Foster care programs, 208-9
Freed, D., 102
Freeman, R., 192

Gault, Gerald, 230
    see also In re Gault
Gault case, see In re Gault
Gaylin, W., 14
Gay men
adoptions by, 339-40
as fathers, 115-24
Gelles, R., 268
Gender identity, 121
Giarretto, H., 333
Gil, D., 268, 269, 277
Girls
circumcision of, 336-37
sexual abuse legislation and, 340
Goins, S., 205
Goodall, J., 266
Goode, W.J., 138
Goodman, G., 313
Goodwin, J., 146
Grandchildren, 127-28
in clinical evaluations, 141-42

in family, 136-41
visitation rights of, 128-36
Grandparents, 68, 127-42, 262-64, 307-7
Green, A., 148
Green, R., 121, 122
Gregory, I., 325
Greif, J., 87
Grisso, T., 29
Group homes, 207-8
Group techniques, 199, 204
for children exposed to violence, 294-99
Guardianship proceedings, 115
Guindon, 197
Guns, 267-68, 275-77
in television violence, 272
used against children, 269

Haddad, W., 87
Hamperion, D., 189-90
Handguns, 267-68, 275-77
Handicapped children
Education for All Handicapped Children
    Act for, 217-26
legal and medical issues involving, 338
Haynes, J.M., 78
Hazen, N., 209
Hearsay evidence
in expert testimony, 318
Tender Years Common Law Doctrine on,
    344
Heroard, 7
Herzog, J., 106-7
Highfields (New Jersey) program, 198-99
Hinckley, John, 277
Hippocratic Oath, 4
Hobbes, Thomas, 285
Hoeffer, B., 120, 122
Hoffman, E., 139
Home visits, in custody disputes, 67-68, 73
Homicide, *see* Murder
Homosexuals
adoptions by, 339-40
as parents, 115-24
Hormones, 103
Hospitalizations
civil commitments to, 170-71
psychiatric, due process in, 231, 234-40
state laws on, 24
Hypnosis, used with children, 328, 329

Illfeld, F., Jr., 88
Illfeld, H., 88
Incest, 145-46, 155
allegations of, 330
    see also Sexual abuse

Indians, American (native Americans), 132-33
Individualized Education Programs (IEPs), 221-22, 225
Infant psychiatry, xviii-xix
Infants (babies)
  in custody of fathers, 110
  social interaction by, 104-5
  as witnesses, 313-23
  see also Children
Information
  collateral, in cases of alleged sexual abuse, 153-54
  in consent, 27
  on crimes, from children, 299-300
  for fathers as single parents, 108
  withheld in research situations, 51-52
Informed consent, *see* Consent
In-home programs, 208-9
In re Gault (1967), 8, 161, 168-73, 219, 230-31, 233
In re Winship (1970), 170, 172
Institute of Judicial Administration, 177
Institutionalized violence, 277-78
Institutional review boards, 47
Integration, of handicapped children, 223
Intelligence tests, 220, 225
Interviews
  in assessment of sexual abuse, 150-51
  child psychiatric, on videotape, 327-28
  of children, under hypnosis, 329
  of children, by police, 299-300
  of child victims or witnesses of violence, 288-94
  in custody disputes, 63-66
  in examinations of juveniles for waivers to adult courts, 187-88
Isaac Ray Center (Chicago), 72-75
Israel, judicial processes involving children in, 343
Itard, J.M.G., 7

Jackson, Robert H., 256
Jewish Community Relations Council, 256-57
Johnson, Lyndon B., 218
Joint custody, 85-92
  children's experience of, 92-94
  children's tasks and demands in, 95-97
  co-parenting agreements for, 80-81
  disputed, 94-95
  emotions of children in, 82
  policy and research implications of, 97-99
Jonestown, 261-62, 336
Judges
  behavior of babies observed by, 320

child witnesses and, 301-2, 304-5, 327
errors of, in contested psychiatric hospitalization cases, 242-44
waivers of juveniles to adult courts by, 184
Juries, 301
Jurisdiction
  of juvenile justice system, 163-66
  waiver of juveniles to adult courts, 180-90
Jury trials, 172
Juvenile delinquents, *see* Delinquents
Juvenile Justice and Delinquency Prevention Act (1974), 192, 193
Juvenile Justice Standards (Joint Commission on Juvenile Justice Standards), 177-78
  on transfer to adult courts, 183-85
Juvenile justice system, 159-62
  adjudication by, 166-67
  alternative treatment programs for, 191-212
  current issues in, 171-77
  disposition in, 167-68
  In re Gault case and, 168-71
  jurisdiction of, 163-66
  origins of, 162-63
  parens patriae doctrine in, 230
  standards of juvenile justice in, 177-78
  waivers of juveniles to adult courts from, 180-90

Kaplan, S., 146
Katan, C., 145
Kellum, S.G., 141
Kelly, J.B., 85
Kennedy, John F., 218
Kenniston, K., 272
Kent v. *United States* (1966), 181, 184, 186
Kidney transplants, 44
Kilpatrick, D., 193
Kinsey, A.C., 332
Kohut, H., 325
Koocher, G.P., 33
Kornhaber, A., 140
Kreiger, M., 146
Kuby, A., 193
Kugel v. *Mid-Westchester Industrial Park* (1982), 326

Lamb, M.E., 103-5
Language
  of cult members, 261
  intelligence testing in, 220, 221
  in sexual abuse allegations, 148, 151
Larry P. v. *Riles* (1972), 220-21

Lawyers, *see* Attorneys
Leaky, Louis, 267
LeBlanc, M., 203
Lebovici, S., 294
Legislation, xix
  on child abuse, 334
  on children, 8
  on compensation for wrongful death, 326-27
  creating juvenile justice system, 163
  current issues in, 340-45
  Education for All Handicapped Children Act, 217-26
  on gun control, 277, 280
  on joint custody, 86-87
  National Child Abuse Prevention and Treatment Act, 7
  on no-fault divorce, 78
  on parental authority in psychiatric commitments, 234
  on visitation rights of grandparents, 127, 131-32
  on waiver of juveniles to adult courts, 183
Lerman, P., 191-92
Lesbians
  adoptions by, 339-40
  as mothers, 115-24
Levine, R.J., 55
Lewis, William A., 262
Lidz, C.W., 29
Limitations, statutes of, 341-42
Lion, J.R., 279
Litigation
  of allegations of sexual abuse of children, 329-30
  on compensation for loss of parental services, 324-27
  of custody, 60-61
  on Education for All Handicapped Children Act, 224-26
  hypnosis with children in, 329
  in joint custody cases, 88
  psychopharmacology and risks of, xviii
  on rights of grandparents, 127
  videotaped child psychiatric interviews used in, 327-28
Loftus, Elizabeth, 313
Long, Michael, 231
Lorenz, Konrad, 266, 267
Luepnitz, D.A., 88

Maccoby, S., 274
McDermott, J.F., Jr., 141
McKeiver v. *Pennsylvania* (1971), 172
McKorkle, Lloyd, 198

Mainstreaming, 223, 224
Malpractice, 341
Mandel, J., 122
Marshak, R., 110-11
Mead, Margaret, 105
Mediation
  in divorce, 76-84
  by psychiatrists in custody disputes, 71
Medical care, for children of cult members, 263
Medical ethics, 3-7
  codes of, 18-19
Medical records, videotape in, 328
Medications, indicated on consent forms, 49-50
Meisel, A., 29
Melton, G.B., 33
Mental health service, minors' access to, 170
Mental illness, definitions of, in contested psychiatric hospitalization cases, 243
Michels, R., 12
Miller, A., 207
Miller, B.L., 14-15
Miller, N., 274-75
Milligan, Billy, 335
Mills, T., 270
Mills v. *Board of Education* (1972), 219
Minority students, segregated as "retarded," 220-21
Minors, *see* Children
Missing Children's Act (1982), 336
Mothers
  automatic custody given to, 61, 101-2
  effect of father custody on, 111
  lesbians as, 115-24
  roles of, 105
  surrogate, 337-38
  violence against children by, 269
Mourning, 325
Movies, as evidence, 317
Mucklow, B., 120
Multiple personality, 334-35
Murder (homicide), 266, 285
  by abuse victims, 335-36
  death penalty and, 277
  effect on children who witness, 325
  by handgun, 275, 276
  by Satanic cults, 336
  witnessed by children, 288
Murray, C., 205

Nadelson, C., 146
National Assessment of Juvenile Corrections (NAJC), 195, 197

National Association of Juvenile Corrections, 184
National Center on Child Abuse and Neglect, 332
National Child Abuse Prevention and Treatment Act (1974), 7
National Coalition on Television Violence, 273
National Commission on the Causes and Prevention of Violence, 268-71
National Institute for Child Health and Human Development, 8
National Rifle Association, 277
Neglect proceedings, 115-16
Neonatal fetal alcohol syndrome, 339
Neugarten, B.L., 139
New Jersey v. *T.L.O.* (1985), 173-74
New York v. *Ferber* (1982), 345
No-fault divorce laws, 78, 85, 101
North American Man/Boy Love Association, 334
North American Transplant Coordination Organization (NATCO), 44

O'Connor v. *Donaldson* (1975), 170
Odel v. *Lutz* (1947), 129
Ohlin, L., 207
Olsen, G.K., 182, 186
Organ transplantation, 5, 23, 44-47
  consent forms for, 48-54
  consent procedures for children for, 54-55
Orne, M.T., 329
Outward Bound wilderness programs (Colorado), 205-6

Pappenfort, D., 193, 195
Parens patriae doctrine, 7, 131, 160, 229-30
  due process requirements and, 172
  juvenile courts and, 162, 163, 165
  Schall decision and, 173
  warrantless searches and, 174
Parental services, compensation for loss of, 324-27
Parents
  abuse of, 270-71
  childhood cancer treatment refused by, 37-43
  consent by, 16, 18, 22
  co-parenting agreements for, 80-81
  of cult members, 252-58
  in custody disputes, 59-61, 64-67
  in divorce mediation, 83-84
  in evaluations of sexual abuse allegations, 151-53

father custody, 100-12
grandparents, 127-42
impact of Education for All Handicapped Children Act upon, 222-23
joint custody by, 85-99
legal responsibilities of, 23
lesbians and gay men as, 115-24
murder of, witnessed by children, 288
psychiatric hospitalization admissions by, 231, 234-40, 245
"psychological," 320-21
status of children to, 345
violence against children by, 269-70
see also Fathers; Mothers
Parham v. *J.L. and J.R.* (1979), xviii, 171, 232-34, 241, 248
Parsons, Talcott, 138
PASE v. *Hannon* (1980), 225
Paternalism, 25
  autonomy versus, 27
  in consent, 14-15
paternity cases, 314
  evidence in, 315-16
Peckham, 220-21
Pedophilia, 333-34, 339, 344-45
Pedophilic Information Exchange, 334
Pennsylvania Association for Retarded Children (PARC), 219
Pennsylvania Association for Retarded Children v.*Commonwealth of Pennsylvania* (1972), 220
People's Temple, 262
Personality, multiple, 334-35
Persons in need of supervision (PINS), 165, 178
Peters, J.J., 146
Phelan, G., 120
Photographs, as evidence, 315, 317
Piaget, Jean, 29, 197, 202
P.L. 94-142, *see* Education for All Handicapped Children Act
Play, in assessment of sexual abuse, 149-50
Ploscowe, M., 102
Plyer v. *Doe* 1982), 225
Pornography, 318-19, 333-34, 345
PORT (Probational Offenders Rehabilitation and Training Programs; Rochester, Minnesota), 203-4
Postdivorce custody issues, 60-61
Post-traumatic stress disorder (PTSD), 286-87, 306, 307, 325
Predivorce custody issues, 60
President's Panel on Mental Retardation (1961), 218
Preventive detention, 172-76

Prison, 305
Probational Offenders Rehabilitation and
    Training Programs (PORT; Rochester,
    Minnesota), 203-4
Project Pride (Denver, Colorado), 207
Prosecutors, 183-84, 302
Proxy consent, 14
Pruett, K.D., 109
Psychiatric interviews, of children, on
    videotape, 327-28
Psychiatric patients
    children and adolescents committed as,
        229-48
    competency of, 25-26, 30-32
    as victims of abuse, 270, 286
Psychic trauma, 294
    civil proceedings on, 306
    discussions with children on, 290-92
    expert testimony on, 319-20
    from exposure to violence, 286-87
    resulting from violence at school, 298
    statutes of limitations for compensation
        for, 342
Psychoanalysts, in litigation for children,
    324
Psychoanalytic theory
    on child's identification with same-sex
        parent, 110
    fatherhood ignored in, 102-3
Psychoeducational (educateur) programs,
    197, 202-3
"Psychological parents," 320-21
Psychopharmacology, xviii
Punishment
    capital, 277
    corporal, 268-70, 277
    in juvenile justice system, 166-67
    sentencing, 305
    in stories by children exposed to
        violence, 292
Putnam, 335

Rada, R., 146
Radecki, T., 274
Rape, 285, 320
Reagan, Ronald W., 277
Reality testing, by children, in sexual abuse
    allegations, 147-48
Rehabilitation, 181, 185-86
    of ex-cult members, 257
    as goal of corrections, 191
Rehnquist, William H., 159, 160, 173
Religion
    cults, 250-64
    female circumcision and, 336-37

in refusal of treatment cases, 38-40
    Satanic, 336
Renee Guyon Society, 334
Research
    consent to, 24
    on organ transplants, 44-55
Residential facilities for delinquents, 193-95,
    210-12
    see also Community-based programs for
        juvenile offenders
Restrictions on visitation rights, 117
Retardation and retarded people, 218
    Baby Jane Doe case and, 338
    educable mentally retarded (EMR) classes
        for, 219-21
Ricker, P., 270
Rights
    "to bear arms," 267
    of children, 8, 11, 229, 233-34
    of cult members, 256
    of grandparents, 127-36
    of handicapped, to life, 338
    to jury trials, 172
    of juveniles, in adult courts, 181
    of juveniles, Supreme Court decisions on,
        168-70
    of psychiatric patients, 231
    of retarded, 219-21
    of state, in parens patriae doctrine, 160
    to be well born, 338-39
Risks, indicated on consent forms, 49-50
Robertson, J.F., 140
Rodham, H., 26, 28
Roman, M., 87
Rosenfeld, A., 146
Ross, J.M., 102-3
Roth, L.H., 29, 31-32
Rounsaville, B., 270
Rudin, M., 262

Sahd, D., 146
Salk, L., 102
Santrock, J., 110-11
Satanism, 336
Schall v. *Martin* (1984), 172-73, 175
Schools
    corporal punishment in, 277
    in joint custody cases, 93
    rights of handicapped in, 217-26
    treatment for violence at, 298-99
    treatment for violence external to, 294-98
    warrantless searches by, 173-74
Schwartz, I., 195
Scranton v. *Hutter* (1973), 134-35
Searches, Supreme Court on, 173-74

Seductiveness, 151, 344
Segregation, 217
    of handicapped, 219
Sentencing, 305
Sex
    age of consent for, 334, 340-41
    of children in custody of fathers, 110-11
    stereotyping by, 279
Sex roles
    of children of homosexual parents, 122
    impact of fathers on, 106-7
    in parenting styles, 120
Sexual abuse, 332-33
    age of consent and, 340-41
    allegations in custody and visitation
        disputes of, 145-56
    babies as witnesses to, 318-20
    child pornography as, 333-34
    conspiracy to commit, 342
    judicial processes involving, 342-45
    litigation over, 329-30
    multiple personality and, 334
    in refusal of treatment cases, 41-42
Sexuality
    lesbian mothers and gay fathers, 115-24
    seductive behavior and, 151, 344
Sexual preference
    adoptions and, 339-40
    in custody cases involving homosexual
        parents, 115-16
Shanas, E., 138
Shepard-Towner Maternity-Infancy Act, 8
Shornhurst, F.T., 181
Siblings
    abuse of, 269
    in custody disputes, 68
Side effects, indicated on consent forms, 50
Silberman, C., 267
Simons, Virginia A., on child custody
        disputes, 59-75
Single parents, fathers as, 107-9
Slawson, P.F., xviii
Slovenko, R., 101-2
Smith, C., 107
Smith, R., 107
Social class, family violence and, 268-69
Social Security Act (1935), 8
Social services, juvenile justice system and,
        168
Solnit, A., 279
Sorrentino, J.N., 182, 186
Spanking, 268-70, 277
Specialized foster care programs, 208-9
Spencer, J.M., 79
Sperry, Willard, 3-4
Sports, violence in, 277-78

Spouses
    abuse of, 270
    in joint custody cases, 94-95
State
    education responsibilities of, 217
    federal role in education, 218
    intervention in family by, 23-24
    parens patriae doctrine and, 160, 163
    violence by, 277
Status offenses, 165-66, 178
Statutes of limitations, 341-42
Steinmetz, S., 268
Stigmatization, of children of homosexual
        parents, 123
Strauss, M., 268-70
Succession of Reiss (1984), 128-29, 132
Suicide, 275
Supreme Court (U.S.)
    on babies as witnesses, 313
    on child pornography, 333, 345
    on due process for juveniles, 172-73
    on minors' competency, 28
    on psychiatric commitments, 232-33
    on right to education, 225
    on rights of children, 170-71, 230
    on segregation, 217
    on state intervention in family, 23-24
    on transfer of juveniles to criminal courts,
        181, 184
    on warrantless searches, 173-74
Surrogate mothering, 337-38
Sutherland, E.H. 199

Tatro v. *Texas* (1981), 225-26
Teachers
    corporal punishment by, 277
    impact of Education for All Handicapped
        Children Act upon, 224
    stress upon, after school violence, 298,
        299
Team approach
    in custody disputes, 64-65, 73
    in divorce mediation, 76, 77
Technology, medical ethics and, 5
Television
    used with children as witnesses in trials,
        303
    violence and, 271-75, 279, 280
    violence in sports on, 278
    see also Videotape
Tender Years Common Law Doctrine, 344
Testimony
    by babies, 313-23
    by child psychiatrists at civil proceedings,
        306
    on childrearing in cults, 263

by children, 300-5, 343
of children, on videotape, 327-28
of children, under hypnosis, 329
in custody cases involving homosexual
parents, 117-18
expert, by infant specialists, 318-20
expert, in transfers of juveniles to adult
courts, 187-89
by psychiatrists in cutody cases, 70
Therapy, *see* Treatment
Third parties, in visitation cases, 133-34
Thomas, Lewis, 3
Toy guns, 276
Transplants, 5, 23, 44-47
consent forms for, 48-54
consent procedures for children for, 54-
55
Trauma, *see* Psychic trauma
Treatment
alternative juvenile justice programs for,
191-212
of children exposed to violence, 288-308
children's decision-making capacities for,
22-33
in contested psychiatric hospitalization
cases, 240, 245-46
for families of cult members, 254-55
refusal of, in childhood cancer, 37-43
Trials
babies as witnesses at, 313-23
children as witnesses at, 300-5
civil, 305-7
detention prior to, 172-76
divorce, 60
by jury, 172
Tribal Child Welfare Act (1978), 132-33
Troll, L.E., 140

UDIS (Unified Delinquency Intervention
Services; Illinois), 204-5
Unemployment, 192, 209
Unification Church, 257
Unified Delinquency Intervention Services
(UDIS; Illinois), 204-5
Uniform Marriage and Divorce Act (states),
78

Videotape
child psychiatric interviews on, 327-28
evidence on, 317
testimony by children on, 343
Vierling, L., 29
Vinter, R., 199
Violence, 266-68, 278-80
in cults, 261-63

in family, 268-71
handguns and, 275-77
institutionalized, 277-78
on psychiatric interventions with children
trauamatized by, 285-308
television and, 271-75
see also Abuse; Murder; Sexual abuse
Visitation
contested, videotape interviews as
evidence in, 327-28
in divorce mediation, 79
by homosexual parents, 115-18
legal standards for, 61
points of legal involvement in, 60
sexual abuse allegations in, 145-56
see also Custody
Vocational Act Amendments (1973), 218
Voir dire, 301-2
Voluntary civil commitments, 170-71
by parents, 231
Vulnerability, 10-11

Waivers of juveniles to adult courts, 180-90
Wald, Patricia, 233
Wallerstein, J.S., 85
Ware, C., 82
Warrantless searches, 173-74
Warren v. *Warren* (1973), 131
Weinberg, M., 118
Weisberger, E., 269-70
Weissman, M., 270
West, J., 277
West, L.J., 256
White, Byron, 345
Wilderness programs (Outward Bound;
Colorado), 205-6
Williams v. *Miller* (1978), 130
Winslade, W.J., 19
Winters v. *Miller* (1971), 25
Wisconsin v. *Yoder* (1972), 28
Witnesses
babies as, 313-23
children as, 300-5
to murder, children as, 325
see also Testimony
Women
abuse of, 270
circumcision of, 336-37
in cults, 263
pregnant, 339
sexually abused as children, 332
Women's movement, 104
Wrongful death litigation, 325

Zaharoff, H.G., 133